Lecture Notes in Computer Science 13917

Founding Editors

Gerhard Goos
Juris Hartmanis

The series Lecture Notes in Computer Science (LNCS), including its subseries Lecture Notes in Artificial Intelligence (LNAI) and Lecture Notes in Bioinformatics (LNBI), has established itself as a medium for the publication of new developments in computer science and information technology research, teaching, and education.

LNCS enjoys close cooperation with the computer science R & D community, the series counts many renowned academics among its volume editors and paper authors, and collaborates with prestigious societies. Its mission is to serve this international community by providing an invaluable service, mainly focused on the publication of conference and workshop proceedings and postproceedings. LNCS commenced publication in 1973.

Lucio Davide Spano · Albrecht Schmidt ·
Carmen Santoro · Simone Stumpf
Editors

End-User Development

9th International Symposium, IS-EUD 2023
Cagliari, Italy, June 6–8, 2023
Proceedings

 Springer

Editors
Lucio Davide Spano ⓘ
University of Cagliari
Cagliari, Italy

Albrecht Schmidt ⓘ
LMU Munich
Munich, Germany

Carmen Santoro ⓘ
ISTI-CNR
Pisa, Italy

Simone Stumpf ⓘ
University of Glasgow
Glasgow, UK

ISSN 0302-9743   ISSN 1611-3349 (electronic)
Lecture Notes in Computer Science
ISBN 978-3-031-34432-9   ISBN 978-3-031-34433-6 (eBook)
https://doi.org/10.1007/978-3-031-34433-6

This Springer imprint is published by the registered company Springer Nature Switzerland AG
The registered company address is: Gewerbestrasse 11, 6330 Cham, Switzerland

Preface

Welcome to the proceedings of the 9th International Symposium on End-User Development (IS-EUD 2023), organised by the University of Cagliari and held during June 6–8, 2023. IS-EUD is a biennial event for researchers and practitioners with an interdisciplinary approach to EUD, including Human-Computer Interaction, Software Engineering, Computer Supported Cooperative Work, Human-Work Interaction Design and related areas.

End-User Development (EUD) aims to empower end-users who are not necessarily experts in technology development, to create their own technology to address their specific needs. These technologies might include mobile, web or software systems, IoT solutions, physical computing devices or machine learning systems. The conference welcomes contributions that describe new, simple and efficient environments for end-user development, describe new processes, methods and techniques for empowering users to create, modify and tailor technology artefacts, present case studies and design implications of challenges and practices of end-user development, or develop theoretical concepts and foundations for the field of end-user development. While originally EUD was conceived as a more general instance of end-user programming, focusing on the entire software lifecycle, nowadays EUD has embraced the problem of defining and modifying the behaviour of smart environments through the Internet of Things (IoT), robotics, cyber-security and artificial intelligence (AI) systems. Therefore, the term 'End-User Development' has acquired a much broader meaning.

IS-EUD 2023 collected research contributions as full papers, short papers, work-in-progress and doctoral consortium papers that presented topics surrounding:

- AI for end-users
- End-user IoT
- Privacy, security and society
- Supporting end-user programming

The paper track originally received 26 submissions of regular and short papers, of which 22 were reviewed. We accepted 11 regular papers and 6 short papers after a rigorous double-blind review process in which, on average, each submission received three reviews.

The program was opened by the keynote speaker Antti Oulasvirta, Professor at Aalto University, Finland, who discussed algorithmic and interactive aspects of Human-In-The-Loop methods for considering human agency and cognition. The closing keynote was given by Nava Tintarev, Professor at Maastricht University, who covered the reasons for developing decision-support systems that can explain themselves, and how to assess whether they successfully support users in making their decisions.

The program also hosted a Doctoral Consortium and three workshops: CoPDA 2023 on Artificial and/or Human Intelligence: Nurturing Computational Fluency in the Digital Age, CSE4IA on Cyber Security Education for Industry and Academia, and EMPATHY on Empowering People in Dealing with Internet of Things Ecosystems.

We thank all the authors and reviewers for their commitment and contribution to make the symposium a successful event!

April 2023

Lucio Davide Spano
Albrecht Schmidt
Carmen Santoro
Simone Stumpf

Organization

Program Committee Chairs

Santoro, Carmen   ISTI-CNR, Italy
Stumpf, Simone   University of Glasgow, UK

Program Committee

Simone Barbosa   PUC-Rio, Brazil
Barbara Rita Barriceli   University of Brescia, Italy
Andrea Bellucci   Universidad Carlos III de Madrid, Spain
Simone Borsci   University of Twente, The Netherlands
Paolo Bottoni   Sapienza University of Rome, Italy
Paolo Buono   University of Bari, Italy
Silvio Carta   University of Hertfordshire, UK
Luigi De Russis   Politecnico di Torino, Italy
Giuseppe Desolda   University of Bari, Italy
Paloma Diaz   Universidad Carlos III de Madrid, Spain
Sebastian Feger   LMU Munich, Germany
Daniela Fogli   University of Brescia, Italy
Thomas Kosch   Humboldt University Berlin, Germany
Rosa Lanzilotti   University of Bari, Italy
Catherine Letondal   ENAC, France
Angela Locoro   University Carlo Cattaneo, Italy
Thomas Ludwig   University of Siegen, Germany
Monica Maceli   Pratt Institute, USA
Marco Manca   CNR-ISTI, Italy
Maristella Matera   Politecnico di Milano, Italy
Alessandra Melonio   Università Ca' Foscari Venezia, Italy
Alberto Monge Roffarello   Università di Torino, Italy
Anders Morch   University of Oslo, Norway
Teresa Onorati   Universidad Carlos III de Madrid, Spain
Fabio Paternò   ISTI-CNR, Italy
Antonio Piccinno   University of Bari, Italy
Fabio Pittarello   Università Ca' Foscari Venezia, Italy
Gustavo Rossi   National University of La Plata, Argentina
Carmen Santoro   ISTI-CNR, Italy

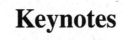

Keynotes

Putting the Human Back in the Loop

Antti Oulasvirta

Aalto University, Finland
`antti.oulasvirta@aalto.fi`

Extended Abstract

Human-in-the-loop (HITL) methods utilize human input to steer a learning or optimization algorithm. *Bayesian optimization* is a method for optimizing complex designs with many tunable parameters [4]. The method has raised interest in human-computer interaction (HCI) thanks to three benefits: First, it guides users in exploring complex decision spaces by proposing which candidates to try next; second, it can optimize opaque functions, enabling applications in cases where objective functions contain subjective elements like human preferences; third, it is sample-efficient – users are minimally bothered. In practice, when used as a HITL method, Bayesian optimization presents candidate designs to a human one at a time. Based on evaluative feedback, it builds a proxy model, which it then uses to decide where to sample next and to approach the optimal solution.

Why is it that – despite the favorable properties – Bayesian optimization and other HITL methods are not as popular in HCI applications as perhaps expected?

In this keynote, I look at Bayesian optimization as an example of using AI as a partner in HCI. The method appears particularly suitable for problems where the problem can be cast in terms of tuning parameters. In such cases, empirical evidence suggests that it can reduce human effort and increase the quality of outcomes. However, I argue that significant improvements can be made by rethinking the foundations of the method, especially its assumptions about humans and their tasks.

I argue that HITL methods should not treat people as mere sources of evaluative feedback. While these methods can help in well-defined design problems, professional users thwart them because of loss of agency and control [1]. I visit some assumptions of Bayesian optimization that are often violated. For example, users often deliberately provide feedback that is biased. As one such case, I discuss 'white lies', or how users exaggerate their inputs in order to steer the optimizer [2]. Moreover, their feedback is non-stationary. For example, design, as an activity, is a process of learning and reflection, which means that the criteria users use evolves over time [3].

In general, the nature of human decision-making and creativity should be more deeply appreciated. Practically all real-world design problems involve multiple objectives. While multi-objective HITL does exist, technically, regular users are not able to deal with concepts like a prior, optimization, or Pareto frontier. HITL methods should simply explain the winning designs and their tradeoffs with indicators of uncertainty. Experts also have a lot of tacit knowledge and best practices that they should be better able to express to the algorithm. They should be able to skip options and steer the optimize to explore options that they find promising. They should be able to strategically provide low-fidelity (fast, inexpensive) evaluations instead of high-fidelity (costly, high accuracy) evaluations. I discuss interaction techniques to this end called *cooperative Bayesian optimization.*

To conclude the keynote, I propose a roadmap for human-centric human-in-the-loop methods. I present a vision for increasing the adoption of Bayesian optimization.

Biography

Professor Antti Oulasvirta leads the User Interfaces research group at Aalto University and the Interactive AI research program at FCAI (Finnish Center for AI). Prior to joining Aalto, he was a Senior Researcher at the Max Planck Institute for Informatics and the Cluster of Excellence on Multimodal Computing and Interaction at Saarland university. He received his doctorate in Cognitive Science from the University of Helsinki in 2006. He was awarded the ERC Starting Grant (2015-2020) for research on computational design of user interfaces.

Acknowledgements. I am thankful to my colleagues Yi-Chi Liao, John Dudley, Per Ola Kristensson, Liwei Chan, and George Mo.

References

1. Chan, L., et al.: Investigating positive and negative qualities of human-in-the-loop optimization for designing interaction techniques. In: Proceedings of the 2022 CHI Conference on Human Factors in Computing Systems, pp. 1–14 (2022)
2. Colella, F., Daee, P., Jokinen, J., Oulasvirta, A., Kaski, S.: Human strategic steering improves performance of interactive optimization. In: Proceedings of the 28th ACM Conference on User Modeling, Adaptation and Personalization, pp. 293–297 (2020)
3. Liao, Y.C., et al.: Interaction design with multi-objective Bayesian optimization. IEEE Pervasive Comput. (2023)
4. Shahriari, B., Swersky, K., Wang, Z., Adams, R.P., De Freitas, N.: Taking the human out of the loop: a review of Bayesian optimization. Proc. IEEE **104**(1), 148–175 (2015)

How Do We Make Explanations Beneficial to Different Users?

Nava Tintarev

Maastricht University and TU Delft, the Netherlands
n.tintarev@maastrichtuniversity.nl

Extended Abstract

Some computer systems operate as artificial advice givers: they propose and evaluate options while involving their human users in the decision making process. For example, a regulator of waterways may use a decision support system to decide which boats to check for legal infringements, a concerned citizen might used a system to find reliable information about a new virus, or an employer might use an artificial advice giver to choose between potential candidates. However, while we need to be able to assess the advice of these AI systems, as users, we do not know when we can rely on these models and predictions, since they typically operate as black boxes. This keynote focuses specifically on such explanations for *advice-giving systems*, such as recommender systems or predictive classifiers. For explanations to be useful, they need to be able to justify the advice in a *human-understandable* way. This creates a necessity for techniques for automatic generation of satisfactory explanations that are *intelligible* for users interacting with the system. However, understanding is rarely an end-goal in itself. Pragmatically, it is more useful to operationalize the effectiveness of explanations in terms of a specific notion of usefulness or explanatory goals such as improved decision support or user trust [6]. One aspect of intelligibility of an explainable system (often cited for domains such as health) is the ability for users to accurately identify, or correct, an error made by the system. In that case it may be preferable to generate explanations that induce appropriate levels of reliance (in contrast to over- or under-reliance) [1], supporting the user in discarding recommendations when the system is incorrect, but also accepting correct recommendations. The domain affects not only the overall cost of an error, but the cost of a specific type of error (e.g., a false negative might be more harmful than a false positive for diagnosing a terminal illness). In domains such as news, or search on disputed topics, a different goal might be more suitable, such as explanations that facilitate users' epistemic goals (e.g., broadening their knowledge within a topic) [5], or mitigate their confirmation bias [4]. Assessing the effect of explanations on given explanatory goals requires systematic user-centered evaluation. To understand which explanation (e.g., with regard to modality, degree of interactivity, level of detail, and concrete presentational choices) for explanations, it is vital to identify which requirements are placed by *individual characteristics*, the *domain*, as well as the *context* in which the explanations are given. For example, in the music recommender domain, personal characteristics such as domain expertise and visual memory have been found to influence explanation effectiveness [2]. Other contextual factors, such as group dynamics, create additional requirements on explanations, such as balancing privacy and transparency [3].

Bio

Nava Tintarev is a Full Professor of Explainable Artificial Intelligence at Maastricht University, and a guest professor at TU Delft. She leads or contributes to several projects in the field of human-computer interaction in artificial advice-giving systems, such as recommender systems; specifically developing the state-of-the-art for automatically generated explanations (transparency) and explanation interfaces (recourse and control). She currently participates in a Marie-Curie Training Network on Natural Language for Explainable AI (October 2019 — October 2024). She is also representing Maastricht University as a Co-Investigator in the ROBUST consortium, selected for a national (NWO) grant with a total budget of 95M (25M from NWO) to carry out long-term (10-years) research into trustworthy artificial intelligence, and co-director of the TAIM lab on trustworthy media. She regularly shapes international scientific research programs (e.g., on steering committees of journals, or as program chair of conferences), and actively organizes and contributes to high-level strategic workshops relating to responsible data science, both in the Netherlands and internationally. She has published over 80 peer-reviewed papers in top human-computer interaction and artificial intelligence journals and conferences such as UMUAI, TiiS, ECAI, ECIR, IUI, Recsys, and UMAP. These include best paper awards at Hypertext, CHI, HCOMP, and CHIIR.

References

1. Cau, F., Hauptmann, H., Spano, D., Tintarev, N.: Effects of AI and logic-style explanations on users' decisions under different levels of uncertainty. TiiS (2023)
2. Jin, Y., Tintarev, N., Htun, N.N., Verbert, K.: Effects of personal characteristics in control-oriented user interfaces for music recommender systems. User Model. User-Adap. Inter. 1–51 (2019)
3. Najafian, S., Delic, A., Tkalčič, M., Tintarev, N.: Factors influencing privacy concern for explanations of group recommendation. In: UMAP (2021)
4. Rieger, A., Draws, T., Theune, M., Tintarev, N.: This item might reinforce your opinion: obfuscation and labeling of search results to mitigate confirmation bias. In: Hypertext (2021)
5. Sullivan, E., et al.: Reading news with a purpose: explaining user profiles for self-actualization. In: Adjunct Publication of the 27th Conference on User Modeling, Adaptation and Personalization, pp. 241–245 (2019)
6. Tintarev, N., Masthoff, J.: Beyond explaining single item recommendations. In: Ricci, F., Rokach, L., Shapira, B. (eds.) Recommender Systems Handbook. Springer, New York (2012). https://doi.org/10.1007/978-1-0716-2197-4_19

Contents

Artificial Intelligence for End-Users

Adaptive and Adaptable Systems: Differentiating and Integrating AI and EUD

Gerhard Fischer[✉]

Center for Life Long Learning & Design (L3D), Department of Computer Science and Institute
of Cognitive Science, University of Colorado, Boulder, USA
gerhard@colorado.edu

Abstract. The framework presented in the paper identifies the promises and pitfalls of *Artificial Intelligence (AI)* and *End-User Development (EUD)* approaches by focusing on two basic system components: (1) *adaptive systems* (grounded in AI) *t*hat change their behavior automatically driven by context-aware mechanisms including models of their users and specific task contexts, and (2) *adaptable systems* (grounded in EUD) that can be adjusted, modified, and extended by their users in order to capture unforeseen and important emergent user needs and aspects of problems. Grounded in an analysis of design trade-offs between the two approaches, arguments, and examples for creating a desirable symbiosis between adaptive and adaptable systems are described and design guidelines for future socio-technical environments are explored contributing to the development of theoretical concepts for the future of EUD.

Keywords: artificial intelligence · adaptive systems · context-aware
interactions · user and task modeling · Personalization · end-user development ·
adaptable systems meta-design · creativity · Auto-Correct · ChatGPT · design
trade-offs · design guidelines

1 Introduction

Research efforts arguing for the need and desirability of socio-technical environments that support users of all ages to think, learn, work, and collaborate in more productive and more creative ways have been the objective of numerous research disciplines including computer science, cognitive science, and the learning sciences [1]. More specifically, the research has been pursued in *Artificial Intelligence (AI)* [2] and *End-User Development (EUD)* [3]. AI and EU are research areas which have multiple meanings and are often used without any detailed descriptions and simple definitions of the two research themes are not sufficiently descriptive. By focusing on *adaptive* approaches (relying primarily on AI) and *adaptable* approaches (relying primarily on EUD), the paper attempts to deepen the understanding of the challenges, promises, pitfalls, and design trade-offs associated with future socio-technical environments contributing to the *quality of life* in the digital age [4–6].

© The Author(s), under exclusive license to Springer Nature Switzerland AG 2023
L. D. Spano et al. (Eds.): IS-EUD 2023, LNCS 13917, pp. 3–18, 2023.
https://doi.org/10.1007/978-3-031-34433-6_1

2 Differentiating AI and EUD Approaches

There is no generally accepted definition for AI and there is no defined boundary to separate "AI systems" from "non-AI systems". Despite this shortcoming AI is currently being considered world-wide as a "Deus ex Machina" and it is credited with miraculous abilities to solve all problems and exploit unique opportunities of the digital age (the most prominent example emerging in late 2022 being ChatGPT that is briefly discussed later in the paper). AI (as characterized by this paper) explores technology-centered approaches, replacing human beings by automating how decisions and conclusions are reached. AI involves the creation of models and algorithms that can analyze data, learn from it, and make predictions or decisions based on that data. These kinds of AI applications include natural language processing, image recognition, self-driving vehicles, and chatbots.

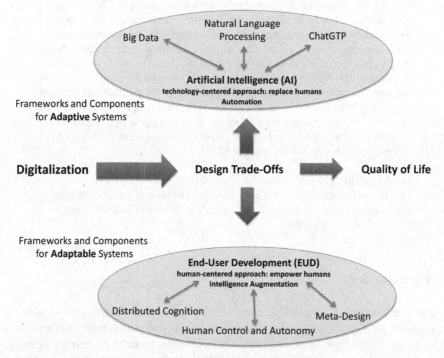

Fig. 1. Differentiating AI and EUD Approaches.

EUD is instrumental for the ability to create and reformulate knowledge, for allowing all stakeholders to express themselves creatively and appropriately, and for producing and generating information rather than simply comprehending existing information. It supports diverse audiences in designing and building their own artifacts by situating computation in new contexts, by generating content, and by developing tools that democratize design, innovation, and knowledge creation [7]. With computers and software becoming pervasive, many domain experts have started to develop or adapt sophisticated software systems as an integral part of their work to fully utilize the power of the computer. They are not professionally educated as software engineers but spend a great deal of their time creating software systems for their own work. Given how domain experts' needs, goals, and education differ from those of professional software engineers, end-user development research should not be based on a scaled-down version of, or a simple transfer from, current software engineering principles [8].

Figure 1 tries to illustrate the relationship between the two approaches.

3 AutoCorrect: A Simple Example for Illustration

The following simple example illustrates the abstract approaches in a specific context. AutoCorrect is a software feature commonly found in word processing programs (such as Microsoft Word). The adaptive part of AutoCorrect detects and corrects misspelled words e.g., (1) "hte" is transformed into "the" and (2) "EHR" into "HER".

Typed Text by the User:
    This letter is written to hte National Science Foundation Agency EHR

Revised Text by the AutoCorrect:
    This letter is written to the National Science Foundation Agency HER

Fig. 2. The adaptive component of AutoCorrect in action.

These modifications are done *automatically* by an AI-based systems relying on 1) an extensive dictionary of correct spellings in the English language, (2) the recognition that "hte" or "EHR" are no English words, and (3) the knowledge that transposition errors are mistakes that people make frequently.

The example shows the fundamental limitations of adaptive features (and AI systems in general): their knowledge of the world is limited. While the change of "hte" to "the" in Fig. 2 is welcome, the replacement of "EHR" is inappropriate in this context. The example documents a real event: by going unnoticed in a communication with the NSF funding agency "Education and Human Resources (EHR)", the change (being unnoticed by the writer) did not leave a good impression of the research team applying for funding by using a wrong abbreviation for the name of the agency.

The designers of AutoCorrect recognized this limitation of the adaptive part of AutoCorrect, and they added an adaptable component (see Fig. 3) that allows users to overwrite existing modifications of the adaptive system. With this extension in place AutoCorrect replaces the original sentence of Fig. 2 correctly.

Beyond adaptive and adaptable components AutoCorrect includes a third heuristic: in cases where it identifies a potential misspelling with the adaptive component, but it is unsure which replacement should be chosen it returns control to the users with a set of possible modification and delegates the control to the user to decide (see Fig. 4). This feature illustrates a simple heuristic for a symbiotic relationship between adaptive and adaptable features (further discussed later in the paper).

Replace:

ehr

With:

Education and Human Resources

• Plain text   ○ Formatted text

effecient	efficient
efort	effort
eforts	efforts
ehr	her
eligable	eligible

[Replace]   [Delete]

Fig. 3. The Interface of Auto-Correct to Support Adaptations by Users.

There are several additional features in AutoCorrect relevant for the theme of AI and/versus EUD including: (1) turning AutoCorrect off completely, and (2) ignoring the suggestions made by the adaptive systems.

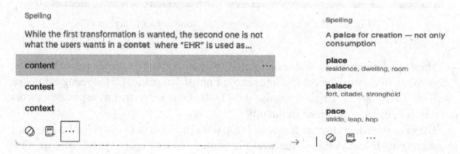

Fig. 4. Two Examples simplifying the adaptable component with suggestions from the adaptive component.

4 Adaptive Systems

Adaptive systems change their behavior automatically, driven by context-aware mechanisms [9] including models of their users and of specific tasks. Adaptive systems are important because the "typical" user of a system does not exist; there are many different users, and the requirements of an individual user usually change with experience [10]. Simple classification schemes based on stereotypes, such as novice, intermediate, or expert users, are inadequate for complex knowledge-based systems because they do not take contexts into account. One of the central objectives of user modeling in Human-Computer Interaction (HCI) [11] is to address the problem that systems will be unable to interact with users cooperatively unless they have some means of finding out what individual users really know, do and intend. Techniques to achieve these objectives are: (1) being told by the users (e.g., by questionnaires, setting preferences, or specification components), and (2) being able to infer it from the user's actions (e.g., by analyzing usage data).

This section will describe some of the more prevalent benefits and drawbacks associated with the development and use of *adaptive* systems.

Benefit: Reducing Information Overload with Personalization. Personalization techniques are widely used in major technological developments; some prominent examples are:

- *Recommender systems* [12] assist customers in buying books or selecting movies of special interest for them. The basic idea of these systems is to present a selection of items to users which correspond closely to their specific interests. The collected data is based on items users have bought, recently viewed, and rated, and suggestions of interesting collaborations as identified by "big data" analyses [13];
- *Intelligent Tutoring Systems* [14] employ adaptive components by dynamically adjusting the level or type of course content based on an individual student's abilities contained in user models. They identify *zones of learnability* [15] by determining the gap between what a student knows and what a student is supposed to learn (e.g. according to defined learning goals) by moving students through a personalized learning path to prescribed learning outcomes and skill mastery.

Benefit: Becoming Aware of Unknown Things with Information Delivery. Information access (based on "pull" approaches) and information delivery (based on "push" approaches) are two approaches for obtaining information [1]. Information access relies on user-initiated searches, while information delivery is a system-initiated presentation of information that is intended to be relevant to the user's task. Information access schemes help the designer *articulate* information needs, while information delivery schemes *infer* information needs. Support for information access is indispensable since designers must have support to search for information when they perceive the need. Information delivery is a complementary approach that is particularly important when users are not motivated to look for information or are not aware of the existence of relevant information.

The fundamental challenge for information delivery systems is not to provide more information "to anyone, at any time, and from anywhere," but to keep them quiet most of the time by exploiting context-aware mechanisms for identifying *"the 'right' information, at the 'right' time, in the 'right' place, in the 'right' way, to the 'right' person."* [9].

Drawback: Personalization Leading to a Lack of Shared Experiences and Common Understanding. Personalization [9] supported by adaptive system components addresses the fundamental issue that the scarce resource in the digital age is not information but human attention. Simon [16] illustrates this fact with convincing examples that design representations suitable for a world in which the scarce factor is information may be exactly the wrong ones for a world in which the scarce factor is attention. Reducing the information is highly desirable but it represents a design trade-off [17] that needs to be taken into account, and the pros and cons need to be carefully evaluated. One of the things that binds a culture together is that people are exposed to the same relevant information presented from different points of view. One of the pitfalls of adaptive systems and user models is that they can and will create filter bubbles and echo chambers [18]. The polarization based on individual universes of information has become a defining characteristic in our world of today. Grounded in interests captured by big data, citizens will be grouped into types and be confronted with information that corresponds to their preferences and conforms to their beliefs which leads to *group think* [19]. There are numerous prominent examples such as (1) people in the USA watching CNN or Fox News will form beliefs and act accordingly as they would live in two different worlds and (2) the Corona virus has split societies around the world in totally opposed camps believing in vaccination or totally opposing it. To address global problems (such as Corona, climate change, digitalization, fake news, and the widening economic divide) requires the efforts of large communities and massive coordination to create a common understanding based on shared experience [20]. Groupthink, filter bubbles, and echo chambers represent serious obstacles for a future world in which people make conscious efforts to create common ground and avoid further polarization.

Drawback: Lack of Meaningful Explanations. Many current systems (specifically AI systems based on correlations within big data sets [13]) are unable to provide understandable explanations about their behavior. The inner workings of such systems are "black boxes": they provide recommendations and answers, but they are unable to explain the underlying rationale needed for empowering users to adapt systems to their needs.

A simple example (encountered a couple of years ago by the author) occurred in the context of using the navigation system of a rental car. The fact that it was a rental car limited our familiarity with the functionality of the navigation system. We programmed the system to guide us the quickest way to our destination. Continuing our trip with the navigation system in operation, it advised us at every exit to leave the freeway. Without any way to query our navigation system and because we were familiar with the geography, we decided not to follow the advice that the system repeated at every exit. Unable to explore the differences between the system's knowledge and ours for choosing the most preferable route, we followed our plan and shut the system off.

The navigation system acting as an adaptive system was unable to describe its intention in a way that we were able to understand. Drivers do not have any way to query these systems and they cannot adopt individual user's perspectives to determine what statement would satisfy them. They cannot convey confidence in the route they have selected (other than giving a probabilistic estimate of the time differential for alternative routes), whereas we wanted them to explain the assumptions they are making for their recommendation.

When we returned the car and described the encountered problem, the rental car agent provided us with an explanation: somewhere deep down in a complex web of options there was a flag "do not use freeways"—and the previous renter had selected this option as part of the adaptable features. An intelligent navigation system would have allowed us to ask the question "why should we leave the freeway" and then guided us to find the flag that was responsible for this behavior.

5   Adaptable Systems

New design methodologies [3, 21] explore that the once sharp distinction between users and developers of software is fading away, and many users are starting to take control of shaping software with adaptable systems to their needs by engaging in end-user development. Adaptable systems provide foundations for "democratizing innovation" as argued by von Hippel [7]: *"Users that innovate can develop exactly what they want, rather than relying on manufacturers to act as their (often very imperfect) agents. Moreover, individual users do not have to develop everything they need on their own: they can benefit from innovations developed and freely shared by others"*. Figure 3 illustrates the adaptable component of Auto-Correct to overwrite the changes made by the adaptive component. Another simple but useful adaptable system component supports the development of macros in MS-Word.

On a global scale, adaptable systems can be supported by: (1) offering task-specific languages supporting human problem-domain interaction with domain-oriented design environments [22]; (2) providing programming environments that protect users from low-level computational drudgery [23]; (3) supporting customization, reuse, and redesign effectively [24]; and (4) tailoring software applications at use time with component-based approaches [25];

This section will describe some of the benefits and drawbacks associated with the development and use of *adaptable* systems.

Benefit: Creating Support Environments for Adaptable Systems with Meta-design. *Meta-design* ("design for designers") [26] is a theoretical framework to conceptualize and to cope in unique ways with design problems. It is focused on open-ended co-design processes in which all the involved actors actively participate in different ways. It is grounded in the fundamental assumption that design is not a matter of getting rid of the emergent, but rather of including it and making it an opportunity for more creative and more adequate solutions to problems by supporting adaptable systems [27].

Research resulted in the following design requirements for encouraging end-users to engage in adaptable extensions [28]: (1) making changes must seem possible; (2) changes must be technically feasible; (3) benefits must be perceived by the stakeholders who do the work associated with the adaptations; (4) low barriers must exist for sharing changes; and (5) the original designers acting as meta-designers must be willing to share control of how systems will be used, which content will be contained, and which functionality will be supported.

Benefit: Putting the Problem Owners in Charge. A challenge for many software systems is the growing importance of application domain knowledge held by domain experts rather than by software developers, who suffer from a "thin spread of application domain knowledge" [29]. Another challenge is the need for open, evolvable systems that can adjust to fluctuating and conflicting requirements.

A interview that we conducted with a geoscientist highlights the importance of these challenges that can be addressed by adaptable components. He uses several existing domain-specific software systems to analyze his research data. However, those systems cannot provide complete solutions to his problems as his research unfolds and his understanding of the problem, data, and results progresses. He said: *"I spend on average an hour every day developing software for myself to analyze the data I collected because there is not any available software. Even if there is a software developer sitting next to me, it would not be of much help because my needs vary as my research progresses and I cannot clearly explain what I want to do at any moment. Even if the software developer can manage to write a program for me, I will not know if he or she has done it right without looking at the code."*

He continued *"so I spent three months to gain enough programming knowledge to get by. Software development has now become an essential task of my research, but I do not consider myself a software developer, and I don't know many other things about software development."*

This example provides evidence for democratizing innovation (see comment from von Hippel [7] earlier in the paper) and that software development is no longer the exclusive activity of professional software engineers. *Domain experts* being the owners of problems such as this geoscientist are engaged in intensive software development and adaptable systems provide important support environments to address this challenge. In education the Scratch project [23] very successfully made it easy for millions of children of all ages, backgrounds, and interests to engage in creating and remixing, and not just in browsing and interacting.

Drawback: Participation Overload. Adaptable systems open unique new opportunities for mass collaboration and social production [30], but these engagements are not without drawbacks. One such drawback is that humans may be forced to cope with the burden of being active contributors in personally irrelevant activities leading to a *participation overload* [31]. "Do-it-yourself" societies empower humans with powerful tools; however, they force them to perform many tasks themselves that were done previously by skilled domain workers serving as agents and intermediaries. Although this shift provides power, freedom, and control to users and customers, it also has urged people to act as contributors in contexts for which they lack the experience that professionals have at their disposal.

Drawback: Complexity and Heterogeneity of End Users. End users are a diverse group with varying levels of technical expertise. The needs and preferences of end users can vary widely depending on the context and domain, making it difficult to design EUD systems that meet everyone's needs.

Drawback: The Tension Between Standardization and Improvisation. Adaptable systems create inherent tensions between standardization and improvisation. The SAP Info [32] argues to reduce the number of customer modifications: *"every customer modification implies costs because it has to be maintained by the customer. Each time a support package is imported there is a risk that the customer modification may have to be adjusted or re-implemented. To reduce the costs of such on-going maintenance of customer-specific changes, one of the key targets during an up-grade should be to return to the SAP standard wherever this is possible."* Finding the right balance between standardization (which can suppress innovation and creativity) and improvisation (which can lead to a Babel of different and incompatible versions) represents an important design trade-off (e.g., in open-source environments, in which forking leads developers in different directions).

Summary. Table 1 summarizes the major distinction between adaptive and adaptable systems.

Table 1. A Comparison and Differentiation between Adaptive and Adaptable Systems.

	Adaptive systems	Adaptable systems
Definition	Suggestions generated by systems for specific tasks and users	Users actively change the functionality of the system leading to distributed control
Knowledge	contained in the system; projected in different ways	Knowledge is curated, modified, and extended by users resulting in living systems
Strengths/Benefits	Little (or no) effort by users; no special user knowledge is required; work *for* people	Users are in control; users know their tasks best; work *with* people
Weaknesses/Drawbacks	Users lack control; shared understanding is reduced resulting in filter bubbles; lack of explainability; skill degradation	Users must do substantial work (participation overload); require a learning effort; create a tool mastery burden; systems may become incompatible
Mechanisms required	Models of users and tasks; context awareness; big data resources; intelligent agents	Meta-design environments supporting modifiability, tailorability, and evolution
Application domains	Recommender systems, intelligent tutoring systems, conversational agents	Open systems, co-designed systems, end-user development
Primary Techniques	automation grounded in Artificial Intelligence (AI) approaches	Human involvement grounded in Intelligence Augmentation (IA) approaches

6   Challenges for the Future

This section will discuss how the framework based on the analysis of adaptive and adaptable systems in the previous sections can provide design ideas and guidelines for differentiating and integrating AI and EUD and thereby contributing theoretical concepts and foundations for the field of end-user development.

6.1   Example: ChatGPT—The Newest "MIraculous" AI Development

As mentioned earlier *ChatGPT* (Chat Generative Pre-trained Transformer; https://en.wikipedia.org/wiki/ChatGPT) is credited with miraculous abilities to create unique and far-reaching new opportunities for Natural Language Understanding, Question Answering, Content Creation, and Education. It is a conversational AI program (a "chatbot") developed by OpenAI and launched in November 2022. It has generated worldwide attention and the initial assessments combine *praise* such as.

- a significant advancement that can produce articles in response to open-ended questions that are comparable to good high school essays;
- the shift to making search engines more conversational being able to confidently answer questions rather than offering links to other websites could change the advertising-fueled search business;
- changing our mind about how we work, how we think, and what human creativity really is;
- OpenAI is gathering data from ChatGPT to further train and fine-tune ChatGPT in the future;

with fundamental criticisms such as,

- it poses risks if it does not get its facts right;
- its fluency is an illusion that stems from the combination of massive amounts of data, immense computing power, and novel processing techniques;
- it is not capable of understanding the context or meaning of the words it generates; it can only produce text based on the probabilities of certain words or sequences of words appearing together, based on the training data it has been given;
- it is difficult for humans to scrutinize the answer produced;
- it will give sometimes answers that are not related to the questions asked, and it will occasionally make up facts or "hallucinate" outputs.

Figure 5 provides an example showing ChatGPT's response to a question relevant to the theme of this paper.

Figure 6 shows an architectural overview diagram of the two examples AutoCorrect and ChatGPT) indicating adaptive AI components and adaptable EUD components.

The same analysis can be applied to understand adaptive and adaptable components of the current version of ChatGPT can provide theoretically grounded design ideas for its future development by exploring questions such as:

- Should further developments of ChatGPT strengthen the adaptive and/or adaptable components (in which way and to which extent)?
- Can users trust the answers provided by ChatGPT?
- Can ChatGPT support and enhance EUD capabilities when learners and workers use its answers not as final results but as additional commentaries and creative prompts enriching their further analysis?

A critical design challenge that has already generated numerous widely diverging views is to understand the implications of ChatGPT for *learning, teaching, and education* [33]. With ChatGPT being around only since late 2022, there are many unknowns about how it will be used, adopted, and further developed in the coming years. To increase our understanding much can be learnt from the controversial assumptions that governed the

Question by a user: How is ChatGPT related to AI and EUD?

ChatGPT's response: ChatGPT is a type of AI (Artificial Intelligence) system that uses Natural Language Processing (NLP) and Deep Learning algorithms to generate human-like responses to user inputs.

EUD (End-User Development) refers to the ability of non-technical users to create, modify, and personalize software applications to meet their specific needs. While ChatGPT is not directly related to EUD, it has the potential to be used as a tool for end-users to interact with software applications in a more natural and conversational way.

For example, a user could interact with a chatbot powered by ChatGPT to perform a task or retrieve information from a software application. By providing a conversational interface, the chatbot could make the application more accessible to users who may not be familiar with its traditional user interface. Additionally, as ChatGPT continues to improve and become more adaptable, it could potentially be used to personalize the user experience of software applications based on a user's language and preferences.

Fig. 5. ChatGPT in action

original discussion of Massive Open Online Courses (MOOCs) when they first appeared a decade ago [34]. Some of the controversial issues are:

- Will ChatGPT enhance or replace the necessity for writing essays?
- Where to draw the line between ChatGPT being used as an assistant for writing (the EUD approach) versus letting it take over the whole process (the AI approach)?
- Will its availability contribute to making the "flipped classroom" a more attainable reality because it makes relevant information readily available?
- Should teachers and learners become informed about the promises and pitfalls of ChatGPT and develop new and different skills?
- Which (current and future) mechanisms are required to turn ChatGPT from a black box into a glass box thereby empowering learners to scrutinize the answers provided?

6.2 Symbiosis Between Adaptive and Adaptable Systems

In the previous sections of the paper and in Table 1, benefits and drawbacks of adaptive and adaptable systems were identified [35]. This analysis can serve as the foundation to create a *symbiosis* between adaptive and adaptable systems [36] and between AI and EUD approaches [37].

An adaptive system can provide valuable input to an adaptable system. As indicated in the AutoCorrect example, the adaptive component could generate a list of suggestions to support the adaptation process by the user to choose the correct choice. Answers generated by the adaptive component of ChatGPT (see Fig. 5) maybe most valuable if not seen as "final", but as starting points and inspirations for users to further adapt and

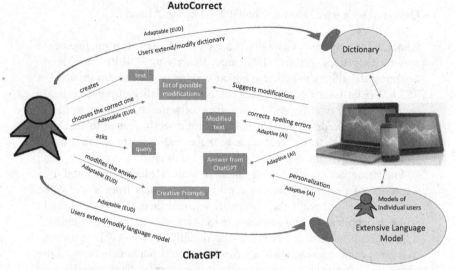

Fig. 6. The Intertwining of Adaptive and Adaptable components in AutoCorrect and ChatGPT << the symbiotic options are colored in orange >>

improve the information content. In adaptive approaches, models of users and tasks can be inferred indirectly from interactions with systems whereas in adaptable approaches they can be described explicitly via specifications component [11].

Another rationale to support the integration is to compare ChatGPT and EUD with the framework of fast and slow thinking [38]. Fast thinking is automatic, intuitive, and effortless but prone to errors and biases. Slow thinking is controlled, rational, creative, and more accurate and reliable. Kahneman's research demonstrates that human cognition is a *mixture* of these two modes of thinking. ChatGPT engages very successfully in "fast thinking" operations and can and should be complemented by the "slow thinking" component of EUD that verifies and transcend the information given [39].

Identifying and exploiting symbiotic relationships between adaptive and adaptable components can contribute to the objective to improve the *quality of life* in the digital age [6]. Digitalization will transform the world, but it does not mandate a single deterministic outcome and design trade-offs can spark efforts toward syntheses that lead to new levels of understanding and can productively exploit the best mixes between opposing choices. Automation (supported by adaptive components and AI approaches) can be a two-edged sword [40, 41]: (1) it is a *servant,* relieving humans of the tedium of low-level operations, and freeing them for higher cognitive functions or (2) it can reduce the status of humans to that of *button pushers,* and can strip their work of its meaning and satisfaction and eliminate learning opportunities.

The desirability of adaptable approaches and EUDs approaches to positively contribute to quality of life objectives is grounded in the fact that human beings value things and relationships for which they have to make an effort in obtaining them and in which they find purpose, enjoyment, and flow states [42]. Humans (in the context of *personally meaningful* tasks) enjoy 'doing' and 'deciding', 'they want control and autonomy, and they enjoy the process, and not just the final product [40]. But these objectives come with a price tag: they require time, engagement, and learning, and may lead (as indicated earlier) to *participation overload* [28, 31] which can be addressed and reduced by carefully designed adaptive components.

6.3 Design Guidelines

Adaptive and adaptable systems will be important components of future socio-technical environments. This section summarizes some *design guidelines* grounded in the frameworks and examples discussed in the paper.

- *Identify the design trade-offs associated with different approaches* including: to understand the benefits and pitfalls of adaptive and adaptable systems their uses must be situated and explored in specific contexts because there are no decontextualized sweet spots in design problems [5].
- *Strengthen the Benefits of Adaptive Systems* including: to reduce information overload, deliver unknown functionality and information, support personalization to focus attention, complement the tool approach with intelligent agents [43].
- *Strengthen the Benefits of Adaptable Systems* including: to create sociotechnical environments that empower domain experts to engage actively in the continuous development of systems rather than restricting them to using existing systems; support meta-design at design time for creating solution spaces in which users can create their own solutions to fit their needs at use time [28].
- *Be aware of the Drawbacks of Adaptive Systems* including being enclosed in filter bubbles and echo chambers; lack of explainability of the algorithmic decisions; and privacy intrusions [18].
- *Be aware of the Drawbacks of Adaptable Systems* including participation overload; incompatible version of systems; lack of rewards and recognition of contributions [5].
- *Give Humans Control over Technology* including: to identify the right mix between computer-based automation (replacing human beings) and human control (empowering human beings) [44].
- *Explore the Opportunities for Creating Symbiotic Relationships between Adaptive and Adaptable Systems* including adaptive systems analyze what exists and can provide foundations for how new functionality can be added with adaptable components; support user-controlled adaptation with system-generated adaptive suggestions [36].

6.4 Implication

Most of the currently existing AI approaches and visions are over-inclusive and reflect the common tendency to use the "AI" label as a catchall marketing phrase. AI is a "suitcase word" to which people attribute multiple meanings [45]. There is a need to differentiate AI and explore complementary approaches such as EUD.

This paper attempts to use the distinction between adaptive and adaptable approaches to show that AI can contribute not only by replacing human beings but in a synergistic fashion empowering them to act as active contributors in EUD to transcend "how things are" by exploring *"how things could or should be"* [16]. An essential challenge is that

AI and EUD will find more new ways to communicate with each other [37]. Because the most fundamental problems that our world is facing are wicked and ill-defined [46], the future must remain something to which all stakeholders can make contributions. Providing all citizens in EUD approaches with the means to become co-creators of new ideas, knowledge, and products in personally meaningful activities presents one of the most exciting innovations and transformations with profound implications in the years to come.

7 Conclusions

To enrich rather than limit human lives with AI and EUD systems, discourses and investigations must not only be focused on technological issues but explore motivation, control, ownership, and autonomy. A better understanding is required of whether the technologies of the future (1) will provide us with more time, less stress, more control, and enhance human creativity or (2) will cause a shift in authority from humans to algorithms (especially with tools that humans do not understand and that cannot provide us with explanations about their actions). The relationship between AI and EUD and between adaptive and adaptable systems should not be conceptualized and driven forward by competition, but by exploiting symbiotic relationships in human-centered design approaches.

While the growth of technologies such as AI and EUD will continue in the years to come, the inevitability of any particular future is not. To improve the *quality of life* in the digital age requires the co-design of social and technical systems and requires models and concepts that exploit the social context in which the systems will be used. The paper documents frameworks and illustrates with real-world examples identified by empirical research how to differentiate and integrate AI and EUD approaches with adaptive and adaptable systems components in socio-technical environments towards achieving these objectives.

Acknowledgments. The author wishes to thank Daniela Fogli, Anders Mørch, Antonio Piccinno, and the three reviewers who provided insightful comments that greatly improved earlier versions of this article.

References

1. Brown, J.S., Duguid, P.: The Social Life of Information, Harvard Business School Press, Boston (2000)
2. Brockman, J.: Possible Minds: Twenty-Five Ways of Looking at AI. Penguin Press, London (2019)
3. Paterno, F., Wulf, V (eds.) New Perspectives in End User Development, Kluwer Publishers, Amsterdam (2017)
4. Calvo, R.A., Peters, D.: Positive Computing —Technology for Wellbeing and Human Potential. MIT Press, Cambridge (2014)
5. Fischer, G.: Design trade-offs for quality of life ACM. Interactions **25**(1), 26–33 (2018)

6. Friedman, B., Hendry D.G.: Value Sensitive Design: Shaping Technology with Moral Imagination. MIT Press Cambridge (2019)
7. von Hippel, E.: Democratizing Innovation, MIT Press, Cambridge (2005)
8. Burnett, M.: What is end-user software engineering and why does it matter? In: Pipek, V., et al. (eds.) End-User Development, pp. 15–28. Springer, Heidelberg (2009)
9. Fischer, G.: Context-aware systems: the 'right' information, at the 'right' time, in the 'right' place, in the 'right' way, to the 'right' person. In: Proceedings of the Conference on Advanced Visual Interfaces (AVI), G.T. et al (eds.) ACM: Capri, Italy (May). pp. 287–294 (2012)
10. Mackay, W.E.: Triggers and barriers to customizing software. In: Robertson, S.P., Olson, G.M., Olson J.S. (eds.) Proceedings of CHI 1991 Conference on Human Factors in Computing Systems, ACM: New York. pp. 153–160 (1991)
11. Fischer, G., User modeling in human-computer interaction. User Model User Adapt. Interact. (UMUAI), 11(1), 65–86 (2001)
12. Terveen, L., Hill, W.: Beyond recommender systems: helping people help each other. In: Carroll, J.M. (ed.) Human-Computer Interaction in the New Millennium, pp. 487–509. ACM Press, New York (2001)
13. Mayer-Schönberger, V., Cukier, K.: Big Data. Houghton Mifflin Harcourt, New York (2013)
14. Mousavinasab, E., et al.: Intelligent tutoring systems: a systematic review of characteristics, applications, and evaluation methods. Interact. Learn. Environ. 29(1), 142–163 (2021)
15. Vygotsky, L.: Thought and Language. MIT Press, Cambridge (1986)
16. Simon, H.A.: The Sciences of the Artificial, 3rd edn. The MIT Press, Cambridge (1996)
17. Fogli, D., et al.: Exploring design trade-offs for achieving social inclusion in multi-tiered design problems. Behav. Inf. Technol. 39(1), 27–46 (2020)
18. Pariser, E.: The Filter Bubble: How the New Personalized Web Is Changing What We Read and How We Think. Penguin Books (2021)
19. Janis, I.: Victims of Groupthink. Houghton Mifflin, Boston (1972)
20. Clark, H.H., Brennan, S.E.: Grounding in communication. In: Resnick, L.B, Levine, J.M., Teasley, S.D. (eds.) Perspectives on Socially Shared Cognition, pp. 127–149. American Psychological Association (1991)
21. Binder, T., et al.: Design Things. MIT Press, Cambridge (2011)
22. Norman, D.A.: Things That Make Us Smart, 290p. Addison-Wesley Publishing Company. Reading (1993)
23. Resnick, M., et al.: Scratch: programming for all. Commun. ACM 52(11), 60–67 (2009)
24. Morch, A.: Three levels of end-user tailoring: customization, integration, and extension. In: Kyng, M., Mathiassen, L. (eds.) Computers and Design in Context, pp. 51–76. MIT Press, Cambridge, MA (1997)
25. Wulf, V., Pipek, V., Won, M.: Component-based tailorability: enabling highly flexible software applications. Int. J. Hum. Comput. Stud. 66, 1–22 (2008)
26. Costabile, M.F., et al.: Advancing end user development through metadesign. In: Clarke, S. (ed.) End User Computing Challenges and Technologies: Emerging Tools and Applications, pp. 143–167. IGI Publishing (2008)
27. National-Research-Council, Beyond Productivity: Information Technology, Innovation, and Creativity. National Academy Press, Washington, DC (2003)
28. Fischer, G., Fogli, D., Piccinno, A.: Revisiting and broadening the meta-design framework for end-user development. In: Paternò, F., Wulf, V. (eds.) New Perspectives in End-User Development, pp. 61–97. Springer, Cham (2017). https://doi.org/10.1007/978-3-319-602 91-2_4
29. Curtis, B., Krasner, H., Iscoe, N.: A field study of the software design process for large systems. Commun. ACM 31(11), 1268–1287 (1988)
30. Benkler, Y.: The Wealth of Networks: How Social Production Transforms Markets and Freedom. Yale University Press, New Haven (2006)

31. Jenkins, H.: Confronting the Challenges of Participatory Cultures: Media Education for the 21st Century. MIT Press, Cambridge (2009)
32. Fischer, G., Nakakoji, K., Ye, Y.: Meta-design: guidelines for supporting domain experts in software development. In: IEEE Software, pp. 37–44, September/October (2009)
33. Collins, A.: What's Worth Teaching: Rethinking Curriculum in the Age of Technology. Teachers College Press, New York (2017)
34. DeCorte, E., Engwall, L., Teichler U (eds) From Books to MOOCs? Emerging Models of Learning and Teaching in Higher Education. Portland Press (Wenner-Gren International Series Volume 88): London (2016)
35. Maes, P., Shneiderman, B.: Direct manipulation vs. interface agents. Interactions **4**(6), 42–61 (1997) ACM Press
36. Oppermann, R.: Adaptively Supported Adaptability. Int. J. Hum. Comput. Stud. **40**(3), 455–472 (1994)
37. Markoff, J.: Machines of Loving Grace (The Quest for Common Ground Between Humans and Robots). Harpercollins (2016)
38. Kahneman, D.: Thinking, Fast and Slow. Farrar, Straus and Giroux, New York (2011)
39. Bubeck, S., Chandrasekaran, V., et al.: Sparks of artificial general intelligence: early experiments with GPT-4 (2023). https://arxiv.org/pdf/2303.12712.pdf
40. Shneiderman, B.: Human-Centered AI. Oxford University Press, Oxford (2022)
41. Carr, N.: The Glass Cage — Automation and US. Norton, New York (2014)
42. Csikszentmihalyi, M.: Creativity — Flow and the Psychology of Discovery and Invention. HarperCollins Publishers, New York (1996)
43. Fischer, G.: Domain-oriented design environments. Autom. Softw. Eng. **1**(2), 177–203 (1994)
44. Fischer, G., Nakakoji, K.: Beyond the macho approach of artificial intelligence: empower human designers - do not replace them. Knowl.-Based Syst. J. Special Iss. AI Des. **5**(1), 15–30 (1992)
45. Minsky, M.: The Emotion Machine. Simon & Schuster (2007)
46. Rittel, H., Webber, M.M.: Planning problems are wicked problems. In: Cross, N. (ed.) Developments in Design Methodology, pp. 135-144. John Wiley & Sons: New York (1984)

End-User Development for Artificial Intelligence: A Systematic Literature Review

Andrea Esposito[✉] ⓘ, Miriana Calvano ⓘ, Antonio Curci ⓘ, Giuseppe Desolda ⓘ,
Rosa Lanzilotti ⓘ, Claudia Lorusso ⓘ, and Antonio Piccinno ⓘ

Department of Computer Science, University of Bari Aldo Moro, Bari, Italy
{andrea.esposito,miriana.calvano,antonio.curci,giuseppe.desolda,
rosa.lanzilotti,antonio.piccinno}@uniba.it,
c.lorusso36@studenti.uniba.it

Abstract. In recent years, Artificial Intelligence has become more and more relevant in our society. Creating AI systems is almost always the prerogative of IT and AI experts. However, users may need to create intelligent solutions tailored to their specific needs. In this way, AI systems can be enhanced if new approaches are devised to allow non-technical users to be directly involved in the definition and personalization of AI technologies. End-User Development (EUD) can provide a solution to these problems, allowing people to create, customize, or adapt AI-based systems to their own needs. This paper presents a systematic literature review that aims to shed the light on the current landscape of EUD for AI systems, i.e., how users, even without skills in AI and/or programming, can customize the AI behavior to their needs. This study also discusses the current challenges of EUD for AI, the potential benefits, and the future implications of integrating EUD into the overall AI development process.

Keywords: Artificial Intelligence · End-User Development · No-Code · Low-Code · AI Customization

1 Introduction

A very recent survey by the McKinsey Global Institute found that by 2022, approximately 50% of the surveyed companies will use AI in at least one function [1]. Furthermore, the recent proliferation of AI products such as Chat-GPT has contributed to the growing popularity of the topic, as evidenced by a possible correlation between the popularity of the two keywords in Google searches [2].

We would like to emphasize that in this paper, unless otherwise specified, we assume a broad definition of AI that includes autonomous systems using machine learning, neural networks, and statistical methods, as well as recommender systems, adaptive systems, and systems for face, image, speech, and pattern recognition.

The motivation for this study lies in the fact that the consequences of the "one size fits all" approach often adopted by AI systems can be an advantage when it comes to reaching a broader audience, thanks to its intrinsic generality. However, such an approach often

L. D. Spano et al. (Eds.): IS-EUD 2023, LNCS 13917, pp. 19–34, 2023.
https://doi.org/10.1007/978-3-031-34433-6_2

renders the overall system inadequate for the specific and situational needs of different users. To clarify the motivation for this study, consider the following two examples. First, physicians might use an AI model to segment histology samples to aid in the diagnosis process, but they may wish to enhance its accuracy by fine-tuning it to target the specific types of cells that require segmentation. Second, a flight recommendation system may have been programmed to prioritize lower cost flights, but a user may prefer shorter flights even if they come at a higher cost. Therefore, the user may choose to personalize the AI model to better align with their preferences.

The full benefits of AI systems can be increased if new approaches are devised to allow non-technical users to be directly involved in the definition and personalization of AI technologies. In this direction, End-User Development (EUD) can provide a solution to these problems, allowing users to customize AI-based systems to their own needs and providing ways to deal with outliers and reduce bias. Another important motivation is that a few literature reviews deal with the topic of EUD for AI. For example, Gresse von Wangenheim et al. provide a comprehensive mapping of tools aiding the teaching of machine learning using visual programming paradigms [3]. Similarly, Hauck et al. provide an overview of the available tools that, using node- or block-based programming, allow the development of smart IoT devices (thus, powered by AI) [4]. An additional list of tools is provided by Queiroz et al., who provide a review of tools that may help teach lay people with a minimum understanding of what AI is [5]. More in line with our study, Li et al. provide a review of no/low code tools for AI; however, they do not cover general techniques, research trends, and challenges, which are important aspects of a Systematic Literature Review (SLR) to drive future activities or the related research area.

To fill these gaps and shed the light on the current state of the applications of EUD for AI, this paper presents an SLR that focuses on solutions that support end-users to develop, customize and tailor AI models, and how such activities may shape the future of AI development. In addition, the SLR discusses the current challenges of EUD for AI, the potential benefits, and the future implications of integrating EUD into the overall AI development process.

This paper is structured as follows: Sect. 2 details the SLR methodology; Sect. 3 describes the dimensions of the analysis; Sect. 4 discusses research challenges; Sect. 5 outlines the threats to the validity of this study, and, finally, Sect. 6 concludes the article.

2   Planning and Conducting the Systematic Literature Review

We conducted a Systematic Literature Review (SLR) via a reproducible and thorough approach to shed the light on the current landscape of EUD for AI systems, i.e., how users, even without skills in AI and/or programming, can customize the AI behavior to their needs. According to Kitchenham, a SLR requires three steps: *planning*, *conducting*, and *reporting* [6]. This section details the first two, while Sect. 3 details the last one.

2.1 Planning the SLR

Planning the SLR includes the following activities [6]: 1) formulation of the research question; 2) definition of the search strings; 3) selection of data sources; 4) definition of inclusion criteria. In the following, we report the details of each activity.

Formulation of the Research Question. The main goal of our SLR is to investigate the current state of research on the EUD for AI systems. With this goal in mind, we formulated the following research question: *How users can perform EUD for AI systems?*

Answering this question allows us to provide insights into how the literature tackles the problem of AI customization and democratization. On the other hand, it will drive the identification of future research respectively by focusing on research trends and by presenting the challenges and limitations identified in the available literature.

Definition of the Search Strings. We defined a total of 9 search strings by deriving terms from the knowledge of the authors of the subject matter. The strings resulted from a combination of the two keywords "end-user development" and "artificial intelligence". To ensure that most of the literature was covered by our search, we decided to also include the concepts of "no-code" and "low-code" (i.e., names for EUD that are common in modern commercial systems [7–9]), as well as the concept of "customization" (i.e., one of the main goals of EUD, as well as one of our interests). Thus, the resulting strings used to query the search engines were:

- EUD AI
- EUD AI customization
- End-user development AI
- End-user development AI customization
- No-code AI
- No-code AI customization
- Low-code AI
- Low-code AI customization
- AI customization

Selection of Data Sources. The chosen search engine is Google Scholar, as it is considered one of the top search engines for scientific researchers and can search the largest databases of scientific publications, ensuring wide coverage of searches.

Definition of the Inclusion Criteria. This step concerns the final selection of the relevant publications based on 3 inclusion criteria:

- *Peer reviewed,* i.e., the article is the result of a peer review process. In the case of journal articles, we included publications that appeared in a journal ranked on Scimago as Q2 or Q1, while publications ranked as Q3 were carefully evaluated. In the case of conference articles, we considered the Core Conference Raking, including publications that appeared in a venue with a score of B, A, and A*, while in the case of score C, we carefully evaluated the publication.

- *Written in English.*
- *Focused on EUD and AI.* Relevance to the topic of EUD for AI is assessed by analyzing the title and abstract of each publication, and introduction if needed.

2.2 Conducting the Literature Review

After the initial planning phase, the literature review is conducted. Following what Kitchenham suggests, we performed two main activities: the literature review execution, and the data synthesis [6], described in the subsequent subsections.

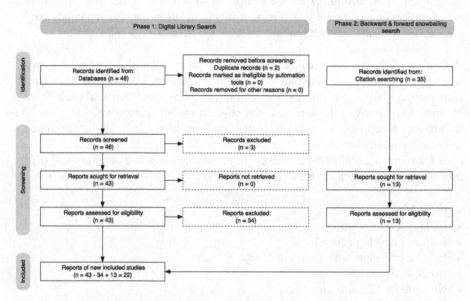

Fig. 1. Flow diagram summarizing the selection of the publications along the 2 search phases.

Literature Review Execution. This activity was performed from December 2022 – January 2023 following the process depicted in Fig. 1, which mainly consists of 2 phases:

- *Phase 1 - Digital library search*: we searched in the Google Scholar digital library using the search strings described in Sect. 2.1;
- *Phase 2 - Backward and forward snowballing search*: we checked references and citations of the publications resulting from the previous phase, as well as publications that cited publications from Phase 1 [10].

The initial search across the digital library yielded a total of 48 potentially relevant publications. After a check for duplicates, a dataset of 46 publications was obtained. A first filtering step brought the exclusion of 3 papers that did not meet the inclusion criteria regarding the publication venue. In the end, this phase resulted in a total of

43 publications. Each publication was then analyzed by reviewing the abstract, the introduction, and the conclusions, considering the other inclusion criteria defined in the previous section. After this step, we excluded 34 publications, thus obtaining a final dataset of 9 publications. Phase 2 allowed us to retrieve further publications, leading the final set to 22 publications. Given the number of selected publications and the fact that all but one were published after 2018, no date constraints were defined.

Data Synthesis. The 22 publications resulting from the search phases are listed in Table 1 and in the References Section. The distribution of the selected publications according to their publication year is shown in Fig. 2.

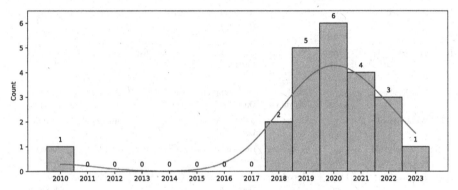

Fig. 2. Publications distribution by year.

3 Reporting and Analyzing the Results

This section reports the analysis of the literature to answer the research question presented in Sect. 2.1. Throughout a deep analysis of the selected publications, we defined 8 dimensions that characterize the existing EUD solutions for AI. This provides an overview of the state of the art, but it also provides an initial framework that may aid the design of novel EUD AI-based systems. A summary of the dimensions and the placement of the publications in such dimensions are reported in Table 1. An overview of the distribution of the set of publications in each dimension category is also shown in Fig. 3.

The resulting dimensions are described in the following paragraphs. For each dimension, we discuss the classification of the publications. Figure 4 provides an overview of the classification framework. It is worth remarking that the dimensions identified for and associated with each publication are not exclusive since a publication can be associated with one or more dimensions.

Dimension 1–Composition Paradigm. EUD researchers proposed several techniques to offer lay users the ability to customize their systems [33]. In the specific context of EUD for AI, we identified 5 techniques that are described in the following paragraphs.

Component-Based. It consists of composing 2D or 3D objects that represent domain-specific concepts [33]: a typical example of this technique is the jigsaw metaphor. For

Table 1. Summary of the 8 dimensions and their values for each publication of the SLR.

Ref	Composition paradigm	Target users	Technology	Domain	Usage	Customization level	Approach Output
[11]	Component-Based	Lay Users	Architecture	AI Model Development	Single	Tailoring	AI Model
[12]	Wizard-Based; Rule-Based; Component-Based	Experts	IoT	Education and Teaching	Collaborative	Tailoring	Teaching Suggestions
[13]	Template-based	Lay Users; Experts	AI models	Domain-Specific Operations	Collaborative	Customization	AI Model
[14]	Rule-Based	Lay Users; Experts	IPA	AI Model Development	Single	Tailoring	AI Model
[15]	Component-Based; Workflow and Data Diagrams	Experts	IPA	Interaction Design	Collaborative	Tailoring	AI Model
[16]	Template-based	Lay Users	Visual Analytics	Domain-Specific Operations	Collaborative	Customization	Visualization Prototype
[17]	Wizard-Based	Lay Users	AI models	Interaction Design	Single	Customization	AI Model
[18]	Template-based	Lay Users	AI models	Domain-Specific Operations	Collaborative	Customization	Business Model
[19]	Template-based	Lay Users	AI models	Domain-Specific Operations	Collaborative	Customization	Business Model
[20]	Component-Based	Lay Users	IoT	Education and Teaching	Single	Customization	AI Model
[21]	Component-Based	Lay Users	AI Models	Education and Teaching	Single	Tailoring	AI Model
[22]	Component-Based; Workflow and Data Diagrams	Lay Users	AI Models	AI Model Development	Single	Customization	AI Model
[23]	Workflow and Data Diagrams	Lay Users	AI Models	Domain-Specific Operations	Single	Tailoring	AI Model
[24]	Component-Based	Lay Users	AI Models	AI Model Development	Single	Customization	AI Model
[25]	Component-Based[1]	Experts	AI Models	AI Model Development	Single	Creation	AI Model
[26]	Component-Based	Lay Users	AI Models	Domain-Specific Operations	Single	Tailoring	AI Model
[27]	Wizard-Based	Lay Users	AI Models	Domain-Specific Operations	Single	Customization	AI Model
[28]	Wizard-Based	Lay Users	Architecture	AI Model Development	Single	Tailoring	AI Model
[29]	Component-Based	Experts	IoT	Education and Teaching	Collaborative	Tailoring	Teaching Suggestions
[30]	Component-Based	Lay Users; Experts	AI models	Domain-Specific Operations	Collaborative	Customization	AI Model

(continued)

---

[1] The publication also presents an approach based on text: for the goal of this study, only the component-based approach is considered interesting.

Table 1. (*continued*)

Ref	Composition paradigm	Target users	Technology	Domain	Usage	Customization level	Approach Output
[31]	Wizard-Based	Lay Users; Experts	IPA	AI Model Development	Single	Tailoring	AI Model
[32]	Component-Based	Experts	IPA	Interaction Design	Collaborative	Tailoring	AI Model

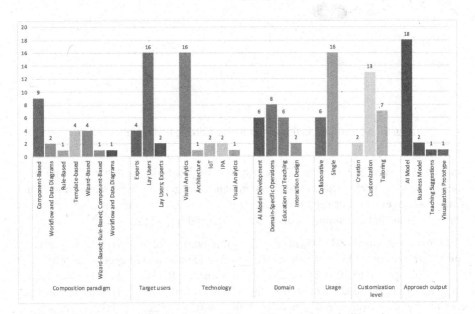

Fig. 3. Frequencies of the distributions of the publications in each dimension category.

example, Piro et al. present an interactive paradigm, which extends an already-existent framework used to build chatbots for conversational AI [15]. The authors' proposal consists in manipulating 2D objects that represent a database's annotation schema and conversation patterns, allowing non-expert programmers to build chatbots from scratch.

Wizard-Based. The wizard-based approach is useful in situations where a task can be simplified to a sequence of simple operations that guide the users throughout the overall activity, thus reducing the cognitive load of the task [33]. An example is the proposal by Rodríguez-García et al., who propose a system that guides the users with a wizard-like interface in the process of the training of an AI model (i.e., dataset creation, training, and testing), providing the possibility of using the trained model in other EUD tools (e.g., Scratch) [27].

Template-Based. It consists of presenting to the end-users pre-made and customizable functionalities, allowing them to edit parameters and/or text to fit their own needs [33].

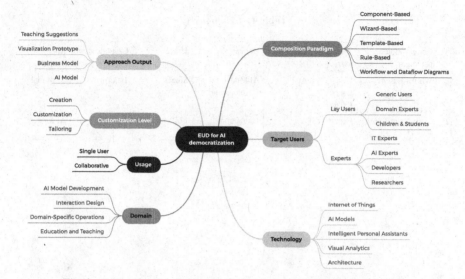

Fig. 4. A classification framework for the existing EUD solutions for AI.

For example, Iyer et al. present *Trinity*, a system for Data Mining that enables the end-users to visually perform three tasks: experiment management, label management, and feature management. For each task, this tool proposes a template with a set of default configurations that can simply be modified by the end users [13].

Rule-Based. It allows end-users to tailor AI components by defining trigger-actions rules for specific purposes [33]. For instance, Rough et al. identify and categorize existing EUD for AI tools applied to the Intelligent Personal Assistant (IPA) domain: they illustrate the opportunity given to end-users in creating their own rules to customize skills or construct routines by composing a rule, after the identification of trigger events and subsequent actions [14].

Workflow and Dataflow Diagrams. This technique concerns the way data are manipulated in the proposed solutions. It consists of using graphical elements, which can be interconnected and intertwined, depending on the needs of the users (i.e., a graph) [33]. The approach can be useful for programmers and developers who do not have a professional or technical background by enabling them to have a visual way to manipulate workflows and data. For example, Godec et al. propose a solution that allows the definition of a pipeline to automatically analyze medical images [23].

Dimension 2–Target Users. One of the key requirements in designing an EUD tool for AI is to carefully identify who the end users will be, considering both their limitations and strengths. The main goal is to facilitate their experience and use of the final tool. The analyzed publications led to the identification of 4 main target users, which are described in the following paragraphs.

Lay Users. They can be defined as people who lack any IT or AI-related skills. In this class, we identified generic users and domain experts. For this review, we consider children and students also as lay users (regardless of their education in IT) as they are not IT or AI experts. Most of the retrieved research focuses on this class of users. For example, Zimmermann-Niefield et al. propose an application that allows its users to train and use ML models that help them during athletic exercises, without requiring any IT or AI knowledge [31]. Another example focused on domain experts is the proposal by Sanctorum et al., who strive to find solutions to help subject matter experts autonomously manage a knowledge base in the toxicology domain [11].

Experts. This category includes users that are experts in IT and/or AI. Here we identified different types of experts, namely *IT experts, AI experts, developers,* and *researchers. IT experts* are users that possess a technical background in IT but do not have any AI or developer skills. Kahn et al. provide a case study, showing that a block-based programming environment may be better for this kind of user [24]. On the other hand, for AI experts we mean users that are experts both in the field of IT and AI, such as AI Specialists and Machine Learning Experts. For instance, Shaikh provides an example of low-code AI customization, geared toward experts in IT that know AI models to choose the best Microsoft Azure services to create an AI-based system [28]. By *developers* we mean users who are capable of programming: for example, Rough and Cowan discuss how the majority of EUD solutions for personal assistants are targeted toward developers, who know how to use Software Development Kits [14]. The last category is *researchers,* i.e., users that adopt this kind of solution for research purposes. For example, Tamilselvam et al. present and test a solution that allows the quick prototyping of neural networks using either tables or a drag-and-drop interface, allowing researchers to quickly create neural networks for further usage [29].

Dimension 3–Technology. The technology defines the constraints, the possibilities, and the context of the use of the proposed solutions. In this context, we identified 5 different types of technologies: the Internet of Things (IoT), AI Models, Intelligent Personal Assistants (IPAs), Visual Analytics, and Architecture.

Internet of Things. The Internet of Things (IoT) is defined as "An open and comprehensive network of intelligent objects that can auto-organize, share information, data, and resources, reacting and acting in face of situations and changes in the environment" [34]. We classify in this category the research that was focused mainly on IoT itself, discussing AI as a secondary subject. For example, Agassi et al. discuss an IoT system that recognizes gestures, and they provide a solution that allows users to customize the recognition model itself [20].

AI Models. We classify as part of this category all research that is mainly focused on the customization, tailoring, or creation of the AI models themselves, regardless of the specific context of use. For example, Xie et al. present an IDE plugin that allows its users to create, through the paradigms of visual programming, and visualize the neural network they are building [30].

Intelligent Personal Assistant. An *IPA* is defined as a user interface, which main interaction method is through speech, that aims at performing tasks requested in natural language [14]. We classify in this category all publications that aim at enabling users to customize chatbots or personal assistants. For example, Rough and Cowan highlight existing EUD opportunities to allow users to customize their personal assistants to make them truly "personal" [14].

Visual Analytics. Visual analytics technology supports the analysis of datasets through sophisticated tools and processes using visual and graphical representations. An example is the solution proposed by Mishra et al., which discuss the development of a prototype tool that enables leaderboard revamping through customization, based on the focus area that the end-user is interested in [16].

Architecture. The last category does not refer to a concrete technology but to an abstract architecture to design EUD systems for AI. For instance, Sanctorum et al. propose an architecture representing the key phases and tasks of knowledge graphs' lifecycle, to guide end-users in the definition of custom knowledge bases [11].

Dimension 4–Domain. With this dimension, we aim at classifying the focus of each publication. The domain of the publication sets its goal, and it may heavily influence the approach used in the publications. A total of 4 dimensions have been identified.

AI Model Development. It represents the class of publications that mainly aim at providing the end-users with a customized AI model that they can use for either a generic task (chosen by them during the customization) or for a predefined task. For example, Carney et al. propose a solution that allows end users to train, through the manipulation of graphical elements, a pre-defined neural network architecture for classification, leaving the users the freedom to choose the classes themselves [22].

Interaction Design. We classify in this domain all the publications that aim at defining the way the interactive system supports users' activities and interacts with them [35]. For example, Bunt et al. try to discover new ways of interacting with AI-based systems, specifically with an AI-enabled recommender system-like tool, which can provide users with suggestions on how to customize graphical interfaces according to their personal preferences [17].

Domain-Specific Operations. This general domain comprises all publications that aim at allowing users to customize or create AI models that are designed to perform a specific task in a specific domain. For example, Jauhar et al. explore how EUD and AI can be used in inventory and supply chains to enable retailers and operators to manage, most coherently and consistently as possible, managing costs, processes, anomalies, and predictions by using machine learning algorithms [36].

Education and Teaching The last domain identified is the one of education and teaching; it concerns how EUD, with its different subtopics, can be taught in various contexts and how awareness can be spread among developers, designers, and engineers. An example is by Paternò, who explores how AI and IT experts need to empower and encourage end users in using and creating daily automations [12].

Dimension 5–Usage. The *Usage* dimension regards the number of people that the sys-tem allows to collaborate during its employment.

Single User. It refers to the use of a system, or a solution, by a single individual. For example, Sanctorum et al. present an approach to let the subject-matter expert alone manually manage a toxicology knowledge base [11].

Collaborative. It refers to the use of a system, or a solution, by a group of individuals with multiple perspectives and experiences. For instance, Iyer et al. propose a system that holds a shared vocabulary and workspace, enabling better collaboration between more end users while recalibrating their skills as if they were equal partners [13].

Dimension 6–Customization Level. This dimension refers to the level of allowed modifications to the AI-based software's components. We identify three possibilities: creation, customization, and tailoring.

Creation. Systems that allow the "creation" of AI models are systems that do not pose any limitation to the personalized system capabilities, nor do they provide a pre-made system that can be adapted to the users' Needs. Examples are by Xie et al. and Tamil-selvam et al., who both define solutions that allow end users to graphically build neural networks [29, 30].

Customization. With customization, we identify all the approaches that allow the users to heavily alter the parameters of an existing AI model. However, the coarse task (e.g., classification) and the model architecture are predefined. For example, the solution proposed by Carney, et al. allows training a pre-defined neural network for classification, providing the ability to customize the dataset and the available labels [22].

Tailoring. We categorize as "tailoring" systems, all solutions that allow end users to *fine-tune* a model for their specific needs, even though the specific task is predetermined. An example is the gesture recognition system proposed by Agassi et al., in which users can change specific gestures, but they are not able to edit other aspects of the AI model [20].

Dimension 7–Approach Output. This dimension was identified to define the types of results and outcomes of the proposed solutions. A total of 4 categories were identified.

Teaching Suggestions Discussion concerning how EUD should be thought about AI is still open. An example of the discussion is in the work by Paternò, who provides suggestions as to how experts should encourage end users in using and creating daily automations [12].

Visualization Prototype. EUD solutions for AI customization may also aid the users by presenting results and metrics in different modalities. For example, Mishra et al. propose visualization techniques that aid the end users in selecting models that are trained and compared fairly [16].

Business Model. The adoption of EUD may aid in undertaking business decisions and may provide new business models to be exploited. This is suggested, for example, by

Redchuk et al., who show that adopting no/low-code AI technologies may shorten the implementation cycles of new systems [18].

AI Model. The main output type concerns the AI model itself. We classify in this category all the approaches that aim at providing the end users with their customized AI model. Most of the publications provide this type of output: for example, Piro et al. allow users to define chatbots that can be deployed immediately [15]. Similarly, Tamilselvam et al. propose a method that allows users to graphically build neural networks for later use [29].

4 Future Challenges

Throughout this SLR, some interesting and relevant challenges emerged that are worth reporting. This section thus discusses relevant open questions that may guide future research in EUD for AI.

Adopt a Human-Centered Artificial Intelligence Approach. In recent years, a new perspective has emerged that aims to reconsider the centrality of humans while reaping the benefits of AI systems to augment rather than replace professional skills: Human-Centered AI (HCAI) is a novel framework that posits that high levels of human control are not incompatible with high levels of computer automation [37]. EUD for AI will play a central role in this direction. As emphasized by Schmidt, AI-based systems should allow humans to have an appropriate level of control by providing EUD approaches for the initial configuration of the system, as well as for reconfiguration of the system at the time of use, to satisfy user needs that cannot be anticipated by the automated system [38]. This is an approach that has not been much explored in the literature, so we believe that EUD can contribute in this direction.

Support Collaborative Activities. Another challenge lies in the collaborative aspect of the EUD for AI. Very little work is available on this aspect: only 6 publications out of the retrieved 22 acknowledge the collaborative aspect of AI development. However, the creation, testing, and deployment of AI models (and AI systems in general) is a collaborative activity that involves multiple actors with different expertise [39]. This highlights the requirement of collaboration in no/low-code AI tools for them to be used in real-case scenarios, especially by experts.

Provide EUD Solutions also for AI Experts. The SLR found that most of the research is focused on lay users, while a few studies target experts. Although EUD for AI could lead to a democratization of AI technologies, it may be interesting to better explore how AI experts can benefit from EUD solutions for AI. In fact, although experts might create or adapt AI systems using technical tools (e.g., Python, R, Weka, etc.), providing an EUD environment might allow them to optimize their resources [18]. An example is Knime, an end-to-end data science platform that provides a graphical user interface based on the graph metaphor to support experts from building analytical models to deploying them without coding [40].

Enable the Creation of AI Solutions Through EUD. A strong limitation of the current research on this topic is the scarce focus on AI system *creation* rather than *customization* or *tailoring*: only 2 out of 22 retrieved publications reach this goal. Furthermore, these 2 publications focus on expert users: research on AI model creation by lay users is, as far as we could find out, completely missing. The lack of the possibility for end users to create rather than adapt the model also affects solutions aimed at experts [27].

Define the Right Composition Paradigm for Each Type of User. At the time of the review, no studies were available on the relationship between EUD programming paradigms and the level of expertise and skills of the users. This is a very important aspect that has been addressed in a similar context. For example, trigger-action programming of IoT devices was found to be easier for non-technical users when using wizard procedures as well as component- or template-based paradigms, while graph-based metaphor was found to be more effective for technical users [41, 42]. Certainly, lessons learned in similar domains can be a good starting point for EUD for AI, but further research is needed to provide the users with the right abstraction mechanisms.

5 Threats to Validity

Several threats to validity can affect the results of a systematic literature review. In the following, we report how we mitigated the most critical ones.

Selection Bias. This occurs when the studies included in the review are not representative of the entire population of studies on the topic. This has been mitigated by i) manually reviewing the publication to ensure their compliance with the SLR goal, and ii) performing two phases, i.e., search on digital libraries and snowballing.

Publication Bias. This occurs when studies that show statistically significant results are more likely to be published than studies that do not. This aspect has been mitigated by manually reading those publications that do not report any result but only a technical solution with preliminary results. Besides the generic inclusion criteria, their relevance for our SLR considered, for example, the number of citations and the novelty of the solution.

Time Lag Bias. This occurs when the review does not include all relevant studies because they were published after the review was conducted. In this case, we can safely assume that this threat is not so evident in our study since the SLR has been performed 2 months before its submission.

Publication Quality. This occurs when studies of poor quality are included in the review. To mitigate this aspect, we defined inclusion criteria on the quality of the venue of the publication, leaving to a manual evaluation of the authors of this SRL the inclusion of publications that appeared in venues of lower quality.

6 Conclusions

This SLR provides an overview of the current state of research in the field of EUD for no/low-code AI creation and customization. The first contribution is the identification of the main topics that are discussed in the community, highlighting potential benefits that lay users or businesses may get from the adoption of EUD technologies. A second contribution, the SLR sheds the light on existing limitations and key challenges that affect the current research landscapes, identifying some insights into possible future research directions. In future work, this SLR might be extended in different directions. First, further digital libraries might be considered, for example, Scholar, Elsevier, and IEEE. Then, other keywords might be defined to increase coverage. Finally, an additional manual search can be performed on Conferences Proceedings and Journals relevant to the topics of the SLR.

Acknowledgment. The research of Andrea Esposito is funded by a Ph.D. fellowship within the framework of the Italian "D.M. n. 352, April 9, 2022" - under the National Recovery and Resilience Plan, Mission 4, Component 2, Investment 3.3 - Ph.D. Project "Human-Centered Artificial Intelligence (HCAI) techniques for supporting end users interacting with AI systems", co-supported by "Eusoft S.r.l." (CUP H91I22000410007).

The research of Rosa Lanzilotti is partially supported by the co-funding of the European union - Next Generation EU: NRRP Initiative, Mission 4, Component 2, Investment 1.3 - Partnerships extended to universities, research centers, companies, and research D.D. MUR n. 341 del 15.03.2022 – Next Generation EU (PE0000013 – "Future Artificial Intelligence Research – FAIR" - CUP: H97G22000210007).

References

1. Chui, M., Hall, B., Mayhew, H., Singla, A., Sukharevsky, A.: The state of AI in 2022—and a half decade in review. Survey, McKinsey Global Institute (2022)
2. Google Trends: AI, chat GPT - Explore - Google Trends. https://trends.google.com/trends/explore?date=2022-11-01%202023-03-14&q=ai,chat%20gpt&hl=en-US. Accessed 14 Mar 2023
3. Gresse von Wangenheim, C., Hauck, J.C.R., Pacheco, F.S., Bertonceli Bueno, M.F.: Visual tools for teaching machine learning in K-12: a ten-year systematic mapping. Educ. Inf. Technol. **26**(5), 5733–5778 (2021). https://doi.org/10.1007/s10639-021-10570-8
4. Hauck, M., Machhamer, R., Czenkusch, L., Gollmer, K.-U., Dartmann, G.: Node and block-based development tools for distributed systems with AI applications. IEEE Access **7**, 143109–143119 (2019). https://doi.org/10.1109/ACCESS.2019.2940113
5. Lacerda Queiroz, R., Ferrentini Sampaio, F., Lima, C., Machado Vieira Lima, P.: AI from concrete to abstract. AI Soc. **36**(3), 877–893 (2021). https://doi.org/10.1007/s00146-021-011 51-x
6. Kitchenham, B.A.: Procedures for Performing Systematic Reviews. Joint Technical Report, Department of Computer Science, Keele University and National ICT, Australia Ltd (2004)
7. Forbes: The most disruptive Trend of 2021: No Code/Low Code. Accessed 15 Mar 2023
8. Bock, A.C., Frank, U.: Low-code platform. Bus. Inf. Syst. Eng. **63**(6), 733–740 (2021). https://doi.org/10.1007/s12599-021-00726-8
9. Sufi, F.: Algorithms in low-code-no-code for research applications: a practical review. Algorithms **16**, J08 (2023). https://doi.org/10.3390/a16020108
10. Wohlin, C.: Guidelines for snowballing in systematic literature studies and a replication in software engineering. In: Proceedings of the 18th International Conference on Evaluation and Assessment in Software Engineering (EASE 2014). Association for Computing Machinery (2014). https://doi.org/10.1145/2601248.2601268

11. Sanctorum, A., et al.: End-user engineering of ontology-based knowledge bases. Behav. Inform. Technol. **41**, 1811–1829 (2022). https://doi.org/10.1080/0144929X.2022.2092032
12. Paternò, F.: teaching end-user development in the time of IoT and AI. In: Ardito, C., et al. (eds.) INTERACT 2021. LNCS, vol. 13198, pp. 257–269. Springer, Cham (2022). https://doi.org/10.1007/978-3-030-98388-8_23
13. Iyer, C.V.K., et al.: Trinity: a no-code AI platform for complex spatial datasets. In: Proceedings of the 4th ACM SIGSPATIAL International Workshop on AI for Geographic Knowledge Discovery, pp. 33–42. Association for Computing Machinery, Beijing, China (2021). https://doi.org/10.1145/3486635.3491072
14. Rough, D., Cowan, B.: Poster: APIs for IPAs? Towards end-user tailoring of intelligent personal assistants. In: 2020 IEEE Symposium on Visual Languages and Human-Centric Computing (VL/HCC), pp. 1–2 (2020). https://doi.org/10.1109/VL/HCC50065.2020.9127267
15. Piro, L., Desolda, G., Matera, M., Lanzilotti, R., Mosca, S., Pucci, E.: An interactive paradigm for the end-user development of chatbots for data exploration. In: Ardito, C., et al. (eds.) INTERACT 2021. LNCS, vol. 12935, pp. 177–186. Springer, Cham (2021). https://doi.org/10.1007/978-3-030-85610-6_11
16. Mishra, S., Arunkumar, A.: How robust are model rankings: a leaderboard customization approach for equitable evaluation. Proc. AAAI Conf. Artif. Intell. **35**, 13561–13569 (2021). https://doi.org/10.1609/aaai.v35i15.17599
17. Bunt, A., Conati, C., McGrenere, J.: Mixed-Initiative interface personalization as a case study in usable AI. AI Mag. **30**, 58 (2010). https://doi.org/10.1609/aimag.v30i4.2264
18. Redchuk, A., Walas Mateo, F.: New business models on artificial intelligence—the case of the optimization of a blast furnace in the steel industry by a machine learning solution. Appl. Syst. Innov, **5**, 6 (2022). https://doi.org/10.3390/asi5010006
19. Sunil Kumar, J., Shashank Mayurkumar, J., Sachin, S.K., Saurabh, P., Amine, B., Shivam, G.: How to use no-code artificial intelligence to predict and minimize the inventory distortions for resilient supply chains. Int. J. Prod. Res.. 1–25 (2023). https://doi.org/10.1080/00207543.2023.2166139
20. Agassi, A., Erel, H., Wald, I.Y., Zuckerman, O.: Scratch Nodes ML: A playful system for children to create gesture recognition classifiers. In: Extended Abstracts of the 2019 CHI Conference on Human Factors in Computing Systems, pp. 1--6. Association for Computing Machinery (2019). https://doi.org/10.1145/3290607.3312894
21. Alturayeif, N., Alturaief, N., Alhathloul, Z.: DeepScratch: Scratch programming language extension for deep learning education. Int. J. Adv. Comput. Sci. Appl. **11** (2020). https://doi.org/10.14569/IJACSA.2020.0110777
22. Carney, M., et al.: Teachable machine: approachable web-based tool for exploring machine learning classification. In: Extended Abstracts of the 2020 CHI Conference on Human Factors in Computing Systems, pp. 1--8. Association for Computing Machinery (2020). https://doi.org/10.1145/3334480.3382839
23. Godec, P., et al.: Democratized image analytics by visual programming through integration of deep models and small-scale machine learning. Nat. Commun. **10**, 4551 (2019). https://doi.org/10.1038/s41467-019-12397-x
24. Kahn, K., Megasari, R., Piantari, E., Junaeti, E.: AI programming by children using Snap! block programming in a developing country. In: Practitioner Proceedings of the 13th European Conference On Technology Enhanced Learning, vol. 2193. CEUR-WS, Leeds, UK (2018)
25. Moin, A., Mituca, A., Challenger, M., Badii, A., Gunnemann, S.: ML-Quadrat & DriotData: a model-driven engineering tool and a low-code platform for smart IoT services. In: Proceedings of the ACM/IEEE 44th International Conference on Software Engineering: Companion Proceedings, pp. 144--148. Association for Computing Machinery (2022). https://doi.org/10.1145/3510454.3516841

26. Rao, A., Bihani, A., Nair, M.: Milo: A visual programming environment for data science education. In: 2018 IEEE Symposium on Visual Languages and Human-Centric Computing (VL/HCC), pp. 211–215 (2018). https://doi.org/10.1109/VLHCC.2018.8506504
27. Rodríguez García, J.D., Moreno-León, J., Román-González, M., Robles, G.: LearningML: a tool to foster computational thinking skills through practical artificial intelligence projects. Revista de Educación a Distancia (RED) **20** (2020). https://doi.org/10.6018/red.410121
28. Shaikh, K.: AI with Low Code. Demystifying Azure AI: Implementing the Right AI Features for Your Business, pp. 151--182. Apress (2020). https://doi.org/10.1007/978-1-4842-6219-1_5
29. Tamilselvam, S.G., Panwar, N., Khare, S., Aralikatte, R., Sankaran, A., Mani, S.: A visual programming paradigm for abstract deep learning model development. In: Proceedings of the 10th Indian Conference on Human-Computer Interaction. Association for Computing Machinery (2019). https://doi.org/10.1145/3364183.3364202
30. Xie, C., Qi, H., Ma, L., Zhao, J.: DeepVisual: a visual programming tool for deep learning systems. In: Proceedings of the 27th International Conference on Program Comprehension, pp. 130--134. IEEE Press (2019). https://doi.org/10.1109/ICPC.2019.00028
31. Zimmermann-Niefield, A., Turner, M., Murphy, B., Kane, S.K., Shapiro, R.B.: Youth learning machine learning through building models of athletic moves. In: Proceedings of the 18th ACM International Conference on Interaction Design and Children, pp. 121--132. Association for Computing Machinery (2019). https://doi.org/10.1145/3311927.3323139
32. Zimmermann-Niefield, A., Polson, S., Moreno, C., Shapiro, R.B.: Youth making machine learning models for gesture-controlled interactive media. In: Proceedings of the Interaction Design and Children Conference, pp. 63--74. Association for Computing Machinery (2020). https://doi.org/10.1145/3392063.3394438
33. Barricelli, B.R., Cassano, F., Fogli, D., Piccinno, A.: End-user development, end-user programming and end-user software engineering: a systematic mapping study. J. Syst. Softw. **149**, 101–137 (2019). https://doi.org/10.1016/j.jss.2018.11.041
34. Madakam, S., Ramaswamy, R., Tripathi, S.: Internet of Things (IoT): a literature review. J. Comput. Commun. **3**, 164–173 (2015). https://doi.org/10.4236/jcc.2015.35021
35. Sharp, H., Rogers, Y., Preece, J.: Interaction Design: Beyond Human-Computer Interaction. John Wiley & Sons (2019)
36. Jauhar, S.K., Jani, S.M., Kamble, S.S., Pratap, S., Belhadi, A., Gupta, S.: How to use no-code artificial intelligence to predict and minimize the inventory distortions for resilient supply chains. Int. J. Prod. Res. 1–25 (2023). https://doi.org/10.1080/00207543.2023.2166139
37. Shneiderman, B.: Human-Centered AI. Oxford University Press, Oxford (2022)
38. Schmidt, A., Herrmann, T.: Intervention user interfaces: a new interaction paradigm for automated systems. Interactions **24**, 40–45 (2017). https://doi.org/10.1145/3121357
39. Kreuzberger, D., Kühl, N., Hirschl, S.: Machine Learning Operations (MLOps): Overview, definition, and architecture. arXiv:2205.02302 (2022)
40. Berthold, M.R., et al.: KNIME: the Konstanz Information Miner. In: Proceedings of the 31st Annual Conference of the Gesellschaft für Klassifikation e.V. (GfKI 2007), pp. 319–326. Springer Berlin Heidelberg, (2007). https://doi.org/10.1007/978-3-540-78246-9_38
41. Desolda, G., Ardito, C., Matera, M.: Empowering end users to customize their smart environments: model, composition paradigms, and domain-specific tools. ACM Trans. Comput.-Hum. Interact. **24**, 12 (2017). https://doi.org/10.1145/3057859
42. Ghiani, G., Manca, M., Paternò, F., Santoro, C.: Personalization of Context-dependent applications through trigger-action rules. ACM Trans. Comput.-Hum. Interact. 24, 14 (2017). https://doi.org/10.1145/3057861

Human-AI Co-creation: Evaluating the Impact of Large-Scale Text-to-Image Generative Models on the Creative Process

Tommaso Turchi[1]([✉]) [iD], Silvio Carta[2] [iD], Luciano Ambrosini[3] [iD],
and Alessio Malizia[1,4] [iD]

[1] Department of Computer Science, Università di Pisa, Pisa, Italy
{tommaso.turchi,alessio.malizia}@unipi.it
[2] Department of Architecture and Design, University of Hertfordshire, Hatfield, UK
s.carta@herts.ac.uk
[3] Independent Researcher, Napoli, Italy
luciano.ambrosini@outlook.com
[4] Molde University College, Molde, Norway

Abstract. Large-scale Text-to-image Generative Models (LTGMs) are a cutting-edge class of Artificial Intelligence (AI) algorithms specifically designed to generate images from natural language descriptions (prompts). These models have demonstrated impressive capabilities in creating high-quality images from a wide range of inputs, making them powerful tools for non-technical users to tap into their creativity. The field is advancing rapidly and we are witnessing the emergence of an increasing number of tools, such as DALL-E, MidJourney and StableDiffusion, that are leveraging LTGMs to support creative work across various domains. However, there is a lack of research on how the interaction with these tools might affect the users' creativity and their ability to control the generated outputs. In this paper, we investigate how the interaction with LTGMs-based tools might impact creativity by analyzing the feedback provided by groups of design students developing an architectural project with the help of LTGMs tools.

Keywords: Generative AI · Creativity · Human-AI · AI-driven design process

1 Introduction

In the past year we have witnessed the rise of impressive AI-based tools capable of generating images from textual descriptions, holding coherent conversations, providing writing suggestions for creative writers, and even writing code alongside a human programmer. All these examples share a common characteristic: the AI does not simply categorize data or interpret text based on predetermined models, but instead it generates something entirely new such as images or designs. This type of work pushes the potential of AI systems beyond problem-solving and towards problem-finding, which often results in the AI functioning as a creative human collaborator and supporter rather than a decision-maker.

L. D. Spano et al. (Eds.): IS-EUD 2023, LNCS 13917, pp. 35–51, 2023.
https://doi.org/10.1007/978-3-031-34433-6_3

These tools are often based on Large-scale Text-to-Image Generative Models (LTGMs), a rapidly evolving class of Artificial Intelligence (AI) algorithms with the ability to generate images based on natural language descriptions, called prompts. These models have shown remarkable capabilities in creating high-quality images from a wide range of inputs, making them powerful tools for non-technical users to tap into their imagination. As the field of LTGMs continues to advance, we are witnessing the growing adoption of a number of tools, such as DALL-E, MidJourney, and Playground, that are leveraging the power of these models to support work in various creative domains.

However, despite their increasing popularity, the impact of LTGMs-based tools on creativity remains largely understudied. The users' ability to effectively direct and control a creative support tool to fit their needs is an essential component of the creation process and plays a crucial role in determining the successful outcome of a project. Therefore, it is important to understand how the interaction and collaboration between humans and AI through these tools might affect creative processes.

In this paper, we address this gap by investigating the impact of LTGMs-based tools on creativity. Our study analyzes post-hoc feedback provided by different groups of design students as they work on an architectural project with the support of some of these tools. We aim to gain insights into how the interaction with LTGMs affects the students' creative process, focusing on the ability to effectively control them to generate new ideas.

Therefore, the research question tackled in this work is: *how does the interaction with LTGMs affect users' creativity?*

This research provides a valuable contribution to the field of End-User development by exploring the impact of Human-AI Co-Creation on users. Our findings will inform the development of future tools and investigate their use in creative work.

2   Related Works

2.1   Generative AI and Text-to-Image Generative Models

Generative AI refers to a new class of Artificial Intelligence models that create new content, as opposed to simply analyzing existing data like Expert Systems do. These Generative Models consist of a discriminator (or transformer) and a generator, trained on a dataset and can map input information into a high-dimensional space, producing novel content on each new trial, even from the same input. Thus, unlike predictive Machine Learning systems, Generative Models can both discriminate information and generate new content [1]. Within the domain of architecture and spatial design, the automated generation of spatial configuration has a long tradition, starting with the seminal work of Shape Grammars [2] in the 1980s, developing with Spatial Synthesis [3], with more recent developments with more sophisticated graph-based models [4, 5]. A detailed account of such developments in architecture can be found in [6].

The recent growth of Generative AI is due to the availability of large datasets and the latest advancements in computing power. Such models can map any input format, like text, to any output format, like video or images, allowing the generation of new media from prompts-like text inputs, or a set of relevant images. The taxonomy of existing systems mapping the different input formats to different outputs is growing day by day, as new models are introduced to jumpstart new domain-specific applications [1].

The availability of massive datasets and a wide range of use cases enabled by their widespread has contributed to the rapid development of Text-to-Image Generative Models, with new tools emerging on a daily basis. These models can be exploited by different disciplines such as architecture or product design, and throughout many phases of the creative process: ideation, sketches, variants building, texture creation, … [7]. They can be used to spark new ideas and inspire innovative designs.

Developing such large-scale Generative AI Models proved to be a challenging task, as the estimation of their parameters requires enormous computational power and a highly skilled and experienced team in data science and engineering [1]. Thus, only a handful of companies have been successful in deploying Generative Models.

Among the firsts, StabilityAI introduced Stable Diffusion in 2022 and its main purpose is to generate highly detailed images based on textual descriptions [8]. Additionally, it can be utilized for other tasks like image editing and image translation. The model is trained on 512x512 images from "2b English language label subset of LAION 5b, a general crawl of the internet created by the German charity LAION"[1]. The model incorporates a fixed CLIP [9] ViT-L/14 text encoder to influence the model's output based on text inputs.

Most notably, OpenAI created DALL-E 2, which is an improvement over its predecessor DALL-E. It generates more lifelike images at higher resolutions and has the ability to blend together concepts, attributes, and styles [8]. DALL-E 2 was trained using approximately 650 million image-text pairs obtained from the Internet. A clear comparison[2] where salient points are summarized in Table 1 below.

Table 1. Comparison between DALL-E 2 and Stable Diffusion models.

DALL-E 2 (OpenAI)	Stable Diffusion (Stability.ai)
code is not open-source	code is open-source
Training data are not disclosed and publicly available	Training data are disclosed and publicly available
The model uses heavily curated data. This results in strict control of the outputs	Training data are generally non-curated. The model can generate uncontrolled images
The model uses GPT-3 and its large number of parameters (over 175 billion machine learning parameters). This allows for a high capability of generation of unseen visuals	The model uses a diffusion technique based on existing data. Outputs are restricted to training images (limited capability of generating unseen visuals)

These two Generative Models were selected and tested in our study with the help of a purposefully-designed tool integrating them into the participants' workflows, as reported in Sect. 3.

---

[1] https://stability.ai/blog/stable-diffusion-public-release.

[2] https://nimblebox.ai/blog/stable-diffusion-ai.

2.2　Human-AI Co-creation

The idea of humans and AI agents collaborating to achieve creative endeavors is becoming increasingly common, stemming from a long tradition of Computer-Supported Cooperative Work and creativity support systems, thanks also to the recent popularity of Generative AI Models. This contributed to the rise of a new research area called Human-AI Co-Creation [10], involving both the human and the AI contributing to the creative process and sharing responsibility for the resulting artefact.

Nonetheless, while powerful Generative AI Models are now commonly available to designers, artists [11], and knowledge workers, there is still much to learn about how to make these tools interactive and design effective user experiences around them. Additionally, little is known about the long-term effects of this technology on creative practices, the overarching role of Generative AI in society as a whole, and the regulations that will govern this area of design [12].

A recent literature survey [13] showed how fostering productive use in Human-AI Co-Creation systems is still a challenge. Researchers found that many such systems failed to achieve positive synergy, which refers to the ability of a Human-AI team to produce superior outcomes compared to either party working alone. In fact, some studies have even found the opposite effect, with Human-AI teams producing inferior results compared to a Human or AI working alone [14].

Furthermore, fostering the safe use of Generative AI is also a challenge due to the potential risks and harms associated with these systems. These risks can stem from how the model was trained [15] or how it is applied [16].

Several theoretical frameworks [17–19] have been proposed to guide the design of these systems and to make sure that the collaboration between Humans and AI is fruitful. However, there is still a limited amount of on-the-field studies investigating how this synergy impacts creative outcomes and affects existing design processes, now more than ever with the rising popularity of new tools. With this study, we aim to collect user feedback on these models and analyze how these tools can impact creative works in a real-world scenario.

3　User Study

This section presents the goals, hypotheses, and description of the user study we carried out, following the guidelines of Wohlin et al. [20].

3.1　Goals

The goal of this study was to collect user feedback on how LTGMs-based tools can affect creative works. The purpose is to evaluate their impact on creativity.

3.2　Research Questions

Large-scale Text-to-Image Generative Models (LTGMs) can generate high-quality images from natural language descriptions, and they are increasingly used to support work in creative domains. However, their impact on creativity remains understudied, and it is important to understand how users can effectively direct and control these tools to generate new ideas.

The main research question derived from this context is: *how does the interaction with LTGMs affect users' creativity?*

3.3 Participants

Overall, 22 students took part in the workshop in mixed groups representing the spectrum of genders, age, discipline (architecture, urban design and interior architecture) and level of study (undergraduate and postgraduate) of the student cohorts in the Department of Architecture and Design at the University of Hertfordshire, UK. Students were divided into 8 groups of 3–4 students. Generally speaking, none of them had prior experience of Generative AI Tools for design, and all had experience in developing architectural projects in both academic and professional settings.

The students were asked to develop design solutions responding to a given design brief called the Art of Bathing. This brief required to create a public repository of water, namely a building serving as a sanctuary for individuals to contemplate, meditate, replenish, and heal, from the daily pressure of life. The students were tasked to design a structure, with a maximum building envelope of 10x10x10m in Stanborough Park, Welwyn Garden City (UK), characterized by a rich sensory experience and spatial configuration. Students were asked to create a building concerned not simply with style, image or beautiful materiality, but resonant with memories of volumetric weight, contiguity and enclosure of space, as well as sound and light effects related to water (Fig. 1).

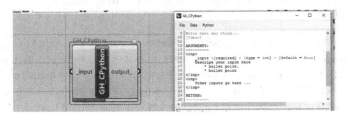

Fig. 1. Example of scripting feature on Grasshopper.

The workshop took place in one of the computer labs at the University of Hertfordshire, UK. In order to facilitate the workshop, we developed a suite of Grasshopper (GH) Components to allow students to experiment with the different options provided by OpenAI and Stability.ai. Grasshopper[3] is a node-based visual programming environment working within McNeel's Rhinoceros 3D software widely used in architecture and design industry and research. Rhino and GH allow for great tool customization by including scripting capability through Visual Basic (VB), C# and Python for developers.

---

[3] https://www.grasshopper3d.com/.

Grasshopper has been used for this workshop since it allowed us to generate ad hoc scripts to introduce diffusion models into the design process, and it also represents a familiar design environment for the students.

The tools used in the Grasshopper (GH) definitions distributed to students belongs to the "AI" subcategory included within the "Ambrosinus-Toolkit" plugin[4]. These services are underpinned by two models: DALL-E 2 [21] and Stable Diffusion [22] respectively. Both the OpenAI and StabilityAI platforms allow students to perform three different types of image generation: Creative mode, Variation mode and Edit mode. The study presented therein will comply with the first two methods which are performed differently by the two aforementioned platforms (Fig. 2).

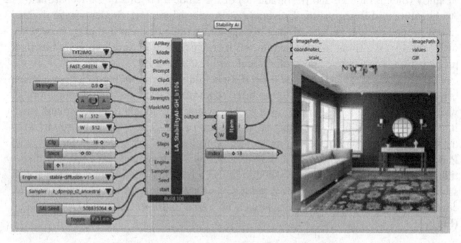

Fig. 2. Grasshopper with Stable Diffusion model.

There are two GH tools that perform these operations[5]: "OpenAI-GHadv" and "StabilityAI-GHadv". The first tool processes images through the neural model called DALL-E (v.2), while the second tool processes images through the neural model called Stable Diffusion. Before quickly illustrating some of the most significant parameters that will be used in this experiment by the students, it is important to underline that the substantial difference between the two neural models is that DALL-E can not discretize the generative process in the current version, while the Stable Diffusion model can and this translates into the possibility of making the outputs, and therefore all the parameters used, completely identifiable and recallable with the same settings.

OpenAI-GHadv main parameters:

- *Mode*: execution mode selector (Create, Variation and Edit);

---

[4] The author of the plugin started to develop and share the Toolkit in November 2022 and the current version is v1.1.6 (2023/02/06). The Main AI components are available from this GitHub page: https://github.com/lucianoambrosini.

[5] The current version of the tool "LA_OpenAI-GHadv" is the build 111 and that one of the tool "LA_StabilityAI-GHadv" is the build 107.

- *BaseIMG* is the source image path, it is required in order to run the Variation and Edit modes;
- *MaskIMG* is the source image-mask path (it will be ignored in this experimentation);
- *DirPath* is the target path where the tool will store the generated image by DALL-E;
- *Prompt* is the textual description passed as input;
- *S* is the image size. The pre-trained model used for the training process of the DALL-E allows only these sizes: 256, 512 and 1024 pixels (it is allowed only squared pictures);
- *N* is the number of images to generate;

StabilityAI-GHadv main parameters[6]:

- *Mode* is the execution mode selector (TXTtoIMG, IMGtoIMG and IMGtoIMG Masking);
- *DirPath* is the target path where the tool will store the generated image by Stable Diffusion;
- *Prompt* is the textual description passed as input;
- *ClipG* is the CLIP guidance mode. It is a tricky procedure executed by the neural network encoder to increase the consistency of the image with the text given as input;
- *BaseIMG* is the source image path, it is required in order to run the IMGtoIMG mode;
- *Strength* is how much "weight" has the text prompt in relation to the initial image (admitted values from 0.0 to 1);
- *MaskIMG* is the source image-mask path (it will be ignored in this experimentation);
- *H* and *W* are the height and width of the output image. Only the size in the range 256 to 1024 pixels with 64px as increment value is admitted;
- *Cfg* scale dictates how closely the engine attempts to match a generation to the provided prompt; v2-x models respond well to lower CFG (eg: 4–8), whereas v1-x models respond well to a higher range (eg: 7–14);
- *Steps* affect the number of diffusion steps performed on the requested generation.
- *N* is the number of images to generate;
- *Engine* current version includes eight engines[7], all selectable by the user;
- *Sampler* is the sampling engine to use. Currently have been implemented in the toolkit nine samplers. They are a sort of statistical samplers that are used in the diffusion model prediction process (especially for the denoising process);
- *Seed* is an integer number useful to discretize all parameters used in the generative process. The toolkit assigns a random value if no slider is connected to the *Seed* input.

Another aspect to take into account concerns the image-to-image mode, i.e. the mode that allows a user to get output variations starting from a source image. Basically, the source image can be generated previously and alternatively by OpenAI or by StabilityAI tools, using DALL-E allows only the source image to be processed as input. On the other hand, using Stable Diffusion lets the user have more control over the image-to-image process (IMGtoIMG) due to the possibility of adding a second text prompt as

---

[6] This workshop focused only on text-to-image and image-to-image procedures, so all "masking" mode parameters have been skipped in this description.

[7] The engines are different neural models that are developed by the use of a specific pre-trained set of images with different sizes. More info here: https://stability.ai/blog/stable-diffusion-v2-release.

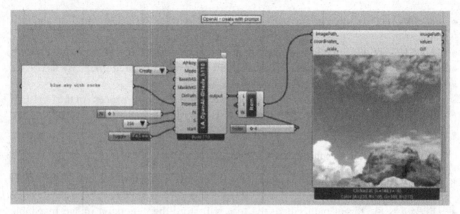

Fig. 3. Grasshopper script with OpenAI model (DALL-E) manually inputted by a prompt.

input besides the source image. Finally, thanks to the parameters *Strength* and/or *ClipG*[8] will possibly shift the weight of the generative process towards text or the source image (Fig. 3).

Both tools mentioned above generate three output formats: a PNG image stored in a subfolder called "IMGs", a TXT text file stored in a subfolder called "TXTs" and finally a Log file in CSV format located in the folder specified in the "DirPath" parameter. This way of managing the output files allows students to keep track of all their design exploration iteratively by archiving the input and output parameters used during the investigative stage, but also to access each metadata stored in the TXTs subfolder.

The script we created for the workshop offered the students multiple options for the task. Students were able to run the 2 models (Stable Diffusion and DALL-E) using different parts of the prepared script. The components allowed for three modes of image generation: creation, variation and prompt editing. Input can be images (generated in previous iterations) or prompts (manually modified by the students as they progress with their tasks).

As students generated different images (examples shown in Fig. 4) manipulating the prompts to achieve a satisfying solution to address the tasks set in the project brief, our model automatically generated a CSV log that records data that helped us to track the entire process. The log includes a timestamp, the prompt used, the mode of creation, along with other metadata like the name and size of the image file saved, and the base and image-mask used.

3.4 Tasks and Procedure

The workshop required students to design a public repository of water that serves as a sanctuary for individuals through the exploration and use of DALL-E-2 and Stable Diffusion models. The aim of the workshop was to introduce design students to the

---

[8] Clip guidance mode (ClipG) works only with the "Ancestral Sampler" models, according to StabilityAI's API documentation. Source, https://platform.stability.ai/docs/getting-started/pyt hon-sdk.

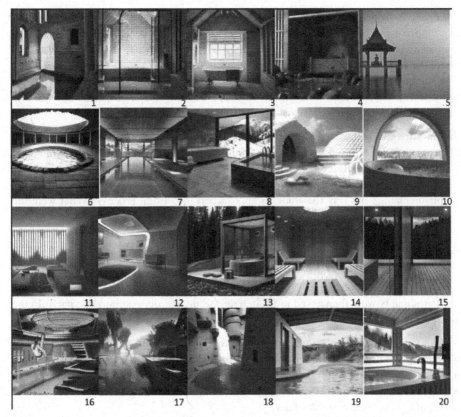

Fig. 4. Example of the work produced by the students. 1–3 Group 7 Stability.ai, 4–5 Group 7 DALL-E; 6–7 Group 2 Stability.ai, 8–10 Group 7 DALL-E; 11–12 Group 3 Stability.ai, 13–15 Group 7 DALL-E; 16–18 Group 5 Stability.ai, 19–20 Group 5 DALL-E.

use of diffusion models and allow them to explore the 'design process' and the 'digital representation' of this novel method. Throughout the course of the workshop, students were asked to reflect on the application of diffusion models in architecture and how they could be used to assist in the design process and enhance their visual presentations.

The workshop ran for 4 h and was divided into: Workshop Introduction (30 min), Phase 1: Groups to develop projects with diffusion models (duration 1.5 h), Phase 2: Groups to fill in the questionnaire template (duration 1.5 h) and finally, the group presentations (duration 30 min).

Phase 1: Once all groups had a solid concept for their building, they started using DALL-E-2 (for the first 45 min) and Stable Diffusion (for the second 45 min) to generate images of their repository of water, by providing models with text-based descriptions. This gave the students a better idea of what their building would look like and allowed them to make any necessary adjustments to their concept. Groups documented and commented on each iteration, explaining their own thinking process per each image generated.

Phase 2: In phase two of the workshop, the students were asked to reflect on their experience using DALL-E-2 and Stable Diffusion within the design process. This phase was an important part of the workshop as it allowed the students to think critically about the tools they have used and how they might be able to apply them in the future. The students combined snippets and comments describing Phase 1 providing an overall reflection on the process.

The students were asked to discuss the following topics:

1. The strengths and weaknesses of using DALL-E-2 and Stable Diffusion in the design process: What worked well and what didn't? What were the limitations of the tools and how did they affect the students' designs?
2. The impact of AI on the design process: How did using DALL-E-2 and Stable Diffusion change the way the students approached the design process? What were the advantages and disadvantages of using these tools compared to traditional design methods?
3. Potential future applications: How might the students use DALL-E-2 and Stable Diffusion in future projects? Are there other industries or fields where these tools could be applied?

Participants were then asked to fill in a questionnaire, divided into two parts. In the first part of the questionnaire we included the following questions:

- Can you briefly describe your experience with using the diffusion models?
- What is the aspect/activity you found more challenging?
- What is the aspect you found more interesting?
- On the basis of your experience today, what are the potentials you see in these models?
- What are the weaknesses/pitfalls?
- How about your learning experience? What did you learn (new) today?
- How would you compare your design activity today with the more conventional design methods (e.g. using CAD, 3D modeling etc. to produce architectural images/concepts)?
- Is there anything in particular that you think you are learning more or differently using diffusion models?
- Is there anything you think you are missing out by using these models?

Students were asked to comment on open-ended questions describing their experience through brief commentaries.

In the second part of the questionnaire, we asked the students to respond to the following questions:

Q1. Can you score (1–5) your experience today with diffusion models within GH?
Q2. How easy or difficult was it to experiment with these tools (1–5)?
Q3. How much the images that were generated differed from each other (1–5)?
Q4. How easy was it to instruct the AI to produce the solutions you had in mind (1–5)?
Q5. How many adjustments did you have to do to each prompt in order to produce a satisfying solution (1–5)?

Q6. To what extent do you feel you had an agency in the entire process? (How much of you as a designer do you think there is in the final results?) (1–5)

The discussion has been guided by the tutors who encouraged the students to share their thoughts and ideas, and provided feedback on their reflections. Overall, this phase of the workshop is an opportunity for the students to think critically about the role of AI in the design process, and how they can use these tools to enhance their creativity and improve their designs in the future.

The workshop was open-ended, meaning there was no specific design requirement, but students were encouraged to explore different design elements, typologies and styles. The workshop was, in fact, process-driven rather than finalized to the design outcome. The project was a great opportunity for students to explore the potential of AI in the design process, come up with creative solutions, and think critically about how the use of AI might shape the future of architecture.

3.5 Results

The data collected in the workshop were mainly a log of the prompts used by each group, the images generated with different models and prompts, and the replies of each student to the questionnaire. We use the latter to run a thematic analysis with an a priori coding [23], stemming from comments of the students in relation to two main topics: (i) usability of the pipeline; and (ii) relationship between automated process and the designer. Two of the authors coded independently the questionnaire's answers, using the following nodes (or codes) with the relative Intercoder Reliability scores [24] (Cohen's Kappa coefficients, with a fair-to-good strength of agreement between 0.41 and 0.75, very good between 0.75 and 1 [25]) as per below:

- Challenges: 0.7445
- Enhancement of Design: 0.8066
- General Opinion (interest surprise): 0.5202
- Limitation in Design: 0.8661
- Representation of ideas: 0.4955
- Usability

  - Awareness: 0.7705
  - Negative: 0.5379
  - Positive: 0.6648

With the relationship between the tool tested and the designer, we wanted to explore the extent to which the students (in their role as designers) felt that the diffusion models were enhancing or hindering their creative process in responding to a given design brief.

The first theme that emerged was the ability of the tools to support the students in **representing** their **design ideas visually**. Overall respondents commented positively on this point, yet they highlight a certain level of discrepancy between what they expected as the outcome and what the tools produced. This was considered positively and in many cases as a surprising product of the process: "[the tools] *gave a different perspective that I wouldn't have taught about in the first place*", yet with the awareness of some difference in the expected final results "*it was great, although the design did not represent what we wanted*". This aspect is also supported by the other emergent theme about the **interest and surprise** generated by the experience. Students seemed to appreciate the short time needed to generate strong visuals to describe and support their design: "*we learn a new way to generate idea in short amount of time*", "*it's good for getting a quick answer*" or "*I learnt how some changes when describing can give off big changes in the design*". Another aspect that has been emphasized in the responses is the **variety of images** that can be easily generated "*how AI creates different images by simply changing one or two words*". However, students realized the importance of words in generating prompts: "*How many vastly different versions it can create from the same prompt*" or "*it makes me focus more on the vocabulary I use to create something I can see in my mind*". Some students felt the need to be able to **manipulate prompts in a more granular way**, perhaps replicating the level of accuracy to which they are used in generating design with traditional tools (pencil while sketching or drafting, or CAD and 3D modeling): "*It would be nice to change one little thing In particular in each image as some were close to what we wanted to create but not exact*".

In our analysis, we noticed two most significant themes that emerged in a very similar measure: the tools as **enhancement of design** and as **hindrance of design**. These two aspects are reflected in two of the codes with highest value of agreement: Enhancement of Design (0.8066) and Limitation in Design: (0.8661). Students appreciated the capabilities of using diffusion models to generate images as a part of their creative process: "*it is great with creating something crazy*", "*[useful] for future use of quicker design and productivity*", "*exploring the potential of my thoughts*" and "*an easy way to communicate our ideas instead of only description. If there was a way of transmitting our sketches as well and from that it could generate a more realistic image*". Students emphasized the power of the used tools in creating unexpected images in a quantity and speed that is appealing and considered a strong addition to their designer toolkit. This is particularly true for early-stage design and representation or investigation of initial concepts.

In the same way, students highlighted the limits of the tools in helping them to produce the expected results: "Unexpected random outcomes, frustrating to communicate, no consistency", "*it was frustrating to* [be able to] *get a final model close to our ideas*", or "*the Dall-e is quite tricky because you have to choose proper words and play with it for a long time to get results you want*". The problems highlighted by the students in answering the brief through the tools proposed can be attributed to the fact that all participants were using diffusion models for the first time during the workshop. We recognise that some of the comments can be associated with any other generative design approach where the designer needs to design a method to produce an outcome. This is in contrast with more traditional What-You-See-Is-What-You-Get (WYSIWYG) approaches (e.g. in 3D and CAD modeling). It would be interesting at this point to run a similar workshop with designers who are used to generative models (like for example, genetic algorithms or other form-finding approaches) to compare the results. This would allow us to isolate the comments about not being able to intervene directly into the final results and appreciate whether they are related to generative processes in general, or to the diffusion models used in our particular case.

More speculatively, we realized that students felt a sense of indirectness in their design process due to the complexity that underpins the AI models used. Students explained that there was a third agent in the creative process (besides them as the designers and the medium as the computer or pen and paper): *"we feel more following the 'machine minds' to interpret things, while in the conventional method we visualize ideas almost purely from our own mind"*. Designers are used to impact directly on their design representations, very often through a lengthy iterative process. The process the students underwent in this workshop forced them to have a mediated approach to the development of their design, where the mediation was represented by an AI agent. While some students embraced this new element in the creative process as an enhancer *"When the images come out right, they are very good and extremely realistic. Producing such an image could have taken weeks"*, others found it somewhat hindering *"it cannot replicate the image you might have in your head and can take time to get the perfect image that the description depicts"*.

Table 2. Results for the second part of the questionnaire.

	Q1	*Q2*	*Q3*	*Q4*	*Q5*	*Q6*
Mean	3.83	3.72	3.61	3.06	**4.00**	**2.67**
Median	4	4	3.5	3	4	2
Max	5	5	5	5	5	5
Min	2	1	1	1	2	1
Range	3	4	4	4	3	4
Standard dev	0.90	0.99	1.01	1.18	0.94	1.25

The findings from the second part of the questionnaire reinforce the concept that AI models alter the notion of agency in the design process. In this part of the questionnaire, students confirm this idea by focusing on the unforeseen and spontaneous (generated/different/interesting) results during the process.

We obtained 18 valid responses from participants, which are summarized in Table 2 above.

The overall findings suggest that there were no extreme attitudes towards the utilization of AI tools during the workshop. The mean values for all 6 questions varied between 4 (highest in Q4) and 2.67 (Q6). While students had a moderate viewpoint on the general experience of using the tools, with values around 3 for Q1–Q4, they expressed a strong opinion on the number of adjustments required to attain the desired outcomes, as indicated by a value of 4 in Q5. The most intriguing outcome was from the question about the students' agency in the design process (Q6), which suggested a low level of feeling in control for the students as designers during the process (mean = 2.67 for Q6).

4 Discussion

The results of our study point out several interesting things about the use of Generative AI tools in the context of creative work to support users.

First, as participants pointed out, the images produced are surprising and interesting, which, together with novelty and utility or value form three basic criteria for evaluating creativity [12]. However, the control over the outputs proved to be more challenging than initially expected, as the importance of the chosen words for each prompt became immediately clear to participants. Controlling the way in which outputs are produced through prompts by tweaking them slightly or completely, as it is used in traditional creative work can be a much-needed improvement. Enabling users to better adjust outputs by means of fixing prompts is a topic that can definitely fit within the End-User Development research area's point of view, as it would enable users to customize these tools to fit their intended use and interact with them more naturally, in turn fostering their widespread use [26]. Also, students felt the need to see a direct relation (or mapping) input (prompt/words) to output (image generated), almost mimicking the node structure that characterizes Grasshopper-like design and programming environments.

The contrast between some participants' feedback in relation to the effects of Generative AI on their design is quite striking. The reported unpredictability of results represents an added value for the initial stages of design when blue-sky concepts are welcome, but can be limiting in later stages when a convergence over an expected solution is sought. This is still an open problem, but it could be mitigated with tools implementing masking actions: for instance, some conditioning procedures acting on the Stable Diffusion's decoder have been implemented using a Neural Network named ControlNET. The latter enables conditional inputs like edge maps, segmentation maps, keypoints to enrich the methods to control Large Diffusion Models and further facilitate related applications. This technology showing promising results [27].

Finally, the key point arising from our results is closely related to the nature of these tools: the sense of indirectness sensed by participants over the results, together with the lack of control of them in order to replicate what they had in mind is rooted into the black-box nature of Artificial Intelligence models. Generative AI tools will have to find ways to properly open up their inner models and allow users to properly direct them if they want to succeed in becoming the next companion of digital creators. Some proposed frameworks [17–19] already point out features needed in terms of Explainability of the models and characteristics of the outputs, but more research is needed in order to investigate proper solutions to these issues.

Finally, the inability to replicate what participants had in mind may cause a significant hindrance to the design process, resulting in frustration and lower creativity. These results have broader implications for the development and implementation of Generative AI Tools for Architecture, calling for a better understanding of the underlying algorithms and the need for greater transparency in the design process. By addressing these challenges, we can create more effective and accessible tools that really support and enhance the creativity and control of architects and designers, rather than be perceived as a tool to replace them, reflecting the true meaning of "Co-Creation".

4.1 Limitations

Although participants provided their feedback autonomously, it's important to recognize the significant role that facilitators played in the workshop. In this study, one of the authors moderated the workshop, but we plan to conduct future ethnographic research studies to increase the results' validity.

Our study aims to examine the impact of Generative AI tools on creativity. However, achieving this goal requires meticulous analysis and testing to ensure the results can be applied generally.

The group formation in the current study may have led to internal biases, which may have skewed certain groups, thereby limiting the results' overall validity. Question formulation could also have impacted the reliability and validity of the collected data. More studies are needed to cross-validate our results with different quantitative data coming from other sources of measure.

Finally, since participants were architecture students, additional research is necessary to evaluate the tools with participants from diverse backgrounds and levels of expertise.

5   Conclusions and Future Work

The rise of AI-based tools capable of generating new content has pushed the potential of AI systems beyond problem-solving and towards problem-finding, where the AI functions as a creative collaborator and supporter. Large-scale Text-to-Image Generative Models (LTGMs) are a rapidly evolving class of AI algorithms that have shown remarkable capabilities in creating high-quality images based on natural language descriptions, making them powerful tools for non-technical users. While the adoption of LTGMs-based tools is growing in various creative domains, their impact on creativity remains understudied.

This paper addressed this gap by investigating the impact of LTGMs-based tools on creativity through post-hoc feedback provided by design students. Our findings provide valuable insights into how the interaction with LTGMs affects the users' creative process, focusing on their ability to effectively control them to generate new ideas. This research contributes to the development of future tools and investigate their use in creative work. As LTGMs continue to advance, it is important to understand how the collaboration between humans and AI through these tools might affect creative processes.

Future works include further analysis of data in relation to the prompts issued by users to highlight, for instance, how many times a single prompt has to be refined in order to obtain a suitable result, as well as comparing the final outcomes with previous work that haven't made use of Generative AI tools. Moreover, involving participants without an architectural background would provide an interesting way of comparing our results outside of this domain and make them more generally valid.

Acknowledgements. The authors would like to thank Ian W. Owen for helping organize the workshop and the other tutors of the Architecture department at Hertfordshire who helped run the activities. We would also like to thank the students who proactively took part in the workshop and provided useful feedback for this study. The work has been organized as follows: TT coordination and leadership, LA developments of the tools, SC workshop, prep of the GH scripts, testing and troubleshooting, data analysis, AM feedback and advice throughout the study.

Research partly funded by PNRR - M4C2 - Investimento 1.3, Partenariato Esteso PE00000013 - "FAIR - Future Artificial Intelligence Research" - Spoke 1 "Human-centered AI", funded by the European Commission under the NextGeneration EU programme.

References

1. Gozalo-Brizuela, R., Garrido-Merchan, E.C.: ChatGPT is not all you need. a state of the art review of large generative AI models (2023). http://arxiv.org/abs/2301.04655
2. Stiny, G.: Introduction to shape and shape grammars. Environ. Plann. B. **7**, 343–351 (1980). https://doi.org/10.1068/b070343
3. Jo, J.H., Gero, J.S.: Space layout planning using an evolutionary approach. Artif. Intell. Eng. **12**, 149–162 (1998). https://doi.org/10.1016/S0954-1810(97)00037-X
4. Park, H., Suh, H., Kim, J., Choo, S.: Floor plan recommendation system using graph neural network with spatial relationship dataset. J. Build. Eng., 106378 (2023).https://doi.org/10.1016/j.jobe.2023.106378
5. Jabi, W., Chatzivasileiadi, A.: Topologic: exploring spatial reasoning through geometry, topology, and semantics. In: Eloy, S., Leite Viana, D., Morais, F., Vieira Vaz, J. (eds.) Formal Methods in Architecture. ASTI, pp. 277–285. Springer, Cham (2021). https://doi.org/10.1007/978-3-030-57509-0_25
6. Carta, S.: Self-organizing floor plans. Harvard Data Sci. Rev. (2021). https://doi.org/10.1162/99608f92.e5f9a0c7
7. Ploennigs, J., Berger, M.: AI Art in architecture (2022). http://arxiv.org/abs/2212.09399
8. Borji, A.: Generated faces in the wild: quantitative comparison of stable diffusion, MidJourney and DALL-E 2. (2022). https://doi.org/10.48550/ARXIV.2210.00586
9. Radford, A., et al.: Learning transferable visual models from natural language supervision. (2021). https://doi.org/10.48550/ARXIV.2103.00020
10. Wu, Z., Ji, D., Yu, K., Zeng, X., Wu, D., Shidujaman, M.: AI creativity and the human-AI co-creation model. In: Kurosu, M. (ed.) HCII 2021. LNCS, vol. 12762, pp. 171–190. Springer, Cham (2021). https://doi.org/10.1007/978-3-030-78462-1_13
11. Lyu, Y., Wang, X., Lin, R., Wu, J.: Communication in human–AI co-creation: perceptual analysis of paintings generated by text-to-image system. Appl. Sci. **12**, 11312 (2022). https://doi.org/10.3390/app122211312
12. Muller, M., Chilton, L.B., Kantosalo, A., Martin, C.P., Walsh, G.: GenAICHI: generative AI and HCI. In: CHI Conference on Human Factors in Computing Systems Extended Abstracts, pp. 1–7. ACM, New Orleans (2022). https://doi.org/10.1145/3491101.3503719
13. Campero, A., Vaccaro, M., Song, J., Wen, H., Almaatouq, A., Malone, T.W.: A test for evaluating performance in human-computer systems (2022). http://arxiv.org/abs/2206.12390
14. Clark, E., Ross, A.S., Tan, C., Ji, Y., Smith, N.A.: Creative writing with a machine in the loop: case studies on slogans and stories. In: 23rd International Conference on Intelligent User Interfaces, pp. 329–340. ACM, Tokyo (2018). https://doi.org/10.1145/3172944.3172983
15. Weidinger, L., et al.: Ethical and social risks of harm from language models (2021). https://doi.org/10.48550/ARXIV.2112.04359
16. Houde, S., et al.: Business (mis)use cases of generative AI (2020). https://doi.org/10.48550/ARXIV.2003.07679
17. Amershi, S., et al.: Guidelines for human-AI Interaction. In: Proceedings of the 2019 CHI Conference on Human Factors in Computing Systems, pp. 1–13. ACM, Glasgow (2019). https://doi.org/10.1145/3290605.3300233

18. Abedin, B., Meske, C., Junglas, I., Rabhi, F., Motahari-Nezhad, H.R.: Designing and managing human-AI interactions. Inf. Syst. Front. **24**, 691–697 (2022). https://doi.org/10.1007/s10796-022-10313-1

19. Weisz, J.D., Muller, M., He, J., Houde, S.: toward general design principles for generative AI applications (2023). http://arxiv.org/abs/2301.05578

20. Wohlin, C., Runeson, P., Höst, M., Ohlsson, M.C., Regnell, B., Wesslén, A.: Experimentation in Software Engineering. Springer, Boston (2000). https://doi.org/10.1007/978-1-4615-4625-2

21. Ramesh, A., Dhariwal, P., Nichol, A., Chu, C., Chen, M.: Hierarchical text-conditional image generation with CLIP Latents (2022). http://arxiv.org/abs/2204.06125

22. Rombach, R., Blattmann, A., Lorenz, D., Esser, P., Ommer, B.: High-resolution image synthesis with latent diffusion models (2021). https://doi.org/10.48550/ARXIV.2112.10752

23. Saldaña, J.: The Coding Manual for Qualitative Researchers. SAGE Publishing Inc, Thousand Oaks (2021)

24. O'Connor, C., Joffe, H.: Intercoder reliability in qualitative research: debates and practical guidelines. Int. J. Qual. Methods **19**, 160940691989922 (2020). https://doi.org/10.1177/1609406919899220

25. Fleiss, J.L., Levin, B., Paik, M.C.: Statistical Methods for Rates and Proportions. Wiley, Hoboken (2003). https://doi.org/10.1002/0471445428

26. Fogli, D., Tetteroo, D.: End-user development for democratising artificial intelligence. Behav. Inf. Technol. **41**, 1809–1810 (2022). https://doi.org/10.1080/0144929X.2022.2100974

27. Zhang, L., Agrawala, M.: Adding conditional control to text-to-image diffusion models (2023). http://arxiv.org/abs/2302.05543

Leveraging Large Language Models for End-User Website Generation

Tommaso Calò[✉][iD] and Luigi De Russis[iD]

Politecnico di Torino, Corso Duca degli Abruzzi 24, 10129 Turin, Italy
{tommaso.calo,luigi.derussis}@polito.it

Abstract. This work introduces an innovative approach that harnesses the power of large language models (LLMs) to facilitate the creation of websites by end users through natural language specifications. Our key contribution lies in a user-oriented method that utilizes prompt engineering, compelling the LLM response to adhere to a specific template, which in turn enables direct parsing of the model's responses, allowing users to focus on refining the generated website without concerning themselves with the underlying code. The engineered prompt ensures model efficiency by implementing a modification strategy that preserves context and tokens generated in the LLM responses, updating only specific parts of the code rather than rewriting the entire document, thereby minimizing unnecessary code revisions. Moreover, our approach empowers LLMs to generate multiple documents, augmenting the user experience. We showcase a proof-of-concept implementation where users submit textual descriptions of their desired website features, prompting the LLM to produce corresponding HTML and CSS code. This paper underscores the potential of our approach to democratize web development and enhance its accessibility for non-technical users. Future research will focus on conducting user studies to ascertain the efficacy of our method within existing low-code/no-code platforms, ultimately extending its benefits to a broader audience.

1 Introduction

The proliferation of the Internet has fundamentally changed the way we live, work, and communicate, leading to a substantial demand for website development. Traditional website development typically necessitates technical expertise, which can be a barrier for many individuals without these skills. In response, researchers and practitioners have sought to develop tools and approaches to enable end-users to create websites without coding. End-User Development (EUD) [2,8,16,21] has emerged as a popular approach to enable non-technical users to create websites [13,17]. Low-code/no-code tools have been developed to support EUD by offering increased ease of use and flexibility [7,9,23,26,28]. These tools enable users to create websites by visually arranging pre-built components, such as buttons, images, and forms, with the underlying code generated automatically. Although these tools have simplified website development, they can be limited in flexibility and may be challenging to use for more complex websites [1,11,12,25]. One of the primary limitations of low-code/no-code tools is the steep learning curve associated with their usage. Users often need to invest significant time learning how to use these tools effectively, which can be a substantial barrier for non-technical users [18].

Recently, there has been growing interest in leveraging artificial intelligence (AI) to enable end users to create websites [22]. Large language models (LLMs) have emerged as a promising approach for generating code based on natural language descriptions provided by end users. LLMs are trained on massive amounts of data and can generate text that closely matches human language, making them well-suited for generating code from natural language input [4,6,29]. However, these approaches have certain limitations, such as not allowing users to refine the output of the LLM with subsequent input or generating multiple pages. These limitations can hinder users from creating websites tailored to their specific needs and preferences.

To address these limitations, we propose a novel approach for leveraging LLMs for EUD using natural language processing to generate code from specifications. This approach is familiar and intuitive for most people, as it utilizes natural language communication [19,30]. Our method is centered around prompt engineering, which constrains the LLM response to follow a predefined template, facilitating the direct parsing of the model's output. This enables users to concentrate on refining their generated websites without the need to delve into the underlying code. Our technique allows users to iteratively adjust the LLM output and create multiple pages, offering greater adaptability and command over the generated code. With minimal technical expertise required, our approach bypasses the necessity to master programming language syntax, structure, or web development tools, considerably reducing the learning curve typically associated with website development. In addition, the approach incorporates an efficient prompting strategy to interact with external LLM APIs [15], which enables generating code that benefits from a larger context window[1] thus enabling refinements that reference earlier parts of the conversation and earlier generated documents. By maintaining a longer context, users can create more complex websites that refer to multiple pages, enhancing the overall functionality and richness of the generated content [15]. The engineered prompt ensures model efficiency by implementing a modification strategy that preserves context and tokens generated in the LLM responses, updating only specific parts of the code rather than rewriting the entire document, thereby minimizing unnecessary code revisions. This method also results in fewer tokens being generated, leading to cost savings, as the cost of API usage is related to the number of generated tokens.

---

[1] The context window refers to the amount of information an LLM can process at once. Preserving context is essential for interactions with LLMs, as it allows user to reference earlier parts of the conversation within the same generation process.

To demonstrate the feasibility of this approach, we present a proof-of-concept implementation where users input textual descriptions of their website requirements, and the LLM processes this input, generating HTML and CSS code to construct the desired website. This proof-of-concept showcases LLMs' potential in automating website development, reducing the time and effort required. In summary, our work builds on the emerging areas of EUD and LLMs, aiming to address existing limitations by empowering users to refine the LLM output with subsequent input and generate multiple pages. Our approach has the potential to democratize website development and significantly help bridge the digital divide.

2   Background and Related Works

End-user development (EUD) has attracted significant attention in recent years, as researchers and practitioners strive to make website development more accessible to non-technical users [2,8,13,16,21,27]. Low-code/no-code tools have emerged as a leading approach to EUD, offering users the ability to create websites without coding expertise [1,7,9,23,26,28]. Despite their popularity, these tools often present limited flexibility and can be challenging to use for developing complex websites [11,12,18,25].

Interestingly, an early prototype of an AI-assisted EUD solution was presented to the AI and HCI community over 50 years ago, referred to as retrieval by reformulation, and had a system called RABBIT as its primary example [24]. This work, although significant, did not gain widespread adoption outside of the research community. Nonetheless, it is important to acknowledge its contribution to the field as it laid the foundation for future developments.

In recent times, large language models (LLMs) have been identified as a promising avenue for EUD [4,29]. LLMs, trained on extensive data, can generate natural language text that closely resembles human language. This capability makes them well-suited for generating code based on textual descriptions provided by end-users.

Several studies have explored the use of LLMs for EUD. Huang et al. [10], for example, proposed a framework that automatically generates website layouts from textual descriptions using LLMs. Chen et al. [6], instead, developed a method for generating code snippets from natural language queries using LLMs. These studies underscore the potential of LLMs for EUD and provide a strong foundation for our research. Our work is unique in its focus on a user-oriented approach that allows end users to refine the LLM output with subsequent input iteratively. This feature empowers users to have greater control over the generated code, ensuring it meets their specific requirements. This refinement process is a critical aspect that differentiates our work from earlier studies on EUD using LLMs. While previous research in EUD using LLMs primarily focused on generating single pages, our work expands this research scope by enabling LLMs to generate multiple pages. It highlights the importance of designing AI systems that ensure high control and high automation, qualities essential for systems interacting with humans.

In addition to the existing body of research on EUD and LLMs, it is essential to consider the relationship between our approach and AI tools that convert hand-drawn website designs into complete systems (e.g., [3,5]). These tools provide an intuitive way for non-technical users to create websites without requiring knowledge of specific website structures and terms. In contrast, our LLM-based approach might still necessitate that users are familiar with technical terms to effectively communicate their design intentions, as illustrated by the use of "navbar" in Fig. 3.

AI services that generate websites based on drawings can offer a more accessible alternative for users who lack knowledge of website terminology. However, our proposed LLM-based approach presents several advantages. By utilizing natural language input, the method encourages iterative refinement of generated code, providing users with greater control and customization options. Moreover, our approach can potentially accommodate a wider range of user preferences and design complexities, as it is not limited to interpreting visual representations.

That said, a discussion comparing the intuitiveness and accessibility of our LLM-based approach and AI tools that convert drawings into websites is warranted. Future research could explore ways to combine the strengths of both methods, creating a more comprehensive and user-friendly solution for EUD. Integrating hand-drawn elements with natural language input could potentially lead to a more intuitive and powerful tool that caters to users with varying levels of technical knowledge and design skills.

To conclude, our research makes a contribution to the EUD and LLM domains by presenting an user-oriented approach that places end-users at the forefront of the website development process. By offering the ability to refine LLM outputs with subsequent input and generate multiple pages, we provide users with a high level of control and customization options [20], thus creating websites tailored to their specific needs and preferences.

3   Methodology

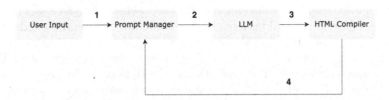

Fig. 1. The interactive website development process: (1) User provides input, (2) Prompt manager processes input, (3) LLM generates HTML code, (4) HTML compiler checks for errors, and if any are detected, the process loops back to the prompt manager for refinement.

In our approach, we utilize a technique that forces the LLM to follow a specific response template, as outlined by the given prompt in Fig. 2. The primary goal is to ensure that the generated code is structured and adheres to the user's specifications. The LLM is guided by a set of rules that dictate the format of the generated responses. By leveraging this template-based approach, end users can focus on their desired website functionality and design without concerning themselves with the underlying code, as the requests and responses are parsed in the specified format and rendered as HTML by the system.

When creating a new document, the LLM follows the response structure: new, ⟨document name⟩, ⟨code⟩. In cases where a document requires modifications, the LLM adheres to a response format that avoids outputting the entire code, opting for a more efficient strategy: ⟨document name ⟩; ⟨add or replace⟩, ⟨n1-n2 range of lines if replace, n1 if add⟩, ⟨code⟩; ... ⟨add or replace⟩, ⟨n1-n2 range of lines if replace, n1 if add⟩ ; ⟨code⟩. This technique ensures that only necessary modifications are made, preserving the original code and avoiding unnecessary API responses. The LLM takes the user's request as input, with the format request: ⟨request⟩, and generates responses according to the aforementioned template. By adhering to the specified format, the LLM efficiently modifies existing documents, only reporting the modification lines and modifications as needed, while leaving unmodified parts of the document untouched.

Furthermore, the technique facilitates error detection and resolution. The structured response format allows the parser to identify any errors in the generated code, providing the user with the necessary information to address these issues. In cases where the LLM generates code with compiling errors, the system can rectify the problem directly by prompting the LLM with the error and the code to correct, as illustrated in Fig. 1. This streamlined approach to error detection and resolution saves time and effort, making the web development process more accessible and efficient for non-technical users.

3.1 Iterative Refinement and Multiple Pages Generation

The methodology allows users to refine the output of the LLM with subsequent input, providing them with greater flexibility and control over the generated code. This iterative process ensures that the final website design closely matches the users' requirements and preferences. Users can provide feedback and request changes in real-time, allowing them to actively shape the development process and avoid time-consuming revisions after the website has been generated. Moreover, the approach enables the generation of multiple pages, further enhancing the user experience and providing a more comprehensive website development solution. Users can create interconnected pages with varying designs and content, allowing for the development of complex and feature-rich websites without needing extensive technical expertise.

3.2 Variety of Design Options

The proposed approach offers users the possibility to choose between a variety of design options in the generated documents. By providing diverse design alterna-

Prompt:
You have been asked to create HTML and CSS code based on the user's specifications. You can create multiple HTML documents, but only one CSS document which will contain the page's style. I will tell you the format of needed responses, you must strictly follow the following response format, and you must not output other words that are not contained in the formats.
If you need to create a new document, your response must be in the form of: new, (document name), (code).
If you need to modify a document already generated in another response, you must not output the whole code, even if the modification is large, you must use the following format for your response:
(document name); (add or replace), (n1-n2 range of lines if replace, n1 if add),(new line); ... (add or replace), (n1-n2 range of lines if replace, n1 if add); (new line).
If no changes are required to a given document you must not output nothing.
You need to specify <add> if the line must be added to the specified line number while <replace> if the line at the specified range must be replaced to accomplish the modification.
Note that the user's request will be inputted as "request:(request)".
Also, if you need to modify an existing document, please only report the modification lines and modification in the format specified above, as efficiently as possible. In order to not rewriting unmodified parts of the document.

Fig. 2. The prompt engineered to create and modify HTML and CSS documents based on natural language specifications, with strict response formats for creating new documents and updating existing ones.

tives, users can explore different aesthetics and layouts for their website, ensuring that the final product aligns with their desired look and feel. This feature adds an extra layer of customization and adaptability to the website development process, empowering users to create a unique and personalized online presence.

To facilitate the selection of design options, the methodology can incorporate predefined templates or design components that the LLM can use as a starting point. Users can then refine and customize these templates based on their preferences, allowing them to quickly create visually appealing websites without starting from scratch. The LLM can also learn from user feedback during the iterative refinement process, further improving the quality of the generated design options and adapting to the users' specific needs.

3.3 Efficient Prompting Strategy

The efficient prompting strategy involves asking the LLM only to respond with the number of lines to modify and the specific modifications, instead of rewriting the entire document. This approach enables the generation of code that benefits from a larger context window, as fewer interactions and tokens are generated. As a result, the LLM can accommodate a more extended sequence of refinements, leading to better model performance and improved user experience.

One of the core challenges in leveraging LLMs for website development is managing the limitations imposed by the maximum token length of the model. Other approaches often involve generating the entire codebase in one go, which may result in exceeding the token limit. By using the efficient prompting strategy, the methodology allows the model to focus on the most relevant portions of the code, thus reducing the likelihood of exceeding the token limit. Minimizing the number of generated tokens is essential for reducing the cost of API usage, as the cost is directly related to the number of tokens generated. This not only makes the methodology more affordable for end-users but also enables more extensive usage of LLM resources for website development.

Additionally, a larger context window allows the model to process longer sequences of text, enhancing its understanding of the user's requirements and improving its ability to generate accurate and contextually relevant code. Maximizing the context window also helps the LLM to maintain coherence across the generated code, ensuring that the resulting website maintains a consistent design and structure. As the LLM has access to more contextual information, it can make better-informed decisions when generating code, improving the overall quality of the generated website.

By generating fewer tokens, the proposed approach leads to cost savings and better resource usage, as discussed in the previous sections. This not only makes the methodology more affordable for end users but also enables more extensive usage of LLM resources for website development. The efficient use of API resources can also lead to faster response times and a more seamless experience for users when interacting with the LLM.

3.4   Proof of Concept

To demonstrate the effectiveness of our approach, we have developed a proof-of-concept implementation using GPT-4 [14], showcasing the technique's practical application. Figure 3 illustrates the sequential website development natural language instructions with the GPT-4 model. The figure highlights the interaction format, enabling readers to understand the structured responses and the methodology applied. Although the actual code in the responses is not shown, the reported responses provide sufficient information to comprehend the template and the format used in the GPT-4 interaction. This proof-of-concept serves as a tangible example of how our approach can be employed in real-world scenarios to create and refine websites using natural language specifications and the power of LLMs, ultimately streamlining the web development process for end users.

4   Conclusion

The proposed methodology consists of an efficient prompting strategy for interacting with external LLM APIs, which optimizes resource usage and enhances the user experience. By focusing on minimizing the number of generated tokens

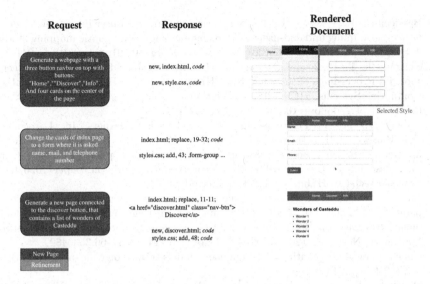

Fig. 3. Sequential website development process visualized in columns and rows: Columns display the Request, Response, and Rendered Page; Rows showcase three requests - the first and third for generating new pages, and the second for refining the existing page. Note that the code in the response is not reported, however, the reported responses should let readers understand the format used to interact with the LLM.

and maximizing the context window, this approach enables cost savings, better resource usage, improved model performance, and more refined control over the generated code.

The provision of a variety of design options and iterative refinement further adds to the customization and adaptability of the website development process. By addressing the core challenges of LLM-based website development, such as token limitations and contextual understanding the proposed methodology is ready to be integrated with existing low-code/no-code tools to enable a wider audience to benefit from the technology.

As a future work, the approach can be integrated with a low-code/no-code platform to ascertain the efficacy and utility of the methodology, through user studies. This integration can also streamline the development process by providing an interface for users to interact with the LLM, further enhancing the overall user experience. The final goal will always be to democratize website development and make it more accessible to users without technical expertise.

References

1. Alamin, M.A.A., Malakar, S., Uddin, G., Afroz, S., Haider, T., Iqbal, A.: An empirical study of developer discussions on low-code software development challenges, pp. 46–57, 05 2021. https://doi.org/10.1109/MSR52588.2021.00018

2. Barricelli, B.R., Cassano, F., Fogli, D., Piccinno, A.: End-user development, end-user programming and end-user software engineering: a systematic mapping study. J. Syst. Softw. **149**, 101–137 (2019). https://doi.org/10.1016/j.jss.2018.11.041

3. Beltramelli, T.: Pix2code: generating code from a graphical user interface screenshot. In: Proceedings of the ACM SIGCHI Symposium on Engineering Interactive Computing Systems. EICS 2018, Association for Computing Machinery, New York (2018). https://doi.org/10.1145/3220134.3220135

4. Brown, T., et al.: Language models are few-shot learners. In: Larochelle, H., Ranzato, M., Hadsell, R., Balcan, M., Lin, H. (eds.) Advances in Neural Information Processing Systems, vol. 33, pp. 1877–1901. Curran Associates, Inc. (2020). https://proceedings.neurips.cc/paper/2020/file/1457c0d6bfcb4967418bfb8ac142f64a-Paper.pdf

5. Calò, T., De Russis, L.: Style-aware sketch-to-code conversion for the web. In: Companion of the 2022 ACM SIGCHI Symposium on Engineering Interactive Computing Systems, pp. 44–47. EICS 2022 Companion, Association for Computing Machinery, New York (2022). https://doi.org/10.1145/3531706.3536462

6. Chen, M., et al.: Evaluating large language models trained on code. arXiv preprint: arXiv:2107.03374 (2021)

7. Di Ruscio, D., Kolovos, D., de Lara, J., Pierantonio, A., Tisi, M., Wimmer, M.: Low-code development and model-driven engineering: two sides of the same coin? Softw. Syst. Model. **21**(2), 437–446 (2022). https://doi.org/10.1007/s10270-021-00970-2

8. Ghiani, G., Paternò, F., Spano, L.D., Pintori, G.: An environment for end-user development of web mashups. Int. J. Hum. Comput. Stud. **87**, 38–64 (2016). https://doi.org/10.1016/j.ijhcs.2015.10.008

9. Gomes, P.M., Brito, M.A.: Low-code development platforms: a descriptive study. In: 2022 17th Iberian Conference on Information Systems and Technologies (CISTI), pp. 1–4 (2022). https://doi.org/10.23919/CISTI54924.2022.9820354

10. Huang, F., Li, G., Zhou, X., Canny, J.F., Li, Y.: Creating user interface mockups from high-level text descriptions with deep-learning models. arXiv preprint: arXiv:2110.07775 (2021)

11. Käss, S., Strahringer, S., Westner, M.: Drivers and inhibitors of low code development platform adoption. In: 2022 IEEE 24th Conference on Business Informatics (CBI), vol. 01, pp. 196–205 (2022). https://doi.org/10.1109/CBI54897.2022.00028

12. Luo, Y., Liang, P., Wang, C., Shahin, M., Zhan, J.: Characteristics and challenges of low-code development: the practitioners' perspective. In: Proceedings of the 15th ACM / IEEE International Symposium on Empirical Software Engineering and Measurement (ESEM). ESEM 2021, Association for Computing Machinery, New York (2021). https://doi.org/10.1145/3475716.3475782

13. Namoun, A., Daskalopoulou, A., Mehandjiev, N., Xun, Z.: Exploring mobile end user development: existing use and design factors. IEEE Trans. Software Eng. **42**(10), 960–976 (2016). https://doi.org/10.1109/TSE.2016.2532873

14. OpenAI: Gpt-4 Technical Report (2023)

15. Ouyang, L., et al.: Training language models to follow instructions with human feedback. arXiv preprint: arXiv:2203.02155 (2022)

16. Rode, J., Rosson, M.B., Qui nones, M.A.P.: End user development of web applications. In: Lieberman, H., Paterno, F., Wulf, V. (eds.) End User Development. Human-Computer Interaction Series, vol. 9, pp. 161–182. Springer, Dordrecht (2006). https://doi.org/10.1007/1-4020-5386-X_8

17. Rosson, M.B., Sinha, H., Bhattacharya, M., Zhao, D.: Design planning in end-user web development. In: IEEE Symposium on Visual Languages and Human-Centric Computing (VL/HCC 2007), pp. 189–196 (2007). https://doi.org/10.1109/VLHCC.2007.45

18. Sahay, A., Indamutsa, A., Di Ruscio, D., Pierantonio, A.: Supporting the understanding and comparison of low-code development platforms. In: 2020 46th Euromicro Conference on Software Engineering and Advanced Applications (SEAA), pp. 171–178 (2020). https://doi.org/10.1109/SEAA51224.2020.00036

19. Sales, J.E., Freitas, A., Oliveira, D., Koumpis, A., Handschuh, S.: Revisiting principles and challenges in natural language programming. In: Virvou, M., Nakagawa, H., C. Jain, L. (eds.) JCKBSE 2020. LAIS, vol. 19, pp. 7–19. Springer, Cham (2020). https://doi.org/10.1007/978-3-030-53949-8_2

20. Shneiderman, B.: Human-centered AI. Oxford University Press, Oxford (2022)

21. Sinha, N., Karim, R., Gupta, M.: Simplifying web programming. In: Proceedings of the 8th India Software Engineering Conference, ISEC 2015, pp. 80–89. Association for Computing Machinery, New York (2015). https://doi.org/10.1145/2723742.2723750

22. Stocco, A.: How artificial intelligence can improve web development and testing. In: Companion Proceedings of the 3rd International Conference on the Art, Science, and Engineering of Programming. Programming 2019, Association for Computing Machinery, New York (2019). https://doi.org/10.1145/3328433.3328447

23. Symmonds, N.: Visual web developer, 01 2006. https://doi.org/10.1007/978-1-4302-0180-9_5

24. Tou, F.N., Williams, M.D., Fikes, R., Henderson, A., Malone, T.: RABBIT: an intelligent database assistant. In: Proceedings of the Second AAAI Conference on Artificial Intelligence, AAAI 1982, pp. 314–318. AAAI Press (1982)

25. Tzafilkou, K., Protogeros, N.: Diagnosing user perception and acceptance using eye tracking in web-based end-user development. Comput. Hum. Behav. **72**, 23–37 (2017). https://doi.org/10.1016/j.chb.2017.02.035

26. Waszkowski, R.: Low-code platform for automating business processes in manufacturing. IFAC-PapersOnLine **52**(10), 376–381 (2019). https://doi.org/10.1016/j.ifacol.2019.10.060. 13th IFAC Workshop on Intelligent Manufacturing Systems IMS 2019

27. Wong, J.: Marmite: towards end-user programming for the web. In: IEEE Symposium on Visual Languages and Human-Centric Computing (VL/HCC 2007), pp. 270–271 (2007). https://doi.org/10.1109/VLHCC.2007.40

28. Woo, M.: The rise of no/low code software development-no experience needed? Engineering **6**(2020). https://doi.org/10.1016/j.eng.2020.07.007

29. Wu, C., Yin, S., Qi, W., Wang, X., Tang, Z., Duan, N.: Visual ChatGPT: talking, drawing and editing with visual foundation models (2023). https://doi.org/10.48550/ARXIV.2303.04671, https://arxiv.org/abs/2303.04671

30. Xu, F.F., Vasilescu, B., Neubig, G.: In-ide code generation from natural language: promise and challenges. ACM Trans. Softw. Eng. Methodol. **31**(2), 1–47 (2022). https://doi.org/10.1145/3487569

Internet of Things for End-Users

Defining Trigger-Action Rules via Voice: A Novel Approach for End-User Development in the IoT

Alberto Monge Roffarello[✉] and Luigi De Russis

Politecnico di Torino, Corso Duca degli Abruzzi, 24, 10129 Torino, Italy
{alberto.monge,luigi.derussis}@polito.it

Abstract. The possibility of personalizing devices and online services is important for end users living in smart environments, but existing End-User Development interfaces in this field often fail to provide users with the proper support, e.g., because they force users to deal with too many technological details. This paper explores novel approaches for personalizing IoT ecosystems via natural language and vocal interaction. We first conducted seven interviews to understand whether and how end users would converse with a conversational assistant to personalize their IoT ecosystems. Then, we designed and implemented two prototypes to define trigger-action rules through vocal and multimodal approaches. A usability study with 10 participants confirms the feasibility and effectiveness of personalizing the IoT via voice and opens the way to integrate personalization capabilities in smart speakers like Google Home and Amazon Echo.

Keywords: End-User Development · Internet of Things · Trigger-Action Programming · Intelligent Personal Assistants

1 Introduction

In the Internet of Things (IoT), end users should be able to customize the behavior of smart devices and online services even without possessing programming skills. To this aim, End-User Development (EUD) interfaces [19] – either commercial platforms or research artifacts – allow the definition of IoT personalizations. These personalizations are typically expressed as trigger-action rules in which an action is automatically executed when a trigger is detected. While trigger-action programming could potentially satisfy most of the behaviors desired by users [20,30], personalizing the IoT through contemporary EUD interfaces is still challenging due to the "low-level" abstraction of the adopted representation models [7]. In these interfaces, smart devices are typically modeled based on the underlying brand or manufacturer. As the number of supported technologies grows, so does the design space, i.e., the combinations between

L. D. Spano et al. (Eds.): IS-EUD 2023, LNCS 13917, pp. 65–83, 2023.
https://doi.org/10.1007/978-3-031-34433-6_5

different triggers and actions, thus generating a problem of information overload [31]. It is, therefore, essential for the user to interact with smart devices in a more abstract way [7, 22].

This paper explores novel approaches for personalizing IoT ecosystems via natural language by exploiting vocal interaction. Such a possibility has been fostered by the growing popularity and adoption of smart speakers like the Amazon Echo or Google Home. Their Intelligent Personal Assistants (IPAs), in particular, allow people to easily connect to their online searches, music, IoT devices, alarms, and wakes [1]. Overall, these IPAs have some end-user personalization capabilities, e.g., the execution of routines in Amazon Alexa[1]. Unfortunately, these capabilities are often segregated in a mobile app and take no advantage of their Natural Language Processing capabilities nor their knowledge of the IoT ecosystem in which the smart speaker is inserted.

To close this gap and initially explore how end users would personalize their IoT ecosystems via voice, we first conducted seven interviews with end users with different occupations and backgrounds. We were interested in understanding whether and how end users are willing to vocally define IoT personalizations, by using which format, and which kind of support they are expecting from the IPAs during the creation process. Results suggest that a balance of automation and human dialogue is necessary when designing an IPA for vocally composing IoT automation, with a trigger-action structure being an effective composition paradigm.

Stemming from the interviews' results, we designed and implemented two different IPA prototypes that allow end users to define trigger-action rules via voice. The first prototype adopts a fully-vocal interaction mechanism through which users can define a rule in a single sentence and refine/correct it through subsequent dialogues in case of errors or misunderstandings. The second prototype, instead, combines the vocal definition of the trigger with an action-specification phase in which the user is asked to reproduce the action to be automated physically.

We evaluated and compared the two prototypes in a usability study with 10 participants. During the study, participants were asked to complete a set of tasks of IoT personalization in a predefined smart-home scenario using both prototypes. Results confirmed the feasibility and effectiveness of personalizing the IoT via voice and highlighted the positive and negative aspects of both solutions. In particular, the fully-vocal interaction mechanism allowed participants to complete the tasks more quickly. However, the multimodal prototype resulted in a higher success rate, with participants that sometimes struggled with defining complex rules entirely via voice.

We conclude the paper by discussing how advances in Natural Language Processing and Artificial Intelligence could further support the integration of personalization capabilities in smart speakers. Finally, we highlight promising

---

[1] https://www.amazon.com/alexa-routines/b?ie=UTF8&node=21442922011,   last visited on February 16, 2023.

areas to be explored, from the management of existing rules to their debugging, to give IPAs a more prominent role in personalizing IoT ecosystems.

2   Related Work

2.1   End-User Development in the IoT

According to Lieberman et al. [24], End-User Development (EUD) refers to creating, modifying, or extending software systems by non-professional developers using various methods, techniques, and tools. Starting from iCAP [20], a rule-base system that allows users to build context-aware applications, EUD approaches and methodologies have been explored in several contexts. Danado and Paternò [14], for example, proposed Puzzle, a mobile framework that enables end users without an IT background to create, modify, and execute applications. Other works explored languages and visual programming for data transformation and mashup [15,23,29]. Smart-home applications have also been an extensively studied context for EUD, and many different tools and approaches have been proposed to customize intelligent home environments [5,17,30].

With the recent technological advances, EUD has become even more relevant, especially in the Internet of Things (IoT) [27]. In this complex scenario made of connected sensors, devices, and applications, EUD methodologies are a viable way to enable users to customize their systems to support personal and situational needs [19]. In the market, cloud-based platforms that support non-technical users in personalizing IoT devices and online services have been proposed in response to this demand. Two of the most famous examples are IFTTT[2] and Zapier[3]. Typically, these platforms enable users to combine the behavior of different entities flexibly by exploiting the trigger-action programming paradigm [19]. Through such a paradigm, users can define trigger-action rules to connect pairs of devices or online services in such a way that when an event (the *trigger*) is detected on one of them, an *action* is automatically executed on the other. Barricelli and Valtolina [4] suggested that trigger-action programming is a simple and easy-to-learn solution for creating IoT applications, and several research works have explored the adoption of trigger-action programming for personalizing smart devices and applications [16,17,30].

Despite their growing popularity, the expressiveness and understandability of current trigger-action programming platforms have been criticized by the HCI community [21,30,31]. Indeed, the models these platforms adopt models and metaphors that are often not well aligned with users' mental models, resulting in misinterpretations between triggers, events, and different action types [21]. Furthermore, platforms like IFTTT require users to manage every IoT device and online service separately. As a result, users must know in advance the involved technologies, and they have to define several rules to program

---

[2] https://ifttt.com/, last visited on February 16, 2023.
[3] https://zapier.com/, last visited on February 16, 2023.

their IoT ecosystems [9]. To overcome these issues, researchers have investigated different approaches, from exploring the adoption of alternative composition paradigms [19] to adopting more abstract representations for defining context-independent rules [9]. This work explores the feasibility and advantages of adopting a specific voice-based paradigm for composing trigger-action rules. The underlying hypothesis is that users are willing to create personalization rules vocally and that conversational assistants could facilitate the composition process, given their knowledge of the IoT ecosystem.

2.2 Programming the IoT via Conversation

Programming the IoT via conversation aims to map a user's natural-language request into the intended automation, e.g., trigger-action rules. Researchers have started to explore conversational agents for trigger-action programming only recently, typically by using users' input to generate some recommended rules. One of the first tools to compose rules via conversation, InstructableCrowd, was proposed by Huang et al. [22]. Through this tool, users can create IF-THEN rules by conversing with crowd workers and asking for suggestions to solve specific problems, e.g., being late for a meeting. RuleBot is instead a conversational agent that uses machine learning and natural language processing techniques to allow end users to create trigger-action rules for automating daily environments such as homes. After the chatbot welcomes, the user can enter a possible trigger or action, then the chatbot provides feedback and asks for the remaining information to complete the rule. Users can also delete the last entered item and asks for a summary of the rule so far created. Similarly, HeyTAP [10] is a conversational platform able to map abstract users' needs to executable trigger-action rules automatically. By exploiting a multimodal interface, the user can interact with a chatbot to communicate personalization intentions for different contexts. In addition, the user can also specify additional information on how to implement their personalization intentions, which are used to guide the suggestion of the rules. HeyTAP[2] [13] is the evolution of HeyTAP and introduces an update of the recommender system so that the application can further understand the user's intention by subsequent refinements. When the user cannot find a rule that fully satisfies their intention, HeyTAP[2] implements a preference-based feedback approach by iteratively collaborating with the user to get further feedback and thus refining the recommendations.

Although some examples mentioned above support vocal commands, all of them are designed as chatbots, thus involving a graphical user interface. Recently, researchers started to investigate the role of IPAs for personalizing the IoT [2,18]. Manca et al. [25] explored how the voice-based support offered by Amazon Alexa could be integrated into a platform to support the creation of trigger-action rules [25]. Instead, Barricelli et al. [3] proposed a new multimodal approach to create Amazon Alexa routines, leveraging Echo Show devices. Nevertheless, these valuable research efforts are often linked to a specific platform or follow fixed and existing metaphors for composing trigger-action rules –

e.g., Amazon Alexa's routine. As such, how to empower users to define trigger-action rules via voice remain an open challenge. For example, how would users recover from errors, or how would they collaborate via voice to select a specific device? Do users prefer composing trigger-action rules entirely via voice, or would they prefer physically acting on specific devices? This work investigates these questions by comparing two different IPA prototypes that exploit different composition paradigms and provide users with different degrees of support.

3 Interviews

We conducted seven interviews with end users with different occupations and backgrounds to explore whether and how they would converse with a conversational assistant to personalize their domestic IoT ecosystem. The main goal was informing the design of novel approaches for creating personalizations through conversation between a user and an IPA, when the IPA is embedded in a smart speaker.

3.1 Methodology

Participants. We recruited participants through convenience and snowball sampling by sending private messages to our social circles. We balanced our population by asking potential participants to complete a demographic survey to minimize self-selection bias. We selected participants to enroll end users with a medium-high interest in home automation. To measure home-automation interest, we used a 5-point Likert-scale question from *1 - not interest at all* to *5 - very interested*. Furthermore, we tried to have a mix of participants using/not using a smart speaker with an IPA, and we balanced our population in terms of occupation, educational background, and tech skills. To measure participants' tech skills, we averaged answers to different 5-point Likert-scale questions from *1 - not able at all* to *5 - I am an expert*. These questions referred to different activities related to using an IPA, from a simple web search to connecting and interacting with external devices, e.g., lights. Our final sample included 3 participants who self-identified as male and 4 who self-identified as female, aged 18 to 52. At the time of the study, three participants worked in the health sector; two were university students with a technical background; the remaining were homemakers and math teachers, respectively. Only 3 participants owned a smart speaker. None of them were programmers. The home-automation interest was 4.14 on average (SD = 0.64), while participants' tech skills was 4.17 (SD = 0.59).

Procedure. All participants completed a two-part study session with a background interview and an imagination exercise. Due to the COVID-19 pandemic, those one-to-one study sessions were conducted partially online (with Zoom) and partially in-person during April 2021. Study sessions lasted from 25 to 40 min.

Background Interview. We first conducted a background, semi-structured interview to understand users' relationships with smart speakers (if they have one) or with IPAs in general. We also asked about the experience that participants have with home automation and IoT devices, providing examples when possible. Questions included: "*Which are the main issues you experienced with a smart speaker?*" and "*In an IoT-powered home, which activities would you like to automate?*"

Imagination Exercise. After the background interview, we conducted an imagination exercise to elicit, directly from the interviewed participants, how they would create personalizations in different scenarios by using a smart speaker. Since not all the participants might have knowledge of end-user personalization in the IoT, we briefly introduced them to the topic. The collected information allowed us to explore the possibilities and approaches an end user would use to create custom personalizations via conversation freely. Participants received a description of a home (i.e., a fully IoT-powered home with a smart speaker for each room) and two personalization goals:

1. "*You want to turn on the main kitchen light every time you enter that room.*"
2. "*You want to close shutters and turn off bedroom lights when you go to bed.*"

Participants had to express, freely but vocally, an instruction for realizing each goal. We then analyzed the vocal inputs with the participants, with the aim of eliciting feedback on how an IPA should react in case of problems or misunderstandings.

3.2   Results

All the participants had some knowledge and experience with smart speakers; as expected, smart speaker owners had a more extended knowledge of the possibilities and limitations of such devices, while the others used them more sporadically, e.g., at a friend's home. They demonstrated, however, to know at least the basic features of smart speakers, especially the Amazon Echo. Regarding home automation and personalization rules, the two participants owning smart-home devices (P2 and P3) declared not to be in charge of configuring devices and creating personalizations at their homes. However, P1, P3, and P7 knew about the personalization capability included in the mobile app of their smart speaker, i.e., the Amazon Echo, although P7 was the only one who created a routine through the Amazon Alexa's app, namely a "goodnight" scenario to be activated on a vocal command.

In the imagination exercise, all participants created personalizations with a structure similar to the **trigger-action** formalism, even if they were not instructed nor primed to do it. As mentioned in previous work about trigger-action programming, also in this case, participants used triggers *one level of abstraction higher* than direct sensors [30].

However, we noticed a clear difference between participants who owned a smart speaker and those who did not, with the former more inclined to provide the IPA with more contextual details. For instance, while speaking with the kitchen's smart speaker to realize the first goal, smart speakers' owners composed the following rule, with minor differences among participants: *"Alexa, every time I walk into the kitchen, turn on the central light."* These participants specified the room where the rule should happen, even if they knew that rule was set in the kitchen and that the smart speaker was in the kitchen. Conversely, participants who did not own a smart speaker composed different rules, such as *"Alexa, turn on the light every time I pass by"* (P3) or *"Alexa, whenever you see someone walk through the door, turn on the main light"* (P6). None of those participants mentioned the kitchen, given that they were speaking with the smart speaker in that same room. This difference is likely due to the participants' experience with smart speakers. Indeed, participants who own smart speakers could have been primed by the current possibilities of these devices, which require them to be very precise in their requests. Instead, participants who did not own a smart speaker seemed to consider that smart speakers may possess some **implicit knowledge**, e.g., about where they are located.

When asked about the possible answers of the speaker after the rule creation, participants preferred to have an **explicit acknowledgment** that the rule was correctly understood, i.e., by having the smart speaker repeat the entire rule in its own terms, with a confirmation at the end.

Finally, participants commented on what should happen if the IPA does not fully understand the rule. They recognized two main options:

- *The composed rule has missing or unclear info (e.g., which lamp to turn on).* In this case, participants would accept either an **auto-complete feature**, if possible (e.g., if there is only one lamp that can be turned on), or an **explicit request** from the speaker (e.g., "which lamp do you want to turn on among these?").
- *The rule has one or more mistakes.* In this case, participants would use a **trial-and-error approach** to rephrase the rule until the IPA understands it correctly.

Key Findings. Overall, the initial interviews highlight the need to introduce the right degree of automation when designing an IPA for vocally composing IoT automation. On the one hand, participants did not consider a fully automated system feasible. In the interviews, they all believed that some dialogue with the IPA was necessary, e.g., to solve mistakes or refine an abstract personalization intention that may not be clear in the first place. On the other hand, participants reacted negatively to the possibility of a non-automated speaker, finding the idea of a long conversation to specify every detail improbably.

Another key finding extracted from our preliminary study is about the composition paradigm: all the participants created rules using a trigger-action structure, confirming that such a paradigm is effective and versatile even for vocally creating IoT automation. Finally, participants' answers – especially from users that did not own a smart speaker – highlight the need to have a straightforward way to provide the IPA with the right contextual details, e.g., to select the suitable device(s) when the user is adopting a high level of abstraction.

4   IPAs Prototypes

Stemming from the results of the interviews, we designed and implemented two different prototypes: an IPA supporting a fully-vocal interaction (*Pr1*, Sect. 4.1) and a multimodal IPA that combines vocal interaction with tangible actions on the smart-home devices (*Pr2*, Sect. 4.2). Our idea was to explore different composition strategies to understand the most promising approaches to define trigger-action rules vocally.

Both prototypes utilize Dialogflow's[4] natural language processing capabilities to capture a user intent – i.e., the Dialogflow's construct that categorizes an end-user's intention – and send requests to a Node.js backend[5] that generates the suitable responses. The conversational agents were integrated into the Google ecosystem by exploiting the Action on Google[6] framework. In the developing phase, the prototypes were tested on a Google Home device and a smartphone with an integrated Google Assistant.

We restricted the two prototypes to work with specific devices in a predefined smart home scenario for testing purposes. In such a scenario, depicted in Fig. 1, a hypothetical smart home comprises six rooms, i.e., bedroom, entrance, kitchen, bathroom, living room, and office. Each environment has a smart speaker, a motion sensor, and some intelligent lights and led strips. Furthermore, except for the bathroom, there are smart thermostats in each room. In addition, there are intelligent blinds in the bedroom, the kitchen, and the bathroom, while the entrance door is locked through a smart door lock. The devices included in the scenario allowed the definition of a restricted set of triggers and actions. For what concern triggers, these were those supported by the two implemented prototypes:

- *Temporal triggers*: events referring specific hours of the day, e.g., "at 9 AM," or more generic time periods, e.g., "in the morning." These triggers were supported by the smart speakers included in each scenario's rooms.
- *Voice commands*: specific keywords or sentences serving as rule-trigger, e.g., "when I pronounce the world 'hello'". Voice commands were supported by the smart speakers included in each scenario's rooms.
- *Movement triggers*: events related to entering or leaving a given place, e.g., "when I enter the living room." All the movement sensors and the entrance smart door lock supported these triggers.

These, instead, were the actions supported by the two implemented prototypes:

- *Lighting actions*: actions for turning on or off a specific light, e.g., "turn on the kitchen's main light."
- *Temperature actions*: actions for setting the temperature on the smart thermostats, e.g., "set up 20° in the bedroom."

---

[4] https://cloud.google.com/dialogflow/docs/, last visited on February 21, 2023.
[5] https://nodejs.org/en/, last visited on February 21, 2023.
[6] https://developers.google.com/assistant/console, last visited on February 21, 2023.

- *Doors and windows actions*: actions for opening or closing the entrance door or the smart blinds, e.g., "close the bedroom's blinds."
- *Audio actions*: actions for reproducing an alarm or an audio message, e.g., "send me an alert." The home's smart speaker supported these actions.

Overall, we developed the two prototypes to understand triggers and actions expressed through different levels of abstraction, as recently called for by recent works [8,12]. For example, the prototypes can detect the two following variations as the same trigger: *"when I enter the living room"* and *"when the living room's motion sensor detects a movement."* For the multimodal prototype (*PR2*, Sect. 4.2), all the controllers of the devices included in the smart-home scenario were simulated through an ad-hoc web application. For each device, in particular, we used a dedicated tablet device that allowed users to interact with the corresponding (simulated) controller. Both prototypes include an "help" command to guide users when they do not know or do not remember how to create a rule. Instructions given by the prototypes also include practical examples, e.g., as in the first message of Fig. 2.

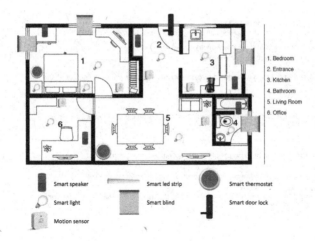

Fig. 1. The smart home scenario that we used to implement the two IPAs prototypes.

4.1   Prototype 1

The first prototype (*PR1*) has been designed and implemented to support full-vocal interaction, enabling users to create rules by using both the trigger and action components in a single sentence.

Figure 2 exemplifies a possible conversational flow of a user that is trying to define a rule in the scenario of Fig. 1 through *PR1*. The exemplified dialogue shows that the conversational flow is divided into four main parts. First, the user can freely specify a trigger-action rule after being introduced with some practical examples (*rule specification*). Following the results of our interviews, the IPA try to **auto-complete** the different parts of the specified rule, e.g., when the user is using a high level of abstraction. When the trigger or the action cannot be unambiguously resolved, instead, the IPA interacts with the user to obtain more details (*rule clarification*). In the reported example, the trigger (*"if I enter the kitchen"*) can be automatically established by the IPA, as the only way to monitor it is by using the kitchen motion sensor. On the contrary, the IPA explicitly asks the user to clarify which light should be automatically turned on, as envisioned by the participants in our interviews. When the user provides the necessary details, there is the *rule confirmation* phase, through which the IPA repeats the rule and asks for confirmation before saving it. The importance of such an **explicit acknowledgement** was mentioned several times in the interviews. If the user is unsatisfied, they can interact with the IPA to fix the trigger, the action, or the entire rule (*rule correction* phase). Such a correction phase adopts a **trial-and-error approach**: after fixing the rule, the user can either confirm it or continue to modify it.

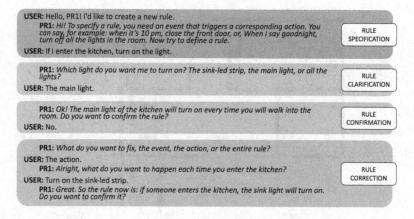

Fig. 2. A dialogue that exemplifies how a user can interact with the first IPA prototype (*Pr1*) to vocally define a trigger-action rule in the scenario depicted in Fig. 1.

4.2   Prototype 2

The second prototype (*PR2*) is a multimodal interface that combines vocal interaction and tangible actions, with users that must physically interact with the home devices to define the actions to be automated.

Figure 3 exemplifies a possible conversational flow of a user that is trying to define a rule in the scenario of Fig. 1 through *PR2*. In this case, *PR2* requires users to specify triggers and actions separately. The first step for the user is the vocal definition of the trigger. To this end, the IPA adopts the same strategies seen in *PR1*. First, the user can specify the event to be monitored (*trigger specification*). In case of ambiguities, *PR2* may ask the user to provide additional details (*trigger clarification*). In the reported dialogue, for example, the IPA needs to know which specific device should be used to define the trigger, i.e., *"each time someone enters the apartment"*. As with *PR1*, there is the possibility of correcting mistakes and misunderstandings (*trigger correction*), although in this case, this phase involves the trigger only. When the user confirms the trigger, it can specify the action. Such an *action specification* phase follows an entirely different approach, asking the user to perform the action that needs to be automatized physically. In the reported example, the user turns on the entrance-main light: the IPA automatically detects the action and links it to the vocally defined trigger. The idea is that such an approach can avoid ambiguity in the definition of actions, thus minimizing the possibilities of long conversations and extensive trial-and-error corrections.

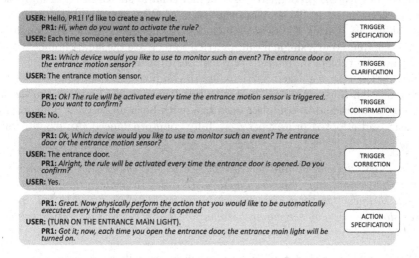

Fig. 3. A dialogue that exemplifies how a user can interact with the second IPA prototype (*Pr2*) to vocally define a trigger-action rule in the scenario depicted in Fig. 1.

5   Usability Study

In this section, we report on a usability study we conducted to evaluate the two implemented prototypes, i.e., *PR1* and *PR2*.

5.1   Methods

Participants. As in our initial interviews, we recruited participants through convenience and snowball sampling by sending private messages to our social circles. Through the same demographic survey used for the interviews, we tried to recruit a sample with a heterogeneous mix of job backgrounds and technological skills and users with a medium-high interest in home automation.

Overall, 10 participants (3 females and 7 males) qualified for the study and took part in the usability test. Participants' ages ranged from 23 to 57 years. Five participants worked in the health and social care sector, two were high-school teachers, one was a production engineer, and one was a housewife. At the time of the study, five owned at least a smart speaker, while the remaining five did not. The average home-automation interest was 4.3 (SD = 0,46). The average participants' tech skills was instead 4.15 (SD = 0,46). All participants currently live in Italy, and the study was conducted in Italian.

Procedure and Metrics. We tested our two IPA prototypes (*PR1* and *PR2*) in an in-the-lab usability study following a within-subject design. We provided participants with the predefined smart home scenario shown in Fig. 1 and asked them to personalize it. To simulate the usage of *PR2*, we provided participants with tablets simulating the devices included in the smart home. Although the test was conducted in a single room, we tried to recreate the smart home scenario by placing the tablets in different physical positions within the lab.

During the test, we asked participants to complete six different tasks of IoT personalization that could be solved with the definition of a single trigger-action rule. Participants had to complete each task with both prototypes. The order of the tasks and adopted prototypes were fully counterbalanced. An example of a task was:

> *It is currently winter, and you would like to save money on your energy bill while improving your sleep quality. In order to achieve this, you may want to lower the room temperature every night before going to bed. You can do this easily by setting an automation that sets the temperature below 22 degrees.*

During each participant's test, we measured the following:

- **Successful task completion:** a task is successfully completed when the user defines a correct rule with a proper trigger and action.
- **Time on task:** the time a participant took to complete the rule.
- **SUS score:** perceived IPA usability, measured at the end of the test through the System Usability Scale (SUS) [6].

5.2   Results

Figure 4 summarizes the most significant quantitative results collected during the study. The chart reports two primary pieces of information: the average *time on task*, i.e., the time participants took to complete each task with the two prototypes successfully, and the *successful task completion* rate, i.e., how many participants in percentage managed to solve each task.

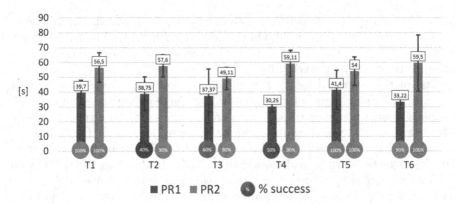

Fig. 4. A summary of the quantitative results from our usability study. The chart shows the average *time on task* for the two tested prototypes, i.e., *PR1* and *PR2*, considering only task instances that have been successfully completed. Times are in seconds. Circles with percentages report *successful task completion* rates.

As shown in the chart, the average time spent by participants for successfully completing a task was greater for *PR2* than for *PR1* for all the tasks. On average, participants took 36,78 s to complete a task with *PR1* (SD = 3,86), while they took on average 55,97 s with *PR2* (SD = 3,56). Such a difference is not surprising: differently from *PR1*, through which rules are entirely created by voice, *PR2* required participants to physically interact with a (simulated) device to establish the action to be automated. In a real-world environment in which devices are located in different rooms, we can expect this time difference to be even larger.

Participants particularly appreciated the ability of both prototypes to map their vocal inputs in concrete triggers and actions without the need to use predefined and structured syntaxes. In particular, both prototypes achieved excellent results when participants defined an action or a trigger that could be implement by a single device in the simulated scenario, e.g., when a trigger referred to activating a motion sensor. Both the prototypes, for example, recognized as valid triggers *"if I enter the kitchen," "if the motion sensor in the kitchen is activated,"* and *"when someone passes through the kitchen door."*

Although the time on task was better for *PR1*, Fig. 4 shows that the successful task completion rate was higher for *PR2* (95%) that for *PR1*. Two tasks in particular – T2 and T4 – turned problematic to be completed with *PR1*, with only 40% and 50% of participants, respectively, who successfully defined a correct rule entirely via voice. Completing these tasks was challenging due to their inherent complexity. In T2, for example, users had to create a detailed rule that involved setting the thermostat of a particular room to a specific temperature and activating the rule at a designated time each day. The many parameters were confusing for most participants. They had to provide a lot of information in a single sentence, and most chose words not recognized by IPA. In other cases, they used intricate phrases that were difficult to understand from IPA, and the

IPA could not react by correcting users and guiding them towards improvement. We found similar patterns in T4. On the contrary, *PR2* solved by nature many of the ambiguities and confusions of complex tasks, asking users to replicate the action to be automated psychically.

One of the reasons why *PR1* resulted in a lower *successful task completion* rate was that the prototype did not always understand the specific device the participant was trying to automate. In some cases, these errors have been solved through the *rule clarification* and *rule correction* phases (see Sect. 4.1). For example, P7 said *"turn on the light in the bedroom"* for defining an action for T6, although the bedroom had more than one light. In this case, the IPA replied *"which light do you want to turn on: main light, bedside lights, or all the lights?"* thus solving the disambiguation problem. However, *rule clarification* and *rule correction* were not always successful: 3 participants, for example, abandoned the current task after having reformulated the same rule twice. Looking at the results of our study and the conversations between users and the prototype, this kind of problems could be minimized by improving the training of the conversational agents, e.g., by including a more extensive set of synonyms for triggers and actions.

Despite the differences in time spent and successful task completion, the SUS score obtained from the participants at the end of the study was similar, with a rating of 71.5 for *PR1* and a rating of 73.3 for *PR2*.

6   Discussion

Overall, our work confirms the feasibility and effectiveness of programming IoT ecosystems through conversational approaches [10,26], and expand such a possibility to a fully-vocal interaction paradigm. The two IPA prototypes that we have developed in our research activity allowed participants – even those without a technical background – to comfortably create personalization rules in a trigger-action format in a smart home scenario. In this section, we first discuss our findings highlighting how Artificial Intelligence and recommendations could support vocal trigger-action programming and mitigate the problems encountered during the usability study, e.g., the low successful task completion rate of the fully-vocal prototype. Then, we discuss the main limitations of our work and highlight promising areas to be further explored to give IPAs a more prominent role in the personalization of IoT ecosystems.

6.1   The Role of Artificial Intelligence and Recommendations

The conversational approaches explored in this paper aim to map a natural-language request of the user expressed via voice into the intended rule. Overall, our work demonstrates that IPAs may support the definition of flexible automation in trigger-action format, allowing users to indicate the desired automation through natural language. However, as demonstrated by our usability study (Sect. 5), conversational approaches - especially the fully-vocal one adopted by the first prototype (*PR1*) - can become challenging due to the ambiguities of natural language. The multimodal IPA of *PR2*, which required users to physically interact with a device to define the action to be automated, solved most of the ambiguities by nature. Nevertheless, such an approach resulted in participants spending more time defining the correct automation and may not be suitable for all situations, e.g., when users need to define automation and they are not physically present in the IoT ecosystem. Consequently, supporting vocal approaches like the one offered by *PR1* is fundamental, and we consider advances in Natural Language Processing (NLP) of primary importance to remove possible ambiguities and allow the users to indicate precisely the desired effects.

As demonstrated by previous works, Artificial Intelligence methods are suitable to effectively map the abstract needs of the user into a lower level of abstraction that can be understood and executed at run-time [10,13]. Stemming from the results of the studies reported in this paper, we see value in supporting fully-vocal solutions like the one implemented by *PR1* with recommendation techniques. In trigger-action programming platforms with graphical user interfaces, recommender systems have been used to help end users define a new rule or complete an existing one. BlockComposer [26], for instance, supports two policies in recommendations while users create rules: i) step-by-step, in which the tool provides suggestions for the next element to include in the rule under editing; or ii) full rule, where complete rules are suggested. TAPrec [11], instead, is a EUD platform that supports the composition of trigger-action rules with dynamic recommendations. By exploiting a hybrid and semantic recommendation algorithm, TAPrec suggests, at composition time, either new rules to be used or actions for auto-completing a rule. Recommendations have also been used to support the composition of trigger-action rules through chatbots, e.g., in HeyTAP [10] and HeyTAP^2 [13].

We hypothesize that recommendations could be used in a fully-vocal IPA, e.g., *PR1*, to proactively suggest an action to be linked to a given trigger - thus solving potential ambiguities without performing any physical interactions. Alternatively, users could ask the IPA for new trigger-action rules to be activated based on their preferences, defined rules, or frequent behaviors in the IoT ecosystem. In the context of smartphones, for example, Srinivasan et al. [28], proposed a platform able to suggest rules based on the user behavior detected through the smartphone sensors. Rules, in particular, are proposed by applying confidence measures of the likelihood of the user performing an action.

6.2   Limitations and Future Works

Although promising, our findings are bounded to some limitations. In particular, the main limitation of our work is that it involved the definition of trigger-action rules in a lab setting. A more ecologically-valid study – during which users define and execute trigger-action rules on their (real) smart devices and online services – is needed to confirm the results reported in this paper. As such, our work suggests that defining trigger-action rules via voice may be a valid alternative to traditional trigger-action programming interfaces.

Future work can enhance the functionality of the developed IPAs to further support users in creating their trigger-action rules via voice. Two potential future implementations include linking multiple actions to a trigger and considering multiple trigger conditions. Besides focusing on *creating* trigger-action rules, we highlight that there are many other challenges and opportunities to be explored towards a better integration of IPAs and smart speakers into EUD:

- The **management of existing rules** might be an interesting effort, especially for those smart speakers not equipped with a screen. Here, the difficulty is not in the command that the end user can provide, but in how to present the list of available rules. Probably, reading all the rules with all their details is inappropriate. Similarly, listing a few pieces of information from the rule (e.g., the title) could provide a limited overview and increase errors. The challenge is to find a balance between these extremes.
- During the **execution of rules**, it is possible to envision a proactive role for IPAs: since smart speakers are always-on devices, they could be aware of what is happening and which rules are currently active. They might allow the user to ask for that information and stop some rules from being executed. It remains to understand whether and how much this is useful and appreciated.
- IPAs could help to **debug problematic rules** during their execution or, more importantly, to explain why a conflict arose. This could be done automatically by the IPA as soon as it identifies an issue or manually by the user if she notices something strange, like a lamp that starts to blink and never stops. The challenge here is, again, at the presentation level: when is it legit to warn the user about a problem? Who is the user to warn? How can the conflict be explained? Options range from describing why a certain rule (or set of rules) is misbehaving, to allowing the user to deactivate one of them, with various levels of details.

7   Conclusions

In this paper, we have explored novel approaches to personalize IoT ecosystems via natural language through vocal interaction. Based on seven interviews with non-programmers, we designed and implemented two different IPA prototypes that allow end users to define trigger-action rules vocally. Results extracted from a usability study with other 10 participants confirmed the feasibility and effectiveness of personalizing the IoT via voice and allowed us to discuss how integrating personalization capabilities in smart speakers could simplify and enhance the personalization process for end users aiming to personalize their smart devices and online services.

Acknowledgments. The authors want to thanks the 17 participants of the studies for their availability, and Carlo Borsarelli who helped with the creation of both prototypes as part of his M.S. thesis.

References

1. Ammari, T., Kaye, J., Tsai, J.Y., Bentley, F.: Music, search, and IoT: how people (really) use voice assistants. ACM Trans. Comput.-Hum. Interact. **26**(3) (2019). https://doi.org/10.1145/3311956
2. Barricelli, B.R., Casiraghi, E., Valtolina, S.: Virtual assistants for end-user development in the internet of things. In: Malizia, A., Valtolina, S., Morch, A., Serrano, A., Stratton, A. (eds.) IS-EUD 2019. LNCS, vol. 11553, pp. 209–216. Springer, Cham (2019). https://doi.org/10.1007/978-3-030-24781-2_17
3. Barricelli, B.R., Fogli, D., Iemmolo, L., Locoro, A.: A multi-modal approach to creating routines for smart speakers. In: Proceedings of the 2022 International Conference on Advanced Visual Interfaces. AVI 2022, Association for Computing Machinery, New York, NY, USA (2022). https://doi.org/10.1145/3531073.3531168
4. Barricelli, B.R., Valtolina, S.: Designing for end-user development in the internet of things. In: Díaz, P., Pipek, V., Ardito, C., Jensen, C., Aedo, I., Boden, A. (eds.) IS-EUD 2015. LNCS, vol. 9083, pp. 9–24. Springer, Cham (2015). https://doi.org/10.1007/978-3-319-18425-8_2
5. Brich, J., Walch, M., Rietzler, M., Weber, M., Schaub, F.: Exploring end user programming needs in home automation. ACM Trans. Comput.-Hum. Interact. **24**(2), 11:1-11:35 (2017). https://doi.org/10.1145/3057858
6. Brooke, J.: SUS: A "quick and dirty" usability scale. In: Usability Evaluation in Industry, pp. 189–194. Taylor and Francis (1996). https://doi.org/10.1201/b15738-26
7. Corno, F., De Russis, L., Monge Roffarello, A.: A high-level semantic approach to end-user development in the internet of things. Int. J. Hum.-Comput. Stud. **125**(C), 41–54 (2019). https://doi.org/10.1016/j.ijhcs.2018.12.008
8. Corno, F., De Russis, L., Monge Roffarello, A.: A high-level semantic approach to end-user development in the internet of things. Int. J. Hum.-Comput. Stud. **125**, 41–54 (2019). https://doi.org/10.1016/j.ijhcs.2018.12.008
9. Corno, F., De Russis, L., Monge Roffarello, A.: Recrules: recommending if-then rules for end-user development. ACM Trans. Intell. Syst. Technol. **10**(5) (2019). https://doi.org/10.1145/3344211
10. Corno, F., De Russis, L., Monge Roffarello, A.: HeyTAP: bridging the gaps between users' needs and technology in IF-THEN rules via conversation. Association for Computing Machinery, New York, NY, USA (2020). https://doi.org/10.1145/3399715.3399905
11. Corno, F., De Russis, L., Monge Roffarello, A.: TAPrec: supporting the composition of trigger-action rules through dynamic recommendations. In: Proceedings of the 25th International Conference on Intelligent User Interfaces, pp. 579–588. IUI 2020, Association for Computing Machinery, New York, NY, USA (2020). https://doi.org/10.1145/3377325.3377499
12. Corno, F., De Russis, L., Monge Roffarello, A.: Devices, information, and people: abstracting the internet of things for end-user personalization. In: Fogli, D., Tetteroo, D., Barricelli, B.R., Borsci, S., Markopoulos, P., Papadopoulos, G.A. (eds.) IS-EUD 2021. LNCS, vol. 12724, pp. 71–86. Springer, Cham (2021). https://doi.org/10.1007/978-3-030-79840-6_5
13. Corno, F., De Russis, L., Monge Roffarello, A.: From users' intentions to if-then rules in the internet of things. ACM Trans. Inf. Syst. **39**(4), 1–33 (2021). https://doi.org/10.1145/3447264

14. Danado, J., Paternò, F.: Puzzle: a mobile application development environment using a jigsaw metaphor. J. Vis. Lang. Comput. **25**(4), 297–315 (2014). https://doi.org/10.1016/j.jvlc.2014.03.005

15. Daniel, F., Matera, M.: Mashups: Concepts. Models and Architectures. Springer, Cham (2014)

16. Daniel, F., Matera, M., Pozzi, G.: Managing runtime adaptivity through active rules: the Bellerofonte framework. J. Web Eng. **7**(3), 179–199 (2008)

17. De Russis, L., Corno, F.: Homerules: a tangible end-user programming interface for smart homes. In: Proceedings of the 33rd Annual ACM Conference Extended Abstracts on Human Factors in Computing Systems, CHI EA 2015, ACM, New York, pp. 2109–2114 (2015). https://doi.org/10.1145/2702613.2732795

18. De Russis, L., Monge Roffarello, A., Borsarelli, C.: Towards vocally-composed personalization rules in the IoT. In: Proceedings of the 2nd International Workshop on Empowering People in Dealing with Internet of Things Ecosystems (EMPATHY 2021) (2021). http://ceur-ws.org/Vol-3053/paper_1.pdf

19. Desolda, G., Ardito, C., Matera, M.: Empowering end users to customize their smart environments: model, composition paradigms, and domain-specific tools. ACM Trans. Comput.-Hum. Interact. (TOCHI) **24**(2), 121–1252 (2017). https://doi.org/10.1145/3057859

20. Dey, A.K., Sohn, T., Streng, S., Kodama, J.: iCAP: interactive prototyping of context-aware applications. In: Fishkin, K.P., Schiele, B., Nixon, P., Quigley, A. (eds.) Pervasive 2006. LNCS, vol. 3968, pp. 254–271. Springer, Heidelberg (2006). https://doi.org/10.1007/11748625_16

21. Huang, J., Cakmak, M.: Supporting mental model accuracy in trigger-action programming. In: Proceedings of the 2015 ACM International Joint Conference on Pervasive and Ubiquitous Computing, pp. 215–225. UbiComp 2015, ACM, New York, NY, USA (2015). https://doi.org/10.1145/2750858.2805830

22. Huang, T.H.K., Azaria, A., Bigham, J.P.: Instructablecrowd: creating if-then rules via conversations with the crowd. In: Proceedings of the 2016 CHI Conference Extended Abstracts on Human Factors in Computing Systems, pp. 1555–1562. CHI EA 2016, Association for Computing Machinery, New York, NY, USA (2016). https://doi.org/10.1145/2851581.2892502

23. Le-Phuoc, D., Polleres, A., Hauswirth, M., Tummarello, G., Morbidoni, C.: Rapid prototyping of semantic mash-ups through semantic web pipes. In: Proceedings of the 18th International Conference on World Wide Web, pp. 581–590. WWW 2009, ACM, New York, NY, USA (2009). https://doi.org/10.1145/1526709.1526788

24. Lieberman, H., Paternò, F., Klann, M., Wulf, V.: End User Development, chap. End-User Development: An Emerging Paradigm, pp. 1–8. Springer, Netherlands (2006). https://doi.org/10.1007/1-4020-5386-X_1

25. Manca, M., Parvin, P., Paternò, F., Santoro, C.: Integrating Alexa in a rule-based personalization platform. In: Proceedings of the 6th EAI International Conference on Smart Objects and Technologies for Social Good, pp. 108–113. GoodTechs 2020, Association for Computing Machinery, New York, NY, USA (2020). https://doi.org/10.1145/3411170.3411228

26. Mattioli, A., Paternò, F.: A visual environment for end-user creation of IoT customization rules with recommendation support. In: Proceedings of the International Conference on Advanced Visual Interfaces. AVI 2020, Association for Computing Machinery, New York, NY, USA (2020). https://doi.org/10.1145/3399715.3399833

27. Munjin, D.: User Empowerment in the Internet of Things. Ph.D. thesis, Université de Genève (2013). http://archive-ouverte.unige.ch/unige:28951

28. Srinivasan, V., Koehler, C., Jin, H.: Ruleselector: Selecting conditional action rules from user behavior patterns. Proc. ACM Interact. Mob. Wearable Ubiquit. Technol. **2**(1), 1–34 (2018). https://doi.org/10.1145/3191767

29. Stolee, K.T., Elbaum, S.: Identification, impact, and refactoring of smells in pipe-like web mashups. IEEE Trans. Softw. Eng. **39**(12), 1654–1679 (2013). https://doi.org/10.1109/TSE.2013.42

30. Ur, B., McManus, E., Pak Yong Ho, M., Littman, M.L.: Practical trigger-action programming in the smart home. In: Proceedings of the SIGCHI Conference on Human Factors in Computing Systems, pp. 803–812. CHI 2014, ACM, New York, NY, USA (2014). https://doi.org/10.1145/2556288.2557420

31. Ur, B., et al.: Trigger-action programming in the wild: an analysis of 200,000 ifttt recipes. In: Proceedings of the 34rd Annual ACM Conference on Human Factors in Computing Systems, pp. 3227–3231. CHI 2016, ACM, New York, NY, USA (2016). https://doi.org/10.1145/2858036.2858556

Language and Temporal Aspects: A Qualitative Study on Trigger Interpretation in Trigger-Action Rules

Margherita Andrao[1,2](✉) [iD], Barbara Treccani[1] [iD], and Massimo Zancanaro[1,2] [iD]

[1] University of Trento, Trento, Italy
{margherita.andrao,barbara.treccani,massimo.zancanaro}@unitn.it
[2] Fondazione Bruno Kessler, Trento, Italy

Abstract. This paper presents a qualitative study that investigates the effects of some language choices in expressing the trigger part of a trigger-action rule on the users' mental models. Specifically, we explored how 11 non-programmer participants articulated the definition of trigger-action rules in different contexts by choosing among alternative conjunctions, verbal structures, and order of primitives. Our study shed some new light on how lexical choices influence the users' mental models in End-User Development tasks. Specifically, the conjunction *"as soon as"* clearly supports the idea of instantaneousness, and the conjunction *"while"* the idea of protractedness of an event; the most commonly used *"if"* and *"when"*, instead, are prone to create ambiguity in the mental representation of events. The order of rule elements helps participants to construct accurate mental models. Usually, individuals are facilitated in comprehension when the trigger is displayed at the beginning of the rule, even though sometimes the reverse order (with the action first) is preferred as it conveys the central element of the rule. Our findings suggest that improving and implementing these linguistic aspects in designing End-User Development tools will allow naive users to engage in more effective and expressive interactions with their systems.

Keywords: End-User Programming · Trigger-Action Paradigm · Mental Models · Language

1 Introduction

End-User Programming aims to enable naive users to create programs to automate the behavior of their digital artifacts [1, 2]. Among different possible solutions [3], Trigger-Action Programming (TAP) is an event-based paradigm in which users can create rules for associating a specific trigger with a particular action to automate the behavior of both hardware and software artifacts [4–7]. These rules are usually expressed in the form of *If < trigger > Then < action >* in research prototypes and in popular automation platforms, such as IFTTT and Zapier [8]. Although quite easy to understand and commercially successful, this approach has the limitation of being well suited just for automating easy tasks by expressing simple rules with one trigger and without limiting or defining conditions

© The Author(s), under exclusive license to Springer Nature Switzerland AG 2023
L. D. Spano et al. (Eds.): IS-EUD 2023, LNCS 13917, pp. 84–103, 2023.
https://doi.org/10.1007/978-3-031-34433-6_6

[7]. Previous works focus, among other aspects, on the distinction between the notion of events and states as a way to facilitate the expression of more elaborated conditions in the if part of the rule [6, 9] suggesting to exploit the lexical difference between *"when"* and *"while"* to differentiate between two aspects. In addition, other linguistic aspects may support people to create different mental representations of states and events. In some languages, for example, a different verbal structure may be more appropriate when describing states rather than events. In Italian, the progressive periphrases might more accurately describe a state (e.g., *"sta piovendo"* which can be translated in English as *"it is raining"*), while a verbal structure that includes the verb *"start"* or *"begin"* emphasizing its punctuality might more accurately describe an event (e.g., *"inizia a piovere"* which can be translated in English as *"it starts to rain"*). Similarly, in other European languages, there are comparable verbal structures to define and distinguish temporal aspects of states and events (e.g., in Spanish, *"está lloviendo"* which is *"it is raining"* and *"empieza a llover"* which is *"it starts to rain"*). In this work, we further elaborate on the idea of exploiting lexical choices by analyzing a larger set of linguistic features such as alternative conjunctions, verbal structures, and order of primitives. In a controlled study involving 11 Italian native speakers participants with no experience in programming, we systematically investigated how the lexical choices impact the participants' mental model of the computational machine, that is, how they imagine a machine could interpret their instructions. The present study employs a thinking-aloud protocol [10] and a qualitative analysis [11] to get a full and rich understanding of the participants' mental processes. It is meant as a first step toward a more robust study which also measures the effectiveness of the proposed solutions proposed. Our results, although still preliminary, suggest that all three different lexical choices investigated (conjunctions, verbal form, and order) contribute to determining the users' mental model, and some combinations of choices foster a proper model while others prompt ambiguity and potential errors. Although the Italian conjunctions and verbal structures used in our study have very similar semantics to their English analogous and the trigger-action rules structure is comparable to the English form (i.e., *"if-then"* is analogous to the Italian *"se-allora"*), which is the most widely used language in existing automation platforms [8], further studies need to investigate linguistic differences.

The lesson learned from our study would suggest that, in order to improve TAP, it is important to offer users lexically accurate interfaces but also it is important to align the ontology (the representation of the domain) of the system to fully and properly represent the distinction between events and states.

1.1 Related Work

TAP is a widely used approach due to its simplicity and intuitiveness, perfectly suitable for people without programming experience [7, 12, 13]. However, the simplicity of this model is also its limitation. For example, IFTTT only allows the creation of basic rules with a single event as a trigger restricting the expressiveness of the programs that users can create [6, 7]. In their study, Ur and coll. [7] analyzed a collection of 1590 trigger-action programs in the domain of Smart homes. Their analysis showed that 77.9% of program behaviors fitted in a single trigger and a single action form, but 16.9% required multiple triggers and possibly multiple actions. People need more expressiveness in trigger composition than those provided by common single-trigger and single-action rules to enable effective programming. Several works on TAP noted this limitation and proposed systems that allow conjunctions of multiple triggers [4, 6, 7, 12, 14]. Trigger conjunctions are meaningful for combining one event trigger alongside multiple conditions [13], similar to ECA (Event-Condition-Action) rules used by expert programmers. These studies showed that users successfully write programs with multiple triggers and actions regardless of prior experience [4, 13, 15]. However, dealing with multiple triggering conditions may be problematic for naive users. According to some results [5, 6], one of the possible causes of ambiguities and errors in rules composition, interpretation, and debugging could be an incomplete or incorrect mental model. Understanding and guiding users' mental models is crucial in Human-Computer Interaction [16, 17]. Indeed, the primary source of confusion in interacting with an artifact is due to users having wrong or inaccurate mental models of the actual functioning of the system.

Mental models are internal structures representing declarative, procedural, and inferential knowledge about the world as well as information extracted by perceptual processes [18]. When interacting with a given system, users rely on their representation of how the system works, its structure, and operations (i.e., conceptual model) stored in long-term memory [17, 18]. The combination of that information and the one extracted by perceptual processes creates a mental representation of the real interaction in working memory [19, 20]. Mental models built in working memory are, by nature, dynamic representations that allow people to simulate the piece of the world they are interacting with, supporting comprehension and reasoning processes, and allowing outcomes prediction of different scenarios. Mental models play a central role in human cognition, and (the creation of) faulty mental models are responsible for most errors in thinking (e.g., [9]). Several studies in psychology of programming and EUD have focused on different factors involved in users' mental model creation. According to Norman [16, 17], effective conceptual models of a system should be implicitly induced (i.e., without explicit instructions) by the system design. However, information and instructions provided to users may be crucial as the systems' complexity increases. Studies investigating the effect of different descriptions on participants' performance suggest that more detailed (albeit more complex) information about system functioning allows users to develop better conceptual models. This results in more effective, as well as more satisfactory, interactions with their digital device and more accurate outcomes predictions (e.g., [21–24]). Moreover, naive users' mental models seem to be influenced by specific properties of the language and structures of rules used for EUP tasks [25, 27]. According to Pane et al. [28], the logical structure of TAP best corresponds to the natural way naive users express rules. Indeed, the authors found that the majority of the statements that non-expert participants produced spontaneously during a programming task started with "*if*" or "*while*".

Dealing with trigger conjunctions led to questions about semantics, temporal features, possible combinations of different types of occurrences, and how these affect users' mental models [5, 6, 21, 22, 29]. Huang and Cakmak [6] emphasized the role of trigger temporal features in the comprehension, interpretation, and composition of trigger-action rules by naive users. The authors defined a minimum of two types of temporal feature-based elements that can be used in triggers: instantaneous events (or simply events) and protracted over time ones (also called states) which are conditions evaluated as true or false at any time. They also observed that users often confused events and states. More specifically, the lack of distinction between different trigger types in the *If < trigger > Then < action >* metaphor may create ambiguities (e.g., the interpretation of when exactly triggers will occur) and undesirable outcomes, especially in the context of trigger conjunctions. The authors thus suggested the following solutions at the interface level that could improve users' mental models: (i) grouping or clearly naming states and events; (ii) using different temporal conjunctions for events (e.g., *"when"*, *"if "*) and states (e.g., *"while"*, *"as long as"*); (iii) employing different verbs to support events (active verbs such as *"turns"*) and states (present tense of the verb *"be"* such as *"I am currently at"*). Overall, they emphasize the need to investigate and implement strategies to communicate to users a clear and categorical distinction between temporal feature-based triggers to facilitate the creation of effective mental models [5, 6, 30]. The distinction between these different types of occurrences is supported implicitly by language [31, 32] grounded in the semantics and codified in lexical choices. When two simultaneous occurrences are present in the same sentence (e.g., states and events), one of them is perceived as the main one (i.e., the figure), while the other one is interpreted as the ground (i.e., the context) [33]. In particular, the longer occurrence is often perceived as the ground, and it is considered more acceptable by participants if introduced by *"while"* instead of *"when"* [33]. Furthermore, in more recent studies, the targeted use of temporal conjunctions (i.e., *"while"* to introduce states, and *"when"* to introduce events) was used to convey a distinction between states and events within trigger-action rules [21, 22, 34]. The results showed that this distinction helped participants create a clearer differentiation between the two kinds of occurrences. Another language-related aspect that might influence mental representations is the syntactic order of temporal sentences [33]. Indeed, the iconicity assumption [35] states that by default, readers/listeners assume that the order of clauses in a sentence corresponds to the actual order of events [36]. In the case of simultaneous events (introduced by temporal conjunction such as *"while"* / *"when"*), representations are always more difficult since it violates the iconicity assumption. De Vega and coll. [33] found that, in multi-clauses sentences, the temporal conjunction indicating simultaneity (*"while"* or *"when"*) is more easily understood by participants when it is at the beginning of the sentence (vs. embedded - at the beginning of the second clause). For example, the sentence *"while you are cooking, the doorbell rings"* is more easily represented in mental models than *"the doorbell rings while you are cooking"* since the first immediately informs of the simultaneity of the two events avoiding people's working memory overload.

Accumulated evidence strongly indicates that linguistic aspects need to be taken into account when designing an interface and choosing the most appropriate verbal primitives in a TAP system. Blackwell [37] suggested that many naive users' difficulties arise from the lack of direct manipulation of the elements involved in the rules and the use of abstract notational elements. Many bugs and difficulties in EUP may arise from the excessive/unnecessary distance between users' mental models and the adopted programming languages [38], together with users' inclination to transfer language knowledge into programming tasks [39].

2 The Study

The study aimed to investigate the role of some specific aspects of language in trigger-action rules composition and interpretation. In particular, we explored the influence of different temporal conjunctions ("*as soon as*", "*when*", "*if*", "*while*", and "*as long as*") and verbal structures (progressive periphrases which are analogous to the present progressive tense in English such as "*it is raining*", specific marks to signal instantaneousness such as "*it starts to rain*", compared to generic forms in present indicative such as "*it rains*") to facilitate the distinct representation of states and events [6]. A second aspect under investigation was the study of the influence of the syntactic order with which trigger and action were presented [33].

The study was organized as individual sessions in which we asked participants, without programming experience, to read a few scenarios illustrating desired states and to compose TA rules aimed at achieving them. The scenarios were carefully prepared to compare different combinations of these variables. The scenarios were presented one at a time and, after reading a scenario description, the participant had to select the language primitives to compose the trigger part of the rule and decide the preferred order of the trigger and the action part. A thinking-aloud technique [10] was used to collect verbal reports on participants' mental models.

2.1 Participants

Seven females and five males, aged between 21 to 33 years (M = 27.67 and SD = 3.49 years; Mf = 27.43 and SDf = 3.41 years; Mm = 28.00 and SDm = 3.41 years), participated in the study. All of them were native Italian speakers with no experience in programming. Three of them were non-degree workers, while nine were university students or just-graduated workers. Participants were recruited by means of a snowball sampling in the surrounding areas of Trento and Brescia (in the north of Italy). Data related to one female participant was excluded due to technical problems during the recording.

2.2 Materials

We created 24 impersonal descriptions of scenarios describing everyday life situations (see Table1). In half of the scenarios, the desiderated outcome could be achieved with a rule triggered by an event and, in the other half, with a rule that should be maintained active during a state. We identified 12 events (for example, "*to rain*") that fit both a state-based, protracted, interpretation ("*it is raining*") and an event-based, instantaneous, interpretation ("*it starts raining*"). For each occurrence (event or state), we defined three verbal structures: an event-specific (preceded by "*it starts to*"), state-specific (progressive form), and generic form (present tense). Then, we defined an associated action for each scenario (e.g., "*keep the umbrella open*" for the state-based scenario, "*close the window immediately*" for the event-based one). All material was designed and presented in Italian.

Table 1. In the table is visible the list of 24 scenarios used in our study and the language primitives (original Italian version and English translation) describing actions and triggers.

Scenario			Language Primitives			
n	occurence	description	action	verb generic	verb state-specific	verb event-specific
1	State	Avoiding clothes getting wet	*tieni l'ombrello aperto* keep the umbrella open	*piove*	*sta piovendo*	*inizia a piòvere*
2	Event	Avoiding water entering the house	*chiudi subito la finestra* close the window immediately	it rains	it is raining	it starts to rain
3	State	Increasing the stimuli for waking up	*tieni alto il volume* keep the volume up	*la sveglia suona*	*la sveglia sta suonando*	*la sveglia inizia a suonare*
4	Event	Having a coffee ready in the morning	*accendi subito la macchinetta del caffè* turn on the coffee machine immediately	the alarm clock rings	the alarm clock is ringing	the alarm clock starts to ring
5	State	Avoiding light entering the room	*tieni le tapparelle abbassate* keep the blinds down	*splende il sole*	*sta splendendo il sole*	*inizia a splendere il sole*
6	Event	Hanging the laundry outside	*invia subito una notifica* send notification immediately	the sun shines	the sun is shining	the sun starts to shine
7	State	Recording Carlo's speech	*tieni il microfono acceso* keep the microphone on	*Carlo parla*	*Calro sta parlando*	*Carlo inizia a parlare*
8	Event	Listening to Carlo's speech	*abbassa subito il volume della musica* turn down the music volume immediately	Carlo speaks	Carlo is speaking	Carlo starts to speak
9	State	Avoiding missing parts of the lesson	*tieni il registratore acceso* keep the recorder on	*il Professore spiega*	*il Professore sta spiegando*	*il Professore inizia a spiegare*
10	Event	Avoiding interrupting the lesson	*attiva subito la modalità silenziosa* turn on silent mode immediately	the Professor teaches	the Professor is teaching	the Professor starts to teach

(continued)

Table 1. (*continued*)

Scenario			Language Primitives			
11	State	Working in an optimal environment	*tieni la temperatura a 18 gradi*	*si lavora*	*si sta lavorando*	*si inizia a lavorare*
			keep the temperature at 18 degrees			
12	Event	Avoiding inappropriate calls	*attiva subito la modalità non disturbare*	one works	one is working	one starts to work
			activate do not disturb mode immediately			
13	State	Increasing concentration in study	*tieni la porta chiusa*	*si studia*	*si sta studiando*	*si inizia a studiare*
			keep the door close			
14	Event	Reducing distractions	*disattiva subito tutte le notifiche*	one studies	one is studying	one starts to study
			turn off all notifications immediately			
15	State	Reducing background noise	*tieni attiva la cancellazione del rumore*	*il cane abbaia*	*il cane sta abbaiando*	*il cane inizia ad abbaiare*
			keep noise cancellation on			
16	Event	Creating a quiet environment	*apri subito la porta*	the dog barks	the dog is barking	the dog starts to bark
			open the door immediately			
17	State	Reaching maximum effort at the sports medical exam	*tieni monitorata la frequenza cardiaca*	*si corre*	*si sta correndo*	*si inizia a correre*
			keep your heart rate monitored			
18	Event	Recording the number of miles of a workout	*attiva subito il conta passi*	one runs	one is running	one starts to run
			activate the step counter immediately			
19	State	Responsible traffic circulation	*tieni i fari accesi*	*la macchina si muove*	*la macchina si sta muovendo*	*la macchina inizia a muoversi*
			keep headlights on			
20	Event	Listening to a podcast in the car	*accendi subito la radio*	the car moves	the car is moving	the car starts to move
			turn on the radio immediately			

(*continued*)

Table 1. (*continued*)

Scenario			Language Primitives			
21	State	Alerting people of a fire	*tieni attivo l'allarme anti-incendio*	*si rileva del fumo*	*si sta rilevando del fumo*	*si inizia a rilevare del fumo*
			keep the umbrella open			
22	Event	Preventing a fire from spreading	*accendi subito gli irrigatori anti-incendio*	one detects smoke	one is detecting smoke	one starts to detect smoke
			close the window immediately			
23	State	Avoiding household accidents	*tieni spenti i fornelli*	*se si dorme*	*si sta dormendo*	*si inizia a dormire*
			keep the stove off			
24	Event	Going to bed safely	*attiva subito l'allarme*	one sleeps	one is sleeping	one starts to sleep
			activate the alarm immediately			

2.3 Methods

Data were collected in a controlled setting using the online platform Qualtrics. Each participant answered all 24 scenarios. Every trial consisted of two different parts: the composition task and the order preference one (see Fig. 1).

In the composition task, participants were instructed to define the language primitives for creating the sentence most appropriate as instructions to realize the scenario proposed. Participants were seated in front of a computer screen. They read the scenario described on the screen. Immediately under this description the action part was presented. Two dropdown lists allowed participants to select the temporal conjunction (among five: "*as soon as*", "*when*", "*if*", "*while*", and "*as long as*") and the verbal structure (among three: generic form, state-specific, event-specific) to compose the rule. Subsequently, in the order preference task, participants were asked to choose the order they perceived as the most natural and accurate to compose an instruction to realize the scenario. In this second screen, participants saw the selected choice in two orders: trigger-first (e.g., "*if it rains close the window immediately*") and action-first (e.g., "*close the window immediately if it rains*"). Finally, participants filled in a short demographic form for age, gender, and previous experience with programming languages. Following a think-aloud protocol, participants were explicitly asked to motivate and elaborate their decision. Each session lasted approximately 45 min and was video and audio-recorded. Session recordings were transcribed and then coded and analyzed using thematic content analysis [11] by two independent researchers.

A. Composition task

[1] Componi la frase nella maniera che ritieni più accurata per realizzare lo scenario. **Ricorda di "pensare ad alta voce".**

> [1] *The instructions displayed: "Compose the sentence in the way you think is most accurate to realize the scenario. Remember to "think aloud".*

[2] Avere un caffè pronto al mattino

> [2] *The scenario description: "Having a coffee ready in the morning".*

accendi subito la macchinetta del caffè   [3] [_____ ∨]   / [_____ ∨]

appena
quando
se
finché
mentre

> [3] *Dropdown to select one conjunction among: "as soon as", "when", "if", "while", and "as long as".*

[4] accendi subito la macchinetta del caffè   [se ∨]   [5] [_____ ∨]

> [4] *The action: "turn on the coffee machine immediately".*

suona la sveglia
inizia a suonare la sveglia
sta suonando la sveglia

> [5] *Dropdown to select one verbal structure among: "the clock alarm rings", "the clock alarm starts to ring", and "the alarm clock is ringing".*

B. Order preference task

[6] Seleziona l'ordine che preferisci per lo scenario: Avere un caffè pronto al mattino

[7]   se suona la sveglia accendi subito la macchinetta del caffè

[8]   accendi subito la macchinetta del caffè, se suona la sveglia

> [6] *The instructions displayed: "Select the order you prefer for the scenario: Having a coffee ready in the morning".*

> [7] *Trigger-first order "if the alarm clock rings turn on the coffee machine immediately".*

> [8] *Action-first order "turn on the coffee machine immediately if the alarm clock rings".*

Fig. 1. Two screenshots from Qualtrics platform showing the two tasks performed by the participants. (A) The top part of the figure shows an example of the composition task for the scenario *"Having a coffee ready in the morning"*. (B) The bottom part of the figure represents the second task to detect the order preference for the same scenario (the light blue boxes contain English translations, and they are not part of the interface).

2.4   Results from Thematic Analysis

A thematic analysis of participants' verbal reports helped us to identify four themes around which to try to understand the relation between lexical choices and participants' mental models of the programming activity.

Theme 1: "As soon as" effectively highlights the instantaneousness of events, especially when associated with the verbal structure "starts to". Participants identified the conjunction *"as soon as"* as the most accurate and precise for describing the timeliness of events. This conjunction helped participants mentally represent a specific instant, as some participants explained:

Participant 3: "'As soon as' makes me think of it as immediate because it is a gesture, an immediate activity".

Participant 9 [referring to scenario n. 6]: "The word 'as soon as' makes me think of an instant [...] the instant when the sun comes out".

Participant 10 [referring to scenario n. 4]: "'As soon as' [...] even though maybe the alarm clock rings for a few seconds, I interpret it as the first second it rings".

Participant 12: "As soon as this thing happens, so at that precise moment".

The conjunction "*as soon as*" seemed to provide confidence to some participants that the action would be carried out effectively. As explicated by participant 8:

Participant 8 [referring to scenario n. 7]: "'As soon as' gives me more confidence in having recorded everything that Carlo has to say."

Often this conjunction was associated with the verbal structure "*starts to*" (event-specific) to reinforce the instantaneousness but also the timeliness of the occurrence. For example, some participant motivated their choices by explaining:

Participant 5 [referring to scenario n. 18]: "because it is 'as soon as one starts to run', immediately activates the step counter [...] to strengthen the sentence".

Participant 8 [referring to scenario n. 6]: "I would choose 'as soon as the sun starts to shine' [...] I need to do the action as soon as the first ray of sunshine enters the room".

For participant 11, the verbal structure "*starts to*" (event-specific) was implicitly associated with the conjunction "*as soon as*" influencing his choices:

Participant 11 [referring to scenario n. 10] "Again, implicitly I add 'the Professor starts to teach' because there is the 'as soon as'".

Nevertheless, for the same participants, this association felt redundant and unnecessary if other elements (e.g., the semantics of the verb) convey the same temporal information:

Participant 11 [referring to scenario n. 4]: "Always 'as soon as' because it tells me the beginning of the action [...] here I would even put without the 'it starts to' but just 'as soon as the alarm rings' because it gives me the idea of a shorter duration this thing [...] the alarm clock lasts up to 10 seconds. If I say, 'as soon as' is enough for me to tell 'as soon as it starts to ring'".

In general, the verbal structure "*starts to*" (event-specific) helped to represent precisely the instant when the action had to be performed. Almost all participants emphasized this aspect several times. While choosing primitives in the composition task, some participants reflected:

Participant 2 [referring to scenario n. 8]: "in my opinion, rather than 'as soon as Carlo speaks', 'as soon as Carlo starts to speak', it is already more precise".

Participant 10 [referring to scenario n. 8]: "Because it is the instant when Carlo starts to speak [...]. So for me, it's instantaneous".

Some participants related the verbal form with the need to promptly perform the action, therefore assuming an impact on the lexical choice in the trigger with the criteria of execution of the action in the TA rule:

Participant 4 [referring to scenario n. 12]: "'One starts to work'. This is the sentence construction when you want the action immediately".

Participant 8 [referring to scenario n. 4]: "'It starts to ring' gives me the idea of something you have to do instantaneously".

Participant 9 [referring to scenario n. 10]: "In this case, because it's an action I have to do immediately, promptly, as soon as the Professor starts to teach, I have to put the silent mode. Yes, it seems that adding the verb to start gives me even more urgency."

Theme 2: "While" effectively highlights the protractedness of events (especially when associated with the progressive form) and "as long as" seems to be more related to the end of the action. The conjunction that best regarded to best express the idea of continuity and duration seems to be the *"while"*:

Participant 4: "When I read 'while' for me it is always something that lasts over time".

Participant 9 [referring to scenario n. 23]: "It has to last the whole time I sleep. So 'while' seems the most appropriate to me".

Participant 11: "I would use 'while' to be even more specifically protracted".

Similar to what emerged for *"as soon as"*, *"while"* was often associated with the progressive form because it reinforced the conception of protractedness. For example, some comments from participants 3, 4, and 5:

Participant 3 [referring to scenario n. 13]: "In this case, 'keep the door close' is more continuous to me, so 'while' is doing an action".

Participant 4 [referring to scenario n. 1]: "maybe 'it is raining' [works better]. It gives more the idea of continuing to do the action".

Participant 5 [referring to scenario n. 7]: "Carlo is speaking. [...] I could also select 'while Carlo is speaking' but 'while' and 'is speaking' give the same sense to the sentence [...] to reinforce the idea of temporality".

Participant 12, on the other hand, preferred not to choose the progressive form and rather used the present tense (the generic form) because, in this participant's view, other elements of the sentence already included the concept of duration:

Participant 12 [referring to scenario n. 11]: "'while one works' and not 'is working' because it seems a repetition to me because 'while' already gives me the idea of something protracted.".

In general, many participants (2, 3, 4, 5, 8, 9, 11, 12) identified the progressive form as reinforcing the representation of a protracted occurrence. For example,

Participant 11 [referring to scenario n. 5]: "Here, the sun shines for a duration of time, I would say 'it is shining' because it's a protracted action".

As participant 3 pointed out, this was the verbal structure to guarantee the action would be performed even after it began:

Participant 3 [referring to scenario n. 19]: "More than 'it starts to move', which means that after you start you can turn off the lights, 'It is moving' gives the obligation to hold them while you are moving".

The conjunction "*as long as*" facilitated participants to represent prolonged occurrence but unlike "*while*", it seems also to suggest or emphasize the end of the action. For example,

Participant 5 [referring to scenario n. 5]: "'as long as the sun shines'. Because 'while' is during, 'as long as' gives it an end".

Participant 4 [referring to scenario n. 13]: "'as long as' is convenient here. [...] 'as long as' gives the idea that until you finish studying, you have to keep the door closed".

Participant 7: "instead of something that is happening, 'as long as' gives me the idea that is going on in time together with the idea of the end".

Presumably related to the semantics of the conjunction, participant 3 associated "*as long as*" with the presence of other rules:

Participant 3 [referring to scenario n. 1]: "it could be: 'as long as it rains'. I basically assume that at one point one opened it [the umbrella] when it started raining, and this [the rule he is composing] is after that moment. Before, there was 'open the umbrella as soon as it starts to rain' and now 'keep the umbrella open as long as it rains'".

Moreover, "*as long as*" led participants to imagine the situation in which the rule might not be triggered. Some examples:

Participant 8 [referring to scenario n. 15]: "as soon as it finishes barking, I'll turn off the noise cancellation mode".

Participant 10 [referring to scenario n.13]: "'as long as', so that then I can also open the door if I'm not studying anymore".

Participant 12 [referring to scenario n. 1]: "'as long as it is raining', if it's not raining, you don't get wet so you can close the umbrella".

Theme 3: "If" and "when" are ambiguous and they do not consistently support the distinction among events with different temporal aspects; similarly, the present tense does not support the definition of temporal aspects and therefore may generate ambiguity. Both "*if*" and "*when*" was used to define indistinctly instantaneousness and continuity of occurrences depending on the context and other temporal elements of the rule including the semantics of the verb associated with the trigger and the duration of the action. The ambiguity of the conjunction "*when*" is apparent because participants used it to express both timeliness and duration, often unaware. For example, initially, participant 2 stated:

Participant 2 [referring to scenario n. 8]: "'when' means as soon as he starts talking".

Then, at one point, he contradicted himself by saying:

Participant 2 [referring to scenario n. 1]: "'when it rains' means something that is protracted in time because it is not as soon as it starts raining".

Other participants explicitly expressed their difficulties with the use of "*when*":

Participant 9: "I feel like I contradict myself".

Participant 10 [referring to scenario n. 8]: "When Carlo speaks, immediately turns down the volume of the music, for me this is tricky".

Participants 11 and 4 were able to recognize that "*when*" does not support individuals in defining events temporally:

Participant 11 [referring to scenario n. 4]: "when the alarm clock rings, however even 'when' is quite unclear".

Participant 4 [referring to scenario n. 4]: "'when the alarm clock rings'. It doesn't sound either like something that happens immediately or an ongoing thing. It's in the middle".

Similar comments were made for the conjunction "*if*". Participant 9, who had associated "*if*" with "*as soon as*" because of its connotation of immediacy, then expressed:

Participant 9 [referring to scenario n. 24]: "Instead, in this case, it's different. [...] because 'if' with the verb sleep sounds like something long. So the 'if' changes according to the verb that comes after."

Other participants expressed uncertainty and difficulty related to the temporal representation of "*if*".

Participant 3 [commented at different moments]: "the ones with the 'if' are the most tricky [...] the if already puts you in an uncertain, doubtful form [...]. In all of them [scenarios] 'if' might also work, however, without giving certainty".

Participant 4 [commented at different moments]: "the 'if' indicates a condition of doubt and uncertainty [...] the 'if' associates well with all scenarios [...] I never used 'if'. The 'if' is too doubtful".

Apparently, the conjunction "*if*" did not help the mental representation of the rule because it was perceived as very general. For example, participant 10 said:

Participant 10 [referring to scenario n. 5]: "This one is difficult. [...] 'If the sun shines' it could be even for a few hours".

Sometimes, however, the flexibility and temporal imprecision of "*if*" is preferred in situations of uncertainty because it limits the temporal boundaries of the rule. For example,

Participant 5 [referring to scenario n. 20]: "it could be 'if the car moves'. Because for listening to a podcast in the car, the 'if' is the option that temporally limits you the least, [...] 'if it moves', when you want you can listen to it [the podcast]".

The present tense for the event verb did not help in assessing the temporal definition of the occurrence, as expressed by participant 8:

Participant 8: "'one runs' [stressing on the present indicative tense] is the concept that meets the 'beginning', the 'while' and the 'end'".

Some participants clarified how the present tense verb defines general situations. For example, participants 7 and 8 explained:

Participant 7 [referring to scenario n. 15]: "'When it barks' not 'when it is barking' because it could bark at any time".

Participant 8 [referring to scenario n. 4]: "'it starts to ring' gives me the idea of something you have to do instantaneously, and 'it's ringing' gives me the idea of a period [...] 'it rings' instead is a broader concept that gives me more space.

Theme 4: The temporal order with the trigger at the beginning of the rule facilitates comprehension yet the most important element to communicate should be at the beginning of the sentence and it is mainly the action. Regarding the order of the trigger and the action part, some participants expressed a preference for the order which corresponds to the actual temporal order, with the trigger at the beginning of the rule (regardless of whether it described a state or an event):

Participant 5 [referring to scenario n. 4]: "I would always select this way [trigger-first], with the right temporal order. That first, it happens that the alarm rings, then I turn on the coffee machine".

Participant 10 [referring to scenario n. 9]: "Again the sentence beginning with 'as long as' [...] it makes me understand that I have to keep it on for the whole duration".

Participant 9 [referring to scenario n. 2]: "Because from the temporal point of view, first, it rains, and then I close the window".

Participant 11 and 10 explained their choices considering the logical consequentiality of condition and action:

Participant 11: "Because it gives me the indication first of the condition and then the action I have to do in this condition. I don't care to know the action if I don't know the condition under which this action should occur".

Participant 10 [referring to scenario n. 2]: "because it gives me more of an idea of why I have to close the window. So it makes you understand immediately".

Nevertheless, from the words of the participants emerged that the elements of the sentence should be ordered by importance. Some participants argued that the trigger was the crucial part since its absence implies that the action won't be performed, as participant 4 expressed:

Participant 4 [referring to scenario n. 2]: "because it gives you the indication, 'as soon as it starts to rain', and then close the window. It seems more important to me to say the first part."

But more participants claimed that the action should be placed at the beginning as it was the main component. Some extracts from verbal reports, as an example:

Participant 7: "The important thing is the action".

Participant 8: "The main diktat [i.e., order or imposition] is 'close the window'. And then there is the part of explaining why. But in the meantime, it [the action] directs you to do something".

Participant 10 [referring to scenario n. 11]: "This one [the action-first order] because it gives us a better understanding of what you need to do, which is to 'keep the temperature at 18 degrees. Then, it is less important to know when, while you are working or studying".

Participant 12 [referring to scenario n. 20]: "But do I care more about the car moving or listening to the radio? Listening to the radio is the thing that interests me. [...] Because normally when people listen to sentences, they lose interest at the end".

In particular, the urgency to start the rule with the action was made explicit for scenarios related to situations of potential danger or harm to safety (fire [scenario n. 21 and 22], road traffic [scenario n. 19], home security [scenario n. 23]). In these cases, almost all participants preferred to place the action at the beginning of the rule rather than the trigger. In this case, the action (placed precisely at the beginning of the sentence) is perceived as the figure, while the trigger remains in the background, as reported by:

Participant 3 [referring to scenario n. 19]: "In this case, however, I would put 'keep the headlights on' first because it seems more important to me [...] the action of keeping the headlights on that [...] is always a safety issue".

Participant 9 [referring to scenario n. 21]: "I would imagine that the alarm siren should sound during the entire period of smoke detection. In that case, I would change my mind [in the other scenarios she preferred the trigger-first order] because the first part of keeping the fire alarm on seems more important to me".

3 Discussion

From our results, it emerges, as already observed by Huang and Cakmak [6], that the use of different temporal conjunctions for events (e.g., *"when"*, *"if"*) and states (e.g., *"while"*, *"as long as"*) facilitated non-programmers in effectively distinguishing occurrences with different temporal features.

The conjunction *"if"* although commonly used to define the event in trigger-action rules (e.g., in IFTTT platform [8]), creates ambiguity, as other studies already highlighted [21, 22, 40]. Indeed, also from our results emerges that individuals perceived *"if"* as ambiguous and they often associated it indistinctly with both events and states.

Recent studies [21, 22, 34] have suggested the use of *"when"* and *"while"* to define events and states, respectively. Our results support the idea that *"while"* is easily associated with prolonged occurrences and this association was stronger when the occurrence was described with the progressive form.

Contrastingly, it appears that *"when"* is not the conjunction that best fits the representation of instantaneous events. Indeed, our results seem to suggest that *"when"* is perceived as imprecise and does not support the temporal definition of events, similarly as *"if"*. The conjunction *"as soon as"* seems to be more appropriate to define punctual events as it spontaneously conveys the idea of an instantaneous occurrence, even more, if associated with the verbal structure *"starts to"*.

Even the conjunction *"as long as"* seems to have a precise and unambiguous representation that leads individuals to mentally represent the end of the event. While in some situations, this focus on the end of an action might be beneficial, it is worth noting that it may also raise unexpected errors.

Similar to the results of other studies [28], our findings support the idea that individuals were likely to prefer the order with the trigger at the beginning of the rule supporting the iconicity assumption, i.e., that the order of elements in a sentence corresponds to the actual order of events and that the conjunction placed at the beginning of the sentence facilitates the understanding of the rule [33].In addition, we found that individuals preferred, in some specific circumstances dealing with personal safety, to reverse the order of the elements when the triggered action is considered the most important part.

In common automation platforms, such as Zapier and IFTTT [8], the order of the trigger and action elements in rule composition and presentation is fixed by displaying first the trigger and then the action, which is the order that facilitated participants' mental representations in our study. But our results also show that more flexible systems on the order of actions and triggers might help naive users to deal with specific danger-related situations.

The lesson learned from our study might be that, in order to improve TAP, it is important to offer users lexically accurate interfaces by favoring *"as soon as"* and *"while"/"as long as"* conjunctions, possibly aligned with redundant verbal forms and a lexical order that focuses the attention on the most relevant aspects of the rule. From an engineering point of view, still, it is also important to align the ontology (the representation of the domain) of the system to fully and properly represent the distinction between events and states. That is, the internal representation of the system should explicitly represent instantaneous events as different from protracted ones even when, as it might be often the case, the difference between the two is merely a matter of representation: for example, because the same sensors can recognize the state (for example, "*it rains*") and the event ("*it starts to rain*") is implicitly derived.

4 Conclusion

In this paper, we presented an explorative qualitative study that investigates the effects of some language choices in expressing the trigger part of a trigger-action rule on the users' mental models.

Although the results need to be validated in a larger study, they seem to suggest that lexical choices play an important role in determining the mental model of naive users engaged in EUD tasks and some combinations of choices foster a proper model while others prompt ambiguity and potential errors. A lesson learned for EUD system engineering would be that users can be facilitated in understanding the semantics of a rule-based system by carefully crafting the ontological definition of the domain (that is, providing an internal representation of instantaneous events paired with the corresponding states, or protracted events, as separate entities) and then properly mapping the domain representation to lexical choices that reduce ambiguity for the naive user.

This study has some limitations, in particular, the limited number of participants and the focus on a specific language (although the linguistic phenomena investigated are not unique characteristics of Italian). Furthermore, other linguistic aspects might play related roles (verb aspect, among others) and different and more variegated scenarios should be investigated. Still, we believe that this study may contribute to an ongoing discussion about user-centered design of EUD systems.

Acknowledgments. This work has been supported by the Italian Ministry of Education, University and Research (MIUR) under grant PRIN 2017 "EMPATHY: EMpowering People in deAling with internet of THings ecosYstems" (Progetti di Rilevante Interesse Nazionale – Bando 2017, Grant 2017MX9T7H). We thank Elia Baccaro for his work in recruiting and testing participants of the study as part of his internship.

References

1. Barricelli, B.R., Cassano, F., Fogli, D., Piccinno, A.: End-user development, end-user programming and end-user software engineering: a systematic mapping study. J. Syst. Softw. **149**, 101–137 (2019). https://doi.org/10.1016/j.jss.2018.11.041
2. Ko, A.J., Myers, B.A., Aung, H.H: Six learning barriers in end-user programming systems. In 2004 IEEE Symposium on Visual Languages - Human Centric Computing, Rome, Italy, 2004, pp. 199–206 (2004). https://doi.org/10.1109/VLHCC.2004.47
3. Paternò, F., Santoro, C.: End-user development for personalizing applications, things, and robots. Int. J. Hum.-Comput. Stud. **131**, 120–130 (2019). https://doi.org/10.1016/j.ijhcs.2019.06.002

4. Bellucci, A., Vianello, A., Florack, Y., Micallef, L., Jacucci, G.: Augmenting objects at home through programmable sensor tokens: a design journey. Int. J. Hum.-Comput. Stud. **122**, 211–231 (2019). https://doi.org/10.1016/j.ijhcs.2018.09.002

5. Brackenbury, W., et al: How users interpret bugs in trigger-action programming. In: Proceedings of the 2019 CHI Conference on Human Factors in Computing Systems, Glasgow Scotland Uk, May 2019, pp. 1–12 (2019). https://doi.org/10.1145/3290605.3300782

6. Huang, J., Cakmak, M: Supporting mental model accuracy in trigger-action programming. In: Proceedings of the 2015 ACM International Joint Conference on Pervasive and Ubiquitous Computing - UbiComp 2015, Osaka, Japan, 2015, pp. 215–225 (2015). https://doi.org/10.1145/2750858.2805830

7. Ur, B., McManus, E., Pak Yong Ho, M., Littman, M.L: Practical trigger-action programming in the smart home. In: Proceedings of the SIGCHI Conference on Human Factors in Computing Systems, Toronto Ontario Canada, 2014, pp. 803–812 (2014). https://doi.org/10.1145/2556288.2557420

8. Rahmati, A., Fernandes, E., Jung, J., Prakash, A.: IFTTT vs. Zapier: A Comparative Study of Trigger-Action Programming Frameworks. arXiv (2017). http://arxiv.org/abs/1709.02788

9. Yarosh, S., Zave, P.: Locked or not?: mental models of IoT feature interaction. In: Proceedings of the 2017 CHI Conference on Human Factors in Computing Systems, Denver Colorado USA, May 2017, pp. 2993–2997 (2017). https://doi.org/10.1145/3025453.3025617

10. Boren, T., Ramey, J.: Thinking aloud: reconciling theory and practice. IEEE Trans. Prof. Commun. **43**(3), 261–278 (2000). https://doi.org/10.1109/47.867942

11. Braun, V., Clarke, V.: Using thematic analysis in psychology. Qual. Res. Psychol. **3**(2), 77–101 (2006). https://doi.org/10.1191/1478088706qp063oa

12. Dey, A.K., Sohn, T., Streng, S., Kodama, J.: iCAP: interactive prototyping of context-aware applications. In: Fishkin, K.P., Schiele, B., Nixon, P., Quigley, A. (eds.) Pervasive 2006. LNCS, vol. 3968, pp. 254–271. Springer, Heidelberg (2006). https://doi.org/10.1007/11748625_16

13. Ur, B. et al.: Trigger-action programming in the wild: an analysis of 200,000 IFTTT recipes. In: Proceedings of the 2016 CHI Conference on Human Factors in Computing Systems, San Jose California USA, May 2016, pp. 3227–3231 (2016). https://doi.org/10.1145/2858036.2858556

14. Ardito, C., Buono, P., Desolda, G., Matera, M.: From smart objects to smart experiences: an end-user development approach. Int. J. Hum.-Comput. Stud. **114**, 51–68 (2018). https://doi.org/10.1016/j.ijhcs.2017.12.002

15. Ghiani, G., Manca, M., Paternò, F., Santoro, C.: Personalization of context-dependent applications through trigger-action rules. ACM Trans. Comput.-Hum. Interact. **24**(2), 1–33 (2017). https://doi.org/10.1145/3057861

16. Norman, D.A: Some observations on mental models. In: Mental Models, Psychology Press, pp. 15–22 (2014)

17. Norman, D.: The Design of Everyday Things: Revised and expanded. Basic books, New York City (2013)

18. Cañas, J.J., Antolí, A., Quesada, J.F.: The role of working memory on measuring mental models of physical systems. Psicológica **22**, 25–42 (2001)

19. Johnson-Laird, P.N.: Mental models, deductive reasoning, and the brain. Cognit. Neurosci. **65**, 999–1008 (1995)

20. Johnson-Laird, P.N.: Mental models and human reasoning. Proc. Natl. Acad. Sci. **107**(43), 18243–18250 (2010). https://doi.org/10.1073/pnas.1012933107

21. Gallitto, G., Treccani, B., Zancanaro, M.: If when is better than if (and while might help): on the importance of influencing mental models in EUD (a pilot study). In: Proceedings CEUR Workshop, vol. 2702, pp. 7–11 (2020)

22. Zancanaro, M., Gallitto, G., Yem, D., Treccani, B. Improving mental models in IoT end-user development. Hum.-Centric Comput. Inf. Sci. **12** (2022). https://doi.org/10.22967/HCIS. 2022.12.048

23. Kulesza, T., Stumpf, S., Burnett, M., Kwan, I.: Tell me more?: the effects of mental model soundness on personalizing an intelligent agent. In: Proceedings of the SIGCHI Conference on Human Factors in Computing Systems, Austin Texas USA, May 2012, pp. 1–10 (2012). https://doi.org/10.1145/2207676.2207678

24. Ngo, T., Kunkel, J., Ziegler, J.: Exploring mental models for transparent and controllable recommender systems: a qualitative study. In: Proceedings of the 28th ACM Conference on User Modeling, Adaptation and Personalization, Genoa Italy, 2020, pp. 183–191 (2020). https://doi.org/10.1145/3340631.3394841

25. Clark, M., Dutta, P., Newman, M.W.: Towards a natural language programming interface for smart homes. In: Proceedings of the 2016 ACM International Joint Conference on Pervasive and Ubiquitous Computing: Adjunct, Heidelberg Germany, 2016, pp. 49–52 (2016). https://doi.org/10.1145/2968219.2971443

26. Galotti, K.M., Ganong, W.F.: What non-programmers know about programming: natural language procedure specification. Int. J. Man-Mach. Stud. **22**(1), 1 (1985). https://doi.org/10. 1016/S0020-7373(85)80073-0

27. Good, J., Howland, K.: Programming language, natural language? Supporting the diverse computational activities of novice programmers. J. Vis. Lang. Comput. **39**, 78–92 (2017). https://doi.org/10.1016/j.jvlc.2016.10.008

28. Pane, J.F., Ratanamahatana, C.A., Myers, B.A.: Studying the language and structure in non-programmers' solutions to programming problems. Int. J. Hum.-Comput. Stud. **54**(2), 237–264 (2001). https://doi.org/10.1006/ijhc.2000.0410

29. Ur, B., McManus, E., Pak Yong Ho, M., Littman, M. L.: Practical trigger-action programming in the smart home. In: Proceedings of the SIGCHI Conference on Human Factors in Computing Systems, Toronto Ontario Canada, 2014, pp. 803–812 (2014). https://doi.org/10. 1145/2556288.2557420

30. Debnath, N.C., Banerjee, S., Van, G.U., Quang, P.T., Thanh, D.N.: An ontology based approach towards end user development of IoT. In: EPIC Sre. Computing, 2022, vol. 82, pp. 1–10 (2022)

31. Casati, F., Castano, S., Fugini, M., Mirbel, I., Pernici, B.: Using patterns to design rules in workflows. IEEE Trans. Softw. Eng. **26**(8), 760 (2000)

32. Pianesi, F., Varzi, A.C.: Events and Event Talk. Speak. Events, pp. 3–47 (2000)

33. de Vega, M., Rinck, M., Díaz, J.M., León, I.: Figure and ground in temporal sentences: the role of the adverbs when and while. Discourse Process. **43**(1), 1–23 (2007)

34. Andrao, M., Desolda, G., Greco, F., Manfredi, R., Treccani, B., Zancanaro, M: end-user programming and math teachers: an initial study. In: Proceedings of the 2022 International Conference on Advanced Visual Interfaces, pp. 1–3 (2022)

35. Givón, T. The grammar of referential coherence as mental processing instructions, pp. 5–56 (1992)

36. Zwaan, R.A.: Time in language, situation models, and mental simulations. Lang. Learn. **58**, 13–26 (2008)

37. Blackwell, A.F.: First steps in programming: a rationale for attention investment models. In: Proceedings IEEE 2002 Symposia on Human Centric Computing Languages and Environments, Arlington, VA, USA, 2002, pp. 2–10 (2002). https://doi.org/10.1109/HCC.2002.104 6334

38. Hoc, J.M., Nguyen-Xuan, A.: Language semantics, mental models and analogy. In: Psychology of Programming, pp. 139–156 .Elsevier (1990)

39. Bonar, J., Soloway, E.: Preprogramming knowledge: a major source of misconceptions in novice programmers. Hum.-Comput. Interact. **1**(2), 133–161 (1985)
40. Desolda, G., Greco, F., Guarnieri, F., Mariz, N., Zancanaro, M.: SENSATION: an authoring tool to support event–state paradigm in end-user development. In: Ardito, C., et al. (eds.) INTERACT 2021. LNCS, vol. 12933, pp. 373–382. Springer, Cham (2021). https://doi.org/10.1007/978-3-030-85616-8_22

Understanding Concepts, Methods and Tools for End-User Control of Automations in Ecosystems of Smart Objects and Services

Margherita Andrao[1] , Fabrizio Balducci[2] , Bernardo Breve[4] , Federica Cena[3] , Giuseppe Desolda[2] , Vincenzo Deufemia[4] , Cristina Gena[3] , Maristella Matera[5] , Andrea Mattioli[6] , Fabio Paternò[6(✉)] , Carmen Santoro[6] , Barbara Treccani[1] , Fabiana Vernero[3] , and Massimo Zancanaro[1]

[1] University of Trento, Trento, Italy
{margherita.andrao,barbara.treccani,massimo.zancanaro}@unitn.it
[2] University of Bari, Bari, Italy
{fabrizio.balducci,giuseppe.desolda}@uniba.it
[3] University of Torino, Torino, Italy
{cena,cristina.gena,fabiana.vernero}@di.unito.it
[4] University of Salerno, Salerno, Italy
{bbreve,deufemia}@unisa.it
[5] Politecnico Di Milano, Milano, Italy
maristella.matera@polimi.it
[6] CNR-ISTI, HIIS Laboratory, Pisa, Italy
{andrea.mattioli,fabio.paterno,carmen.santoro}@isti.cnr.it

Abstract. The continuously increasing number of connected objects and sensors is opening up the possibility of introducing automations in many domains to better support people in their activities. However, such automations to be effective should be under the user control. Unfortunately, people often report difficulties in understanding the surrounding automations and how to modify them. The goal of this paper is to provide a multi-perspective view of what has been done in terms of design, tools, and evaluation in the area of end-user control of automations in ecosystems of smart objects and services. For each aspect we introduce the main challenge, the current possible approaches to address it, and the issues that still need further investigation.

Keywords: End-User Development · Internet of Things · User Experience

1 Introduction

Over the last few years, we have witnessed a wide diffusion of the so-called smart objects, which have become relatively common in our daily environments. These objects are characterised by the presence of integrated sensors and actuators, and the capability of exchanging data over the Internet. Through the pervasiveness of these technologies, the vision of an Internet of Things (IoT) has become a reality, where physical objects

L. D. Spano et al. (Eds.): IS-EUD 2023, LNCS 13917, pp. 104–124, 2023.
https://doi.org/10.1007/978-3-031-34433-6_7

are capable of communicating among themselves and with people and can sense and react to changes in the environment. According to Statista[1], this trend will continue to grow in the next few years. In this evolving landscape, many challenges concerning the interaction of people with these digital ecosystems are emerging. A crucial aspect is how to support people to understand and use these technologies to satisfy their information and automation needs. Indeed, there is considerable academic and commercial interest in providing users with platforms to personalise their environments by IoT without requiring them to write code.

Trigger-Action Programming (TAP) is an End-User Development (EUD) approach aimed at allowing people who may not be expert programmers to specify automations based on the "rule metaphor". In a TAP rule, the trigger part describes the situation (as recognized by sensors or services) that, when occurring, causes the action part (for instance, a change in the state of a device or the activation of a service) to be actuated. There is growing evidence that TAP basics can easily be grasped by end users. Yet, this approach presents nuances that become apparent - and critical - in complex and realistic situations. For instance, configuring smart environments with multiple active automations [22] or dealing with temporal sequences are complex tasks to master by rules. Even the formulation of a single rule can be challenging, because of the interactions among its different parts. Other problematic aspects can emerge for security issues from automations that do not execute as the user expects. There is therefore the need to better focus on the end-user creation and management of automations in everyday environments. This is a required step to fully leverage the potential and social benefits of the interaction of people with smart environments [63].

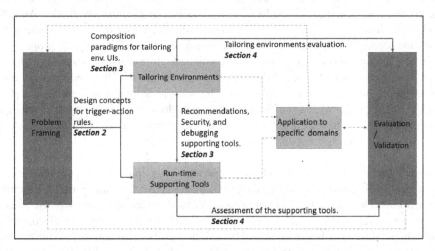

Fig. 1. The structure of the EMPATHY Project.

In this paper, we report the reflections and the experiences on the research activities pursued as part of the EMPATHY project involving six academic groups in developing

---

[1] https://www.statista.com/statistics/1183457/iot-connected-devices-worldwide/, last accessed 2023/04/12.

EUD solutions for IoT in several domains. Figure 1 shows the structure of the EMPATHY project. There are some parts not considered in this paper indicated with dashed lines. The discussion is structured along three axes: what the main aspects of automation rules to consider when designing trigger-action rule languages (Sect. 2), which type of EUD tools for TAP can be relevant (Sect. 3), and what metrics and evaluation strategies can be considered to assess the outcome of the EUD work (Sect. 4). The overall goal is to foster a discussion about the state in the area of end-user control of automation in ecosystems of smart objects and services, along with its current challenges, and possible solutions. This discussion can be useful for improving overall understanding of the state of art and identifying areas that require further research efforts.

2 Design of Trigger-Action Languages

2.1 How to Represent Rule Structures

TAP has demonstrated to be relevant in emerging IoT ecosystems as a paradigm that while it does not seem to require specific programming or algorithmic abilities, it allows for the definition of varying behaviours that users can find useful [70]. Triggers can be formulated in terms of events and conditions, and their expression is a key aspect to consider to avoid users creating automations resulting in unexpected behaviours [41]. Several studies investigated how to extend the TAP syntax using more flexible rule for-mulations. For instance, Desolda and colleagues [30] describe a model with operators for allowing the specification of multiple events and actions, and temporal and spa-tial constraints on rule elements such as "when" and "where". The model is based on the cause–effect schema, enriched with questions inspired by the 5W model. An iOS application that allows inhabitants to customise the behaviour of a smart home with rules and scenes is introduced by Fogli and colleagues [35]. The goal is to propose an approach capable of modelling automation with enough expressive power through the event-condition-action syntax while unwitting this complexity, by guiding users dur-ing the definition of the various rule parts. The work of Salovaara and colleagues [63] aims at discovering "what smart-home automation do technically competent families actually ideate, implement, use, and – most importantly – need?". To this goal, the study involved various steps (creativity workshops, home automation toolkit installa-tion, and actual use of the environment). Participants could define automations using an extended TAP syntax supporting advanced operators (e.g. time counters, accumulators). Corno and colleagues [21] analysed the levels of abstraction that can be used to describe automations. They argue that current approaches for connecting IoT devices use a one-to-one, low-level mapping, sometimes dependent on the brand of objects involved, while users should instead be better supported by a higher level of abstraction. For this reason, they introduce the EUPont ontology for EUD in the IoT context, which was integrated into a EUD platform and evaluated with a user study, demonstrating the feasibility and understandability of the approach.

Another recent solution [4] based on the use of semantic properties to simplify the creation of ECA rules has been proposed through a design approach that allows domain experts, not necessarily IT experts, to visually specify, for each IoT device, the semantic properties closer to their expertise. An extension of this work reports the results of an analysis of trade-offs in frameworks for the design of smart environments [3]. The main contribution was a framework consisting of a set of trade-offs identified between various dimensions that characterise the quality of software environments for ECA rule design (Creativity, Workload, UX, Engagement, Utility, Completeness and Ease of Use). A recent extension of this research has also explored the use of a system that, through a tangible user interface integrated with pattern recognition and computer vision techniques, assists Cultural Heritage experts in creating smart interactive experiences by properly tailoring the behaviour of the smart objects involved [6].

2.2 Distinguishing Between Events and Conditions

The structure of the temporal aspect of the trigger part of an automated procedure is critical for allowing more evolved behaviours, and it is one of the main sources of errors in TAP [8]. To limit possible ambiguities in the formulation and interpretation of TAP rules, it is necessary to clearly support the correct definition of temporal specifications. Brackenbury and colleagues classified the temporal aspects of the triggers, identifying three different compound structures (event-event, event-condition, condition-condition). EUD platforms can implement all these different combinations, however, it is not immediate how to apply them in a way that is clear for users. For instance, the event-event combination makes sense only when the "OR" operator is used (because an AND would imply that the events should occur at the same time, which is unlikely), or when a time window for the second event to occur is specified. The event-condition structure, although non-ambiguous, can be misunderstood by users.

Huang and Cakmak [44] highlighted that it is possible to distinguish at least two types of triggers based on temporal features: instantaneous occurrences (events) and occurrences protracted over time (conditions on states). They noted that users often confused events and conditions on states and remarked that the lack of distinction between different trigger types may create ambiguities (e.g., the interpretation of when exactly triggers will occur) and undesirable outcomes. The considerations raised by Huang and Cakmak have been taken into account in [41], where a rule editor distinguishing between events and condition triggers is described. Events are associated with the 'becomes' keyword (linked to when an attribute changes its value), while conditions are related to the 'is' keyword. An interactive natural language description of the automation is used to further bring attention to this distinction.

Language use implicitly supports the distinction between these different types of occurrences [13, 59]. De Vega and colleagues [29] observed that, when temporal sentences involve two simultaneous occurrences (e.g., conditions on states and events), one is generally interpreted as the main one, while the other one is considered as the ground (i.e., the context). They also showed that: (i) participants tended to perceive the longer occurrence as the ground; (ii) they found this occurrence more acceptable when introduced by "while" vs. "when". In some recent studies, temporal conjunctions (i.e., "while" before conditions on states and "when" before events) have been used to distinguish more intuitively conditions on states and events in trigger-action rules. Gallitto et al. [36] and Zancanaro et al. [76] observed an improvement in the accuracy of participants' mental models, and in understanding rule behaviour when different conjunctions ("when" and "while") introduced triggers with different temporal features (events and conditions on states) instead of using more general conjunction ("if"). Indeed, using "when" and "while" to introduce the trigger part of the rule might facilitate users in distinguishing events and conditions on states and understanding their semantics. Desolda et al. [31] designed and evaluated an authoring tool for EUD, which adopted "while" and "when" to explicitly support the distinction of events and conditions on states in trigger-action rules creation. Their results revealed that the when-while structure is effective and manageable by naive users without complicating the tasks. Natural language description and the when-while structure were also employed to create EUD systems for therapists [2] and math teachers [1]. According to all these studies, employing the when-while rule structure allows a clear representation of different types of triggers.

Future studies should further investigate other linguistic cues (temporal conjunctions, syntactic order, verbal structure) for designing EUD interfaces to support and guide non-expert users in taking effective mental models.

3 Tools for EUD

3.1 Composition Paradigms

In general, composition paradigms indicate how tools represent the relevant concepts and interact with users, and how they support the development process. Several composition approaches are possible for creating and modifying rules in TAP: form-based approaches (based on Wizard-like support), block-based, dataflow, conversational, and augmented-reality are the most investigated so far. The form-based approach has been used in commercial platforms such as IFTTT, Zapier, Alexa app but also in various research-based approaches [e.g. 30, 41]. The composition of automations using this approach exploits visual structures that conceptually group functionalities and the filling of fields. Such approaches have the advantage to guide the user through a well-defined procedure, and, as such, they are typically regarded as easy to use. However, their rigidity can be perceived as too limited in some cases, and therefore not suitable for dealing with more complex scenarios and task automation [7].

Another approach is block-based programming, which has long been considered in EUD for various domains. A well-known example is Scratch [60], a programming environment primarily targeting children. Using a block-based approach, the definition of a program occurs by connecting blocks of various sizes and shapes, dragging and dropping them in a workspace area. Being less restrictive than form-filling languages, applications based on block programming can leave more space for users' creativity.

An example in the TAP domain proposed a block-based rule editor [54] where the event-condition distinction is highlighted using a box with a corresponding icon and description. Inspired by the block-based paradigm, and aimed to amplify educational contexts, Gennari et al. [40] introduced IoTgo, a "phygital" toolkit offering smart cards representing sensors and actuators, and hardware and software tools (an ad-hoc scanner and web app), for reading cards and automatically generating scripts running on the most common micro-controllers. The aim of this toolkit is to empower younger generations to explore, empathise with the design context and ideate novel smart things, to deepen IoT programming and communication with certain design patterns.

One further category of visual language commonly adopted in EUD is data-flow. Differently from the previous approaches, the process-oriented nature of data-flow languages makes them more suitable to represent complex use cases [11]. Process-oriented notations can provide more expressiveness, which however is often coupled with complex user interfaces.

Although visual-based paradigms are common interaction modalities and have been extensively studied in the literature, they present some weak points that can make the tools not engaging and immediate to understand. For instance, selecting which items to use in a rule can be time-consuming [41], a source of errors [38], and require users to know some specific technical details.

Recent technological progress provides novel functionalities that can be used to allow for different interactions with devices and services: among others, the conversational paradigm and augmented reality are promising alternatives. An example of a tool that supports the conversational interface is RuleBot [37]. The platform operates by linking the user input to possible triggers and actions, using the defined intents and additional context information. After the first welcome sentence from the chatbot, the user can enter a rule element or an entire rule. The bot provides feedback and asks for further information to complete the automation, if necessary. The system uses natural language techniques to split the user input in parts that are analysed with the support of DialogueFlow for identifying intents and entities. Another approach based on the conversational paradigm is HeyTAP [24], which proposes a set of IF-THEN rules relevant to user's inputs, also considering further, optional higher-level preferences expressed by the user (i.e. energy saving, security). These concepts are modelled using an extension of the EUPont ontology model.

Another technological innovation that can be used to control smart environments is Augmented Reality (AR). The idea of AR is to create an enhanced space where digital components are blended in a natural way in the users' field of view. Visualisations can make perceivable relations between the devices and decrease the cognitive distance between the physical objects and the representation used for rule creation. In the context of tailoring environments, AR can be used to allow for opportunistic and situated rule editing. A solution to support user control of automations using the smartphone as AR device is SAC [5]. It allows end users to frame a relevant sensor or object using the smartphone camera, obtain the rules currently associated with it, edit them or create a new one. It also allows monitoring of the state of sensors or rules involving a whole environment. An approach with a different goal and target users is MagiPlay [67], a serious game aimed at cultivating children's computational thinking through the personalisation of an augmented environment. AR is used to allow young learners to capture object visualisations and then combine 3D bricks into automation rules. In this area an interesting future work is the design of augmented reality solutions able to show recommendations of possible automations. Another important future direction is to explore how applications of transformers [75] and Large Language Models, such as ChatGPT, will impact the EUD for the IoT ecosystem, for instance, assessing whether such applications are capable of accurately generating automation programs that mirror user intents expressed using natural conversation.

3.2 Security

The definition of automations by users without programming experience can pose serious risks both for the privacy of the user and/or the security of the smart environment [17]. In fact, rules can trigger unexpected behaviours that may be unnoticed by non-technical users [72, 77]. The need for mitigating such risks foster studying and classifying the type of inconsistencies that can be produced [68]. Furthermore, efforts have also been spent on the definition of specific solutions that can support end-users in the identification of security and privacy risks at design time [10, 57]. Chen et al. [15] have proposed a threat model that indicates the various levels at which security issues can emerge in environments where TAP platforms are deployed:

- *Network sniffing*: an attacker can monitor traffic in the IoT network to leak device state or sensitive data from the TAP platform.
- *Privilege escalation attack*: an attacker can exploit over-privileged vulnerabilities to access IoT devices they should not have access to.
- *Malicious automation*: an attacker can create a malicious automation to manipulate triggers and actions to leak sensitive data from IoT device settings.
- *Rule logical attack*: an attacker can manipulate TAP rules to harm the user, cause damage, or facilitate a real-world crime.
- *Unintentional rule logical attack*: legitimate users can unintentionally harm themselves or cause damage by creating TAP rules with logical errors.

Given the high popularity TAP has acquired in the last years, researchers have also focused on investigating how much the users are aware of and concerned about the severity of the risks that might arise from the unintentional creation of risky procedures. The study conducted by Saeidi et al. [62] involved an online survey of 386 participants who were presented with 49 popular rules from the IFTTT platform that had potential security and privacy risks. Participants were asked to evaluate their level of concern for each rule on a scale from 1 to 5, and the results showed that participants were not fully aware of the risks. The top 5 rules for which users expressed the most concern involved acquiring, processing, or sharing their location. The study suggests that there is a need to support users in understanding privacy and security risks while creating trigger-action rules. A recent approach [10] has proposed a classification model for identifying security and privacy violation of rules with one trigger and one action, while a further contribution [9] presents an explainable AI solution that offers textual explanations for the potential hazards linked to a risky rule. Further research is required to explore other areas, such as providing users with effective ways to mitigate the risks associated with these rules. Another important aspect analysed in Saeidi [62] is the impact that contextual factors, i.e., the addition of information related to the execution context in which the rules might execute, have on the overall ability of end users to specify the rules. The results demonstrated that, if asked to focus on a specific and detailed context in which a certain rule could be activated, the users may significantly increase their attention to risk factors. Among the contexts which impacted the most, the authors found that security and privacy implications resulted particularly evident, i.e., which entity can activate the rule and who can observe its action. The results of this study suggest investigating mechanisms for providing contextual information of the defined rule. As an example, a TAP might generate contextual factors based on rule information and user's habits.

3.3 Recommendations

Recommender systems (RS) are designed to help users make better choices from large content catalogues [46]. These systems can show users a personalised list of items tailored to their preferences, which can be derived from implicit (such as clicking, purchasing or device usage behaviours) or explicit feedback (a direct rating on an item). Since the creation of an IoT automation is not a "one-shot" operation but consists of multiple selection and configuration steps [26], recommendation support can be used to help users by providing them with relevant objects or services during the various phases. Two main strategies for generating recommendations can be identified in this context. The first is using automations previously created by other users as the building blocks for providing relevant recommendations to the current user. Another viable strategy is to mine some frequent patterns from the user behaviours and derive one or more rules to automate this behaviour. For the former approach, a relevant example is RecRules [23]. The authors put forward a hybrid collaborative and content-based recommender system that considers semantic features to suggest automations based on their functionality (the final purpose for which the person is creating the automation). This solution leverages a reasoner to enrich the automations of semantic information. Through the hierarchical structure of an ontology, a structure of classes and subclasses is applied to items, allowing to uncover functionality and technological relations between them. Then, a collaborative filtering mapping is applied to leverage the community's appreciation or not appreciation of rules. Finally, a learning-to-rank algorithm is trained on the enriched data.

Early examples of the latter approach can be found in PBE (Programming By Example) systems such as EAGER, Dynamic Macro, and APE [27, 53, 61], which continuously observe user's actions to find repetitions over which they can learn a looping program to complete the user's task. Since automation was recommended directly within the user's workflow, users programmed the system without necessarily being aware of it. A more recent example of this strategy is RuleSelector [66], where a mobile interactive tool is used to allow users to select TAP rules from a short summarised list. The engine of Rule-Selector first uses frequent itemset mining to discover contexts that often occur together (such as "watch TV" and "at home"). From these contexts, a list of candidate rules is generated using three selection metrics (confidence, contextual specificity, and interval count). The last step of the algorithm is to summarise the rule list using a total action coverage criteria defined by the authors. Another aspect to consider is whether to generate and show complete rule recommendations, or just rule parts that fit the automation a user is currently editing in a sort of autocomplete fashion. It should be noted that while the step-by-step approach is easy to integrate into the rule composition process, and hence can be beneficial for beginners, the full rule suggestions provide a wider overview of the personalization capabilities [55]. In this area, an important direction for future work is how to combine state-of-the-art recommendation methods with context and user data. The integration between the recommendations generated by automations and those derived from usage patterns can provide more effective results.

Automation Rules Datasets for Recommendations. To generate relevant recommendations and, in general, to provide intelligent support to users, EUD platforms include some "sub-systems" devoted to analysing previous data to extract patterns or other useful information. These sub-systems rely on collected datasets of information relevant to the specific goal of the platform. Regarding recommendations for smart home personalization platforms, the crucial data source is the automation rules dataset. The first publicly available dataset of (IFTTT) automation rules was crawled and curated by Ur and colleagues [69]. The authors scraped all the programs shared publicly on the IFTTT website at that time (67169 rules) and analysed them to investigate the practicality of letting average users customise smart-home devices. The generated recipes dataset contains the following fields: an "if channel" and its trigger condition and any parameters, a "then channel" and its selected action and any parameters, a recipe id, an author id, and statistics on when it was shared and how many other users have activated it. In a subsequent study [70], the authors proposed a new version of the dataset containing the 224,590 programs shared publicly on IFTTT as of September 2015. The dataset includes recipes from more than 100.000 users (most of whom created only one or two of them) and contains many duplicate programs. The dataset[2] was publicly released. Mi and colleagues [56] collected data from the IFTTT website for six months (from November 2016 to April 2017) and performed controlled experiments on these data using a custom testbed. The dataset was generated first obtaining the full list of available services. Then the authors reverse-engineered the URLs of applets' pages, using this address to fetch more than 300K public applets. For each applet, they obtained its name, description, trigger, trigger service (the service that the trigger belongs to), action name, action service, and add count (the number of this applet being installed by users). The collected data and the testbed[3] are publicly available. A more recent effort was carried out by Yu and colleagues [74]. The focus of the dataset is specifically on rules designating smart space interactions. Another goal is to characterise behaviours that users encapsulate in automation rules in IFTTT. The authors collected 50,067 publicly shared IFTTT recipes, and then filtered them based on their popularity, relevance to IoT applications, and ease of automated parsing. The final dataset consists of 2,648 IoT-relevant rules. This dataset[4], including the preliminary pre-filtered versions and the scripts used to analyse it, is publicly available. The features of the rules in the dataset are rule name, rule id, services (e.g., 'weather', 'hue'), service names ('Weather Underground', 'Philips Hue'), description, service owner (a Boolean indicating whether the rule is provided by the manufacturer), pro features (a Boolean indicating whether a pro subscription to IFTTT is required), and install count. Another recent effort in regard to rule datasets collection was carried out to obtain automation rules in a less limiting format compared to the traditional IFTTT syntax (allowing i.e. to define automations consisting of multiple conditions and actions, or to use the "NOT" Boolean operator). Another objective was to obtain more contextual information about the automation, such as the role of the rule creator (domain expert, platform expert, or student) and the rule's goal (e.g. comfort, health, security). Rules are described by the fields: author, rule name, goal, natural language description, real name (the name of the device or service), parent (a broader classification of the functionality),

---

[2] https://www.upod.io/datasets.html, last accessed 2023/04/12.

[3] https://www-users.cse.umn.edu/~fengqian/ifttt_measurement/, last accessed 2023/04/12.

[4] https://doi.org/10.5281/zenodo.5572861, last accessed 2023/04/12.

operator, value, next operator (what connects a rule element to the next one). The dataset currently contains 638 rules and is available on GitHub[5].

3.4 Debugging and Explainability of Automation Rules

The End-User Development (EUD) paradigm has allowed non-technical users without programming skills to customise the behaviour of their devices and applications [28], empowering users and letting them benefit from the potential of IoT. The relative simplicity and applicability of EUD paradigms to IoT – such as TAP - have attracted great interest [58]. One important aspect to consider is the possible issues derived from interferences between multiple automations. Indeed, despite its ease of use, non-programmers still make numerous mistakes in composing TA rules, like loops, inconsistencies, and redundancies [25]. That is important because poor or conflicting rule settings can lead to unsatisfactory or potentially dangerous behaviour for the user. For example, Chen et al. [15] discuss three possible categories of logical errors in these cases, providing associated examples. *Rule prevention* occurs when the execution of one rule unintentionally prevents the trigger of another rule. For example, if rule 1 is "if nobody is home, turn off the smart outlets" with the intention of saving energy, and rule 2 is "if it's 10AM, turn on the smart pet feeder". If the pet feeder is powered from one of the smart outlets and nobody is home at 10AM, the pet will not be fed. *Rule collision* occurs when the actions of two rules are conflicting, for example: if rule 1 is "if the kitchen sensor detects smoke, open the window" and rule 2 is "if it is dark outside, close the window", when there is something burning in the oven (thereby there is smoke in the kitchen) and it is night, the window may not open because of the rule collision. *Unexpected rule chain* occurs when one rule may trigger another rule unexpectedly. For instance, if rule 1 is "if the temperature in my room is below 20 °C, turn on the heater in my room", and rule 2 is "if the temperature in my room is above 25 °C, open the window". After executing the first rule, the temperature might rise above 25 °C and activate rule 2, which can cause the window to open unexpectedly. In the section about debugging and explainable automations we discussed possible ways to address such issues.

Only recently, a few studies have been carried out that focused on the problem of rule errors in EUD and explored debugging approaches to support end-users in customising their IoT devices [42]. However, while many efforts have been directed toward debugging for mashup programming, spreadsheet, and rule analysis, little work has investigated debugging in TAP [22, 28]. Some of these works, inspired by and extending the Interrogative Debugging paradigm of Ko and Myers [47], proposed tools and approaches that allow end-users to simulate their own rules and identify errors [22, 28, 51]. Specifically, these pioneering works developed and tested different EUD interfaces able to simulate the rules created, detect potential errors, and return explanations of those errors to the user to support them in correcting them. Although preliminary, these studies' results seem to suggest that this type of solutions can support end-users in dealing with and better understanding errors in the composition of trigger-action rules. In particular, ITAD [51] provides the possibility to indicate a specific context of use and

---

[5] https://github.com/andrematt/trigger_action_rules, last accessed 2023/04/12.

automatically check whether certain rules can be triggered in the given context, with the possibility to know why or why not that automation can be executed. FortClash [18] has a different approach, using visual timelines associated with contextual elements and rules highlighting when the contextual items change state in order to better analyse them and control possible conflicts.

However, several aspects remain to be clarified. In particular, we still do not know much about how end-users approach debugging and what strategies they adopt [22]. The meagre extant literature on end-user debugging of TA rules is limited mainly to tools to support bug identification, with limited end user involvement and not delving into user and interaction characteristics. Therefore, a possible research direction could be the study of the strategies exploited by users and the exploration of their mental models during debugging tasks. Knowing more about end users' debugging strategies is essential to inform the design of better tools to support this important task [42]. In a recent pilot study [52], the authors explored the strategies adopted by non-programmer users for testing and debugging a trigger-action rule set focusing on the mental models that users initially have in facing a debugging task. Results highlighted different debugging strategies, partly similar to those already observed in novice programmers [33, 34, 48]. Another aspect is the similarity of these issues with those emerging in explainable artificial intelligence: the set of automations created can be considered a kind of black box that should be made transparent to the users who can ask several questions [49] to better understand the resulting behaviour.

4 Evaluation

4.1 Metrics

It seems fruitful to consider which metrics can be used and when some methods are more suited in the context of EUD for IoT. As introduced in Sect. 2.1, one aspect to assess is how the temporal elements of an automation are perceived by users, and whether their expectations and descriptions correspond to the actual automation execution. The counting of errors during the editing of automations can be used to assess different aspects of a tailoring platform, such as whether its design correctly conveys the concepts of events and conditions or if a debugging tool can decrease the issues in pre-defined automations. For this goal, first, the types of errors should be defined, such as wrong triggers or actions, wrong rule parameters, or incorrect specification of logical operators. A severity index for the errors can also be defined. From these, an "error table" can be designed and used by researchers to assign a score to an automation after they agree on its classification. For instance, in [38] four categories of errors were identified within the rules produced by the participants of a user test and thereby analysed. These categories are: the incorrect definition of triggers and of actions; the incorrect association of a trigger with an event vs a condition; the incorrect application of the NOT operator; and the incorrect use of composition operators (AND/OR) to combine different triggers. The authors assigned a weight (1 point indicating a severe error and 0.5 a moderate one) to the errors according to the defined scheme. The severity of an error was established based on the "distance" between the content and the outcome of the automations (generated using tailoring environments that implement different composition paradigms) and their natural language descriptions. For instance, in the rule "When the user is in bed and the bedroom light level is daylight, send a notification to the user and turn off all the lights in the bedroom", using "bed movement" as a trigger instead of "bed occupancy" is a moderate error, whilst not using any bed-related is a severe error. An analysis of the errors in the generation of automation rules has been performed [30], where the mistakes were categorised as 1) wrong events or actions in a rule; 2) wrong parameters in the specification of events and actions; 3) using a wrong logical operator (AND instead of OR). A score between 1 and 3 was assigned to each type of error, where 3 is the most serious one.

Another measurable aspect to consider is time-to-tasks. In this context, time recordings can be helpful to assess whether a tool more efficiently supports end users in carrying out rule creation and modification tasks [12]. For conversational-based approaches, an evaluation can also be based on the number of conversational turns [45]. Another use of time in assessments can be to set a time limit and check within this interval for the number (and eventually variety) of generated automation to check if one approach is able to stimulate creativity more than another. A similar assessment (but without the time limit) was performed in [25]. A final aspect to consider is users' motivation. There are studies (for instance, [39]) that analyse the components that have a positive or negative impact on the intention to use IoT technologies making reference to the technology acceptance model (TAM). Another aspect is to analyse how these technologies are used after their deployment (as in [50]), supporting analytics to show which object or service is found more useful, or examining the actual usage of automation rules, or whether there is a loss of interest in the platform after some time.

4.2 Assessment of the Different Composition Paradigms

Another aspect to investigate is whether a different composition paradigm has an impact on the user experience on a tailoring platform. For instance, Valtolina and colleagues [71] reported on a study evaluating the benefits of a chatbot in comparison to traditional GUI, specifically for users with a poor aptitude for using technologies. They considered applications in the healthcare and smart home fields and found that for the user experience the chatbot application appears to be better than the GUI-based one. A similar comparison has been carried over in the assessment of the RuleBot [37] platform. RuleBot is a conversational agent that uses machine learning and natural language processing techniques to allow end users to create automations according to a flexible implementation of the trigger-action paradigm, and thereby customize the behaviour of devices and sensors using natural language. The usability of the solution was assessed with a user test that presented users with scenarios of increasing difficulties, requiring them to compose from simple to complex rules using RuleBot (chatbot-based) and the TAREME (wizard-based) platform. After the composition task, users had to compile a questionnaire, assigning scores on a 1 to 5 scale to statements associated with each task. These questions were repeated for each tool. It turned out that for simple rules the wizard style was found more efficient than the chatbot because the users were driven to select the relevant elements, while in the chatbot there was some initial conversational turn to allow users to better understand how to formulate the desired rule. Vice versa, in more structured rules, the chatbot was more efficient since users understood how to indicate them and it was thus quite immediate while with the wizard they still had to navigate across the various sections to find the relevant items.

A similar study but related to a different interaction paradigm was performed in [64]. In the study, a platform (HoloFlows) aimed at enabling users to exploit Augmented/Mixed Reality to simplify the modelling and the configuration of IoT workflows is introduced. The platform exploits concepts from the BPM (Business Process Modelling) domain to allow users to automate tasks involving one or more IoT devices. The assessment of the approach consisted of a user study comparing HoloFlows with other two approaches to model IoT processes based on GUI, Node-RED and Camunda Modeler. The dependent variable was the task completion time. The workload of each tool was examined using the NASA-TLX questionnaire. However, it should be noted that it is not always appropriate to compare the performance of users when using a traditional Web-based tailoring environment and when using an augmented-reality approach because there are fundamental differences between them [5]. The Web-based solutions require explicit access to the tailoring platform, whilst a mobile AR platform can be used more opportunistically. Also, the AR app can remove the necessity to browse the logical organization of triggers and actions available in the editor, hence making less relevant a comparison on task completion times. Other aspects to consider when assessing the user experience of an AR application for personalization rules are whether the selected device is appropriate (e.g., smartphone, tablet, or a dedicated device); if the representations used are understandable (e.g., 3D visualizations that reproduce real objects, or more abstract representations); whether the designed way to interact with the objects is easy to understand; what is the added value of the AR approach, i.e., if it enables functionalities that would not be possible or would be challenging with a different user interface (in this regard, Clark and colleagues [16] assessed the interaction with IoT devices in unfamiliar spaces).

4.3 User Experience

Another aspect to consider is the impact on the user experience of supporting tools such as debuggers or recommendations. When an IoT platform is deployed in a real environment, the interactions between rules may generate some unwanted situations, such as the conflictual triggering of actions, or the specified rule behaviour may result different from the intended one [51].. Hence, a debugging support tool that can test the correctness of rules and possibly identify errors in them (e.g. triggers or actions that they might have forgotten or inappropriately added in the current rule specification). A user-oriented evaluation of such tools could be focused on assessing to what extent the debugging can support non-programmer users. For instance, researchers can generate a dataset of automation that presents different types of errors, such as flipped triggers, or actions that cause loops. Then, users are asked to perform some tasks aimed at checking to what extent they can solve issues in bugged rules under two different conditions: by using the tool and by not using the tool ("control" case). A similar assessment for a debugging tool has been carried out [51] in which participants were provided with some tasks (describing the desired outcome situation) and a set of rules to use to reach the behaviour described in the tasks, which presented some inconsistencies (compared to the intended behaviour). In the 'control' case, they had to write down in natural language the result of their analysis, identifying the rule(s) to edit and the kind of changes to do on one or more rules for specifying the expected behaviour. In the other case, they had to edit/fix the concerned rule(s) by exploiting the simulator functionality and the why/why-not buttons developed in the tool. Another aspect to consider is whether using the support tool can lead to a better understanding of the future system's functioning. For instance, FORTNIoT [19] aims to extend the intelligibility of a system also to the predicted future behaviour of an environment, to allow users to better understand what actions will happen and why. The assessment of the platform has been done through remote interviews, where participants had to use the platform with and without the prediction engine. Participants were asked to think aloud and report what will happen in a scenario and why, also using a 5-point Likert scale to express their confidence in the answer.

A user-centered assessment can be performed on a recommendation system specific to this setting. Besides assessing their user experience on the platforms, other aspects that can be evaluated are the perceived relevance, novelty and diversity of recommendations, and overall satisfaction. To provide a reliable measure of the quality of an algorithm, these user-centered metrics should be combined into a single score [32]. A specific way to assess recommender systems can be to ask users to perform some tasks and check during these tasks whether the presented recommendations are selected [43]. Another relevant aspect that can be tested is if the proposed recommendations speed up the rule generation process or make it easier. It should be noted that a recommender system may increase the time to complete a task, suggesting users some interesting alternatives. Hence, it should be analysed how to correctly integrate the recommender system with the users' operation on the tailoring platform to propose a convenient solution. Another consideration is whether recommendations fit the users' desires concerning long-term preferences, such as convenience, sustainability, security, or privacy. This aspect can be assessed with a match with an inserted or derived user profile, using as a baseline an algorithm that does not consider the user profile (as in [73]).

Another not yet widely considered aspect is the impact of psychological constructs (such as personality traits, locus of control, mindset,...) on user perceived recommendation usefulness as well as on their performance in configuration tasks where they could use recommendations. Cena et al. [14] for example carried out an experiment in the context of home automation where they found that the personality traits of Need for Cognition and Self-efficacy may play an important role in assessing the perceived usefulness of recommendations, and they have some relation in conjunction with the performance of the task.

5 Conclusions

This paper discusses recent proposals in the EUD field addressing the control of IoT automations in ecosystems of smart objects and services. The discussion is structured along the main aspects of automation rules to consider in the design phase, the current relevant tools for EUD in smart ecosystems, and which approaches can be used to assess the outcome of the user interaction with these platforms.

The first part of the discussion focuses on how to represent the rule structure, and how to allow users to correctly interpret the timing aspects of the automation triggers. Regarding the former aspect, novel contributions indicate the feasibility of designing extensions and using different TAP abstraction levels while retaining their understandability. There is a gap between commercial applications, usually not offering much flexibility in rule creation, and advanced home automation systems that require programming skills, e.g. Node-RED. This divide should be investigated more, and to this end, it is of crucial importance to better understand what kind of automations users need, and how these personalization intents are expressed, as well as better grasp the users' mental models about TAP [65]. Another characteristic that emerges [20, 35, 63] is that not much consideration has been given to how different people sharing the same space interact with the automations. This can raise conflicts based on different personal preferences, but it also presents new possibilities, for instance socially-oriented automations aimed towards the well-being of families, which require the cooperation of more people to be achieved. This aspect should be considered while designing possible extensions for TAP rules, providing operators, structures and functionalities that also consider these possible situations, while also keeping in mind the heterogeneity of the actors that can co-participate in the creation of the automation programs. Concerning the distinction between states and events in TAP rules composition, recent studies ([36, 75]) take into account that this distinction can be expressed in natural language [13, 59] and observe that the choice of more specific temporal conjunctions (when-while) leads to an improvement in their understanding. Implementations of EUD systems for different use cases [1, 2, 31] employing the when-while rule structure demonstrated that it enabled clear representation of event and condition triggers. Future work should investigate which other linguistic cues EUD interfaces should use to better support users.

We have also investigated the tools for EUD. The first considered aspect is which composition paradigms are currently used for creating and modifying TAP rules. Visual-based paradigms have been studied in the literature, where their main strengths and weaknesses have been analysed. Recent technological progress allows for new approaches exploiting different interaction modalities, such as tangible, conversational and AR. However, there are not many studies where these approaches are compared with visual tools, or where they are analysed in a context of realistic use over longer periods of time. Studies are needed to better assess how they impact the understanding, definition and control of automations in IoT settings and the long-term engagement of potential users with the system. Concerning the security aspects, different levels of threats can emerge from automations rules and can put at risk the privacy of the user and/or the security of the smart environment. Furthermore, these unexpected behaviours may go unnoticed by non-technical users. Some work has started to investigate users' concerns in IFTTT rules [62], and how to classify the different threats [10] also using textual descriptions to explain why a rule can be dangerous [9]. There are however further aspects that impact how users perceive the risks related to rules, in particular the context where rules might be activated. Context-awareness could be helpful in providing personalized recommendations. Current approaches mainly use two recommendation strategies: they rely on automations created by other users or try to mine some frequent patterns from the user behaviours and derive rules to automate this behaviour. A challenging future direction is an approach capable of combining the two strategies, e.g. considering automations created by others but completing them with the values from the context of the user. Concerning the debugging and explainability of TAP rules, some pioneering works started to investigate how to simulate the rules execution, identify potential errors, and return explanations of those errors. Although preliminary, the results seem to indicate that these tools can support users in composing TAP rules and in understanding the errors that may emerge. However, several aspects remain to be clarified, for instance about how end-users approach debugging and what strategies they adopt [22].

The last section considers the approaches for usability and user experience evaluation. It shows that while some general purpose evaluation methods can be applied in this area, there is a need for specific methods that capture its specific aspects, such as how to identify and assess errors in creating automation rules. In general, this area would benefit from more studies on how to motivate non-technical users to create their automations, and in more extended trials in the wild to better investigate the adoption of EUD approaches.

Acknowledgements. This work has been supported by the PRIN 2017 "EMPATHY: Empowering People in Dealing with Internet of Things Ecosystems", https://www.empathy-project.eu/. Balducci acknowledges the support by the REFIN grant, POR Puglia FESR FSE 2014–2020 "Gestione di oggetti intelligenti per migliorare le esperienze di visita di siti di interesse culturale".

References

1. Andrao, M., Desolda, G., Greco, F., Manfredi, R., Treccani, B., Zancanaro, M.: End-user programming and math teachers: an initial study. In: Proceedings of the 2022 International Conference on Advanced Visual Interfaces, pp. 1–3 (2022)
2. Andrao, M., Treccani, B., Zancanaro, M.: Therapists as designers: an initial investigation of end-user programming of a tangible tool for therapeutic interventions. In: Proceedings of the 2nd International Workshop on Empowering People in Dealing with Internet of Things Ecosystems co-located with INTERACT 2021, Bari, Italy, Online / Bari, Italy, September 30, 2021(CEUR Workshop Proceedings, vol. 3053). CEUR-WS.org, pp. 38–42 (2021). http://ceur-ws.org/Vol-3053/paper_8.pdf
3. Ardito, C., Desolda, G., Lanzilotti, R., Malizia, A., Matera, M.: Analysing trade-offs in frameworks for the design of smart environments. Behav. Inf. Technol. **39**(1), 47–71 (2020)
4. Ardito, C., et al.: User-defined semantics for the design of IoT systems enabling smart interactive experiences. Pers. Ubiquit. Comput. **24**(6), 781–796 (2020). https://doi.org/10.1007/s00779-020-01457-5
5. Ariano, R., Manca, M., Paternò, F., Santoro, C.: Smartphone-based augmented reality for end-user creation of home automations. Behav. Inf. Techno. **42**(1), 124–140 (2023)
6. Balducci, F., Buono, P., Desolda, G., Impedovo, D., Piccinno, A.: Improving smart interactive experiences in cultural heritage through pattern recognition techniques. Pattern Recogn. Lett. **131**, 142–149 (2020)
7. Bellucci, A., Vianello, A., Florack, Y., Micallef, L., Jacucci, G.: Augmenting objects at home through programmable sensor tokens: a design journey. Int. J. Hum. Comput Stud. **122**, 211–231 (2019)

8. Brackenbury, W., et al.: How users interpret bugs in trigger-action programming. In: Proceedings of the 2019 CHI Conference on Human Factors in Computing Systems (CHI 2019). Association for Computing Machinery, New York, NY, USA, Article Paper 552, p. 12 (2019). https://doi.org/10.1145/3290605.330078

9. Breve, B., Cimino, G., Deufemia, V.: Towards explainable security for ECA rules. In: Proceedings of the 3rd International Workshop on Empowering End-Users in Dealing with Internet of Things Ecosystems (EMPATHY), CEUR-WS, vol. 3172, pp. 26–30 (2022)

10. Breve, B., Cimino, G., Deufemia, V.: Identifying security and privacy violation rules in trigger-action IoT platforms with NLP models. IEEE Internet Things J. **10**(6), 5607–5622 (2023)

11. Brich, J., Walch, M., Rietzler, M., Weber, M., Schaub, F.: Exploring end user programming needs in home automation. ACM Trans. Comput. Human Interact. (TOCHI) **24**(2), 1–35 (2017)

12. Cabitza, F., Fogli, D., Lanzilotti, R., Piccinno, A.: Rule-based tools for the configuration of ambient intelligence systems: a comparative user study. Multimed. Tools Appl. **76**(4), 5221–5241 (2016). https://doi.org/10.1007/s11042-016-3511-2

13. Casati, F., Castano, S., Fugini, M., Mirbel, I., Pernici, B.: Using patterns to design rules in workflows. IEEE Trans. Softw. Eng. **26**(8), 760–785 (2000)

14. Cena, F., et al.: Incorporating personality traits in user modeling for EUD. In: 3rd International Workshop on Empowering People in Dealing with Internet of Things Ecosystems, CEUR Workshop Proceedings, vol. 3172, pp. 41–48 (2022)

15. Chen, X., et al.: Fix the leaking tap: a survey of trigger-action programming (TAP) security issues, detection techniques and solutions. Comput. Secur. 102812 (2022)

16. Clark, M., Newman, M.W., Dutta, P.: ARticulate: one-shot interactions with intelligent assistants in unfamiliar smart spaces using augmented reality. Proc. ACM Interact. Mob. Wearabl. Ubiquit. Technol. **6**(1), 1–24 (2022)

17. Cobb, C., et al.: How risky are real users' IFTTT applets? In: Proceedings of the Sixteenth Symposium on Usable Privacy and Security (SOUPS 2020), pp. 505–529 (2020)

18. Coppers, S., Vanacken, D., Luyten, K.: FortClash: predicting and mediating unintended behavior in home automation. Proc. ACM Human Comput. Interact. **6**(EICS), 1–20 (2022). https://doi.org/10.1145/3532204

19. Coppers, S., Vanacken, D., Luyten, K.: Fortniot: Intelligible predictions to improve user understanding of smart home behavior. Proc. ACM Interact. Mob. Wearabl. Ubiquit. Technol. **4**(4), 1–24 (2020)

20. Corcella, L., Manca, M., Paternò, F.: Personalizing a student home behaviour. In: Barbosa, S., Markopoulos, P., Paternò, F., Stumpf, S., Valtolina, S. (eds.) End-User Development. LNCS, vol. 10303, pp. 18–33. Springer, Cham (2017). https://doi.org/10.1007/978-3-319-58735-6_2

21. Corno, F., De Russis, L., Roffarello, A.M.: A high-level semantic approach to end-user development in the Internet of Things. Int. J. Hum Comput Stud. **125**, 41–54 (2019)

22. Corno, F., De Russis, L., Roffarello, A.M.: Empowering end users in debugging trigger-action rules. In: Proceedings of the 2019 CHI Conference on Human Factors in Computing Systems, pp. 1–13 (2019)

23. Corno, F., De Russis, L., Roffarello, A.M.: RecRules: recommending IF-THEN rules for end-user development. ACM Trans. Intell. Syst. Technol. **10**(5), 1–27 (2019). https://doi.org/10.1145/3344211

24. Corno, F., De Russis, L., Roffarello, A.M.: HeyTAP: bridging the gaps between users' needs and technology in IF-THEN rules via conversation. In: Proceedings of the International Conference on Advanced Visual Interfaces, pp. 1–9 (2020)

25. Corno, F., De Russis, L., Roffarello, A.M.: TAPrec: supporting the composition of trigger-action rules through dynamic recommendations. In: Proceedings of the 25th International Conference on Intelligent User Interfaces, pp. 579–588 (2020)

26. Corno, F., De Russis, L., Roffarello, A.M.: Devices, information, and people: abstracting the internet of things for end-user personalization. In: Fogli, D., Tetteroo, D., Barricelli, B.R., Borsci, S., Markopoulos, P., Papadopoulos, G.A. (eds.) End-User Development. LNCS, vol. 12724, pp. 71–86. Springer, Cham (2021). https://doi.org/10.1007/978-3-030-79840-6_5

27. Cypher, A.: Eager: programming repetitive tasks by example. In: Proceedings of the SIGCHI Conference on Human Factors in Computing Systems, pp. 33–39 (1991)

28. De Russis, L., Roffarello, A.M.: A debugging approach for trigger-action programming. In: Extended Abstracts of the 2018 CHI Conference on Human Factors in Computing Systems (2018). https://doi.org/10.1145/3170427.3188641

29. de Vega, M., Rinck, M., Diaz, J.M., León, I.: Figure and ground in temporal sentences: the role of the adverbs when and while. Discourse Process. **43**(1), 1–23 (2007). https://doi.org/10.1080/01638530709336891

30. Desolda, G., Ardito, C., Matera, M.: Empowering end users to customize their smart environments: model, composition paradigms, and domain-specific tools. ACM Trans. Comput. Human Interact. (TOCHI) **24**(2), 1–52 (2017)

31. Desolda, G., Greco, F., Guarnieri, F., Mariz, N., Zancanaro, M.: SENSATION: an authoring tool to support event–state paradigm in end-user development. In: Ardito, C., et al. (eds.) Human-Computer Interaction – INTERACT 2021. LNCS, vol. 12933, pp. 373–382. Springer, Cham (2021). https://doi.org/10.1007/978-3-030-85616-8_22

32. Epifania, F., Cremonesi, P.: User-centered evaluation of recommender systems with comparison between short and long profile. In: 2012 Sixth International Conference on Complex, Intelligent, and Software Intensive Systems, pp. 204–211. IEEE (2012)

33. Fitzgerald, S., et al.: Debugging: finding, fixing and flailing, a multi-institutional study of novice debuggers. Comput. Sci. Educ. **18**(2), 93–116 (2008)

34. Fitzgerald, S., McCauley, R., Hanks, B., Murphy, L., Simon, B., Zander, C.: Debugging from the student perspective. IEEE Trans. Educ. **53**(3), 390–396 (2010). https://doi.org/10.1109/TE.2009.2025266

35. Fogli, D., Peroni, M., Stefini, C.: ImAtHome: Making trigger-action programming easy and fun. J. Vis. Lang. Comput. **42**, 60–75 (2017)

36. Gallitto, G., Treccani, B., Zancanaro, M.: If when is better than if (and while might help): on the importance of influencing mental models in EUD (a pilot study). In: Proceedings of the 1st International Workshop on Empowering People in Dealing with Internet of Things Ecosystems co-located with International Conference on Advanced Visual Interfaces (AVI), Ischia Island, Italy, 2020, pp. 7–11 (2020)

37. Gallo, S., Paterno, F.: A conversational agent for creating flexible daily automation. In: Proceedings of the 2022 International Conference on Advanced Visual Interfaces, pp. 1–8 (2022)

38. Gallo, S., Manca, M., Mattioli, A., Paternò, F., Santoro, C.: Comparative analysis of composition paradigms for personalization rules in IoT settings. In: Fogli, D., Tetteroo, D., Barricelli, B.R., Borsci, S., Markopoulos, P., Papadopoulos, G.A. (eds.) End-User Development. LNCS, vol. 12724, pp. 53–70. Springer, Cham (2021). https://doi.org/10.1007/978-3-030-79840-6_4

39. Gao, L., Bai, X.: A unified perspective on the factors influencing consumer acceptance of internet of things technology. Asia Pac. J. Market. Logist. **26**(2), 211–231 (2014). https://doi.org/10.1108/APJML-06-2013-0061

40. Gennari, R., Matera, M., Morra, D., Melonio, A., Rizvi, M.: Design for social digital well-being with young generations: Engage them and make them reflect. Int. J. Human Comput. Stud. **173**, 103006 (2023). https://doi.org/10.1016/j.ijhcs.2023.103006

41. Ghiani, G., Manca, M., Paternò, F., Santoro, C.: Personalization of context-dependent applications through trigger-action rules. ACM Trans. Computer-Human Interaction (TOCHI) **24**(2), 1–33 (2017)

42. Grigoreanu, V., Burnett, M., Wiedenbeck, S., Cao, J., Rector, K., Kwan, I.: End-user debugging strategies: a sensemaking perspective. ACM Trans. Comput. Human Interact. (TOCHI) **19**(1), 1–28 (2012)

43. Gunawardana, A., Shani, G., Yogev, S.: Evaluating recommender systems. In: Recommender systems handbook, pp. 547–601. Springer US, New York, NY (2012)

44. Huang, J., Cakmak, M.: Supporting mental model accuracy in trigger-action programming. In: Proceedings of the 2015 ACM International Joint Conference on Pervasive and Ubiquitous Computing - UbiComp 2015, pp. 215–225. ACM Press, Osaka, Japan (2015). https://doi.org/10.1145/2750858.2805830

45. Jain, M., Kumar, P., Kota, R., Patel, S.N.: Evaluating and informing the design of chatbots. In: Proceedings of the 2018 Designing Interactive Systems Conference, pp. 895–906 (2018)

46. Knijnenburg, B.P., Willemsen, M.C., Gantner, Z., Soncu, H., Newell, C.: Explaining the user experience of recommender systems. User Model. User-Adap. Inter. **22**, 441–504 (2012)

47. Ko, A., Myers, B.: Designing the whyline: a debugging interface for asking questions about program behavior. In: Proceedings of the SIGCHI Conference on Human Factors in Computing Systems, pp. 151–158. ACM (2004)

48. Li, C., Chan, E., Denny, P., Luxton-Reilly, A., Tempero, E.: Towards a framework for teaching debugging. In: Proceedings of the Twenty-First Australasian Computing Education Conference on - ACE 2019 (2019). https://doi.org/10.1145/3286960.3286970

49. Liao, Q.V., Gruen, D., Miller, S.: Questioning the AI: informing design practices for explainable AI user experiences. In: Proceedings of the 2020 CHI Conference on Human Factors in Computing Systems, pp. 1–15 (2020)

50. Manca, M., Paternò, F., Santoro, C.: Remote monitoring of end-user created automations in field trials. J. Ambient Intell. Human. Comput. **13**(12), 5669–5697 (2021). https://doi.org/10.1007/s12652-021-03239-0

51. Manca, M., Paternò, F., Santoro, C., Corcella, L.: Supporting end-user debugging of trigger-action rules for IoT applications. Int. J. Hum. Comput. Stud. **123**, 56–69 (2019)

52. Manfredi, R., Andrao, M., Greco, F., Desolda, G., Treccani, B. Zancanaro, M.: Toward a better understanding of end-user debugging strategies: a pilot study. In Proceedings of the 3rd international workshop on empowering people in dealing with Internet of Things ecosystems co-located with AVI 2022, Frascati, Rome, Italy, June 06, 2022. (CEUR Workshop Proceedings, vol. 3172). CEUR-WS.org, pp. 31–35 (2022). https://ceur-ws.org/Vol-3172/short6.pdf

53. Masui, T., Nakayama, K.: Repeat and predict—two keys to efficient text editing. In: Proceedings of the SIGCHI Conference on Human Factors in Computing Systems, pp. 118–130 (1994)

54. Mattioli, A., Paternò, F.: A visual environment for end-user creation of IoT customization rules with recommendation support. In: Proceedings of the International Conference on Advanced Visual Interfaces, pp. 1–5 (2020)

55. Mattioli, A., Paternò, F.: Recommendations for creating trigger-action rules in a block-based environment. Behav. Inf. Technol. **40**(10), 1024–1034 (2021)

56. Mi, X., Qian, F., Zhang, Y., Wang, X.F.: An empirical characterization of IFTTT: ecosystem, usage, and performance. In: Proceedings of the 2017 Internet Measurement Conference, pp. 398–404 (2017)

57. Paci, F., Bianchin, D., Quintarelli, E., Zannone, N.: IFTTT privacy checker. In: Saracino, A., Mori, P. (eds.) Emerging Technologies for Authorization and Authentication. LNCS, vol. 12515, pp. 90–107. Springer, Cham (2020). https://doi.org/10.1007/978-3-030-64455-0_6
58. Paternò, F., Santoro, C.: End-user development for personalizing applications, things, and robots. Int. J. Hum Comput Stud. **131**, 120–130 (2019)
59. Pianesi, F., Varzi, A.C.: Events and event talk: an introduction. In: Speaking of Events, pp. 3–47. Oxford University Press, New York, NY (2000)
60. Resnick, M., et al.: Scratch: programming for all. Commun. ACM **52**(11), 60–67 (2009). https://doi.org/10.1145/1592761.1592779
61. Ruvini, J.-D., Dony, C.: Learning users' habits to automate repetitive tasks. In: Your Wish is My Command, pp. 271-XIV. Morgan Kaufmann (2001) https://doi.org/10.1016/B978-155 860688-3/50015-4
62. Saeidi, M., Calvert, M., Au, A.W., Sarma, A., Bobba, R.B.: If this context then that concern: exploring users' concerns with IFTTT applets. In: Proceedings on Privacy Enhancing Technologies, vol. 2022(1), pp. 166–186 (2021)
63. Salovaara, A., Bellucci, A., Vianello, A., Jacucci, G.: Programmable smart home toolkits should better address households' social needs. In: Proceedings of the 2021 CHI Conference on Human Factors in Computing Systems, pp. 1–14 (2021)
64. Seiger, R., Kühn, R., Korzetz, M., Aßmann, U.: HoloFlows: modelling of processes for the Internet of Things in mixed reality. Softw. Syst. Model. **20**(5), 1465–1489 (2021). https://doi.org/10.1007/s10270-020-00859-6
65. Soares, D., Dias, J.P., Restivo, A., Ferreira, H.S.: Programming IoT-spaces: a user-survey on home automation rules. In: Paszynski, M., Kranzlmüller, D., Krzhizhanovskaya, V.V., Dongarra, J.J., Sloot, P.M.A. (eds.) Computational Science – ICCS 2021. LNCS, vol. 12745, pp. 512–525. Springer, Cham (2021). https://doi.org/10.1007/978-3-030-77970-2_39
66. Srinivasan, V., Koehler, C., Jin, H.: RuleSelector: Selecting conditional action rules from user behavior patterns. Proc. ACM Interact. Mobile. Wearabl. Ubiquit. Technol. **2**(1), 1–34 (2018)
67. Stefanidi, E., et al.: MagiPlay: an augmented reality serious game allowing children to program intelligent environments. Trans. Comput. Sci. XXXVII: Spec. Issue Comput. Graph. 144–169 (2020)
68. Surbatovich, M., Aljuraidan, J., Bauer, L., Das, A., Jia, L.: Some recipes can do more than spoil your appetite: analysing the security and privacy risks of IFTTT recipes. In: Proceedings of the 26th International Conference on World Wide Web (WWW 2017), pp. 1501–1510 (2017)
69. Ur, B., McManus, E., Yong Ho, M.P., Littman, M.L.: Practical trigger-action programming in the smart home. In: Proceedings of the SIGCHI Conference on Human Factors in Computing Systems, pp. 803–812 (2014)
70. Ur, B., et al.: Trigger-action programming in the wild: An analysis of 200,000 IFTTT recipes. In: Proceedings of the 2016 CHI Conference on Human Factors in Computing Systems, pp. 3227–3231 (2016)
71. Valtolina, S., Barricelli, B.R., Di Gaetano, S.: Communicability of traditional interfaces VS chatbots in healthcare and smart home domains. Behav. Inf. Technol. **39**(1), 108–132 (2020)
72. Wang, Q., Datta, P., Yang, W., Liu, S., Bates, A., Gunter, C.A.: Charting the attack surface of trigger-action IoT platforms. In: Proceedings of the ACM Conference on Computer and Communications Security, pp. 1439–1453 (2019)
73. Yang, F., Kalloori, S., Chalumattu, R., Gross, M.: Personalized information retrieval for touristic attractions in augmented reality. In: Proceedings of the Fifteenth ACM International Conference on Web Search and Data Mining, pp. 1613–1616 (2022)
74. Yu, H., Hua, J., Julien, C.: Analysis of IFTTT recipes to study how humans use internet-of-things (iot) devices. In: Proceedings of the 19th ACM Conference on Embedded Networked Sensor Systems, pp. 537–541 (2021)

75. Yusuf, I.N.B., Jamal, D.B.A., Jiang, L., Lo, D.: RecipeGen++: an automated trigger action programs generator. In Proceedings of the 30th ACM Joint European Software Engineering Conference and Symposium on the Foundations of Software Engineering, pp. 1672–1676, November 2022

76. Zancanaro, M., Gallitto, G., Dina, Y., Treccani, B.: Improving mental models in IoT end-user development. Human-centric Comput. Inf. Sci. **2**, 48 (2022)

77. Zheng, S., Apthorpe, N., Chetty, M., Feamster, N.: User perceptions of smart home IoT privacy. In: Proceedings of the ACM on Human-Computer Interaction, vol. 2, CSCW, pp. 1–20 (2018)

Understanding User Needs in Smart Homes and How to Fulfil Them

Andrea Mattioli[1,2](✉) and Fabio Paternò[1]

[1] CNR-ISTI, HIIS Laboratory, Pisa, Italy
{andrea.mattioli,fabio.paterno}@isti.cnr.it
[2] Department of Information Engineering, University of Pisa, Pisa, Italy

Abstract. Smart homes are becoming a widespread reality given the increasingly available number of connected objects and sensors. However, it is still unclear what people expect from automations that are made possible by this technological evolution. In addition, it is unclear whether current trigger-action programming (TAP) languages offer sufficient operators and constructs to specify the desired automations. In this paper, we report on a study aiming to provide useful elements to address such issues. It involved 34 users without experience in IoT programming who created 204 desired home automations. We discuss an analysis of such results in terms of the relationships found between smart-home components and of the requirements for novel operators in TAP languages.

Keywords: Smart Homes · End-User Development · Trigger-action Programming · User Requirements

1 Introduction

Personalizing smart homes, which are spaces where objects and devices capable of connecting to the Internet are often used in conjunction with online services, has recently gained popularity. Over the last few years, the widespread of these objects has led to the growth of the Internet of Things (IoT) vision. It is a pervasive technology that according to Statista [30] will continue to expand in the next few years. A relevant approach to capitalize on the new possibilities that this landscape offers is Trigger-Action Programming (TAP), which is an End-User Development (EUD) approach that allows people who are not experts in programming to generate custom automations to reach their goal using the rule metaphor. TAP has shown to be an effective approach [5, 32] to configuring automations including objects, devices and services that behave in a concerted manner. A TAP rule includes a "trigger part", that can be formulated in terms of events and conditions, and an "action" part, defining what will be activated at the occurrence of the trigger part. Although there is evidence that TAP is understandable by most end users, there are still problems with the EUD platforms for personalization [12]. In general, understanding how users interpret and use automations requires more research [5, 9, 28]. It is currently unclear, for example, how aware users are of the advantages and the hazards of these platforms. For instance, users can create automation

© The Author(s), under exclusive license to Springer Nature Switzerland AG 2023
L. D. Spano et al. (Eds.): IS-EUD 2023, LNCS 13917, pp. 125–142, 2023.
https://doi.org/10.1007/978-3-031-34433-6_8

with problems deriving from misunderstandings of the temporal relations of triggers and actions [5] and from the complex interactions between rules [36]. They can also inadvertently create automations harmful to their privacy and to the security of their environments [6]. It is hence crucial how to assist them in better orchestrating behaviours involving more objects and automation rules. Analyzing what potential users anticipate from home automation systems in terms of rule functionalities, constructs and operators can be a first step to designing systems and languages more capable of matching users' mental models, and ultimately lead to the clarification of these issues.

2 Related Work

2.1 TAP Rules and Extensions

Different studies investigated the possibility of expanding TAP syntax with further functionalities introducing more flexible rule formulations. These efforts focused on various aspects, for instance, introducing contextual information such as "when" and "where" [14, 17], designing the possibility of using the fuzziness concept and other space and time aspects in trigger and actions specification [4], explicating the "not" and "revert" operators [25], introducing new operators such as time counters, accumulators and rule chaining [28], or allowing to define automations that refer to more or less abstract levels of abstraction [10]. One of the goals of these efforts is to allow users to generate automations that fit their needs more precisely. At the same time, it is crucial to consider how to balance the expressivity of the rule specification language with its easiness of use [32]. More expressivity can hinder the adoption of the platform because it can become more difficult to understand and use it, but there is still the need to be able to express the desired behaviours. Hence, one relevant aspect is understanding what functionalities users expect, and then it is useful to analyse the more spontaneous natural language descriptions of their intents to derive the necessary operators and constructs that a language for trigger-action rules should support. Indeed, such languages are evolving in order to more flexibly support users' needs. For example, IFTTT started as a language supporting only single trigger/single action rules and recently has introduced in a professional version the possibility of multiple actions and filters to select the actions to perform through specific scripts.

2.2 Eliciting Users' Preferences

Prior work in characterizing users' behaviour within smart home systems followed different approaches, ranging from online surveys to extended experiments that require a full smart home installation. A way to directly elicit users' preferences from the products of their interaction with automation personalization systems is the crawling and then analysis of publicly available automation rules [26, 32–34]. Another approach involves potential users through online surveys, probing their expectations about home automation systems. Examples of this approach are in the first part of the study in [32], where the authors collected five desired smart-home behaviours from respondents to the survey. Then, they analysed if it would be possible to implement these desires with trigger-action programming and whether it would require multiple triggers or actions. In one contribution [27] the authors exploited an online survey to investigate users' desires for smart devices and features at home, focusing on situations where participants wished for a more intelligent device or service. In another one [29] the authors collected home automation scenarios using a survey. They provided participants with a fixed house model and devices list, intending to gather as many possible diverse smart home scenarios while maintaining a level of plausibility with real-world installations. An approach based on a more ecological setting can be providing users with a way to describe and collect automation rules at their homes during a longer period [23]. In a study [12] the authors devised a pen-and-paper kit to allow participants to note down a possible automation whether it comes to their mind during their daily activities. After a first home appointment, participants had one week to collect automations in the given structure, which permits the definition of rules with one trigger and one action, eventually enriched by contextual attributes such as "where", "who", "when", and "which". Brich and colleagues [7] conducted a one-week study where participants had to define automations using two notation kits, one rule-based and the other process-based. The study started with a tour, where participants were introduced to the concept of automation and could start to formulate use cases in a free-form manner. Then, participants were acquainted with the kits, and during the week they could come up with more automation ideas. The main goal of the inquiry was to assess the benefits and drawbacks of the two notations. In another study [28] the authors ideated, implemented and installed in the participants' houses a smart-home toolkit, and organized creativity workshops with the recruited families to facilitate the ideation and writing of automations. The families then configured and used the system for six weeks. A crucial aspect emerging from this research is that social aspects are not considered enough in current home automation systems.

2.3 Research Objectives Definition

Some common traits can be drawn from an analysis of the literature. Different studies aimed at eliciting users' preferences or patterns in device uses are based on a posteriori analysis of automation datasets. Other studies surveyed how potential users describe automations. However, only a few have involved participants with indications aiming at eliciting the desired automations, at times using a guiding template, such as an environment and devices list, or a rule structure, allowing them to write rules creatively and freely in their spaces. Also, little attention has been devoted to investigating the final objective (such as comfort, well-being, security, or energy saving) of the users' automations composition, and the relations between the immediate (such as illumination in a room) and the long-term objectives. Another aspect that previous work focused on is defining extensions to the TAP operators and structure, by designing and assessing interfaces (and the underlying systems) for this goal. Nonetheless, few prior works aimed at understanding how people think and use rule operators, values, and connectors between rule parts. A way to inquire about these aspects can be letting participants compose automations through a template that allows the definition of both simple and advanced automations (e.g., including multiple triggers and actions), also letting them define the notation elements for formalizing the operators and the relations between rule elements in a way most suitable for them. To contribute to addressing such issues, we defined the following research objectives to drive our study:

- What functionalities do potential users expect from automations in a smart home setting?
- What TAP constructs and operators are necessary to specify these desired behaviours?

3 The User Study

Our goal was to investigate which functionalities would people who are not programming experts expect in a home automation system, and to find whether any relationships emerge between these functionalities, or between these and users' long-term preferences. Another goal was to understand how they would define these desired behaviours, for instance, which operators they would use, or if there are any specific rule constructs that participants use for describing them. As described in the previous section, some existing work has been concerned with eliciting the personalization features that people expect or desire in smart home environments. A small number of these [7, 12] have developed kits to allow participants to define automations during their daily activities. However, to our knowledge, there is a lack of a study where participants could describe automations using a syntax that is both expressive and realistic (implementing Event-Condition-Action rules) and extensible according to their needs (e.g., defining new operators). Furthermore, there is no study where the automations are also analysed from a linguistic point of view, where the descriptions in natural language can be compared with their formalized versions. For these reasons, we carried out a one-week user study where we collected automation rules from participants in a format that allowed us to subsequently analyse them.

3.1 Tasks

The tasks that participants were asked to carry out were first to compile a list of automations that they imagine could be useful in their living place, expressing these automations using a natural language description. After that, they also had to formalize them using a provided rule template. To address the first research objective, participants could imagine having any IoT device installed in their homes and could integrate them using web services or apps. Hence, they were not forced to use a predefined list of devices and services, or only technology that they know is already available commercially, but they could include technologies that they expected to be available currently or shortly. We adopted this approach to balance the plausibility of the gathered automations with their capability of matching the participants' needs. Participants were given one week to complete the automation list.

3.2 Rule Template

To allow participants to define automations in a non-ambiguous manner, but at the same time avoid forcing them to use a specific language, we provided them with a document including a template and some examples of common automations, such as "When the

Table 1. An example of automation is described using the template, where each row represents a rule element. The title of this automation is "Garden Light", the goal is "Comfort", and the context is "Spring".

ECA	Environment	Channel	Functionality	Operator	Value	Next Op
Event	No	Position	User position	Equal	Garden	And
Condition	No	Date and Time	Time	Between	19:00 - 05:00	
Action	Garden	External Light	Light on	Equal	TRUE	

user is in the garden and it's between 19:00 and 05:00, turn on the garden lights" (See Table 1 for the corresponding description in the template).

The template's header contains three fields related to the whole rule, namely its title, the long-term goal, and the context of actuation, a more high-level description of the scenario in which the automation could be activated. The template's body comprises seven fields specific to each trigger and action. These fields are the "ECA" class (the only field with fixed values the participants had to choose from, which are Event, Condition or Action); the environment (such as a specific room, valid for the entire house, or the room user is currently in); the channel, which can be a more or less specific description of an object or device (such as "door sensor", "smartphone" or "Alexa"), as well as a service (such as "weather forecast"); the specific functionality of the channel (for instance, "room temperature" or "is raining"); the desired value and operator; and a Next operator (which connects a rule element to the next one). The "Context" and "Next Operator" fields were labelled as optional, as we considered the former as additional information not crucial to the understanding of the rule, and the latter as not always needed, and eventually derivable from the rule elements or from the natural language descriptions. However, participants could leave a field blank if it was not pertinent to the automation, such as the "Environment" field in the first two rows of the example.

This structure is partially inspired by the IFTTT syntax, which is organized into channels (the available device or service), functionalities and then user-defined details of the automation, and on the hierarchical organization of the HomeKit dataset [17]. We adopted the Event-Condition-Action syntax because it allows expressing behaviours with adequate expressiveness for the smart home context [3, 8, 13, 16], and because of its widespread adoption in smart home systems. In the considered template, the event is what causes the system to activate the action part. If one or more conditions are present, these are checked after the event verification to assess whether the state of the environment is satisfactory for the activation of actions. In the case of condition(s) without an event, the beginning of the condition is considered an event. To gather information about the second research objective, we did not put hard constraints on the syntax. Hence, participants could use as many rule elements as desired, ordering them as they prefer (for instance, adding another "event" check after an action). They could link them freely by defining the "next operator" as they prefer, and also complete the other field in a way that better fits their automation idea. In this way, using a plausible but flexible syntax, we could elicit participants' desired automations and which operators would be necessary to formalize them, without restricting this process to a specific language or user interface.

3.3 Participants

The participants in the user study were recruited from a Digital Humanities degree course. Thirty-four users (eleven males) with ages ranging between 23 and 29 years were involved in the study. During their degree studies, they were exposed to Web Programming courses, but they had no experience in IoT (besides using widespread devices such as Amazon Echo) or trigger-action programming.

During the first encounter, which occurred in person, participants were introduced to the interactions with the Internet of Things and to trigger-action programming. They were presented with key concepts such as the distinction between events and conditions and with some examples of common automations. In a second briefer meeting, the key concepts from the first one were recalled, and then they were instructed about their tasks.

3.4 Collected Data

Participants overall produced 204 automations, comprised of the structured and natural language descriptions of the functionality they wanted to express. The structured rules included overall 735 "rule elements" (every single row in the rule structure table, on average 3.603 elements per rule). The dataset containing the automations generated in both structures has been uploaded on GitHub [20].

Some high-level observations can be made from a first look at the natural language descriptions. Two main strategies were used in describing the automations. Participants used both a direct style, as if they were asking the system to perform the actions ("then activate"; "make the fridge suggest recipes from its contents"; "tell Alexa to do this"), and a more impersonal style, describing the situation in the environment that results when the actions execute ("the watering mechanism is activated"; "the cameras turn on and alarm notifications are activated"). We can also distinguish between automations described using a rule-like style ("if this, then do that") and with a more descriptive style ("assuming the house has an entrance door with a smart handle, make sure that…"). Furthermore, in some cases they described the rule indicating that its triggering directly depends on the user, environment, or device state or action, without the mediation of a sensing layer ("if the user is studying"; "if it's raining"; "when it's 8:00"; "if the kitchen temperature is below 17 degrees"), while in other they specify that the sensor is the subject that is performing the check that may lead to the triggering of the automation ("when the bed sensor detects the user"; "when the sensor measures soil humidity below 60%"). Participants seldom used specific brands of devices, mostly for voice assistants, cleaning robots and gaming consoles (respectively 14, 3 and 2 occurrences). In some cases, participants used vague descriptions, both for the trigger part ("when the courier is near", "the house is not yet warm and it is cold outside") and the action part ("make the water very cold"). We counted 4 definitions of this kind, while in most cases, they specified a precise value. Other preliminary observations concern how users used the optional context field. Eight users have used this field to further describe their automations.

Examples of these descriptions are "every morning", "any morning when an alarm is set", "winter months only", and "term time".

To make data more understandable, we then analyse these automations to define some classes to group them. We defined a new "Use case category" class from a combination of the "Channel" and the "Functionality" columns. This new definition comprised 22 "middle level" categories (higher than the single functionality but more concrete than the final goal), obtained by grouping the most frequent and conceptually near functionalities defined by participants. This classification has been done considering the gathered data, and how channels have been combined in related work [12, 32]. For analysing the "Goal" and "Environment" fields, we instead directly use the user-assigned keywords (1 or at most 2 in the case of "Goal"), merging them when they represent the same concept (e.g. "Marco's room" and "Kid room"). Then, we analysed the relations between categories, goals and environments.

3.5 Limitations

About the limitations of this study, one aspect to note is that participants have similar backgrounds. This could have impacted the variety and the choice of functionalities in the automation rules that they produced. Another thing to consider is that participants may have been influenced by the example automations and by the rule structure provided to them. However, having one week to collect the automations should have allowed them to reflect on their daily situations instead of repeating examples. Also, we asked them to define first the rule in a spontaneous way using natural language, and not using the specific rule language to prevent its structure from affecting the reasoning.

4 Analysis

After having provided an overview of the collected data, in this section we will analyse them considering both the structured rules and the natural language descriptions generated by participants.

4.1 What Functionalities Do People Expect from a Smart Home System?

Once a categorization for the functionalities was defined, we started to analyse the relations between them. In the case of doubts, we cross-checked the rule structure with its natural language description to disambiguate the behaviour intended by the participant. Some initial insights can be obtained by considering the frequencies and percentages of the classes in all positions of a rule, in the trigger part, and in the action part (see Table 2).

It can be observed that participants defined the trigger parts making wide use of the "presence" and "scheduling" classes, together accounting for more than 40% of all trigger instances. Rules using the presence trigger involved mainly checking if the user is at home, but also in a specific room or position such as near the window, and also to indicate a generic person (e.g. for detecting a presence in the garden). The scheduling trigger has been used both as a condition (limiting the execution of an automation to a specific

Table 2. The identified classes with their use in frequency and percentage in the trigger and action part of the rules.

	count (all)	% (all)	count (t)	% (t)	count (a)	% (a)
Feeding	30	4.1	18	4.7	12	3.4
Alarm	11	1.5	3	0.8	8	2.3
Hygiene	42	5.7	18	4.7	24	6.9
Device	48	6.5	17	4.4	31	8.9
Door and window	45	6.1	19	4.9	26	7.4
Temperature	45	6.1	21	5.5	24	6.9
Air and humidity	16	2.2	13	3.4	3	0.9
Gardening	9	1.2	1	0.3	8	2.3
Lights	50	6.8	7	1.8	43	12.3
Notification	81	11	0	0	81	23.1
Systems	31	4.2	9	2.3	22	6.3
User detection	30	4.1	30	7.8	0	0
Smart object	27	3.7	13	3.4	14	4
Personal device	11	1.5	7	1.8	4	1.1
Communication	9	1.2	0	0	9	2.6
Kids	12	1.6	6	1.6	6	1.7
Scheduling	91	12.4	82	21.3	9	2.6
Presence	73	9.9	73	19	0	0
Pets	18	2.4	11	2.9	7	2
Entrances	30	4.1	17	4.4	13	3.7
Data	13	1.8	7	1.8	6	1.7
Weather	13	1.8	13	3.4	0	0

time) as well as an event (to start the further condition checks or the action part). For the action part, the "notification" functionality and, to a lesser extent, the "light" controls were the most used. An insight into the relations between the classes can be obtained by considering, for each automation, when a class is found together with another and then assessing the phi correlation between them (see Fig. 1). A weak positive correlation has been found between the "gardening" and "air and humidity" functionalities (due to the relatively common automations that activate the sprinklers when the humidity of the terrains is under a certain value), and a weak negative correlation between the "notifications" and "lights". Since these two classes represent the most used actions, we can infer that a good portion of automations gravitates around one or the other of these functionalities.

There are other positive and negative relations that, although do not represent a correlation or are very weak, can give some insight into other common use cases. Some

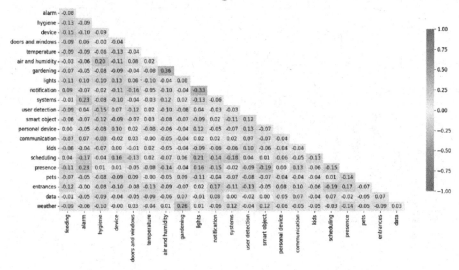

Fig. 1. Phi correlation between the classes, calculated from the frequencies of their joint occurrences in automations.

examples are between "alarms" and "systems" (mostly representing safety and security rules, activating alarms and other prevention systems when users leave home or making emergency calls when problems in the house are detected), "air and humidity" and "hygiene" (mostly automations to circulate air in the house, to prevent mould or smells) "scheduling" and "devices" (e.g., activating the robot cleaner or the music player at a specific time, or dimming the light when the ebook reader is in use in the evening), "gardening" and "weather" (often related to not activating sprinklers when it is raining).

To further analyse the automations, we then look for relations between functionality classes and rule goals, and functionalities and environments. Regarding the class–goal relation, considering the absolute number of occurrences (see Fig. 2) we can observe the high presence of the "comfort" goal, being the most selected in most of the classes (all except alarms, systems, communication, kids, and entrances). Other connections (total occurrences equals or more than 15) emerge between "presence" with "energy saving" and "safety" rules, "well-being" with "temperature", and "security" with "presence" and "entrances".

Considering the frequency count, the top-3 most common functionality classes for each goal are respectively scheduling, lights and devices (11 and 5 occurrences) for the social goal; temperature, notifications, scheduling and presence (15, 14, and 10) for wellbeing; scheduling, devices and notifications (8, 6 and 5) for organizing; scheduling, presence and notification (58, 32 and 30) for comfort; notifications, kids and systems (12, 9 and 9) for safety; notifications, user detections and temperature (14, 10 and 9) for health. Regarding relations between environments and categories, we observed stronger ties between "no specific location" with the "scheduling" and "notification" classes (57 and 50 occurrences respectively). Other relations are in "kitchen" rules with feeding (28 occurrences), "entire home" with "presence" (22) and "doors and windows" (21), "bathroom" rules with "hygiene" (21), "living room" with "devices" (19) and "bedroom"

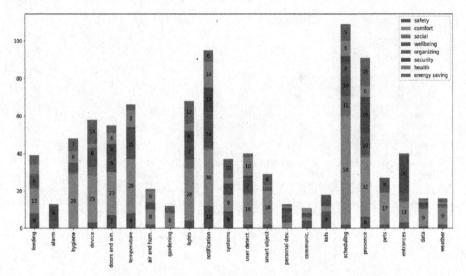

Fig. 2. Frequencies for the goals in each class (only counts >5 are shown).

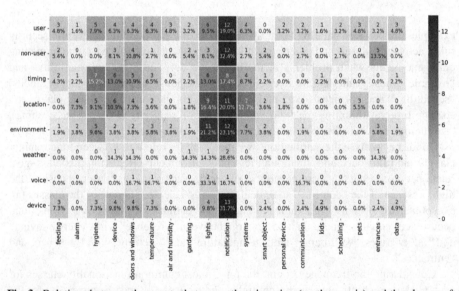

Fig. 3. Relations between the events that cause the triggering (on the y-axis) and the classes of actions (x-axis).

with "scheduling" (16). Another investigated relation is between the events that could trigger the rule and the category of the actions in that rule. From Fig. 3, it can be observed that the "notification" action can be found transversally in all triggering classes. This is not the case for the other actions, which are overall less present and more sparse.

4.2   Which TAP Operators and Structures are Necessary to Express These Behaviours?

Operators for Values and Between Rule Elements. Regarding how participants defined the "next operator" field, the "and" operator was by far the most common. It was commonly used to connect both elements in the trigger (170 occurrences) and in the action part (109 occurrences). By comparison, the "or" operator was found only 11 times. Other used operators were the "iteration"/"every X minutes" (to specify how often a trigger check or an action should be repeated), the "while t < T" (to indicate that an action should remain active for a given period), and the "and after X minutes". The "do" operator was used five times, to indicate when the end of the trigger part and the start of the action, or to signal multiple actions. Also, the "while" operator was used two times to indicate a sustained action [22] temporally linked to a condition, for instance, "while the user is cooking activate the hob extractor fan". Considering also the natural language descriptions, "While" was overall used six times, all the times with this connotation. Regarding the operator field, the "equal" operator was the most used (577 times). Other commonly used operators were more and less than, more equal and less equal, not, and between. Besides these standard operators, the "for" was used in 3 occurrences to indicate a period associated with conditions ("for 10 min").

Standard and Non-Standard Rule Constructs. To further analyse the rules constructs, we needed to define some properties to allow us to discriminate between "standard" and "peculiar" user-generated automation. After reviewing the relevant literature to understand how automations are typically composed, we set the list of properties that defines a "standard" rule, which is:

- Rules comprised by one or more events joined by the "or" operator, with optionally one or more conditions joined by the "and" or the "or" operator, and one or more actions, joined implicitly by the "and" operator, or by another operator if specified.
- Alternatively, rules comprised of one or more conditions joined by the "and" or the "or" operator, and one or more actions, joined implicitly by the "and" operator.
- Rules including basic operators to characterize a value, such as equal, more/more equal than, less/less equal than, between (e.g., between 9 AM and 10 AM), and the negation and the "different from" operators (e.g., if it is not raining).
- Rules that do not require more structured (such as making another event check after an action) and advanced constructs (e.g., call to external routines that synchronize actions).

Overall, 50 out of the 204 automations produced were "non-standard". To describe these functionalities, participants used and modified the standard keywords and constructs, for instance adding "and (after 5 min)" as "next operator" between two actions or adding a new event after an action. The recurring constructs identified in these peculiar rules will be discussed in the following.

Timing Aspects of Triggers. The most conspicuous aspect is the frequent presence of automations that require some advanced temporally based check. Overall, 19 of these non-standard rules identified needed an additional precise temporal specification in the trigger part. Among these, common cases were automations requiring a check (that may eventually lead to rule activation) to be performed at the end of a defined period. This interval can be indicated by a condition (Fig. 4, example 1) or by the non verification of an event (Fig. 4, example 2).

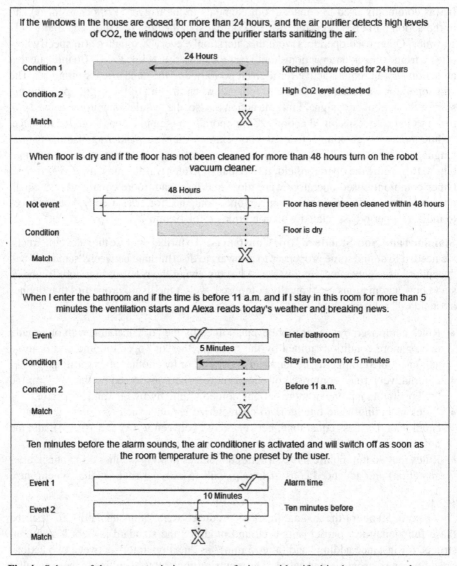

Fig. 4. Scheme of the common timing aspects of triggers identified in the user-created automations.

From a structural perspective, in these cases, the same automation can be written using a condition or negated event (referring to the first two examples in Fig. 4, the alternatives are "the windows have never been opened in the last 24 h" and "the robot cleaner has been off within the last 48 h"). also, in some cases, the temporal audit was made in relation to another event. these checks were described both as "forward" (see Fig. 4 example 3, where the system should check for the state of a condition within a time frame, starting from when another event occurred) or "backward" (whether the temporally bounded event verifies in an interval before the other one, as the example 4 in Fig. 4).

Non-explicit Timing Aspects of Triggers. Another timing aspect of the trigger part was found in automations that did not set a specific time interval but used or implied some timing operator, such as a sequence between the parts of the trigger (for instance indicated by "after that" or "before that") or a time buffer. Without this specification, the rule could not be activated or would not behave as the user expected. For instance, "I don't want the stoves to be turned off each time I exit the kitchen, but only when I forget to turn them off." This automation hence implies a period where stoves are on and unattended. We considered rules where participants used the terms "forgot" or "remains" to describe these types of behaviours (4 instances), and automations that require that the check between the triggers not be immediate but wait for the other trigger to happen, or occur in a non-fixed period before the other (2 occurrences). Another used description is to perform an action at the end of a state (4 occurrences). Below are some examples of user-created automations with these constructs.

- If the refrigerator remains open, send a message to your cell phone.
- When (after that) the car enters the garage, and if the parked car does not move for 10 s, the garage door closes automatically, and the lights come on.
- When I finish taking a shower, turn on the stove in the room at 25°.

Timing Aspects of Actions. Temporal aspects can also be found in actions (8 occurrences). This type of rule involves for instance setting a delayed notification or programming a set of actions in the future (such as opening the blinds gradually at time intervals). For example:

- When it is 21:00, if the user has not yet called the home number of his grandparents, send a text message with the words «How are you?», then after 5 min turn off the TV and start a call to their number.
- If the backrest is raised and our user does not get up, then after five minutes the alarm goes off, and the backrest starts to vibrate.

Programming-like Constructs. A different class of structures (6 occurrences) involves some more advanced, programming-like constructs, such as "if-then-else" (when the trigger verifies, if this condition is true then do this, else if this other condition is true...), parenthesis to defining compound Boolean conditions in the trigger part, or counters and accumulators. Below are some examples of these constructs (the first is an "if-then-else" rule, the second needs parentheses, and the last one use a counter of how many times an action has been activated during the day). For example:

- When the user passes his hands under the automatic soap dispenser, if the soap is finished a small red light turns on; if instead the soap is present a small green light turns on and the soap is dispensed.

- When it is 11 pm on a weekday or 2 am on a public holiday, if the user is not at home, turn off the lights, and lock the windows and the door.
- When the button on the bowl is pressed and if daily food dispenses are less than three then the bowl speaker voice notification says "Bravo" and releases food.

Routines and Rules Concatenations. In this group of automations (n = 7) participants envision the possibility of using advanced synchronizations of triggers or actions, such as a digital assistant that can interact with online services to buy the required medicines after the doctor sends the prescription, or create routines consisting of other triggers that have to be checked after the actions of the first part of the automation have completed. For example:

- If the house temperature is not higher than 17°, turn up the heating and then check the air humidity level, if the humidity is lower than 35% activate the humidifier.
- If the user has not taken the medicines between 08:00 and 09:00, send a notification to the smartphone, and if the user has not given any confirmation of reading, activate the voice notification from the Bluetooth speakers.
- When the user is unwell, if the Smart Watch reports a body temperature above 37°, send a text message to the doctor to get a prescription for a medicine and (then) contact the pharmacy to have it sent home.

Groups. In three rules, participants imply the possibility of creating groups for types of objects and services, for instance, "all the children's devices" or "all the social media platforms".

- When it's 11 pm, and the kids' devices are in use, turn off the lights and send a reminder to turn off devices and go to bed.

5 Discussion and Conclusions

The analysis of the automation rules defined by the participants allowed us to identify some general implications that can support the design of new tailoring environments for TAP that are more capable of matching users' needs. The first is that more attention should be paid to how users can define the timing aspects between rule elements, especially in the trigger part. Participants expressed many behaviours that require different types of temporal occurrences, but often commercial products such as IFTTT do not allow the specification of temporal relations such as "at the end of a period", or "if this does not occur within this period". Furthermore, these aspects have also received little attention from research. A first approach for defining complex timing relations that also consider how end users can understand and use these constructs in a smart home context is CCBL [31]. The prototype handles temporal aspects using a subset of Allen's interval Algebra [1] operators, but can only manage automations based on a hierarchical organization of states. Another possible approach could be using the set of temporal operators for detecting complex events defined in [19] and tested in [2, 21]. In addition to the temporal aspects, participants defined automations that require concepts more advanced than the ones usually definable with ECA syntax, such as the "if-then-else" construct, complex Boolean conditions requiring parenthesis, using iterators or performing some further event check after the activation of an action. Although these possibilities can enrich the expressive capabilities of the TAP rules, it should be considered whether the introduction of these further capabilities would impact the easiness to use of the platform for all users. For instance, a balanced solution could offer both simple and more complex modelling options [7, 32]. This makes also critical the research of tools to simplify the management of automations, such as debuggers [11, 24] or visualizations [36] for making the rule-checking sequence more perceivable and graspable. Another related aspect that emerges is that participants used different approaches for describing the behaviour they wanted to implement using natural language. For instance, they described conditions linked to sustained actions using both the "while" and the "if" terms. Also, no uniqueness emerges for selecting a keyword for events and conditions, and although the terms "when" and "if" were the most frequently used, participants sometimes mixed them. Indeed, it is still not completely clear how to transmit the fundamental concept of the distinction between events and conditions. Recent work [15, 35] started to clarify which terms lead to a better understanding of this distinction, but also other linguistic cues could be used to guide users in shaping effective mental models. These observations should be taken into account when specifying how the platform displays the automations, or in designing conversational agents for creating automation rules. Regarding the user-specified context, a limited number of participants defined this field. Although not particularly used in this study, this specification could be helpful in realistic situations to understand when a rule should be enabled. For instance, one user indicated "school time" as context for an automation that activates Alexa to ask the student whether he really wants to play with the Playstation when it is study time, which should be deactivated during the summer, hence reducing the possible interferences [18] and simplifying the monitoring and debugging of the active automations. Concerning the rule goals, an observation is the wide-spreading of the "comfort" goal. Another is that only the "well-being" and the "comfort" goals have a complete overlap of the top-3 most frequent functionality classes. This means that the final goal of a rule can give us some hints on the functionalities that will be required. Together with the patterns between the functionality classes that emerged, these are clues that a recommender system exploiting these patterns could be useful to speed up and simplify the rule composition.

Regarding the directions for future work, this analysis shows that there is a gap between the apparent simplicity of the trigger-action rules and the nuanced functionalities that it could be possible to implement with them, for example by using in combination events, conditions, and temporal operators. There is hence the need to further investigate how to enable users to take advantage of these features. Another aspect to investigate is whether a solution where these interactions are explained in detail (for example, showing how the system carries out the "check" of an automation) is more effective or whether it would be better to abstract this complexity from the users and manage it automatically. Also, how to personalize these approaches for a specific user (for instance, providing recommendations/explanations and gracefully increasing the available options) should be inquired. Finally, further studies should consider novel approaches to TAP, for instance, combining EUD paradigms with AR/VR and conversational-based interaction technologies, assessing their strong and weak points, and implementing them into novel EUD platforms.

In conclusion, we have presented the design and the results of a study aimed at exploring the functionalities that users expect from smart homes, and the constructs and operators necessary to specify these behaviours. From the analysis of the created automations, we identify some common functionalities that users expect, the long-term goals for which they created these rules, and the relations between goals and functionalities. Furthermore, the analysis provides indications of the "non-standard" constructs necessary to implement these functionalities. We believe that this information can be useful in designing future EUD systems for smart home environments.

Acknowledgements. This work has been supported by the PRIN 2017 "EMPATHY: Empowering People in Dealing with Internet of Things Ecosystems", https://www.empathy-project.eu/.

References

1. Allen, J.F.: Maintaining knowledge about temporal intervals. Commun. ACM **26**(11), 832–843 (1983)
2. Augusto, J.C., Chris, D.N.: The use of temporal reasoning and management of complex events in smart homes. In: ECAI, vol. 16, p. 778 (2004)
3. Bak, N., Chang, B.M., Choi, K.:Smart block: a visual programming environment for smart-things. In: 2018 IEEE 42nd Annual Computer Software and Applications Conference (COMPSAC), vol. 2, pp. 32–37. IEEE (2018)
4. Barricelli, B.R., Valtolina, S.: Designing for end-user development in the internet of things. In: Díaz, P., Pipek, V., Ardito, C., Jensen, C., Aedo, I., Boden, A. (eds.) IS-EUD 2015. LNCS, vol. 9083, pp. 9–24. Springer, Cham (2015). https://doi.org/10.1007/978-3-319-18425-8_2
5. Brackenbury, W., et al.: How users interpret bugs in trigger-action programming. In: Proceedings of the 2019 CHI Conference on Human Factors in Computing Systems (CHI '19). Association for Computing Machinery, New York, NY, USA, Article Paper 552, vol. 12 (2019). https://doi.org/10.1145/3290605.330078
6. Breve, B., Cimino, G., Deufemia, V.: Identifying security and privacy violation rules in trigger-action IoT platforms with NLP models. IEEE Internet Things J. **10**(6), 5607–5622 (2023)
7. Brich, J., Walch, M., Rietzler, M., Weber, M., Schaub, F.: Exploring end user programming needs in home automation. ACM Trans. Comput-Hum. Interact. (TOCHI) **24**(2), 1–35 (2017)
8. Cabitza, F., Daniela, F., Rosa, L., Antonio, P.: Rule-based tools for the configuration of ambient intelligence systems: a comparative user study. Multimedia Tools Appl. **76**, 5221–5241 (2017). https://doi.org/10.1007/s11042-016-3511-2
9. Chen, X., Xiaolu, Z., Michael, E., Xiaoyin, W., Feng, W.: Fix the leaking tap: a survey of trigger-action programming (tap) security issues, detection techniques and solutions. Comput. Secur. **120**, 102812 (2022)
10. Corno, F., De Russis, L., Roffarello, A.M.: A high-level semantic approach to end-user development in the internet of things. Int. J. Hum Comput Stud. **125**, 41–54 (2019)
11. Corno, F., De Russis, L., Roffarello, A.M.: Empowering end users in debugging trigger-action rules. In: Proceedings of the 2019 CHI Conference on Human Factors in Computing Systems, pp. 1–13 (2019)
12. Corno, F., Luigi De, R., Alberto, M.R.: How do end-users program the internet of things?. Behav. Inf. Technol. **41**(9), 1865–1887 (2022)
13. Demeure, A., Caffiau, S., Elias, E., Roux, C.: Building and using home automation systems: a field study. In: Díaz, P., Pipek, V., Ardito, C., Jensen, C., Aedo, I., Boden, A. (eds.) IS-EUD 2015. LNCS, vol. 9083, pp. 125–140. Springer, Cham (2015). https://doi.org/10.1007/978-3-319-18425-8_9

14. Desolda, G., Ardito, C., Matera, M.: Empowering end users to customize their smart environments: model, composition paradigms, and domain-specific tools. ACM Trans. Comput.-Hum. Interact. (TOCHI) **24**(2), 1–52 (2017)

15. Desolda, G., Greco, F., Guarnieri, F., Mariz, N., Zancanaro, M.: SENSATION: an authoring tool to support event–state paradigm in end-user development. In: Ardito, C., et al. (eds.) INTERACT 2021. LNCS, vol. 12933, pp. 373–382. Springer, Cham (2021). https://doi.org/10.1007/978-3-030-85616-8_22

16. Fogli, D., Matteo, P., Claudia, S.: Smart home control through unwitting trigger-action programming. In: Proceedings of the 22nd Conference on Distributed Multimedia Systems (DMS), pp. 194–201 (2016)

17. Fogli, D., Peroni, M., Stefini, C.: ImAtHome: making trigger-action programming easy and fun. J. Vis. Lang. Comput. **42**, 60–75 (2017)

18. Funk, M., Chen, L.-L., Yang, S.-W., Chen, Y.-K.: Addressing the need to capture scenarios, intentions and preferences: interactive intentional programming in the smart home. Int. J. Des. **12**(1), 53–66 (2018)

19. Galton, A.: Eventualities. Foundations of Artificial Intelligence, pp. 25–58 (2005). https://doi.org/10.1016/S1574-6526(05)80004-5

20. GitHub. https://github.com/andrematt/trigger_action_rules. Accessed 14 Apr 2023

21. Gómez, R., Juan, C.A., Antony, G.: Testing an event specification language. In: SEKE, pp. 341–345 (2001)

22. Huang, J., Cakmak, M.: Supporting mental model accuracy in trigger-action programming. In: Proceedings of the 2015 ACM International Joint Conference on Pervasive and Ubiquitous Computing - UbiComp 2015, pp. 215–225. ACM Press, Osaka, Japan (2015). https://doi.org/10.1145/2750858.2805830

23. Manca, M., Fabio, P., Carmen, S.: Remote monitoring of end-user creat-ed automations in field trials. J. Ambient Intell. Hum. Comput. **13**, 1–29 (2021). https://doi.org/10.1007/s12652-021-03239-0

24. Manca, M., Paternò, F., Santoro, C., Corcella, L.: Supporting end-user debugging of trigger-action rules for IoT applications. Int. J. Hum Comput Stud. **123**, 56–69 (2019)

25. Mattioli, A., Paternò, F.: A visual environment for end-user creation of IoT customization rules with recommendation support. In: Proceedings of the International Conference on Advanced Visual Interfaces, pp. 1–5 (2020)

26. Mi, X., Feng, Q., Ying, Z., XiaoFeng, W.: An empirical characterization of IFTTT: ecosystem, usage, and performance. In: Proceedings of the 2017 Internet Measurement Conference, pp. 398–404 (2017)

27. Prange, S., Florian, A.: I wish you were smart (er): investigating users' desires and needs towards home appliances. In: Extended Abstracts of the 2020 CHI Conference on Human Factors in Computing Systems, pp. 1–8 (2020)

28. Salovaara, A., Bellucci, A., Vianello, A., Jacucci, G.: Programmable smart home toolkits should better address households' social needs. In: Proceedings of the 2021 CHI Confer-ence on Human Factors in Computing Systems, pp. 1–14 (2021)

29. Soares, D., Dias, J.P., Restivo, A., Ferreira, H.S.: Programming IoT-spaces: a user-survey on home automation rules. In: Paszynski, M., Kranzlmüller, D., Krzhizhanovskaya, V.V., Dongarra, J.J., Sloot, P.M.A. (eds.) ICCS 2021. LNCS, vol. 12745, pp. 512–525. Springer, Cham (2021). https://doi.org/10.1007/978-3-030-77970-2_39

30. Statista, Number of IoT connected devices worldwide 2019–2021 with forecasts to 2030. https://www.statista.com/statistics/1183457/iot-connected-devices-worldwide/. Accessed 12 Apr 2023

31. Terrier, L., Alexandre, D., Sybille, C.: Ccbl: a language for better supporting context centered programming in the smart home. In: Proceedings of the ACM on Human-Computer Interaction 1, no. EICS, pp. 1–18 (2017)

32. Ur, B., McManus, E., Pak Yong Ho, M., Littman, M.L.:Practical trig-ger-action programming in the smart home. In: Proceedings of the SIGCHI conference on human factors in computing systems, pp. 803–812 (2014)
33. Ur, B., et al.: Trigger-action programming in the wild: an analysis of 200,000 ifttt recipes. In: Proceedings of the 2016 CHI Conference on Hu-man Factors in Computing Systems, pp. 3227–3231 (2016)
34. Yu, H., Jie, H., Christine, J.: Analysis of ifttt recipes to study how humans use internet-of-things (iot) devices. In: Proceedings of the 19th ACM Conference on Em-bedded Networked Sensor Systems, pp. 537–541 (2021)
35. Zancanaro, M., Gallitto, G., Dina, Y., Treccani B.: Improving mental models in IoT end-user development. Hum.-Centric Comput. Inf. Sci. **2**, 48 (2022)
36. Zhao, V., Lefan, Z., Bo, W., Shan, L., Blasé, U.: Visualizing differences to improve end-user understanding of trigger-action programs. In: Extended Abstracts of the 2020 CHI Conference on Human Factors in Computing Systems, pp. 1–10 (2020)

Privacy, Security and Society

Democratizing Cybersecurity in Smart Environments: Investigating the Mental Models of Novices and Experts

Bernardo Breve[1], Giuseppe Desolda[2(✉)], Francesco Greco[2], and Vincenzo Deufemia[1]

[1] Computer Science Department, University of Salerno, Fisciano, Italy
[2] Computer Science Department, University of Bari Aldo Moro, Bari, Italy
giuseppe.desolda@uniba.it

Abstract. As the Internet of Things (IoT) technology continues to grow, more and more people with no technical expertise are demanding the ability to get the most out of smart devices according to their level of knowledge. To meet user needs, task automation systems (TAS) are used to customize the behavior of IoT devices by defining trigger-action rules. However, while TASs allow different types of behavior to be defined, they do not address the aspects that can make smart devices vulnerable to security and privacy threats. To truly democratize cybersecurity in smart environments, TAS should enable end users (both experts and novices) to protect their devices from external threats. To design TASs that are effective for both types of users, it is necessary to investigate how they differ in the definition of rules in natural language. This research aims to contribute to this issue by investigating the mental models of cybersecurity novices and experts when faced with the need to protect their smart environment from security and privacy threats through the definition of security-oriented rules.

Keywords: Task Automation Systems · Cybersecurity · IoT · Design Principles

1 Introduction

Smart home environments today are characterized by the presence of several interconnected devices, called smart objects, favored by the breakthrough revolution provided by the Internet of Things (IoT). These devices, through a combination of sensors and actuators, can interact, more or less autonomously, with smart environments and their users, creating complex ecosystems [1]. Thanks to this new technological paradigm, tasks such as being able to access the recordings of a smart camera, or automating the turning on of lights when motion is detected, have become a well-established reality, allowing for the simplification of tasks previously thought to be complex to accomplish [2].

The wide diffusion of this new technological paradigm has also seen the involvement of that user group characterized by individuals with little to no technical knowledge of IT, who need to be able to access these features even though they do not fully understand the

L. D. Spano et al. (Eds.): IS-EUD 2023, LNCS 13917, pp. 145–161, 2023.
https://doi.org/10.1007/978-3-031-34433-6_9

logic of their operation. To this end, the deployment of Task Automation Systems (TASs) has provided end-users with a set of tools to simplify the definition of interoperability mechanisms between smart devices by means of Trigger-Action Programming (TAP), which facilitates the visual definition of the so-called Event-Condition-Action (ECA) rules. The TAP paradigm enables the definition of automatic behaviors by specifying the action to be performed in response to an event for which the condition is satisfied [3]. This paradigm has been also proposed to define the behavior of complex smart environments [4].

However, the ease of use of TAS and IoT devices, in general, is not without risks attributable to security and privacy. Indeed, the need for compact, wireless, and easily usable devices for all categories of users makes these devices an attractive target for malicious individuals [5]. This is further exacerbated if we consider the average level of knowledge possessed by end-users, who are very often unaware of the vulnerabilities to which smart environments are exposed and are not motivated in taking action in protecting their devices from external threats [6]. Moreover, sometimes is the user, when defining behaviors through TASs, that creates automations that introduce vulnerabilities leading, for example, to the leakage of sensitive data or tampering with an IoT device [7, 8].

Recently, approaches for usable security and privacy issues in TASs have received considerable attention from researchers, proposing end-user-oriented solutions for safeguarding smart environments [9–11]. Among them, in [11], the authors proposed a visual paradigm allowing end-users to create ECA rules that serve as a countermeasure against cyberattacks on IoT devices. By using an ad-hoc device to monitor the security state of a smart environment, the authors allow the end-users to define, through a TAS, rules such as "IF there is a virus threat for a smart device, THEN turn off the device". The authors conducted a user study to evaluate the performance of both users that were experts in cybersecurity and IT and lay users with no programming experience. The results showed that both types of users were able to create correct rules to defend their smart environments against cyberattacks: the sole difference resided in the greater amount of time spent by lay users to compose some of the rules.

Despite providing a valuable comparison between the capability of novices to achieve the definition of rules as an expert user would do, the study presented in [11] evaluates both the category of users under the same circumstances, as the type of events available is strictly dependent on the constructs made available by the proposed visual paradigm. Moreover, the security-related events that the participants could use in their rules were the result of a card-sorting process, and not of a user study. Two out of the six events were indeed considered ambiguous and led to confusion among the participants.

Considering the limitations identified in the literature, to foster a wider democratization of cybersecurity in smart environments, the study presented in this paper explores the mental models of cybersecurity novices and experts. Specifically, we aim to understand how users with different backgrounds in cybersecurity would design the so-called "security-event triggered rules". Specifically, we conducted a study in the form of a survey to understand the differences in the mental models of both cybersecurity experts and novices in creating ECA rules that define security in a smart home. The survey involved 32 participants (18 experts, 14 novices), and the results were evaluated through a thematic analysis. The emerged themes lead to the identification of 5 lessons learned for the design of EUD systems that allow users to manage the security of their smart environments.

The paper's contributions are organized as follows: related works are discussed in Sect. 2. In Sect. 3, we present the design of our study. In Sect. 4, we present the results of the thematic analysis, while in Sect. 5 we propose the lesson learned in terms of possible applications for designing TASs enabling end-users to secure smart environments. Finally, in Sect. 6, we draw the conclusion and future directions of our research.

2   Background and Related Work

In this section, we briefly review the state of the art concerning two main research topics at the base of this study, namely, the relationship between IoT and Cybersecurity, and the advancement of End-User Development (EUD) solutions to Cybersecurity concerns.

2.1   IoT and Cybersecurity Concerns

Concerns and related risks arising from the use of IoT devices have been widely addressed in the literature, which has highlighted several vulnerabilities that have led to the definition of concrete threat models [12, 13].

Providing adequate protection for devices that are limited in computation, power, and storage is a particularly complex task to achieve [14, 15]. These vulnerabilities become even more significant when taking into account end users' perceptions of these risks. For instance, Ion et al. conducted a study on the security measures deemed crucial by both experts and novices for safeguarding their security within smart environments and also online [16]. These measures encompassed software updates installation, antivirus software usage, account security (utilizing password managers, writing down passwords, changing passwords frequently, and applying two-factor authentication), as well as mindfulness (visiting only known websites, verifying if HTTPS is being used, deleting browser cookies, and adopting safe email habits). The findings revealed significant variations in the security practices regarded as most important by experts and novices, with the latter deeming such countermeasures unnecessary or overly conservative. This study was then taken up 4 years later by [17], who extended the study by assessing end users' perceptions of certain security practices. The results showed that there was no significant difference in the improvement of the mental model by end users, believing that the usable security community failed in its intent to convey sufficient awareness of the severity of cyberattacks.

According to [5], IoT environments should improve users' technology threat models, which enable the conscious management of privacy or security risks and communicate best practices suitable for smart spaces. In their study, the authors aimed to investigate end-users' perceptions of privacy risks and the measures taken to protect privacy from external entities, identifying recurring themes such as users' preference for convenience and connectedness influencing their privacy-related behaviors.

He et al. propose the use of a capability-centric model to match access control and authentication mechanisms to the different capabilities and features of smart objects

[18]. This model enables more precise and restricted access, such as allowing users to perform only specific actions, like turning a device on or off or updating software, instead of granting complete access. Additionally, contextual factors, such as the user's proximity to the smart space, should be taken into account when determining access to smart objects' capabilities.

2.2 End-User Development for Cybersecurity

TASs can pose serious risks to both user privacy and the security of smart environments, as rules created through these platforms may hide unexpected behaviors that end-users may not notice due to their lack of technical knowledge [9, 19]. Understanding how users perceive these risks is crucial, and various studies have been conducted to investigate this topic.

Surbatovich *et al.* [7] analyzed a dataset containing 19k + IFTTT rules, utilizing a multi-level lattice that assigns security labels to IFTTT triggers and actions. They applied information flow analysis to identify any potential secrecy or integrity violations caused by the rules. Their findings indicated that approximately half of the applets analyzed were deemed unsafe. Additionally, they manually classified a random subset of applets based on the potential issues they could cause, with around 60% of them being involved in some form of violation.

Their study has been further deepened in [19] where the authors incorporated two additional factors when identifying harmful rules - the context in which the rules are applied and users' privacy preferences. The results of a user study involving 28 IFTTT users and 732 rules showed a significant decrease in the number of the ones initially deemed harmful when considering users' opinions in comparison to the earlier study.

The impact of contextual factors has been evaluated also in the study by Saeidi *et al.* [20], where the authors surveyed 386 participants on 49 smart-home IFTTT rules and found that users were generally not very concerned about using the rules. However, several concerns arose for certain types of rules, where users were asked to consider also contextual factors, such as those involving location data. To address the need for end-users to effectively manage and comprehend the security and privacy risks associated with creating trigger-action rules, efforts have been dedicated to developing ad-hoc solutions that enable end-users to identify and mitigate these risks.

Breve *et al.* proposed the application of NLP techniques for identifying security and privacy issue underlying ECA rules by analyzing their textual components [8, 21], on the other hand, presented two information flow analysis techniques aimed at identifying rules that inadvertently breach users' privacy by distributing personal photos [21].

iRULER is a system proposed by Wang *et al.* that can detect various interference conditions between trigger-action rules, such as action loops (when a rule is cyclically activated) or condition blocks (when a rule's condition is unsatisfiable) [22].

A3ID is a tool developed by Xiao *et al.*, that can detect implicit interferences between rules, where two or more rules are activated at the same time, resulting in conflicting effects on the environment [10]. A3ID utilizes NLP techniques to extract information from knowledge graphs about smart devices, such as their functionality, scope, and effect; such information is then combined to identify any threat.

Finally, ProvThings is a tool that tracks data provenance to provide explanations for the chain behavior of rules [9].

3   Method

The analysis of the literature highlights that TAP programming is widely used to allow novices to define the behavior of IoT devices, especially in smart environments. We also highlighted the high cybersecurity risks that the proliferation of this technology creates. Therefore, it is important to enable all users, both experts and especially novices, to be aware of such risks and, in general, to refine countermeasures.

These motivations led us to explore the mental model of both cybersecurity experts and novices in defining security countermeasures for smart environments by using TAP programming. A mental model is an individual's internal representation of the world, including beliefs, assumptions, and expectations about how things work [23]. In the context of human-computer interaction (HCI), mental models are particularly relevant because they influence how users interact with technology, interpret feedback, and make decisions. By eliciting mental models, designers and researchers can gain insight into users' thought processes and develop interfaces that better match their mental models, leading to improved usability and user experience.

The final goal of this study is to understand how the mental models of cybersecurity experts and novices differ and therefore what TAP solutions should be provided to each of them. This is an aspect that has never been studied before and that deserves attention to truly democratize cybersecurity in smart environments. More formally, our work addresses the following research question: *How does the mental model of novices and experts translate into EUD solutions for the cybersecurity of smart environments?*

To answer our research question, we performed a questionnaire study, which is adequate in eliciting the user's mental model. Then, we carried out an inductive thematic analysis [24] on the qualitative data, i.e., the transcriptions of the participants' answers.

3.1   Participants

A total of 32 participants (F = 7, M = 25) have been recruited through convenience sampling [25] on the social circles of the authors of this article. All participants are Italian. Their mean age was 28.0 years ($\sigma = 8.9$, min $= 20$, max $= 55$). Regarding the participants' level of education, around 90.63% already have a High School Diploma, 68.75% have a bachelor's degree, 18.75% have a master's degree, and 9.38% have a Ph.D. A total of 3 participants (representing the remaining 9.38%) did not provide any information. Regarding the participants' skills, according to the results of the "U.S. Cybersecurity Knowledge" questionnaire [26], 18 participants were experts in cybersecurity while 14 were not. Novices declared that they had a medium experience with IT ($\mu = 2.92/5$, $\sigma = 0.92$, min $= 1/5$, max $= 4/5$) and that they frequently use IoT devices ($\mu = 2.77/5$, $\sigma = 1.12$, min $= 1/5$, max $= 4/5$). Experts, instead, declared that they had a high experience with IT ($\mu = 4.06/5$, $\sigma = 0.85$, min $= 2/5$, max $= 5/5$) and that they frequently use IoT devices ($\mu = 3.61/5$, $\sigma = 1.25$, min $= 2/5$, max $= 5/5$).

3.2 Tasks

A total of 6 attack tasks of increasing complexity have been designed by three authors of this study, both experts in cybersecurity and HCI, taking into account the most common and useful activities that might be required in smart environments to protect IoT devices, as well as the most important attacks against IoT devices in smart homes. Each task was characterized by a short description of the attack, the request to the participant, an ECA rule to be completed, and two optional fields that ask the participant to *i*) motivate the answer and *ii*) indicate if they prefer other ECA rules for the same scenario. For example, the short description of task 1 was "A security camera in Andrea's home could be a target for malicious attackers", the request was "Complete the following rule by defining the action you think should be taken to defend against this attack", and the partial rule to be completed was "Alexa, IF you detect an attack on security cameras, THEN […]". Moreover, for participants that were screened as experts, a further 3 more technical tasks have been proposed. The complete list of all the tasks is reported in Table 1.

3.3 Apparatus and Material

We conducted the study remotely by administering the questionnaire in an online platform that we built specifically for this study. The platform was developed using Laravel 9 and deployed on a virtual machine hosted under the ReCaS cloud infrastructure of the University of Bari. All participants' answers were stored in a MySQL database.

Participants' skills in cybersecurity have been measured by administering the U.S. Cybersecurity Knowledge questionnaire [26]. It is, to the best of our knowledge, the only valid questionnaire used in the literature to distinguish between cybersecurity experts and non-experts. It includes 13 questions that focus on key concepts and basic building blocks that cybersecurity experts consider critical to protecting users online. This questionnaire was integrated into our platform and used to administer the additional 3 tasks to those participants that resulted to be cybersecurity experts, i.e., who scored 8/10 or higher.

3.4 Procedure

The platform guided the participants through the 5 steps required to complete the study. Figure 1 summarizes the workflow of the study. As the first step, when participants opened the link we sent them by email, they were immediately asked to digitally sign a privacy policy. It is worth noting that our universities only require ethics committee approval for medical and clinical studies. For other studies, such as ours, they require written or digital consent from the subjects, so we informed the participants of all the details of the study and asked them to agree before the study began. All agreed.

After giving consent, as the second step, they were asked to complete a demographic questionnaire that asked them their gender, level of education, and age, as well as to answer two 5-point Likert questions about their IT experience and frequency of IoT devices usage. As the third step, they were asked to fill in the U.S. Cybersecurity Knowledge questionnaire [26], which measures cybersecurity skills.

Then, in the fourth step, they were introduced to the basic concepts behind the study, i.e., what is an IoT device, how and why this technology is useful in smart homes, what

Table 1. Summary of all the tasks administered during the questionnaire.

Scenario	Description	ECA rule
1	A security camera in Andrea's home could be a target for malicious attackers	"Alexa, IF you detect an attack on security cameras THEN [...]"
2	The smart TV Andrea has in her living room may be infected with a virus	"Alexa, IF [...] THEN "quarantine" the files on the smart TV and back up the data"
3	Andrea's robot vacuum cleaner could be attacked to steal data and, for example, to reconstruct a map of the house	"Alexa, IF you detect data theft from the robot vacuum cleaner, THEN [...]"
4	An attacker could attempt to break into one of Andrea's smart devices by trying to access it with a variety of username and password combinations	"Alexa, IF [...] THEN [...]"
5	Andrea's router could be scanned by a hacker looking for vulnerabilities and access points to her home network	"Alexa, IF [...] THEN [...]"
6	Alexa can recognize unusual or suspicious activity on devices in the home, such as, for example, opening windows in the middle of the night while Andrea sleeps	"Alexa, IF [...] THEN [...]"
1 expert	One device that a hacker could attack is the smartwatch since it stores sensitive data of the wearer, such as knowing if the wearer is sleeping	"Alexa, IF [...] THEN isolate the smartwatch and send me a notification on the smartwatch"
2 expert	A criminal might try to perform attacks by exploiting an open router port, such as port 22, commonly used for SSH service	"Alexa, IF [...] THEN close router port 22, and set port 2222 for SSH service"
3 expert	Alexa can detect illicit attempts to authenticate to your smart devices (e.g., by detecting connections from unknown IPs) and administrator login activities	"Alexa, [...]"

is TAP programming and how it can be done by defining ECA rules, also providing some examples of ECA rules. In addition, to facilitate the task requests, we presented participants with a scenario that has been carefully designed because it introduces cybersecurity concepts that might result as complex for novices. Specifically, the scenario presented a situation where Andrea has several smart devices in her smart home that can be commanded through Alexa, such as "Alexa, turn on the lights in the living room". The Alexa example was created to project participants into a situation familiar to them and easy to understand. Then, the scenario presents two new (fictional) features that Alexa has introduced. The first concerns the ability to vocally define event-condition-action rules to manage the behavior of smart objects in the home, for example, by saying "Alexa, IF it is raining, THEN close the blinds". The second feature concerns the protection that Alexa offers to all devices connected to the home network, i.e., its ability to monitor all the IoT devices installed in the smart home to detect attacks against them. In the scenario, to introduce participants to the request for the creation of ECA rules, we explained that Alexa also allows Andrea to protect her smart devices by defining ECA rules on security aspects (some basic examples of ECA rules that protect IoT devices were listed in the scenario).

After presenting the scenario, at the fifth and last step, participants were invited to complete the tasks reported in Sect. 3.2. The entire procedure, the scenario, and the 9 tasks have been iteratively validated by further 4 experts and 4 novices. The procedure lasted around 22 min for each participant.

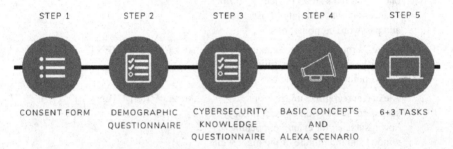

Fig. 1. Workflow of the questionnaire study.

3.5 Data Analysis

The questionnaire responses were analyzed in a systematic qualitative interpretation using inductive thematic analysis. Two researchers, who are co-authors of this study and experienced in qualitative data analysis, followed the 6-step procedure proposed by [24], which includes data familiarization, coding, theme generation, theme verification, theme naming and theme description. Finally, a set of themes was proposed for each item that represented a different dimension for analyzing participants' behavior.

After familiarizing with the data, the researchers started the initial coding independently splitting them into 2 two groups, i.e., by participants expertise. Once all the data were coded, the set of initial codes was further refined by merging similar codes. The identified code groups were then used to extract the main themes. Finally, the sets of codes and themes obtained by each researcher were compared to identify similarities and differences. The initial reliability value was 91%, thus the researchers discussed the differences and reached a full agreement. The process of the grouping of codes is reported in Fig. 2. The code groups that were not grounded in the data (with low support) were discarded. The themes had the goal of answering the research question by highlighting as much as possible the differences between the two user groups. The themes were iteratively refined by the two analysts jointly and were each given a temporary name that would reflect the respective code group's name. The final themes presented here were derived from a joint naming session conducted by all of the authors of this study.

4   Results

The thematic analysis resulted in the description of five themes (Fig. 2), which are presented in the following paragraphs. For each theme, significant quotes from participants are reported. For the sake of brevity, we will refer to participants as 'P' followed by the participant number. Tasks accomplished by the participants will be indicated with a 'T' followed by the task number: T1-T6 are the tasks in common to both expert and novice participants, while T7-T9 are the tasks done by expert participants alone.

Theme 1. Users want to be aware of potential threats. All users, both novices and experts, want to receive alerts about any potential attack that may occur within the smart environment. Sometimes it is even sufficient for them to just receive a notification, without performing any action; for example, P5 (expert) defined for T1 the rule "*call me on the phone and send me a message containing attack information*" to protect themselves from attacks to security cameras. Often, the user creates a rule without specifying the message to be notified, assuming that the EUD system is aware of the broader context of the smart environment and can provide the information that they expect to receive (like in the latter example of P5). Moreover, the user rarely specifies the device to which to send the notification. Only in sporadic cases, participants specified "smartphone", "smartwatch", or "phone" as a device on which to receive communications.

The communication is specified with an AND statement in the actions when some other action is defined. Sometimes, the expert prefers to be promptly notified to make a personal evaluation of what happened and implement appropriate countermeasures; for example, P5 (expert) in T3 defined "*block the [vacuum] robot until I unlock it*", while P2 (expert) specifically explained in T2 "*I would like to personally verify an eventual error or infected file, or if I can personally solve the problem*".

Theme 2. Users heavily rely on the system to understand the context of the rule. Both expert and novice users rely on contextual information during the rule definition, by referring to other parts of the rule, omitting information that they give for granted after being specified once throughout the rule. Participants generally refer to information related to the event in the actions. For example, P8 (expert) defined the rule "*IF you detect connection attempts from the outer network via non-authenticated devices, THEN block them*"; analogously, P32 (novice) defined the rule "*IF you detect an attack to security cameras THEN turn them off and do not allow the access to already archived videos*", referring to videos of the security cameras.

Another common behavior of both types of users is not specifying the device or account of the event and/or the action(s). This is more pronounced in the cases of multiple actions (the device is likely specified for the first action only, and not for the consequent ones) and in the cases of notification (like already mentioned in *Theme 1*). As an example, P3 (expert) in T1 wrote "*[…] send a notification to the smartphone AND turn off the security cameras AND block suspicious connections*", presumably referring to suspicious connections arriving at the cameras.

Theme 3. All users customize their rules, but experts do it more. Both types of users expect events to be monitored under certain conditions, specifying constraints for the rule to activate, like the specification of devices type (e.g., P14 (novice) in T5"*IF there is an access to the router from a new device* [...]*")*, the definition of a time constraint, specification on the event (e.g., P13 in T7"*IF you detect port 22 is open* [...]"), time constraints (e.g., P24 in T6 "IF you detect window opening between *01:00 AM and 07:00 AM* [...]") or situational constraints (e.g., P10 (expert) in T1 "*IF an attack is detected AND I am home* [...]"). Novices tend to specify these conditions in a discursive way, while experts use logical operators such as "AND" or "OR".

Expert users, as expected, highly customize their rules, specifying multiple actions in a rule, usually in conjunction clauses with "AND", using commas, or using the word "moreover" (e.g., "[...] *AND send diagnostic data* [...]. *Moreover, ask me to reset the actions tied to vocal commands")*. Also, they specify multiple events in disjunction clauses with "OR", like P21 (expert) in T2 that wrote, "*Alexa, IF you detect a suspicious activity or an unauthorized access on the smart TV* [...]". Finally, they also define multiple rules for obtaining a single behavior, as P29 (expert) did in T6:

1) Alexa IF you detect suspicious activity on the windows THEN turn on all the lights and make the smartwatch ring/vibrate

2) Alexa IF you detect suspicious activity on the windows THEN send an SMS to the surveillance service and make the smartwatch ring/vibrate".

Novices as well customize their rules with custom parameters, but they generally tend to keep their rules simpler. E.g., P19 (novice) specified an emergency number to call in T1, and P1 (novice) in T4 defined the exact number of login attempts before the lockout.

All users often specify to apply the rule to a generic "smart device", like P22 (expert) in T4: "*Alexa, IF you detect more than 3 failed login attempts on a smart device* [...]".

Theme 4. All users make use of abstract statements: novices, as expected, make use of very abstract actions and events; for example, P24 in T2 defined the trigger "*IF you notice that the TV automatically logs out from an app* [...]", which is an ambitious command, to say the least. Even if expert users require different degrees of customization to specify parameters and additional constraints (as we stated in *Theme 3*), they sometimes require keeping things at a very high level as well; experts make use of abstract statements also in combination with precise events/actions, e.g., P25 (expert) in T9 defined the rule "*Alexa IF there are excessive attempts of accessing the devices [THEN] change the password to XXX*": we can see that the definition of "excessive" is very ambiguous, while the action is quite concrete (even if the device is not specified). Very high-level actions are likely used, like P18 (expert) in T3 "*Block eventual suspicious connections, [AND] close the router's non-essential access points*". Nonetheless, events are defined more abstractly than actions overall, as users very commonly make use of abstract statements like "*IF you detect a malicious access*" - P7 (novice) in T5. Moreover, both types of users express events based on the situation and the observable factors and not the technology behind them. For example, an event triggered when a window is opened is expressed as "*IF the* window opens [...]" (P26 (expert) in T6) rather than "*if the window sensor detects its opening*".

Theme 5. Novices tend to define drastic actions in response to attacks: novices tend to perceive actions that physically intervene on threatened devices as more secure. E.g., they may specify to delete their data if an attack is detected, like P24 in T3 ("*Alexa IF you detect a data theft from the robot vacuum, THEN turn off the robot vacuum and perform a factory reset on the robot*"), or disconnect/turn off the attacked device, like P32 in T1, who specified to "*deactivate the cameras*". Actions with very strong countermeasures can surely protect users but also carry heavy implications: e.g., the availability of their network can be limited, or their data can be lost, making the attack successful to some extent.

On the other hand, expert users require the adoption of countermeasures that involve services to also avoid future attacks, such as changing access credentials to the account; for example, P29 (expert) in T3 to protect their robot vacuum defined to "*Turn off the device, send me a notification on the smartphone and ask me to change the access credentials*".

5   Lessons Learned

In this Section, we answer the research question of this study, i.e., *How does the mental model of novices and experts translate into EUD solutions for the cybersecurity of smart environments?*, by presenting possible implications for the design of TAS that allow users to manage the security of their smart environments. Despite the specific goal of this study, we believe that some of the following principles might also benefit the design of EUD systems in general.

Alert the User by Default. Based on the findings of Theme 1, a TAS that allows defending a smart environment should communicate the attack information to the user in a prompt manner and, most importantly, by default. The system should indeed let the user easily set the devices on which they want to receive notifications of possible threats, or even let the user set a default device to be used for communications. Similarly, the user should be able to define custom messages and any additional contacts to reach out beside themselves: authorities in the case of serious emergencies, customer service to ask for technical assistance and/or send diagnostic data, and so on. Of course, they should be able to disable notifications altogether. These customizations can increase the user's possibility to define the perceived urgency of the situation. Sonification (a form of nonspeech auditory displays), e.g., can be used to effectively capture the user's attention [27] and represent and convey information intuitively [28, 29]; therefore, a user could prefer sonification for the communication of potential threats. Evidence of this aspect resulted from this very study: in T6, for example, participants had to defend themselves against night housebreakings. In this context, many users created rules that included in the actions the activation of alarms and/or sirens; some users also specified to turn on all

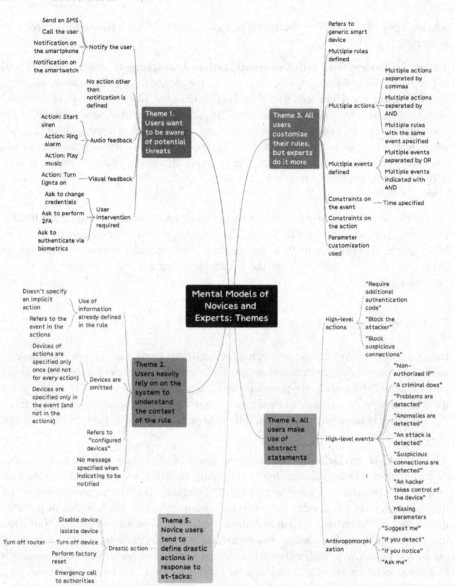

Fig. 2. Codes hierarchically grouped into the 5 Themes

the lights in their house, defining yet another means of being alerted, i.e., through visual feedback.

Compensate Missing Information in Rules. In theme 2 it emerged that users (both experts and novices) are not naturally prone to be rigorous, e.g., they do not repeat themselves by specifying, for each action, the involved device or the attack at issue, as they are already specified in other parts of the rule. To address missing information during rules creation, TAS should heavily make use of auto-completion technology to facilitate the user in defining their rules in the most natural way possible. An example could be automatically considering the device of the rule's event and selecting it as the object of the rule's action(s). Artificial Intelligence (AI) approaches could help achieve what has been discussed beforehand. Whether AI will further enhance the possibilities and support for EUD is an open question and has been the focal point of the research community in very recent years [30–32]. One of the major problems regarding AI integration in EUD systems is enabling informal languages while still maintaining formality on the system's side [32], to safeguard the correct functioning of the system. While, on the one hand, research is trying to bridge the gap between traditional EUD approaches and modern AI, on the other hand, the recent phenomenon of ChatGPT (https://chat.openai.com) has shown the world the potential of generative language models. The latter might indeed allow the user to provide the system with their goal in natural language, which would produce an intermediate representation of the utterance through the use of AI. This could be a very interesting point of debate for the EUD community, as generative language models have raised the bar about what we can expect from AI and query-answering methodologies.

Allow the Creation of Complex Rules Even for Novices. Theme 3 suggests that TAS should give, independently of the expertise level of the users, the possibility to define optional parameters (custom messages, number of login attempts before lockout, etc.), conditions on the event (time, type of device, etc.), multiple events and actions and multiple rules that work together to accomplish a security goal. EUD systems should also allow users to define rules that apply to either an individual device or to multiple devices in their smart environments; users should also be able to specify generic rules that work for every device in their network. To adopt a similar approach and provide every type of user with the same customization options, designers of EUD system user interfaces should employ well-known design principles [33] to reduce the risk of cognitive overload for novices.

Abstract Security Triggers Should be Available also for Experts. Theme 4 suggests that EUD systems for smart home security might benefit from including events that represent the situation to detect, more than the low-level conditions to be verified to provoke an event. In other words, we should use more high-level events that comprehend a large gamma of attacks and situations that could indicate an attack. This is not only valid for novices, as there is evidence from our study that the majority of expert users as well naturally make use of abstract security-related events. Anyway, in some cases (like it happened in T8), expert users made use of fine-grained events. Therefore, EUD systems should include abstract events by default, but allow the definition of parameters to constrain the rules' events. Some of the abstract events that were defined by many participants and might be included in a EUD system are: *detection of illicit login attempts*, *detection of unknown devices*, *virus detection*, and, more generally, *detection of anomalies and generic attacks* on devices. These events are comparable to the ones reported in the study of Breve *et al.* [11], in which the authors defined 6 security triggers for the protection of a smart environment through an EUD platform.

Accompany Novices in the Choice of Less Drastic Solutions. To address what emerged in Theme 5, the EUD system might suggest to the user alternatives to a drastic action (e.g., turning off a device completely, or disconnecting it from the network), to protect them more efficiently and without losing functionality. To do this, the system should understand what are the actions that can protect the user from most common attacks, based on known cybersecurity procedures (e.g., closing unused open ports rather than turning off the router altogether). In the literature, some works have addressed the issue of recommending certain sets of rules by prioritizing aspects related to security and privacy [34, 35]. What we suggest, instead, is to recommend users rules to achieve a trade-off between security and functionality which may vary depending on the conformation of their smart environment. For example, the system could suggest the user not turn off the security cameras in presence of a cyber threat, if there are no perimetral security devices (e.g., proximity sensors) as a backup.

6 Conclusion and Future Work

In this work, we addressed the problem of understanding how the mental models of experts and novices differ when defining the security behavior of IoT devices in smart environments. This aspect has never been studied before and deserved attention to truly democratize cybersecurity in smart environments. Therefore, we conducted a survey study with 32 participants (18 experts and 14 novices) to investigate their mental models. Then, we performed a thematic analysis to find out recurrent themes in the answers of different types of users. Finally, we came up with 5 different lessons learned (one for each emerged theme) for the design of new TAP solutions aimed at expert and novice users for the defense of their smart environment. We found a lot of points in common between the two types of users: for example, they both frequently use abstract security-related events and they both customize their rules with parameters, conditions, and multiple actions/events. Another factor that emerged is that, when defining rules in natural language, users are very prone to leave out information that might be implicit in the context but is essential for the system to work. We, therefore, propose to shift towards the adoption of more intelligent EUD systems which can predict the users' intention when defining incomplete rules and filling in the missing information. The EUD community has already shown great interest in integrating AI into traditional EUD paradigms [30–32] and would benefit from research going in this direction.

Some of the limitations of this study regard the constraining of using the ECA paradigm that we imposed on the users with the questions of our survey. We explicitly asked the participants to define ECA rules to have data more easily analyzable. Another limitation of this study may reside in the lack of visual support to the participants for the creation of the rules. Indeed, they were asked to freely write their rules in plain textboxes.

This was necessary to elicit the definition of rules solely based on their mental models but may have represented an obstacle for some of the participants. Finally, a limitation consists of the classification of the participants into two flat categories (experts and novices) based on the results of the "U.S. Cybersecurity Knowledge" questionnaire [26]. In future studies, it could be useful to classify users with a fuzzier criterion, considering that they may be mediumly competent in cybersecurity, even if not experts.

For future work, we will evaluate the findings we have discussed in Sect. 5, applying them to a novel TAS for helping users define security behaviors in their smart environments. It will be important to evaluate the system with users with different expertise to assess the validity of the lessons learned that emerged in this study since they focus on similarities and differences between expert and novice users. In addition, we will also investigate possible abstraction mechanisms to further facilitate the definition of ECA rules, for example, by exploiting semantic defined codified in ontologies [36] or by users themselves [4, 37, 38].

Acknowledgment. This work is partially supported by the Italian Ministry of University and Research (MIUR) under grant PRIN 2017 "EMPATHY: Empowering People in dAling with internet of Things ecosYstems" and with the co-funding of the European union - Next Generation EU: NRRP Initiative, Mission 4, Component 2, Investment 1.3 – Partnerships extended to universities, research centres, companies and research D.D. MUR n. 341 del 5.03.2022 – Next Generation EU (PE0000014 - "Security and Rights In the CyberSpace - SERICS" - CUP: H93C22000620001).

The research of Francesco Greco is funded by a PhD fellowship within the framework of the Italian "D.M. n. 352, April 9, 2022"- under the National Recovery and Resilience Plan, Mission 4, Component 2, Investment 3.3 - PhD Project "Investigating XAI techniques to help user defend from phishing attacks", co-supported by "Auriga S.p.A." (CUP H91I22000410007).

References

1. Atzori, L., Iera, A., Morabito, G.: The internet of things: a survey. Comput. Netw. **54**, 2787–2805 (2010)
2. Krishna, A., Le Pallec, M., Mateescu, R., Salaün, G.: Design and deployment of expressive and correct web of things applications. ACM Trans. Internet Things **3**, 30 (2021)
3. Desolda, G., Ardito, C., Matera, M.: Empowering end users to customize their smart environments: model, composition paradigms, and domain-specific tools. ACM Trans. Comput.-Hum. Interact. **24**, 58 (2017)
4. Balducci, F., Buono, P., Desolda, G., Impedovo, D., Piccinno, A.: Improving smart interactive experiences in cultural heritage through pattern recognition techniques. Pattern Recogn. Lett. **131**, 142–149 (2020)
5. Zeng, E., Mare, S., Roesner, F.: End user security & privacy concerns with smart homes. In: Thirteen Symposium on Usable Privacy and Security, pp. 65–80. USENIX Association (2017)
6. Alqhatani, A., Lipford, H.R.: There is nothing that i need to keep secret: sharing practices and concerns of wearable fitness data. In: Proceedings of the Fifteenth USENIX Conference on Usable Privacy and Security, pp. 421–434. USENIX Association (2019)
7. Surbatovich, M., Aljuraidan, J., Bauer, L., Das, A., Jia, L.: Some recipes can do more than spoil your appetite: analyzing the security and privacy risks of IFTTT recipes. In: Proceedings of the 26th International Conference on World Wide Web, pp. 1501–1510. International World Wide Web Conferences Steering Committee (2017)

8. Breve, B., Cimino, G., Deufemia, V.: Identifying security and privacy violation rules in trigger-action IoT platforms with NLP models. IEEE Internet Things J. **10**, 5607–5622 (2023)

9. Wang, Q., Hassan, W., Bates, A., Gunter, C.: Fear and logging in the internet of things. In: Network and Distributed Systems Symposium, pp. Medium: X. The Internet Society (2018)

10. Xiao, D., Wang, Q., Cai, M., Zhu, Z., Zhao, W.: A3ID: an automatic and interpretable implicit interference detection method for smart home via knowledge graph. IEEE Internet Things J. **7**, 2197–2211 (2020)

11. Breve, B., Desolda, G., Deufemia, V., Greco, F., Matera, M.: An end-user development approach to secure smart environments. In: Fogli, D., Tetteroo, D., Barricelli, B.R., Borsci, S., Markopoulos, P., Papadopoulos, G.A. (eds.) IS-EUD 2021. LNCS, vol. 12724, pp. 36–52. Springer, Cham (2021). https://doi.org/10.1007/978-3-030-79840-6_3

12. Rizvi, S., Pipetti, R., McIntyre, N., Todd, J., Williams, I.: Threat model for securing internet of things (IoT) network at device-level. Internet of Things **11**, 100240 (2020)

13. Seeam, A., Ogbeh, O.S., Guness, S., Bellekens, X.: Threat modeling and security issues for the internet of things. In: Conference on Next Generation Computing Applications, pp. 1–8. IEEE (2019)

14. Alrawi, O., Lever, C., Antonakakis, M., Monrose, F.: SoK: security evaluation of home-based IoT deployments. In: 40th IEEE Symposium on Security and Privacy, San Francisco, CA, pp. 1362–1380. IEEE (2019)

15. Atamli, A.W., Martin, A.: Threat-based security analysis for the internet of things. In: International Workshop on Secure Internet of Things, Wroclaw, Poland, pp. 35–43. IEEE (2014)

16. Ion, I., Reeder, R., Consolv, S.: "...no one can hack my mind": comparing expert and non-expert security practices. In: Eleventh Symposium on Usable Privacy and Security, pp. 327–346. USENIX Association (2015)

17. Busse, K., Schäfer, J., Smith, M.: Replication: no one can hack my mind revisiting a study on expert and non-expert security practices and advice. In: Fifteenth Symposium on Usable Privacy and Security, pp. 117–136. USENIX Association (2019)

18. He, W., Golla, M., Padhi, R., Ofek, J., Fernandes, E., Ur, B.: Rethinking access control and authentication for the home internet of things (IoT). In: USENIX Security Symposium, pp. 255–272. USENIX Association (2018)

19. Cobb, C., et al.: How risky are real users' IFTTT applets? In: Sixteenth Symposium on Usable Privacy and Security, pp. 505–529. USENIX Association (2020)

20. Saeidi, M., Calvert, M., Au, A., Sarma, A., Bobba, R.: If this context then that concern: exploring users' concerns with IFTTT applets. In: Privacy Enhancing Technologies Symposium, pp. 166–186 (2021)

21. Paci, F., Bianchin, D., Quintarelli, E., Zannone, N.: IFTTT privacy checker. In: Saracino, A., Mori, P. (eds.) ETAA 2020. LNCS, vol. 12515, pp. 90–107. Springer, Cham (2020). https://doi.org/10.1007/978-3-030-64455-0_6

22. Wang, Q., Datta, P., Yang, W., Liu, S., Bates, A., Gunter, C.A.: Charting the attack surface of trigger-action IoT platforms. In: Proceedings of the 2019 ACM SIGSAC Conference on Computer and Communications Security, pp. 1439–1453. ACM (2019)

23. Norman, D.A.: Some observations on mental models. In: Gentner, D., Stevens, A.L. (eds.) Mental Models, p. 8. Psychology Press, New York (1983)

24. Braun, V., Clarke, V.: Using thematic analysis in psychology. Qual. Res. Psychol. **3**, 77–101 (2006)

25. Etikan, I., Abubakar, S., Musa, R., Alkassim, S.: Comparison of convenience sampling and purposive sampling. Am. J. Theor. Appl. Stat. **5**, 1–4 (2016)

26. Olmstead, K., Smith, A.: U.S. Cybersecurity knowledge-what the public knows about cybersecurity. Pew Research Center (2017)

27. Wogalter, M.: Communication-human information processing (C-HIP) model. In: Forensic Human Factors and Ergonomics, pp. 33–49. CRC Press (2018)

28. Datta, P., Namin, A.S., Jones, K.S., Hewett, R.: Warning users about cyber threats through sounds. SN Appl. Sci. **3**(7), 1–21 (2021). https://doi.org/10.1007/s42452-021-04703-4

29. Walker, B.N., Nees, M.A.: Theory of sonification. In: Hermann, T., Hunt, A., Neuhof, J.G. (eds.) The Sonification Handbook, pp. 9–40. Logos Publishing House, Berlin (2011)

30. Fischer, G.: End-user development: empowering stakeholders with artificial intelligence, meta-design, and cultures of participation. In: Fogli, D., Tetteroo, D., Barricelli, B.R., Borsci, S., Markopoulos, P., Papadopoulos, G.A. (eds.) IS-EUD 2021. LNCS, vol. 12724, pp. 3–16. Springer, Cham (2021). https://doi.org/10.1007/978-3-030-79840-6_1

31. Barricelli, B.R., Fogli, D.: Exploring the reciprocal influence of artificial intelligence and end-user development. In: Sixth International Workshop on Cultures of Participation in the Digital Age (2022)

32. Paternò, F., Burnett, M., Fischer, G., Matera, M., Myers, B., Schmidt, A.: Artificial intelligence versus end-user development: a panel on what are the tradeoffs in daily automations? In: Ardito, C., Lanzilotti, R., Malizia, A., Petrie, H., Piccinno, A., Desolda, G., Inkpen, K. (eds.) INTERACT 2021. LNCS, vol. 12936, pp. 340–343. Springer, Cham (2021). https://doi.org/10.1007/978-3-030-85607-6_33

33. Quiroga, L., Crosby, M., Iding, M.: Reducing cognitive load. In: Annual Hawaii International Conference on System Sciences, Big Island, HI, USA, vol. 37, p. 9. IEEE (2004)

34. Huang, T.-H.K., Azaria, A., Bigham, J.P.: InstructableCrowd: creating IF-THEN rules via conversations with the crowd. In: Proceedings of the 2016 CHI Conference Extended Abstracts on Human Factors in Computing Systems, pp. 1555–1562. ACM (2016)

35. Corno, F., De Russis, L., Monge Roffarello, A.: HeyTAP: bridging the gaps between users' needs and technology in IF-THEN rules via conversation. In: Proceedings of the International Conference on Advanced Visual Interfaces, p. 9. Association for Computing Machinery (2020)

36. Corno, F., Russis, L.D., Roffarello, A.M.: A high-level approach towards end user development in the IoT. In: CHI Conference Extended Abstracts on Human Factors in Computing Systems, Denver, Colorado, USA, pp. 1546–1552. ACM (2017)

37. Ardito, C., et al.: User-defined semantics for the design of IoT systems enabling smart interactive experiences. Pers. Ubiquit. Comput. **24**(6), 781–796 (2020). https://doi.org/10.1007/s00779-020-01457-5

38. Ardito, C., Desolda, G., Lanzilotti, R., Malizia, A., Matera, M.: Analysing trade-offs in frameworks for the design of smart environments. Behav. Inf. Technol. **39**, 47–71 (2020)

On the User Perception of Security Risks of TAP Rules: A User Study

Bernardo Breve[1]([✉]), Gaetano Cimino[1], Giuseppe Desolda[2],
Vincenzo Deufemia[1], and Annunziata Elefante[1]

[1] Computer Science Department, University of Salerno, Fisciano 84084, Italy
{bbreve,gcimino,deufemia,anelefante}@unisa.it
[2] Computer Science Department, University of Bari Aldo Moro, Bari 70121, Italy
giuseppe.desolda@uniba.it

Abstract. Trigger-Action Platforms (TAPs) provide users with enhanced control to automate interactions between IoT devices using rules that consist of trigger conditions and actions that get executed when the triggers are fired. To better describe the behavior of these rules from the perspective of reuse and sharing, end-users can provide natural language descriptions. Unfortunately, TAPs do not assess these descriptions, which can result in unintentional exposure of sensitive information about the user's smart environment, and consequently, pose significant security and privacy threats. In this paper, we present a study involving end-users to evaluate the plausibility of cyberattacks that leverage information inferred from rules of the IFTTT platform, also known as *applets*. The study recruited 30 participants of varying technical proficiency, to investigate the degree of perceived risk when exposed to attack scenarios involving specific smart objects. ChatGPT was utilized to automatically generate descriptions of potential cyberattacks based on sensitive information inferred from applets by using NLP techniques. The findings highlight that users, particularly experts, considered attack scenarios highly plausible, especially given the ease of access to such sensitive information as a user's routine schedule or home environment. Qualitative analysis revealed that users were overall very concerned about how information in trigger-action rule descriptions could give malicious individuals important clues to plan cyberattacks. Finally, based on the study results, we draw some recommendations to the EUD community to improve the security of the interaction with TAPs.

Keywords: Trigger-action rules · security and privacy · end-user perception

1 Introduction

The Internet of Things (IoT) has revolutionized home appliances by transforming physical objects into intelligent and connected devices that can acquire, process, and transmit data over the Internet through sensors and actuators [4,19].

L. D. Spano et al. (Eds.): IS-EUD 2023, LNCS 13917, pp. 162–179, 2023.
https://doi.org/10.1007/978-3-031-34433-6_10

As the adoption of IoT devices continues to grow, it has become increasingly important to provide users having different levels of expertise with the ability to manage these devices and establish connections between them to create automations that simplify their daily lives [11,21]. To this end, we witnessed the birth of End-User Development (EUD) platforms, which empower end-users to create the desired smart environment's behaviors by means of an abstraction expressed in the form of Trigger-Action rules [1,2,5,10,12,17,24]. These platforms, also known as Trigger-Action Platforms (TAPs), implement the trigger-action paradigm through ad-hoc interfaces and various steps for rule creation [8]. Typically, defining a rule almost always requires the end-user to select the trigger component, which describes the event whose occurrence triggers the rule, and the action component, which describes the operation to be performed to complete the behavior. An example of a rule might be the following: "IF I leave the house THEN turn off the lights in the living room", which automates the turning off of lights, relieving the user from having to perform the operation manually each time.

In addition to the specification of trigger and action components, some TAPs allow users to specify natural language textual descriptions, making it easier for users to remember the behavior of their rules. This is the case with the If-This-Then-That (IFTTT) platform[1], the most commercially deployed TAP, which provides users with the ability to describe in a few words the behavior they have just generated through their interface [15]. In fact, this system requires users to first assign an appropriate title to the rule and then provide additional information in its description to further clarify the behavior. Such a text will allow the end user not only to remember for themselves the rules (a.k.a. applets) created, but also to make it easier for other users of the platform to understand the behavior. Indeed, on IFTTT, users are given the opportunity to share the applets they create with the rest of the community, which are added to a public catalog and presented through that description. For example, a description of the previous rule might be: "*Make sure you don't unintentionally leave the light on when you're not home. This applet turns off Hive Active Light when you leave the house*".

The writing of rule descriptions in Trigger-Action Platforms (TAPs) is not supervised, which may result in users unintentionally exposing confidential details about their smart environment, such as the types and brands of devices used, as well as their functions. Even seemingly harmless rule descriptions may include a considerable amount of sensitive information, posing serious privacy and security risks. This information can be easily used by malicious individuals to plan cyberattacks, which may go unnoticed by unsuspecting users.

Several works in the literature have assessed the security and privacy concerns related to TAPs and their rules [9,16,18]. The analyses have been conducted either by the authors themselves through a painstaking evaluation of the rules and the risks they imply [9,18], or by means of user studies that analyze user perceptions based on the characteristics of the rules [16]. In this paper we

---

[1] https://ifttt.com.

present a user study that evaluates the user's perception by means of real cyber-attacks generated by information inferred from the rules descriptions defined on the IFTTT platform. We defined an NLP-based strategy to automatically extract information from the descriptions of all IFTTT applets created by a single user. In particular, the proposed strategy allows the identification of details such as which devices the user owns, their location, and when they are triggered. To demonstrate how this information can be easily exploited to formulate cyber-attacks, we use ChatGPT, an advanced chatbot created by OpenAI. Specifically, the information inferred from the rules is then injected into a template leading to the query for ChatGPT, which outputs scenarios where a malicious individual could leverage the information to cause harm.

A group of 30 participants with various levels of expertise in cybersecurity was selected for the plausibility study. Our aim was to understand the risk level perceived by the users when exposed to attack scenarios involving specific smart objects. Moreover, by including users with different levels of technological knowledge, we sought to investigate if the level of perceived risk varied based on the participants' technical backgrounds. The results of the study confirm the feasibility and simplicity of generating attacks against a user in their day-to-day life and demonstrate that the perceived level of risk is higher for the category of expert users examined in the study.

The paper is organized as follows: Sect. 2 reviews the current state-of-the-art. Section 3 provides an overview of the methodology defined for inferring sensitive information from trigger-action rules and generating a textual description of cyberattacks. Section 4 presents the user study design and the obtained results. Section 5 discusses strategies for providing protection to the end-users from leaking sensitive data through trigger-action rules. Finally, Sect. 6 summarizes the conclusions drawn from the research and proposes directions for future work.

2   Related Work

As TAPs become increasingly popular, it is essential to comprehend the potential privacy and security risks that come with these platforms [3,9,18]. Understanding how users perceive these risks is crucial, resulting in numerous studies that investigate user attitudes and behaviors toward granting third-party access to their personal data and devices.

Saeidi et al. surveyed 386 participants on 49 smart-home IFTTT applets, revealing that users generally were not very concerned about using the rules, with location data-related rules being of greater concern [16]. Zheng et al. conducted 11 semi-structured interviews with smart homeowners, identifying recurring themes including users' preferences for convenience and connectedness influencing their privacy-related behaviors and lack of awareness of the privacy risks from inference algorithms [25]. Cobb et al. analyzed 732 applets installed by 28 users and their responses to survey questions, finding that participants did not express significant concerns about security and privacy risks, but were aware of the possibility of such risks and stressed the importance of security and privacy for their applets [9]. Zeng *et al.* conducted a study to investigate the security and privacy concerns of users who utilize smart home platforms and devices [23]. The study involved in-depth, semi-structured interviews with 15 smart home users, which revealed that the threat models of the participants were sparse and depended on their technical mental models. Furthermore, the study found that many smart home users were aware of potential security and privacy issues but were not generally concerned, and there may be tensions between multiple residents in a smart home. Based on these findings, the authors provided recommendations for the designs of future smart home platforms and devices. Finally, Morgan *et al.* performed two experiments for exploring the adoption of trigger-action rules in smart homes and the influence of security and privacy priming on user behavior [14]. The experiments were conducted with the help of a Delphi study and used narrative descriptions of domestic smart devices. The results show that priming promotes safer rule adoption, especially when explicit, but there is an asymmetry in the effects of privacy and security priming. The study also found that perceived benefits of technology and preexisting trusting beliefs in online companies are two aspects of user attitudes that shape riskier rule choices. The findings suggest that perceived trust and benefits should be considered when designing safety messaging for smart home users.

In conclusion, a comprehensive and meticulous study of the risks associated with trigger-action rules is critical to ensure the safe and reliable operation of TAP-based systems. By identifying and analyzing potential vulnerabilities, it is possible to develop effective solutions that can mitigate these risks and create a more secure and privacy-preserving environment for users. However, it is important to note that the proposed solutions offer limited feedback on the identified risks [7,20]. Therefore, it is necessary to prioritize continuous evaluation and feedback to ensure that the implemented solutions are effective in mitigating the identified risks. In doing so, the confidence of users in the security and reliability of TAP-based systems is increased, enabling their widespread adoption.

3 Methodology

The proposed methodology for extracting end-user information from applet behavior descriptions and generating attack scenarios is shown in Fig. 1. The inference module, which takes in input a trigger-action rule, utilizes NLP techniques to identify relevant entities such as IoT devices used in the applets and triggers and actions events that regulate the automation. Subsequently, the attack generation module uses the information gathered by the inference module on applet-related entities to generate attack scenarios that may compromise the privacy and security of users.

In the following, we describe the dataset of IFTTT applets that we employed in our study, followed by comprehensive technical specifications for implementing the inference and attack generation modules.

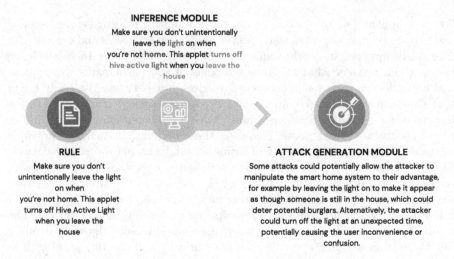

INFERENCE MODULE

Make sure you don't unintentionally leave the light on when you're not home. This applet turns off hive active light when you leave the house

RULE

Make sure you don't unintentionally leave the light on when you're not home. This applet turns off Hive Active Light when you leave the house

ATTACK GENERATION MODULE

Some attacks could potentially allow the attacker to manipulate the smart home system to their advantage, for example by leaving the light on to make it appear as though someone is still in the house, which could deter potential burglars. Alternatively, the attacker could turn off the light at an unexpected time, potentially causing the user inconvenience or confusion.

Fig. 1. Overview of the proposed methodology to define cyberattacks from rules' descriptions.

3.1 IFTTT Applet Dataset

We used the dataset proposed in [6], which consists of a collection of 79,214 applets crawled from the IFTTT.com site. More specifically, each applet is provided with several features: a title (*Title*) and a description (*Desc*) describing the applet's behavior, the event triggering the applet (*TriggerTitle*) defined by a specific channel (*TriggerActionChannel*), the action to be performed (*ActionTitle*) selected from the corresponding channel (*ActionChannelTitle*), and the username of the applet creator (*Creator Name*). In addition, applets are classified into four macro-classes according to the potential damage they could cause to users (*Target*). In particular, the categories are:

- "*Innocuous*", which includes applets that do not pose any damage or risk;
- "*Personal*", which consists of applets that may result in the loss or compromise of sensitive data. This risk is solely due to the user's behavior;
- "*Physical*", which includes applets that have the potential to cause physical harm or damage to goods. Such damage is inflicted externally by third parties;
- "*Cybersecurity*", which includes applets that have the potential to disrupt online services or distribute malware. The damage caused by these applets is also external.

As an example, Fig 2 shows an applet created by the user "*Sanny*" whose behavior consists in the execution of the "*Add file from URL*" action from the Dropbox channel when the "*Any new attachment in inbox*" trigger from the Gmail channel is activated. This applet is classified under Cybersecurity as an attacker could exploit it to send a malicious attachment via email, which would then be automatically uploaded to Dropbox, thereby increasing the likelihood of the user opening it.

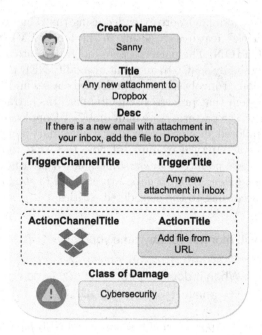

Fig. 2. An example of a risky applet.

3.2   Inference Module

The inference module leverages a *Named-Entity Recognition* (NER) model for recognizing and categorizing entities present within the behavior descriptions of IFTTT applets. This is performed by using the spaCy Python library, which provides a list of pre-trained models for processing and analyzing text data.

The NER model provided by spaCy is a pre-trained model that employs advanced deep learning techniques, including convolutional and recurrent neural networks. It has undergone meticulous training on extensive labeled data, enabling it to accurately identify various types of entities, such as products (labeled as **PRODUCT**), locations (referred to as **LOC**), organizations (labeled as **ORG**), and different categories of events (identified with the label **EVENT**) from textual data. However, due to the lack of knowledge about the smart house domain in the library, we developed a customized version of the NER model. Specifically, by manually analyzing the values of the "Title", "Desc", "TriggerChannelTitle", "ActionChannelTitle" features of a randomly selected subset of 1000 applets, and crawling web pages selected through IoT domain keywords such as "sensor" and "digital technology", we incorporated supplementary information into the existing entities of interest. The resulting NER model specifies smart devices with the label PRODUCT, their manufacturer with the label ORG, and their location within the environment with the label LOC. Furthermore, to enable the model to detect the parts of text pertaining to the trigger and action events of an applet, the patterns for the EVENT label of the pre-trained model were extended using the values of the "TriggerTitle" and "ActionTitle" features, resulting in the labels **EVENT_TRIGGER** and **EVENT_ACTION**. The patterns were integrated into a specialized *EntityRuler*, a factory used by spaCy to augment or modify NER patterns for specific entities. In particular, it involves a set of preloaded classes and methods and acts as a rule-based system that processes semantic patterns extracted from textual data. In our context, the patterns were built on IFTTT applet information, yielding an NLP tool tailored specifically for identifying smart home-related entities. Figure 3 illustrates a practical example of how the NER module works. The text *"This Applet will monitor for any time your Wyze camera detects abundant smoke in the kitchen. When it does, expect Wyze to start recording an alert video"* is labeled according to the considered entities.

This Applet will monitor for any time your Wyze (ORG) camera (PRODUCT) detects abundant smoke (EVENT_TRIGGER) in the kitchen (LOC). When it does, expect Wyze (ORG) to start recording (EVENT_ACTION) an alert video (PRODUCT).

Fig. 3. Application of the customized NER model.

3.3 Attack Generation Module

To generate a series of potentially feasible attack scenarios against users' privacy and security based on the information extracted by the inference module, we utilized ChatGPT[2], an advanced chatbot developed by OpenAI. The decision to use a chatbot was based on its ability to function as a computer program that emulates human conversation, rendering it accessible to a wide range of users.

Interacting with a chatbot typically entails creating specific templates to guide the conversation. This is due to chatbots' reliance on structured data to understand and respond to user input. The use of templates can ensure that users provide the necessary information in a format that the chatbot can interpret. Once a template is submitted to the chatbot, it employs NLP techniques to analyze the data and extract relevant information such as the user's intent, context, and specific requests. Once this data has been extracted, the chatbot can generate a response that is appropriate and contextually relevant. For this reason, the approach involved the creation of a template containing details about the user's devices, location within the environment, the trigger utilized to activate them, and the desired action to be taken, gathered through the application of the inference module. The template is represented as follows:

---

[2] https://openai.com/blog/chatgpt.

> *"Suppose a user has a rule concerning a {PRODUCT}, which is situated in the {LOC}, and is triggered when {EVENT_TRIGGER}, leading to the execution of the {EVENT_ACTION} action, what attack could an attacker perform?"*

We performed a series of queries on the chatbot, which began with a focus on individual rules and then culminated in concatenated queries that combined information on multiple rules using the AND operator. As an example, the resulting template for two rules is represented as follows:

> *"Suppose a user has a rule concerning a {PRODUCT}, which is situated in the {LOC}, and is triggered when {EVENT_TRIGGER}, leading to the execution of the {EVENT_ACTION} action **AND** a rule concerning a {PRODUCT}, which is situated in the {LOC}, and is triggered when {EVENT_TRIGGER}, leading to the execution of the {EVENT_ACTION} action, what attack could an attacker perform?"*

The answers generated from the queries were collected using the Google extension "Save ChatGPT" and then examined by a group of end-users in the following user study.

4   User Study

We conducted a user study to evaluate the feasibility and level of risk associated with attack scenarios generated by ChatGPT. The study exclusively examined scenarios that were deemed as potentially feasible to execute, to ensure that the analysis outcomes accurately reflect the participants' perceptions and are not influenced by the inherent implausibility of the attacks.

The study involved a group of 30 participants, including 20 undergraduate and graduate computer science students from the University of Salerno with programming experience. The study aimed to answer two key research questions, namely:

- **RQ1**: To what extent are the attack scenarios generated through a dialogue by ChatGPT considered plausible?
- **RQ2**: How does the perception of risk vary between users with programming knowledge and those without?

To evaluate the plausibility of the attack scenarios produced by the chatbot, participants were presented with the responses generated by ChatGPT via an online questionnaire. The questionnaire was designed to systematically assess the viability of each attack scenario, incorporating a series of carefully crafted questions to ensure a comprehensive evaluation. Participants were encouraged to provide detailed explanations to support their assessments, allowing for a thorough analysis of the results.

4.1 Participants and Study Design

The user study consisted of a total of 30 participants, consisting of 23 male and 7 female participants. The study participants were stratified into two groups, Experts and Non-experts, based on their academic backgrounds and expertise. The expert group was composed of 20 participants, recruited from computer science students pursuing a master's or bachelor's degree at the University of Salerno. The experts' age ranged from 18 to 30 years, with a mean age (MD) of 25.45 years and a standard deviation (SD) of 1.47. The selection of experts with programming experience aimed to elicit critical perspectives on the potential vulnerabilities of the proposed attack scenarios. Conversely, the non-expert group was comprised of 10 participants with no programming knowledge, who were recruited from business or medical students. The non-expert group's age ranged from 18 to 40 years, with a mean age (MD) of 23.8 years and a standard deviation (SD) of 2.71. The inclusion of the non-expert group aimed to ensure an unbiased and diverse representation of the population and provide contrasting perspectives on the plausibility of the attack scenarios. Overall, the study's sample size and participant selection criteria were carefully selected to ensure a comprehensive evaluation of the attack scenarios' plausibility while minimizing sampling bias.

Both the Experts and Non-experts groups received the same online questionnaire, consisting of two parts. The preliminary part aimed to elicit demographic information from the participants, including their age and educational qualifications. The second part comprised 20 multiple-choice questions pertaining to the attack scenarios generated by ChatGPT. The participants were required to assess the plausibility of each attack scenario by selecting one of the following options:

1. **very plausible** - the proposed attack is deemed to be probable or has already occurred within the context of smart homes
2. **plausible** - the proposed attack could be true or possible within the context of smart homes
3. **not very plausible** - the proposed attack may occur but with a low probability within the context of smart homes
4. **implausible** - the proposed attack is unlikely to occur, with a very low or negligible chance of happening within the context of smart homes

These four response options were mapped into *plausibility scores* of 1, $\frac{2}{3}$, $\frac{1}{3}$, 0, respectively [13]. In particular, the plausibility score for a given response R_i is computed according to the following formula:

$$ps_{R_i} = (0 \cdot ip_{R_i}) + (\frac{1}{3} \cdot nvp_{R_i}) + (\frac{2}{3} \cdot p_{R_i}) + (1 \cdot vp_{R_i})$$

where ip_{R_i}, nvp_{R_i}, p_{R_i}, vp_{R_i} represent the number of times the options "implausible", "not very plausible", "plausible", "very plausible" were selected, respectively. The questionnaire consisted of several illustrative attack scenarios against smart devices owned by a user. These scenarios were generated by providing ChatGPT with applet information in the form of a question. An example of such a question is as follows:

> *"Suppose a user has a rule concerning a voice command, which is situated in the **kitchen**, and is triggered when the user says a special word, leading to the execution of the turn on the light action, what attack could an attacker perform?"*

The response generated by ChatGPT was:

> *"An attacker could potentially perform a **voice command injection** attack, where they mimic or imitate the special word or phrase used to trigger the voice command. This could cause the attacker to gain control over the device and potentially execute any action they want, such as turning on/off the lights or accessing other connected devices in the network. Another possible attack is a **man-in-the-middle** attack, where the attacker intercepts the communication between the device and the cloud service provider and sends its own malicious voice commands to the device. This can be done by compromising the network, stealing credentials, or exploiting vulnerabilities in the device or cloud service."*

For each question in the questionnaire, participants were also given the opportunity to provide a reason for their answer, allowing for a deeper understanding of their reasoning and thought processes. This provided valuable insights into their perspectives on the plausibility of attack scenarios. By including the attack scenarios and motivation section, the study aimed to offer a thorough examination of the plausibility of these scenarios in a real-world context.

4.2 Data Collection

The study was designed to create a natural setting and encourage a greater number of participants to take part. To accomplish this, we conducted an uncontrolled study with the aim of reducing any potential biases that could affect participant performance and yield more reliable and truthful results. In particular, the questionnaire was disseminated through a unique link sent via popular instant messaging services, such as WhatsApp and Telegram, allowing effortless access to the questionnaire via smartphones or personal computers. The completion time for each participant was approximately 25 min.

We collected a set of qualitative data to comprehend the thought processes and justifications of participants in assessing the proposed attacks generated by ChatGPT. The data were acquired through an online questionnaire and stored in an Excel spreadsheet , enabling further analysis to extract a wide array of information relevant to the study's objectives.

4.3 Results

Data analysis comprised both qualitative and quantitative methods. Qualitative data analysis yielded significant insights into the participants' thought processes and concerns when assessing the plausibility of attack scenarios, especially by examining the motivations offered by the participants. Conversely, quantitative data analysis allowed for the calculation of response frequency and average plausibility scores for each attack scenario, both in total and for individual scenarios. The combination of qualitative and quantitative data analysis proved to be an effective approach in evaluating the efficacy of ChatGPT in suggesting attack scenarios and obtaining a more accurate estimate of the risks associated with releasing sensitive information on EUD platforms. Indeed, it facilitated a deeper understanding of the participants' concerns, providing valuable insights for answering the research questions.

The first research question was answered through a two-stage review process. The process started with the calculation of the mean plausibility score from the responses of all 30 completed questionnaires, resulting in a value of 63%. Then, a qualitative analysis was performed on the open-ended responses provided by participants, where some examples are shown in Table 1, to identify their concerns regarding the privacy and security risks associated with the use of TAP platforms. The analysis revealed that participants expressed concerns about the possibility of malicious individuals exploiting these platforms to access information or carry out cyberattacks. After calculating the mean plausibility score for all questionnaire responses, a plausibility analysis was performed for each individual question's scenario to gain a more accurate understanding of the cyberattacks generated by querying ChatGPT.

Table 1. Some of the rationales provided by the participants.

ID question	Expert motivation	Non-expert motivation
Q1	Very likely since with voice commands the device may not notice the difference in voice and give the attacker potential confidential information	All devices are connectable, and many people use the same password for everything, although security levels are different
...	...	...
Q10	The attack is complicated and fails to capture relevant information	It does not seem to report any particular advantages for the malicious party
Q11	By causing problems of this kind, it can isolate the family from the outside causing inconvenience and gaining the ability to enter the system	This type of attack is particularly advantageous for the attacker if he can carry it out

Analysis of the proposed attack scenarios revealed different levels of plausibility. The average plausibility score for each scenario is illustrated in the plot in Fig. 4, where it can be seen how the score changes between the different types of proposed attacks. Scenario Q10 for example received a score of 40%, while Q11 received a score of 79%, indicating significant differences between the scenarios. Participant feedback played a key role in identifying the reasons behind these variations. Participants reported that ChatGPT responses did not always provide adequate and accurate information to generate credible or feasible cyberattacks. In addition, the type of smart device involved in the attack affected the plausibility of the scenario. For example, scenario Q10, which described an attack on a dishwasher, was considered impractical and unhelpful by many participants. In contrast, scenario Q11, which listed various attacks that could be carried out by an attacker with access to a user's home Wi-Fi, was considered more realistic and effective in a real-world context.

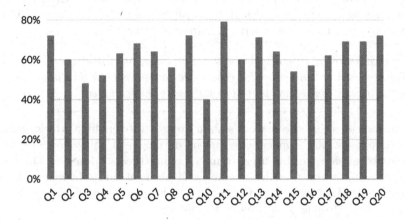

Fig. 4. Summary bar plot of mean plausibility scores for each attack scenario.

As regards the second research question, the mean plausibility score was calculated for each group of participants, obtaining the following scores:

- Experts: 65%.
- Non-experts: 58%.

The results of our study revealed a difference in the approach taken by participants with and without a programming background in assessing the plausibility of proposed attack scenarios. In fact, the average plausibility of lay users resulted slightly lower compared to expert ones. This is probably due to the fact that the former relied more on their personal interpretation to assess the plausibility of attacks, without considering their technical aspects, resulting in users judging them as not credible. On the other hand, participants with a programming background, having already dealt with cyberattacks, tended to assess the feasibility based on their technical knowledge or past experiences. As an example, a participant belonging to the expert group motivated a high plausibility score for a voice command injection attack with the following answer:

> "*A voice assistant generally does not perform a speaker ID check so it seems highly plausible to me that such a scenario could occur.*"

demonstrating technical understanding of a typical vulnerability of to-date voice assistants [22].

These results, therefore, suggest that technical knowledge and experience in cybersecurity are important factors in accurately assessing the plausibility of attack scenarios, but that nevertheless, the possibility of real risks is visible to both types of participants.

Conducting a separate analysis of the two groups of participants, an additional significant finding emerged. In particular, responses from the Non-expert group stood out for expressions of amazement at ChatGPT's ability to generate attack scenarios that appeared highly plausible in a real-world context. One of the reasons cited by a Non-expert participant is reported as follows:

> "*I have heard of cyberattacks before, but I am amazed at the ease with which even a person without a cyber base can simply ask the chatbot and get an attack that seems plausible and easily implemented.*"

This indicates that the chatbot's ability to generate credible attack scenarios could have significant implications for the development of cybersecurity measures aimed at safeguarding users from emerging threats. Moreover, the results emphasize the crucial need for ongoing enhancement and refinement of input mechanisms in TAP platforms, which can enable better protection for users and faster responses to potential threats in real-time.

We also conducted a thorough evaluation of our user study and sample selection by analyzing both internal and external validity. Internal validity pertains to the degree to which our study accurately measures the variables of interest, without any confounding variables. However, due to the absence of a control group in our uncontrolled study, we were unable to verify the veracity of participants' behavior and the presence or absence of extraneous variables in the procedure, thus limiting the internal validity. In contrast, external validity refers to the extent to which the results of our study can be generalized to other populations or contexts. We ensured the external validity of our results by recruiting a diverse sample of participants with varying levels of experience and expertise in programming and cybersecurity concepts. Although our study was conducted outside the laboratory, increasing external validity, we acknowledge the possibility of other factors that could influence the results. For instance, self-selection bias may have affected the representativeness of our sample, and the geographic region where the study was conducted may limit the generalizability of our results to other cultural contexts.

In conclusion, while our study had several strengths in terms of internal and external validity, there are limitations that should be considered when interpreting our findings. Nevertheless, the results provide valuable insights into the significance of user privacy and security in EUD platform design and development, emphasizing the requirement for future research in this field to minimize potential harm to users. Subsequent investigations in this area should focus on developing strategies to mitigate these perceived risks and improve transparency and control over the use of personal data by these platforms.

5   Discussion

In this section, we present possible implications for the EUD community to take into account when designing TAPs.

Supervising Input into Unstructured Text Fields. The presence of unstructured text fields, such as the description of a rule, is a component that is as fundamental as it is underestimated. Through these fields, the user is given full freedom to describe the behavior of the rule in the way he deems most appropriate. However, this choice must be subject to a process that verifies, at the time of insertion, that the user is not communicating sensitive information that could potentially be exploited by malicious individuals. In fact, for lay users, typing not only details about their devices but also contacts such as email addresses and telephone numbers, may not pose any risk, perhaps because they ignore that other people may also have access to such data. Furthermore, recently, platforms such as IFTTT have decided to facilitate the end-user in writing descriptions, completing these fields automatically, through the generation of a structured string taking the reference from the trigger and action components.

Fig. 5. An applet's title containing sensitive information automatically generated by IFTTT during applet's creation.

As an example, Fig. 5 shows the generated text for an applet that notifies a user via email whenever they are tagged on Facebook. We can observe that the text contains several confidential user information items (obfuscated for privacy reasons), including the user's first and last name and the designated email address for receiving tag notifications. Therefore, this process adds extra risk for the user, as they are unlikely to modify the generated text, and thus, may unintentionally reveal sensitive information. One possible solution is to introduce automated methods that identify and report the presence of sensitive information in rule descriptions.

Security and Privacy Risks. Most participants in the user study expressed concern about potential privacy and security issues that may arise from using a high-level model system, particularly because of the abstract nature of its representation. It is imperative to carefully evaluate and address privacy and security concerns when implementing high-level representations such as those found in EUD platforms.

The study used a mixed sample of participants, which helped confirm the risks associated with the disclosure of personal information through EUDs. The research aimed to raise awareness of the ease with which such data can be exploited to compromise an individual's privacy and security, even by malicious individuals without a background in programming. The findings of the study showed that participants with a background in computer science had a heightened awareness towards the potential harm resulting from the inadvertent disclosure of sensitive information through EUD platforms. When exposed to realistic attack scenarios, these individuals acknowledged the plausibility and severity of the risks involved.

Similar findings, although sometimes less informed, were observed among participants without a background in IT, as they reconsidered revealing their data unconsciously despite initially advocating the use of such platforms. Assistance in promoting safe and responsible usage of high-level systems can be provided through the implementation of robust privacy and security measures and by educating users on the potential risks and best practices for safeguarding their personal information. By taking these measures, we can help mitigate the privacy and security concerns that arise with using platforms EUD and promote the responsible use and protection of personal information.

6   Conclusion and Future Work

In this paper, we aimed to assess end users' perception of the risk posed by cyberattacks that exploit sensitive information contained within trigger-action rule descriptions. We conducted a user study with 30 participants, seven of whom were female, to evaluate the plausibility of cyberattacks generated by ChatGPT, a freely available chatbot developed by OpenAI. We selected participants from both expert and non-expert backgrounds to evaluate the potential impact of technical knowledge on user perception. Our results showed that, on average, users - particularly those with technical expertise - rated the generated attack scenarios as highly plausible, with a plausibility score exceeding 50% for both groups. A subsequent qualitative analysis revealed that users were particularly concerned about the ease with which seemingly insignificant information within trigger-action rule descriptions could provide valuable insights to malicious individuals. Based on our findings, we offer some recommendations to the EUD community for designing solutions guaranteeing a more secure interaction for TAPs users.

In the future, we would like to extend this research by conducting an extensive analysis of trigger-action rule datasets available in the literature in order to evaluate the degree of sensitive information that users unwittingly share through TAPs. Furthermore, we would also like to analyze users' perception also in scenarios of rule interferences. Such scenarios occur when multiple rules are linked together, leading to combined execution that generates harm without users' knowledge, as discussed in [20].

Acknowledgements. This work has been supported by the Italian Ministry of University and Research (MUR) under grant PRIN 2017 "EMPATHY: Empowering People in deAling with internet of THings ecosYstems" (Progetti di Rilevante Interesse Nazionale − Bando 2017, Grant 2017MX9T7H).

References

1. Ardito, C., Desolda, G., Lanzilotti, R., Malizia, A., Matera, M.: Analysing trade-offs in frameworks for the design of smart environments. Behav. Inf. Technol. **39**(1), 47–71 (2020). https://doi.org/10.1080/0144929X.2019.1634760
2. Ardito, C., et al.: User-defined semantics for the design of IoT systems enabling smart interactive experiences. Pers. Ubiquit. Comput. **24**(6), 781–796 (2020). https://doi.org/10.1007/s00779-020-01457-5
3. Atlam, H.F., Alenezi, A., Walters, R.J., Wills, G.B., Daniel, J.: Developing an adaptive risk-based access control model for the internet of things. In: Proceeding of 2017 IEEE International Conference on Internet of Things (iThings) and IEEE Green Computing and Communications (GreenCom) and IEEE Cyber, Physical and Social Computing (CPSCom) and IEEE Smart Data (SmartData), pp. 655–661 (2017)
4. Atzori, L., Iera, A., Morabito, G.: The internet of things: a survey. Comput. Networks **54**(15), 2787–2805 (2010)
5. Balducci, F., Buono, P., Desolda, G., Impedovo, D., Piccinno, A.: Improving smart interactive experiences in cultural heritage through pattern recognition techniques. Pattern Recogn. Lett. **131**, 142–149 (2020). https://doi.org/10.1016/j.patrec.2019.12.011
6. Breve, B., Cimino, G., Deufemia, V.: Identifying security and privacy violation rules in trigger-action IoT platforms with NLP models. IEEE Internet Things J. **10**(6), 5607–5622 (2023)

7. Breve, B., Desolda, G., Deufemia, V., Greco, F., Matera, M.: An end-user development approach to secure smart environments. In: Fogli, D., Tetteroo, D., Barricelli, B.R., Borsci, S., Markopoulos, P., Papadopoulos, G.A. (eds.) IS-EUD 2021. LNCS, vol. 12724, pp. 36–52. Springer, Cham (2021). https://doi.org/10.1007/978-3-030-79840-6_3

8. Caivano, D., Fogli, D., Lanzilotti, R., Piccinno, A., Cassano, F.: Supporting end users to control their smart home: design implications from a literature review and an empirical investigation. J. Syst. Softw. **144**, 295–313 (2018)

9. Cobb, C., et al.: How risky are real users' IFTTT applets? In: Proceedings of the Sixteenth USENIX Conference on Usable Privacy and Security, pp. 505–529 (2020)

10. Corno, F., De Russis, L., Monge Roffarello, A.: My IoT puzzle: debugging IF-THEN rules through the jigsaw metaphor. In: Malizia, A., Valtolina, S., Morch, A., Serrano, A., Stratton, A. (eds.) IS-EUD 2019. LNCS, vol. 11553, pp. 18–33. Springer, Cham (2019). https://doi.org/10.1007/978-3-030-24781-2_2

11. Desolda, G., Ardito, C., Matera, M.: Empowering end users to customize their smart environments: model, composition paradigms, and domain-specific tools. ACM Trans. Comput-Hum. Interact. TOCHI **24**(2), 1–52 (2017)

12. Ghiani, G., Manca, M., Paternò, F., Santoro, C.: Personalization of context-dependent applications through trigger-action rules. ACM Trans. Comput. Hum. Interact. (TOCHI) **24**(2), 1–33 (2017)

13. Marasović, A., Beltagy, I., Downey, D., Peters, M.E.: Few-shot self-rationalization with natural language prompts. arXiv:2111.08284 (2021)

14. Morgan, P.L., Collins, E.I., Spiliotopoulos, T., Greeno, D.J., Jones, D.M.: Reducing risk to security and privacy in the selection of trigger-action rules: implicit vs. explicit priming for domestic smart devices. Int. J. Hum.-Comput. Stud. **168**, 102902 (2022)

15. Rahmati, A., Fernandes, E., Jung, J., Prakash, A.: IFTTT vs. Zapier: a comparative study of trigger-action programming frameworks. arXiv:1709.02788 (2017)

16. Saeidi, M., Calvert, M., Au, A.W., Sarma, A., Bobba, R.B.: If this context then that concern: exploring users' concerns with IFTTT applets. Proc. Priv. Enhancing Technol. **2022**(1) (2021)

17. Saunders, J., Syrdal, D.S., Koay, K.L., Burke, N., Dautenhahn, K.: "Teach Me—Show Me"—End-user personalization of a smart home and companion robot. IEEE Trans. Hum.-Mach. Syst. **46**(1), 27–40 (2016)

18. Surbatovich, M., Aljuraidan, J., Bauer, L., Das, A., Jia, L.: Some recipes can do more than spoil your appetite: analyzing the security and privacy risks of IFTTT recipes. In: Proceedings of the 26th International Conference on World Wide Web, pp. 1501–1510. WWW 2017, ACM Press (2017)

19. Ur, B., McManus, E., Pak Yong Ho, M., Littman, M,L.: Practical trigger-action programming in the smart home. In: Proceedings of the SIGCHI Conference on Human Factors in Computing Systems, pp. 803–812 (2014)

20. Xiao, D., Wang, Q., Cai, M., Zhu, Z., Zhao, W.: A3ID: an automatic and interpretable implicit interference detection method for smart home via knowledge graph. IEEE IoT J. **7**(3), 2197–2211 (2019)

21. Yang, H., Lee, H., Zo, H.: User acceptance of smart home services: an extension of the theory of planned behavior. Ind. Manag. Data Syst. **117**, 68–89 (2017)

22. Yuan, X., et al.: All your Alexa are belong to us: a remote voice control attack against echo. In: 2018 IEEE Global Communications Conference (GLOBECOM), pp. 1–6. IEEE (2018)

23. Zeng, E., Mare, S., Roesner, F.: End user security and privacy concerns with smart homes. In: Symposium on Usable Privacy and Security (SOUPS), vol. 220 (2017)

24. Zhao, V., Zhang, L., Wang, B., Lu, S., Ur, B.: Visualizing differences to improve end-user understanding of trigger-action programs. In: Extended Abstracts of the 2020 CHI Conference on Human Factors in Computing Systems, pp. 1–10. ACM (2020)
25. Zheng, S., Apthorpe, N., Chetty, M., Feamster, N.: User perceptions of smart home IoT privacy. In: Proceedings of the ACM on Human-Computer Interaction, vol. 2(CSCW), pp. 1–20 (2018)

ConnectivityControl: Providing Smart Home Users with Real Privacy Configuration Options

Sebastian S. Feger[(✉)], Maximiliane Windl, Jesse Grootjen,
and Albrecht Schmidt

LMU Munich, Munich, Germany
`sebastian.feger@ifi.lmu.de`

Abstract. Smart home devices become increasingly popular as they allow to automate tedious tasks and often provide a wide variety of entertainment features. Yet, this increase in comfort comes at the cost of exposure to privacy risks as connected devices in smart homes capture most sensitive user data, including video, audio, and movement data of the inhabitants and guests. Smart home owners and bystanders typically have very limited control over these recordings. While few devices do provide physical artifacts to block individual sensors, deactivating recording and transmission capabilities typically requires powering devices off or disconnecting them from the network, typically rendering these smart home appliances useless. In response, we created *ConnectivityControl*, a framework that allows users to switch between four device connectivity levels: Offline, Access Point mode, Local Network mode, and Online. *ConnectivityControl* features a privacy label that depicts how those modes impact device features and privacy exposure. The label can be used to inform purchase decisions and to monitor devices across their lifetime. In this paper, we detail the system architecture and the interaction design and showcase *ConnectivityControl*'s implementation in the context of two common smart home systems: a smart camera and an environmental sensing unit. Finally, we discuss how *ConnectivityControl* and its labels can transform the way smart home users configure their systems to match individual privacy needs.

Keywords: Privacy label · ConnectivityControl · ConnectivityLabel · Effective smart home privacy configuration

1 Introduction and Related Work

The number of installed smart home devices has been growing rapidly in recent years. These devices provide comfort by automating tasks and creating supportive environments. They are also fitted with an increasing number of sensors and actuators to further benefit their users. The evolution of smart speakers makes for a good example: initially focused on microphones and speakers, some modern versions additionally come with cameras, displays, and even motors to adapt to

© The Author(s), under exclusive license to Springer Nature Switzerland AG 2023
L. D. Spano et al. (Eds.): IS-EUD 2023, LNCS 13917, pp. 180–188, 2023.
https://doi.org/10.1007/978-3-031-34433-6_11

users moving in their homes. While any additional sensor and actuator promises an increase in the number of features and the level of comfort provided, they also pose severe privacy threats to both smart home inhabitants and bystanders [4].

Three principal strategies exist to mitigate privacy risks and to configure devices according to users' preferences: (1) adapting device behavior through software settings; (2) physically disabling individual sensors; and (3) disconnecting devices.

Concerning the first strategy, software settings, we note that it foremost requires manufacturers to provide such control options. Also, it requires users to trust the device manufacturer in respecting their wishes as they have little control in knowing, for example, whether a microphone is actually still used to record audio or not. In contrast, the second option, physically disabling sensors, can provide such assurance [7]. Webcam shutters represent one of the most commonly known classes of physical interventions that are often integrated into modern camera-based smart home devices. Such covers can even be turned into smart devices that automatically block cameras when they are not in use [2]. Other examples include wearables that automatically deactivate nearby microphones [1] and a special hat that prevents smart speakers from listening [6]. Yet, they require additional external devices to configure the primary smart home device, rendering such solutions less usable for mass adoption. In summary, tangible smart device control is still mostly limited to built-in camera shutters [7].

The third option, disconnecting devices, applies to all smart home appliances. Users can always disconnect them from the network or turn off their power. While this represents the most effective strategy to mitigate privacy risks, it comes at the expense of losing device features and desired comfort, rendering this option typically unacceptable to most users. However, we note that there are several device connectivity options between complete *offline* and *online* modes, such as *access point* or *network-only* connections. Yet, smart home devices typically provide features only when being fully connected to the internet.

We developed ConnectivityControl, to depict how a smart home ecosystem that designs specifically for the four connectivity modes *offline*, *access point*, *network-only*, and *online*, can benefit users by giving them real smart home privacy configuration options that let them weigh comfort and privacy exposure. In this paper, we provide a detailed overview of the four connectivity modes, the two prototype devices, and the web interface.

Contribution Statement

We present a prototype system, ConnectivityControl, that increases the control of smart home end users over data sharing practices of their devices. This improvement in end-user privacy control is achieved in three ways: 1) by extending devices' typical connectivity spectrum with *network-only* and *access point* modes; 2) by allowing end users to weigh between features and risks of devices across the connectivity spectrum; and 3) by introducing a tangible mechanism that is easy to use and interpret among smart home owners and bystanders. We discuss our vision of turning ConnectivityControl, with the support of manufacturers and the research community, into a larger smart home ecosystem that returns smart home privacy control to end users.

2   System

In this section, we first describe in detail the four connectivity modes and the ConnectivityLabel. Next, we present the two key components of Connectivity-Control: (1) the devices and their specific interfaces; and (2) the web platform. We conclude this section with an overview of the system architecture.

2.1   Connectivity Modes

Online refers to full internet access and represents the connectivity mode that most modern smart home devices require by default. Devices can send and retrieve data by communicating with remote web servers.

Network-only mode limits data exchange to devices that are within the same network. In a typical smart home with a single access point, this means that data can be shared across devices in this home, but should not leave the physical boundaries of the house. We note that assuring this desired communication behavior requires network devices that support package filtering and is increasingly difficult in more complex network setups.

Access point mode refers to the ability of a network device to set up its network interface specifically for direct connections with other devices. In most cases, data exchange on these network interfaces is limited to the connected communication partners. Some smart home devices use this mode for initial setup, allowing a user to connect with their mobile phone or computer to provide credentials

Connectivity	Features		Privacy Threats
Online	👆 ⚙ ◉ 🛠	Remote Diagnosis and Support	Remote device control and status tracking
Network-only	👆 ⚙ ☕	Speech-based Preparation	Misuse and data intercept by close-by people with network access
Access point	👆 ⚙	Advanced Settings	Third-party configuration
Offline	👆	Manual	None
Smart Coffee Maker TX2441 Label issued for Firmware Version 3.23.13b			

Fig. 1. The ConnectivityLabel informs users about the privacy/feature tradeoffs of each connectivity mode. A large icon in the *Features* column highlights features enabled by the corresponding connectivity level. We note that this is a prototypical label for a fictional device that will be refined through user testing.

for connecting to the home network. In contrast, ConnectivityControl foresees exchanging actual usage data during the device lifetime in this mode.

Offline means that a device cannot exchange any data over network interfaces. It does not use any cable or wireless network interface.

2.2   ConnectivityLabel

Emami-Naeini et al. [3] proposed static device labels that detail principal security and privacy considerations of smart devices. The labels are expected to support users in making informed purchase decisions. Inspired by these, ConnectivityLabel revolves around the four connectivity modes and contrasts device features (i.e., comfort) with corresponding privacy implications and threats. Figure 1 depicts an example ConnectivityLabel for a fictional smart coffee maker.

2.3   Device Level

ConnectivityControl prescribes the following physical interfaces that must be implemented by devices within the ecosystem.

Four-State Switch. As shown in Fig. 2, each device must have a physical interface that shows the current connectivity mode of the device and that allows the user to change the mode. Four LEDs are used to visually highlight the currently active mode. The slider is positioned close to the corresponding LED. The motorized slider can either be manipulated manually by the user or programmatically be repositioned through ConnectivityControl's web platform. This feature can be used when a device owner wants to remotely change device connectivity from *online* mode to any lower connectivity level. Note that programmatically switching back to a higher connectivity mode requires that the user has corresponding access to the device.

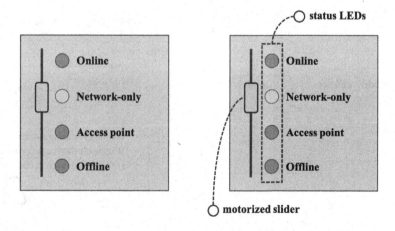

Fig. 2. Devices integrated into the ConnectivityControl ecosystem must feature a physical interface that allows changing between the four connectivity modes and that shows the current state.

QR Codes. Each device is uniquely identifiable through a QR code attached to the device itself. This code is used to connect the specific device with the owner's ConnectivityControl account. This private QR code is accessible only after opening the package of the device. In contrast, a second QR code publicly attached to the device package allows users to retrieve information about the device connectivity modes and corresponding features before purchasing the device. This takes inspiration from the static privacy and security labels proposed by Emami-Naeini et al. [3].

2.4   Web Platform

The React Native web platform enables ConnectivityControl device users foremost to create an account and to manage the devices they own. The platform is accessible on mobile devices and computers. After adding a device through the private and unique device QR code, users can always review the latest ConnectivityLabel associated with this device. In a future iteration, they are also expected to receive email notifications whenever a label associated with a user's device gets updated to reflect new device features or adjusted privacy considerations.

In case a selected device is currently in *online* mode, the users can invoke the dedicated *online* devices features and lower the connectivity level.

2.5   Architecture

Figure 3 provides an overview of the key components introduced in this section and their interplay.

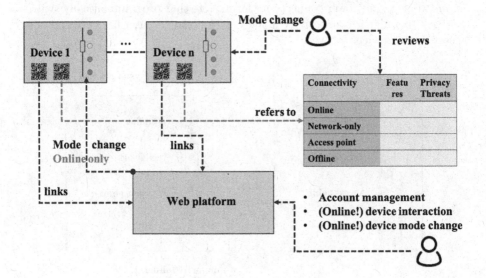

Fig. 3. High-level overview of ConnectivityControl's system architecture.

We note that the web platform is the central hub for account management and provides device control features. However, the device management features are only available for devices that are in *online* mode at the time of platform interaction. Users can always review the ConnectivityLabel of devices, irrespective of their connectivity level and even before actual device purchase/registration. Further, users can always physically manipulate the connectivity level of smart home devices. The same is true on the web platform for *online* devices.

3 Prototypes

Currently, ConnectivityControl includes two prototype devices that showcase the different uses of diverse sensors across the connectivity spectrum. Figure 4 shows the environmental sensing unit and a camera module. Both prototypes are based on the popular low-cost WiFi microcontroller ESP32. The tangible connectivity user interface is based on a linear motorized potentiometer commonly used as a fader in mixing consoles.

In *offline* mode, the environmental sensing unit, shown on the left, displays the temperature and humidity on an integrated LED matrix. In any other mode, it transmits those data digitally. In *network* or *online* mode, the data can be used to control a connected off-the-shelves thermostat. The camera module, in the center, provides recordings on a removable SD card in *offline* mode. Recordings are transmitted according to the connectivity settings in the other three modes. The web interface of ConnectivityControl allows users to contrast features with risks for each corresponding device across the connectivity spectrum.

Fig. 4. The two prototype devices (left: environmental sensing unit; center: camera) share the same four-stage connectivity interface that characterizes ConnectivityControl. Right: The web interface shows the ConnectivityLabel for the environmental sensing unit, contrasting features and risks across the four connectivity levels.

Figure 5 depicts two web interface views, displayed on a mobile device. Users can select among their registered devices (left) for detailed information about the smart home appliance and its data. In the case of the environmental sensing unit (right), the user can review temperature history for those periods in which the device was in *online* mode.

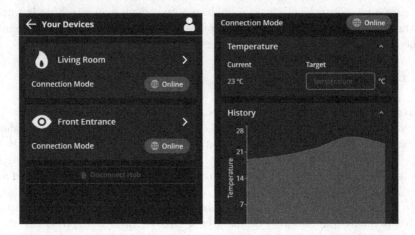

Fig. 5. Some of the principal views of ConnectivityControl's web interface. Left: Overview of the registered devices and their connectivity states. Right: Detailed view of a selected device.

4   Discussion and Future Work

Smart home devices become increasingly attractive due to the multitude of features they provide. Yet, smart home inhabitants and bystanders typically have little control over these devices. Actually disconnecting them from the power outlet or the internet network remains in most cases the only real configuration option, rendering the devices useless. ConnectivityControl envisions an entirely new class of smart device configuration that is based on four network connection levels and clear ConnectivityLabels that allow users to weigh comfort and privacy implications. In this context, we note that the system focuses on TCP/UDP-based data exchange and does not currently consider additional communication schemes and technologies like service-based Bluetooth Low Energy or NFC.

Our latest prototype ecosystem features two devices: one ESP32-based camera and a smart thermostat with environmental sensors. We note that the user-centered development and evaluation of ConnectivityControl requires the future integration of additional device types and models that represent actual smart home configurations to the largest extent possible. Therefore, we hope that the presented physical and web prototypes will spark discussions and interest among device manufacturers and the research community, forming an initiative that develops smart home device ecosystems that highly value diverse device connectivity options. It will be particularly interesting to see how designers deal with lower-than-usual connectivity, in particular *offline* modes. Related to the environmental sensing unit, we deal with this challenge by integrating a display. More complex devices like smart access control systems might need to integrate alternative physical mechanisms like manual locks as secondary interaction modalities.

Besides researching and integrating advanced built-in tangible sensor blockers, we consider the presented strategy highly promising for returning actual smart home privacy control to end users. While we commit to adding smart lighting systems and motorized window blinds to our ecosystem next, we hope for wider contributions from research and practice that will quickly allow running long-term studies on the adoption and use of connectivity-based smart home control systems.

In this context, we note the following user-centered requirements and opportunities for future work. First, extensive user testing will enable the design of a ConnectivityLabel that can be used uniformly across devices. This label must be intuitive for all smart home users and clearly allow weighing between features and risks in relation to the four connectivity levels. While the communication of device features, as illustrated in Fig. 1, might be rather straightforward, the intuitive and detailed communication of privacy threats in such a label remains a research and design challenge. Related work on privacy and security labels [3,5] focused mostly on providing a high-level assessment. Second, future work should explore actual ConnectivityControl user behavior in real smart homes and thoroughly document circumstances and motivations for interaction with the connectivity control interface. This includes dimensions such as the type of user initiating the change (i.e., smart home owner or bystander), the type of device, the origin of interaction (i.e., physical intervention or remote change through the web interface), and the social setting in which the change occurred. Based on the sum of findings from these user-centered research threads, we are confident that future smart home systems sharing control mechanisms as envisioned by ConnectivityControl and its associated ConnectivityLabel will be able to transform how smart home end users, i.e., owners and bystanders, weigh devices' features and risks and take informed decisions.

References

1. Chen, Y., et al.: Wearable microphone jamming. In: Proceedings of the 2020 CHI Conference on Human Factors in Computing Systems, CHI 2020, pp. 1–12. Association for Computing Machinery, New York (2020). https://doi.org/10.1145/3313831. 3376304
2. Do, Y., et al.: Smart webcam cover: exploring the design of an intelligent webcam cover to improve usability and trust. Proc. ACM Interact. Mob. Wearable Ubiquitous Technol. 5(4) (2022). https://doi.org/10.1145/3494983. https://doi-org. emedien.ub.uni-muenchen.de/10.1145/3494983

3. Emami-Naeini, P., Dixon, H., Agarwal, Y., Cranor, L.F.: Exploring how privacy and security factor into IoT device purchase behavior. In: Proceedings of the 2019 CHI Conference on Human Factors in Computing Systems, CHI 2019, pp. 1–12. Association for Computing Machinery, New York (2019). https://doi.org/10.1145/3290605.3300764

4. Obermaier, J., Hutle, M.: Analyzing the security and privacy of cloud-based video surveillance systems. In: Proceedings of the 2nd ACM International Workshop on IoT Privacy, Trust, and Security, IoTPTS 2016, pp. 22–28. Association for Computing Machinery, New York (2016). https://doi.org/10.1145/2899007.2899008

5. Oser, P., et al.: Safer: development and evaluation of an IoT device risk assessment framework in a multinational organization, vol. 4, pp. 1–22. ACM, New York (2020)

6. Tiefenau, C., Häring, M., Gerlitz, E., von Zezschwitz, E.: Making privacy graspable: can we nudge users to use privacy enhancing techniques? (2019). https://doi.org/10.48550/ARXIV.1911.07701. https://arxiv.org/abs/1911.07701

7. Windl, M., Schmidt, A., Feger, S.S.: Investigating tangible privacy-preserving mechanisms for future smart homes (2023)

Designing for a Sustainable Digital Transformation: The DEA Methodology

Barbara Rita Barricelli[1] ⓘ, Daniela Fogli[1](✉) ⓘ, and Angela Locoro[2] ⓘ

[1] Department of Information Engineering, University of Brescia, Brescia, Italy
{barbara.barricelli,daniela.fogli}@unibs.it
[2] Department of Theoretical and Applied Sciences, University of Insubria, Varese, Italy
angela.locoro@uninsubria.it

Abstract. In this paper, we present the DEA (Design for EUDability) methodology, which is derived from the need to design End-User Development (EUD) environments for specific domains and workplaces, by taking into account workers' Computational Thinking (CT) skills. After introducing the concept of EUDability, we outline the phases of the DEA methodology and how they should be iteratively performed. These phases rely on the study of several aspects of a sustainable digital transformation—among others: the domain of application, the work environment, and the ability of people to manage CT practices—and on the characterization of the EUD techniques that could be applied to support the modification, extension, and creation of digital artifacts.

Keywords: End-User Development · Human Work Interaction Design · Sustainable Digital Transformation · Socio-technical design

1 Introduction

A sustainable future requires that anyone possesses adequate skills to interact with the digital world that surrounds us. In this vein, a huge literature in education and Computational Thinking (CT) fosters coding with different kinds of tools in K-12 curricula [3,10,14]. However, there is currently a problem, which will probably worsen in the next few years, due to the digital transformation: that of adults, already inserted in the professional work sectors (35-55-year-old), who do not yet align with the adequate kind of computational literacy [7] necessary to cope with the changes that are coming.

Several studies state that, in the next future, many tasks currently performed by human workers will be performed by machines and several jobs will be replaced by other jobs with higher added value [23,30]. In particular, workers will be more and more asked to carry out problem-solving activities [15,19], which may require the creation, extension and customization of digital artifacts (e.g., software applications, smart environments). These activities should not expect from workers advanced CT skills but should be possibly supported by

L. D. Spano et al. (Eds.): IS-EUD 2023, LNCS 13917, pp. 189–199, 2023.
https://doi.org/10.1007/978-3-031-34433-6_12

tools that favor their gradual acquisition. We believe that End-User Development (EUD) [16,22] may represent the right approach to sustain human workers in the next decade and foster such a transition at the workplace. In [5] the most used EUD techniques and their crossover with a new conveyed model of Computational Thinking have been analyzed and characterized. Then, the authors defined a new construct, EUDability, to capture the quality dimensions of EUD systems suitable to work scenarios where better roles and better tools for individuals may be shaped. EUDability has to do with identifying and assessing the difficulties of using a EUD environment on one side and the CT skills held by individuals on the other side.

We propose here the DEA (Design for EUDability) methodology supporting the introduction of EUD in work settings where EUD techniques are not adopted yet, but where they could potentially improve effectiveness and efficiency of the workers, as well as having a positive impact on the organization. The aim of the paper is to identify and describe the phases of the methodology that lead to the design of EUD environments ensuring a high degree of EUDability.

2 Background and Related Work

According to the original definition reported in [16], End-User Development is "a set of methods, techniques, and tools that allow users of software systems, who are acting as non-professional software developers, at some point to create, modify, or extend a software artifact". The definition of EUD highlights two important aspects: i) the need of users, and especially domain experts, while using digital artifacts, to tailor them to their work and preferences; ii) the different types of EUD activities that users may ask or be required to perform, from simple modification (adaptation) of a system, to system extension with new features, until the more complex activity of artifact creation. The former aspect has been deepened in literature by presenting applications of EUD methods and techniques in various domains, e.g., business and data management [6], healthcare [26], e-government [29] and industrial contexts [18], often delineating users' profile and presenting laboratory usability studies of the proposed EUD solution [27]. The latter aspect has been explored in the surveys of Paternò [21], Maceli [17] and Barricelli et al. [4]. The paper [21] underlines the need to balance the complexity of the EUD activity and the learning effort required to the users. The author also reflects on the generality of the EUD approach, the coverage of main interactive aspects, and the use of abstraction to hide implementation details. Maceli [17] classifies and describes the EUD technology tools proposed in literature by highlighting how few works considered novel interaction modalities based on tangible and voice interfaces. The systematic mapping study presented in [4] analyzes the different EUD techniques found in the literature and classifies them on the basis of the type of interaction or metaphor adopted in the user interface. As a result, 14 techniques are presented in the paper, from the most frequent used to the less frequent ones: *component-based* (also known as block-based), *rule-based, programming-by-demonstration, spreadsheet-based, wizard-based, template-based, natural language, workflow and dataflow diagrams, model-based, text-based, digital sketching, annotation-based, assertion-based,* and *gesture-based.*

User-centered design (UCD) [1,20] and participatory design (PD) [25] have been traditionally proposed as methodologies suitable to the design of complex interactive systems. Both of them prescribe that representative users are involved (more or less actively) during the design phase. However, EUD aims to transfer to end users those activities that software developers usually carry out at use time, such as system customization to users' preferences or its extension with new functionalities. For this reason, meta-design [8,9] has been proposed as a framework to conceive interactive systems as seeds that may evolve in the users' hands. The meta-design framework plays a fundamental role in the conceptualization of a EUD environment, but it does not describe the concrete design phases to be put in place. A contribution in this direction is provided in [12], where the authors introduced an approach to designing EUD environments for multi-tiered proxy design problems structured in three phases: i) a meta-design phase based on meta-modeling, ii) a design phase based on instantiating the meta-model, and iii) a use phase. However, that approach is neither applicable to all types of design problems that require a EUD environment nor detailed enough with respect to the choice of the most suitable EUD techniques for the target end-user developers.

We propose here a design methodology, in the frame of meta-design, which aims to provide a concrete account of the activities that the design team should perform with representative users to build a EUD environment that is not only usable but also "EUDable".

3   EUDability

EUDability is a novel construct introduced in [5] defined as *the degree of concreteness, modularity, structuredness, reusability, and testability fostered by a EUD environment designed for specified end-user developers, with a specified goal to be pursued in a specified context.* The five dimensions of EUDability have been identified by intersecting EUD techniques with the most significant and frequent Computational Thinking skills described in literature, namely: Abstraction, Decomposition, Algorithm Design, Generalization, and Evaluation. Paraphrasing [5], EUDability dimensions are characterized as follows:

- *Concreteness:* it is the capability of a EUD environment of presenting concepts and requests in a concrete way, without asking highly-developed abstraction skills;
- *Modularity:* it is the availability in a EUD environment of different components, blocks, or elements, which help end-user developers decompose a problem into sub-problems to find a solution;
- *Structuredness:* it is the capability of a EUD environment to support the structuring of a solution in a step-by-step process and the connection between the input and output of the different steps;

– *Reusability*: it is the possibility of reusing the outcome of a EUD activity carried out with a EUD environment in other situations and by other end-user developers;
– *Testability*: it is the availability, within the EUD environment, of features for testing the outcome of the EUD activities.

The *end-user developers* considered in the definition of EUDability are human workers with different CT skills, who are called on to carry out EUD activities for the sake of their work. These end-user developers might pursue different types of goals related to EUD, namely: i) *modification* of an existing digital artifact, as in the case of the definition of behaviors of an industrial IoT ecosystem by means of a rule-based EUD environment [18]; ii) *extension* of a digital artifact with new features, as when new objects or manipulations are defined in the context of collaborative robotics where robot tasks can be defined by operators without programming or robotics knowledge [11]; iii) *creation* of a new digital artifact, as when physiotherapists define exercises based on a tangible display, which are personalized to their patients [26].

4   The DEA Methodology

The design methodology proposed in this paper is iterative and structured along 5 phases (see Fig. 1). Phases 1, 2 and 4 recall typical phases of UCD and Design Thinking (DT) methodologies. They are herewith extended with specific activities related to the design of EUD environments. Phases 3 and 5 are more characteristic of the novel design approach presented, relying on the peculiar nature of EUD, i.e., a bunch of "brick and mortar" assets to be applied in varied problem-solving modalities. The phases are carried out sequentially until the results from the EUDability evaluation are available. If the results suggest that the degree of EUDability of the environment can be improved, one or more of the first four phases will be carried out again to solve any existing issues and improve the EUDability of the designed artifact. Such iteration could occur several times until the desired degree of EUDability is reached. At the end of the iterative execution of the DEA methodology's phases, development and subsequent usability and user experience analyses occur.

4.1   Phase 1: Context of Use Analysis

In this phase, the application domain should be analyzed by delineating the nature of the EUD activities that users should perform to pursue their work. This phase can be accomplished gathering insights with questionnaires and interviews on business processes by involving key informants (i.e., domain experts). After the business process as-is analysis, the designer must identify the digital transformation that could be applied, with a particular attention to the type of EUD that could support it. The type of EUD refers to the nature of the activity that is performed through EUD, namely: modification, extension or creation of a digital artifact.

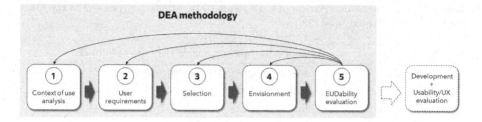

Fig. 1. The five DEA methodology's phases. Development and Usability/UX evaluation are not included in the DEA methodology.

In this phase, it is also crucial to analyse the physical context where the work activities are carried out, by gathering information about environment space, noise and lighting, as well as about the type of workers' equipment, which may include gloves or glasses that may potentially interfere with some types of interaction needed to perform EUD activities.

4.2 Phase 2: User Requirements

In this phase of the DEA methodology, the users are observed during their activities and are interviewed to gather a picture of what they potentially need to accomplish their tasks with digital tools. In this phase, their Computational Thinking level should also be assessed. The direct observation of users at work is essential to identify how they interact with the work environment, the activities that they are normally attending, and the kind of tasks and routines that imply some sort of repetitive behaviour, semi-automatization or configuration-like completion. With interviews with users, researchers aim to acquire as much knowledge as possible about the users' background, education, abilities, work experience, role, and preferences. The CT level should emerge as a property of the users' experience and potential to manage a EUD approach for accomplishing their tasks. In this respect, the Tsai's Computational Thinking Scale (CTS) assessment test [28] is firstly administered to users. It will subsequently be taken into account when considering the tasks potentially requiring one or more of the CT skills identified for EUD. The CTS assessment items are reported in Table 1, together with the CT skills activated during EUD usage and management. The CTS assessment test is exploited to determine the degree of users' experience in practicing the EUD activities identified in Phase 1, namely: modification, extension, and creation of digital artifacts. At the end of this phase, it is established the degree of expertise of EUD prospective users in relation to their habitual tasks, their work environment, and their CT skills for EUD.

4.3 Phase 3: Selection

The third phase of the methodology relies on the designers' competence in the EUD field: they must draw on their previous experience in designing interactive

Table 1. A synthetic description of CTS items to be assessed in phase 2 of the DEA methodology (adapted from [28]).

Skills	Items (What users perceive they are able to do)
Abstraction	1. see the whole point, not the details
	2. identify relations
	3. find key points
	4. see common patterns
Decomposition	1. decompose a problem into pieces
	2. structure a problem
	3. know how to split a problem into smaller problems
Algorithmic Thinking	1. figure a step-by-step solution
	2. find an effective solution
	3. layout the steps
	4. figure how to execute a step
Generalization	1. solve problems based on one's experience
	2. use a common way to solve problems
	3. apply a given solution to a new problem
	4. apply a familiar solution to new problems
Evaluation	1. find a correct solution
	2. think of the best solution
	3. find the most effective solution
	4. think of the fastest solution

systems for EUD and also capitalize on the expertise of the EUD community reported in the scientific literature. This phase aims to select one or more EUD techniques best suited to the application domain and the specific type of activity to be performed in the project under consideration.

It should be noted that, in this phase of the DEA methodology, the preliminary choice of potential valid techniques is not influenced by the level of users' CT, determined in the previous phase: the objective of the Selection phase is to exclude those techniques that do not suit the final goals, the environmental conditions in which the EUD activity is to be performed, or the application domain in which it operates (e.g., white-collar workers may have different needs than blue-collar workers, since EUD techniques for data management are usually different from those used for operating on robotic devices).

In [4] the use of specific EUD techniques in interactive systems has been explored considering several application domains. The analysis of the scientific literature on EUD reported in fact that some techniques are more recurrently used in some domains than others. With a more precise characterization, the EUD techniques identified in [4] can be conceived as different EUD paradigms, which can be implemented in EUD environments using a specific interaction

Table 2. Suitability of EUD paradigms with respect to the different types of EUD.

EUD paradigm	Modify	Extend	Create
Component-, Text- based, and Workflow/dataflow diagram	●	●	●
Programming-by-demonstration/example		●	●
Rule- and Spreadsheet- based	●	●	
Wizard with form-based interaction	●		●
Template- and Assertion- based	●		
Model-, Annotation-, Card- based, and Digital Sketching			●

style. The interaction styles that are usually offered to the user are direct manipulation and conversational interaction or, more recently, augmented reality [2]. Therefore, the classification of EUD techniques proposed in [4] can be improved by removing the categories *natural language* and *gesture-based*, which refer to the interaction style rather than to the EUD paradigm; indeed, the former can lead back to the *conversational interaction* style, the latter to the *direct manipulation* style. In addition, further research carried out in the EUD field in the last years (e.g., [13,24]) yield the proposal of a new EUD paradigm that we may call *card-based*. It consists of supporting users with physical or virtual cards that suggest them how to combine sensors and actuators, and their respective input and output, to create interactive smart objects in an intuitive and joyful way.

The suitability of the resulting 13 paradigms is evaluated in the Selection phase with reference to the type of EUD activities required in the given domain that emerged in the Context of Use and User Requirements Analysis phases. Based on our experience in the field and on the literature review in [4], we propose Table 2 as a starting point for selecting the most suitable EUD paradigm for the case at hand.

4.4   Phase 4: Envisionment

In the fourth phase, the designers exploit the results obtained in the previous phases to choose how to implement the EUD environment in terms of interaction style. Once the final EUD technique (i.e., the combination of EUD paradigm and interaction style) is identified, the designer will proceed with the envisionment activity by creating a prototype that can be used in the last phase of the DEA methodology (i.e., EUDability evaluation). Should more than one EUD technique be compatible with the case at hand, the designer can proceed in two ways: 1) make a choice dictated by factors such as cost or time required for implementation, or 2) proceed with prototyping multiple alternatives and defer the final decision to the evaluation phase.

4.5   Phase 5: EUDability Evaluation

In this last phase, the design process proceeds with a predictive evaluation for measuring the EUDability of the prototypes (or prototype, in case just one has been realized) resulting from the Envisionment phase. The assessment method is inspective, carried out by experts in Human-Computer Interaction and particularly in EUD, and is focused on exploring the EUDability of prototypes in their entirety by compiling the 15-item checklist shown in Table 3.

Table 3. Checklist for EUDability evaluation.

Dimensions	Items to check (Y/N forced choice)
Concreteness	The EUD environment:
	1. represents the domain concepts as elements for problem solving
	2. does not require to know the low-level details of each element
	3. uses the language that is more familiar to the end user
Modularity	The EUD environment allows:
	4. the identification of elements that may compose a problem solution
	5. organizing the elements in meaningful categories
	6. freely exploring each category of elements
Structuredness	The EUD environment suggests:
	7. the steps to be performed for problem solving
	8. the order of the steps to be performed for problem solving
	9. the connectedness between different steps of the problem solution
Reusability	The outcome resulting from a EUD activity can be:
	10. saved in a library
	11. included in another EUD project
	12. modified to be adapted to another EUD project
Testability	The outcome resulting from a EUD activity can be:
	13. executed within the EUD environment
	14. inspected by the user
	15. represented in alternative ways

5   Conclusion

In this paper, we introduced the DEA methodology, aimed at supporting the design of EUD environments and their evaluation with respect to the EUDability dimensions, to be deployed in work scenarios requiring a digital transformation. Sustainability of the digital transformation is ensured by the assessment of human workers' CT skills and the selection of the most adequate EUD techniques for the case at hand.

The DEA methodology represents a novel contribution with respect to the approaches to designing interactive systems (i.e., UCD, PD, and DT), and to the approaches specifically oriented to EUD, such as meta-design. In particular, it aims to provide concrete indications for introducing EUD in work domains where end users could not possess high CT skills or the characteristics of the environment could or could not foster certain implementations of EUD paradigms. We are planning to validate the DEA methodology in the next future through its application in a real case in the healthcare domain, where domain experts will be required to define tasks for collaborative robots supporting their work. In the meanwhile, this paper would like to solicit a discussion within the EUD community about EUDability for EUD environments, and how to pursue it through the DEA methodology.

References

1. Abras, C., Maloney-Krichmar, D., Preece, J., et al.: User-centered design. In: Bainbridge, W. (ed.) Encyclopedia of Human-Computer Interaction, vol. 37, no. 4, pp. 445–456. Sage Publications, Thousand Oaks (2004)

2. Ariano, R., Manca, M., Paternò, F., Santoro, C.: Smartphone-based augmented reality for end-user creation of home automations. Behav. Inf. Technol. **42**(1), 124–140 (2023). https://doi.org/10.1080/0144929x.2021.2017482

3. Barr, V., Stephenson, C.: Bringing computational thinking to k-12: what is involved and what is the role of the computer science education community? ACM Inroads **2**(1), 48–54 (2011). https://doi.org/10.1145/1929887.1929905

4. Barricelli, B.R., Cassano, F., Fogli, D., Piccinno, A.: End-user development, end-user programming and end-user software engineering: a systematic mapping study. J. Syst. Softw. **149**, 101–137 (2019). https://doi.org/10.1016/j.jss.2018.11.041

5. Barricelli, B.R., Fogli, D., Locoro, A.: Eudability: a new construct at the intersection of end-user development and computational thinking. J. Syst. Softw. **195**, 111516 (2023). https://doi.org/10.1016/j.jss.2022.111516

6. Dax, J., Ludwig, T., Meurer, J., Pipek, V., Stein, M., Stevens, G.: FRAMES – a framework for adaptable mobile event-contingent self-report studies. In: Díaz, P., Pipek, V., Ardito, C., Jensen, C., Aedo, I., Boden, A. (eds.) IS-EUD 2015. LNCS, vol. 9083, pp. 141–155. Springer, Cham (2015). https://doi.org/10.1007/978-3-319-18425-8_10

7. DiSessa, A.A.: Computational literacy and "the big picture" concerning computers in mathematics education. Math. Think. Learn. **20**(1), 3–31 (2018)

8. Fischer, G., Fogli, D., Piccinno, A.: Revisiting and broadening the meta-design framework for end-user development. In: Paternò, F., Wulf, V. (eds.) New Perspectives in End-User Development, pp. 61–97. Springer, Cham (2017). https://doi.org/10.1007/978-3-319-60291-2_4

9. Fischer, G., Giaccardi, E.: Meta-design: a framework for the future of end-user development. In: Lieberman, H., Paternò, F., Wulf, V. (eds.) End User Development, pp. 427–457. Springer, Dordrecht (2006). https://doi.org/10.1007/1-4020-5386-X_19

10. Fletcher, G.H.L., Lu, J.J.: Human computing skills: rethinking the k-12 experience. Commun. ACM **52**(2), 23–25 (2009). https://doi.org/10.1145/1461928.1461938

11. Fogli, D., Gargioni, L., Guida, G., Tampalini, F.: A hybrid approach to user-oriented programming of collaborative robots. Robot. Comput.-Integr. Manuf. **73**, 102234 (2022). https://doi.org/10.1016/j.rcim.2021.102234

12. Fogli, D., Piccinno, A.: Co-evolution of end-user developers and systems in multi-tiered proxy design problems. In: Dittrich, Y., Burnett, M., Mørch, A., Redmiles, D. (eds.) IS-EUD 2013. LNCS, vol. 7897, pp. 153–168. Springer, Heidelberg (2013). https://doi.org/10.1007/978-3-642-38706-7_12

13. Gennari, R., Matera, M., Melonio, A., Rizvi, M., Roumelioti, E.: The evolution of a toolkit for smart-thing design with children through action research. Int. J. Child-Comput. Interact. **31**, 100359 (2022). https://doi.org/10.1016/j.ijcci.2021.100359

14. Grover, S., Pea, R.: Computational thinking in k-12: a review of the state of the field. Educ. Res. **42**(1), 38–43 (2013). https://doi.org/10.3102/0013189X12463051

15. Kaasinen, E., et al.: Mobile service technician 4.0: knowledge-sharing solutions for industrial field maintenance. Interact. Des. Archit.(s) **2018**(38), 6–27 (2019)

16. Lieberman, H., Paternò, F., Wulf, V.: End User Development. Human-Computer Interaction Series, Springer, Heidelberg (2006). https://doi.org/10.1007/1-4020-5386-X

17. Maceli, M.G.: Tools of the trade: a survey of technologies in end-user development literature. In: Barbosa, S., Markopoulos, P., Paternò, F., Stumpf, S., Valtôlina, S. (eds.) IS-EUD 2017. LNCS, vol. 10303, pp. 49–65. Springer, Cham (2017). https://doi.org/10.1007/978-3-319-58735-6_4

18. Manca, M., Paternò, F., Santoro, C.: End-user development in industrial contexts: the paper mill case study. Behav. Inf. Technol. **41**(9), 1848–1864 (2022). https://doi.org/10.1080/0144929X.2022.2089597

19. Merisotis, J.: Human Work in the Age of Smart Machines. RosettaBooks, New York (2020)

20. Norman, D.A., Draper, S.W.: User Centered System Design. New Perspectives on Human-Computer Interaction. L. Erlbaum Associates Inc., USA (1986)

21. Paternò, F.: End user development: Survey of an emerging field for empowering people. ISRN Softw. Eng. (2013). https://doi.org/10.1155/2013/532659

22. Paternò, F., Wulf, V. (eds.): New Perspectives in End-User Development. Springer, Cham (2017). https://doi.org/10.1007/978-3-319-60291-2

23. PwC: Workforce of the future: The competing forces shaping 2030 (2018). https://www.pwc.com/gx/en/services/people-organisation/workforce-of-the-future/workforce-of-the-future-the-competing-forces-shaping-2030-pwc.pdf

24. Roumelioti, E., Pellegrino, M.A., Rizvi, M., D'Angelo, M., Gennari, R.: Smart-thing design by children at a distance: how to engage them and make them learn. Int. J. Child-Comput. Interact. **33**, 100482 (2022). https://doi.org/10.1016/j.ijcci.2022.100482

25. Schuler, D.C., Namioka, A.: Participatory Design: Principles and Practices. CRC Press (1993)

26. Tetteroo, D.: Tagtrainer: end-user adaptable technology for physical rehabilitation. In: Proceedings of the 11th EAI International Conference on Pervasive Computing Technologies for Healthcare, PervasiveHealth 2017, pp. 452–454. Association for Computing Machinery, New York (2017). https://doi.org/10.1145/3154862.3154901

27. Tetteroo, D., Markopoulos, P.: A review of research methods in end user development. In: Díaz, P., Pipek, V., Ardito, C., Jensen, C., Aedo, I., Boden, A. (eds.) IS-EUD 2015. LNCS, vol. 9083, pp. 58–75. Springer, Cham (2015). https://doi.org/10.1007/978-3-319-18425-8_5

28. Tsai, M.J., Liang, J.C., Hsu, C.Y.: The computational thinking scale for computer literacy education. J. Educ. Comput. Res. **59**(4), 579–602 (2021)

29. Valtolina, S., Barricelli, B.R., Fogli, D., Colosio, S., Testa, C.: Public staff empowerment in e-government: a human work interaction design approach. In: Barbosa, S., Markopoulos, P., Paternò, F., Stumpf, S., Valtolina, S. (eds.) IS-EUD 2017. LNCS, vol. 10303, pp. 119–134. Springer, Cham (2017). https://doi.org/10.1007/978-3-319-58735-6_9
30. World Economic Forum: The future of jobs report 2020 (2020). https://www.weforum.org/reports/the-future-of-jobs-report-2020

Supporting End-User Development

Exploring Visual Languages for Prototyping Interactive Behaviors for Tangible Virtual Reality

Andrea Bellucci(✉)[iD], Paloma Díaz[iD], and Ignacio Aedo[iD]

Department of Computer Science and Engineering, Universidad Carlos III de Madrid,
Avenida de la Universidad 30, 28911 Leganés, Madrid, Spain
{andrea.bellucci,mpaloma.diaz,ignacio.aedo}@uc3m.es

Abstract. We explore potentials and limitations of visual programming environments to prototype Tangible Virtual Reality interactive behaviors, a technically complex task that requires the integration of real-time tracking hardware as well as software to program what happens in the virtual world given the position and orientation of physical objects. We created a plugin and an ad-hoc library to ease the integration of tracking hardware in the Unreal Blueprints visual environment and facilitated a one-day contextual inquiry workshop with six designers and researchers (with textual programming expertise) programming interactive behaviors using our library. Observations and contextual interviews with participants involved in two design activities uncovered areas of development for future visual end-user tools: provide different layers of abstraction, embrace liveness, foster in situ immersive programming and enable the use of interactive machine learning to program behaviors via users' physical demonstration.

Keywords: tangible virtual reality · visual programming languages · interactive behaviors

1 Introduction

Tangible Virtual Reality (VR) is a form of Mixed-Reality that incorporates physical objects and surfaces into a virtual world to create a more immersive and embodied interactive experience [19], as users can physically manipulate virtual objects through physical proxies and haptic feedback devices [10]. Tangible VR has showed potential for enhancing real-world training and simulations [11], as well as to support spatial cognition and skills [7] or to enable more engaging game experiences [13].

Creating Tangible VR *interactive behaviors*, that is, programming anything that happens in the virtual environment as a response to a user interaction with a physical object, however, is more technically complex than traditional VR. It requires the integration of hardware that can track physical objects in real time (e.g., markers and sensors that provide position and orientation of an object

© The Author(s), under exclusive license to Springer Nature Switzerland AG 2023
L. D. Spano et al. (Eds.): IS-EUD 2023, LNCS 13917, pp. 203–219, 2023.
https://doi.org/10.1007/978-3-031-34433-6_13

inside a tracking area), together with creation tools, editors and game engines to program what happens in the virtual world, given the position and orientation of physical objects in the physical world [13]. For instance, rendering virtual elements that are anchored to a physical proxy, managing collision of physical objects with virtual elements or, making the virtual environment reacting to users' interaction with a physical object.

Text-based languages, such as C# or C++, have been the standard for programming interactive behaviors in VR, since the task inherently make use of programming concepts such as conditionality (e.g., a behavior that happens if an object is at a certain distance of another object) or loops (e.g., a behavior that happens as long a user is touching an object). Recently, the use of node-based visual languages has gained traction thanks to their integration in popular game engines: Unreal Engine offers the Blueprints[1] visual scripting environment and the Bolt[2] environment is shipped with the Unity Editor.

Visual programming involves creating visual graphs of interconnected nodes to represent the logic and behavior of an application and has showed potential to lower the barrier for the creation of interactive behaviors through the manipulations of graphical elements [8]. High-level visual programming languages can foster creativity and rapid prototyping by allowing designers to quickly try out different ideas and to experiment with different configurations [8]. This is especially crucial in the complex design space of physical interactions in virtual environments, as the user experience depends on the purposeful integration of diverse factors for which design guidelines are underdeveloped, such as interaction methods (e.g., physical controllers, gestures, full body movement), navigation techniques, sensorial feedback and affordances of physical objects.

In this work, we report the results of contextual inquiry observations and interviews [4] with six designers and researchers with programming experience during a workshop we facilitated with the goal to *uncover potentials and limitations of current visual tools to program interactive behaviors for Tangible VR with physical objects as proxies of virtual objects*. Such physical proxies are also known as passive haptics in the literature [1]. We provide insights in terms of designers' preferences and highlight four areas of development for future visual-based programming tools for Tangible VR: provide layers of abstraction, support liveness, foster in situ immersive programming and exploit interactive machine learning for physical demonstration.

2   Related Work

Our work builds upon the literature on visual programming languages for creating interactive behaviors, either in virtual reality or for live performances (e.g., live coding), as well as research methods to inquiry users' preferences.

---

[1] https://www.unrealengine.com/es-ES/.

[2] https://assetstore.unity.com/packages/tools/visual-scripting/bolt-163802.

2.1   Visual Programming Languages for Interactive Behaviors

Visual programming languages (VPLs) allow the creation of software programs using a visual interface rather than a text-based syntax. Code is represented as graphical blocks that can be dragged and dropped onto a canvas and connected together to compose a program [21]. VPLs are generally easier to learn and use, as they rely on direct manipulation of graphical elements and, thus, they do not require to memorize abstract syntaxes. They can also be more intuitive and provide a more immediate feedback loop, as programmers can see the results of their code in real-time.

Due to their potential to lower the barrier for non-programmers, VPLs have been long object of research in the End-User Development community in different domains, from the Scratch block-based programming environment to develop fluency with computational concepts [25], to CoBlox [29], a block-based visual environment for programming the behavior of a robotic arm, to the Node-Red low-code, data-flow environment for connecting devices, applications and services [18].

Data-flow programming has been proposed as a key technology for enabling digital artists' self-expression in virtual reality [26]; it allows to use a graphical interface to design software systems by connecting visual nodes that represent data sources, processing algorithms, and outputs. Data-flow programming tools, such as Node-Red [18], provide libraries of pre-built nodes for common operations, as well as the ability to create custom nodes for specific applications. This approach to visual programming has successfully enabled interactive performances that require live coding and real-time control over the program in execution, for instance in the music-making and New Interfaces for Musical Expression (NIME) community [14]. Previous works have explored the potential of flow-based VPLs for virtual and mixed-reality applications. For instance, the X-Reality Toolkit proposed an interface to create simplified visual trigger-action rules to program cross-reality environments [3]. EntangleVR [8] provides a reactive visual programming interface as a plugin for the Unity game engine to generate virtual reality interactive behaviors that uses the entanglment quantum effect as design metaphor. Chu and Zaman [9] proposed a plugin for the Unreal Engine Blueprints visual scripting language to support rapid prototyping through the exploration of alternative ideas, such as exploring multiple variants of a game mechanic, game objects, different scenarios that can be seen in the game, or multiple combinations of game mechanics. FlowMatic [31] implements an ad-hoc, simplified flow-based visual language to program interactive behaviors while immersed in the virtual environment, showing that immersive authoring is a promising paradigm for creating interactive behaviors, compared to textual, imperative programming. While immersive programming could engage users, fostering liveness and natural interaction, other EUD authoring environments such as VREUD [30] showed that simple interactive VR scenes can be easily prototyped by non-technical users through a desktop authoring environment and a menu-based interface to configure trigger-action interactions with conditions.

Despite the interest of the academia as well as the industry, the potential and drawbacks of VPLs for programming interactive behaviors with physical objects in virtual environments has not yet been investigated.

2.2 Inquiring Designers' Preferences

Different research methods have been applied in the literature to understand designers, developers and researchers' needs, behaviors, and preferences with respect to programming tools for interactive systems. Krauß et al. [16] interviewed practitioners (n = 17) to uncover needs for future XR tools from the industry perspective. They, however, recognized that online interviews was a limiting factors, and further research would benefit from direct observation and participatory inquiry methods. Myers et al. [20] applied contextual inquiry [4] to gather insights on how designers (n = 13) program interactive behaviors by observing and interacting with them in their natural environment, while they were engaged in their work process. They employed retrospective and walk-throughs, and assessed their results with a large scale (n = 259) online survey. In another study, one-to-one, semi-structured, *in situ* interviews with HCI researchers (n = 9) were conducted employing the critical incident technique [12] to uncover the needs of researchers when prototyping new interaction techniques and how well existing toolkits and frameworks support them [23]. Bellucci et al. [2] proposed the extreme co-design tactic to run *in situ* design workshops with families, interleaved with short cycles of implementations of desired features and use of the resulting prototype. Workshops with (re)programmable prototypes have been proposed by Borowsky and Larsen-Ledet [5] to understand how to engage end-users (n = 13) in the modification and customization of high-fidelity interactive prototypes.

In our study, we combined contextual inquiry in a workshop setup, applying the recommendations distilled by Borowsky and Larsen-Ledet [5] on familiarization, expectations, exploration and levels of programming experience when working with programmable prototypes.

3   Method

We facilitated a one-day, four-hours workshop with six designers and HCI researchers with expertise and interest in virtual reality programming environments and applications. Participants completed a design activity, programming a puzzle for a mixed-reality escape room, using the Unreal Engine Blueprints visual scripting language together with the Antilatency[3] positional tracking system and a software library we crafted to offer high-level visual functions that ease the integration of physical tracked objects in a VR application.

---

[3] https://antilatency.com/.

3.1   Unreal Engine Blueprints Visual Scripting

The Blueprints language allows the creation of 3D gameplay mechanics and interactive systems without writing code. It consists of a set of nodes that represent various functions, events, and variables within the Unreal Engine 3D authoring tool. Blueprints are arranged by connecting nodes together to create a flowchart-like structure. Each node performs a specific action, such as moving a character or playing a sound effect, and can be customized with various inputs and outputs to control how the action is executed. There are several types of nodes available, including: event (triggered by specific events, such as when a button is pressed or a character enters a certain area), action (i.e., perform a specific action, such as moving a character or spawning an object), branch (to split the flow of execution based on a condition, such as if a certain variable is true or false), variables (representing data values that can be stored and manipulated within the script) and functions. Function nodes allow developers to create custom behaviors that can be called from other parts of the Blueprint.

While Blueprints covers the needs of developers to create complex 3D interactive environments without requiring in-depth programming knowledge, it does not offer predefined functions and nodes to integrate physical objects as proxies for virtual objects, and program their interactive behavior. To create a low-threshold starting point for participants, we developed a Blueprints plugin (TangibleVR) for adding tracked physical objects in room-scale mixed-reality experiences.

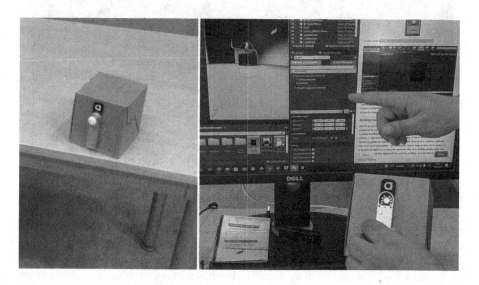

Fig. 1. The Antilatency Alt and a socket for tracking physical objects.

3.2   The TangibleVR Plugin and the XRoom Library

We built our TangibleVR plugin on top of the Antilatency optical tracking system that offers small-sized IR trackers (the *Alt*) and supports modular design through the combination of different sockets (Fig. 1). The sockets provide wireless tracking capabilities for Head-Mounted displays (HDM socket) and physical objects (Tag socket) as well as hands or other body parts (Bracer socket). Thus, the Alt attached to a physical object through the Tag socket, provides real-time spatial mapping data (position and orientation) of the object with respect to a tracking area. The plugin follows the Entity-Components-System pattern typical of 3D authoring tools. At its lowest level, it allows to add a tracked physical proxy to the 3D scene by a special pawn[4] Entity called *ALItem* (Fig. 2), which corresponds to an Antilatency Tag socket with its Alt tracker. A designer can link a tracked object to its virtual representation in the world by manually configure the id of the socket in a text field of the *BP_AltTrackerTag* Component.

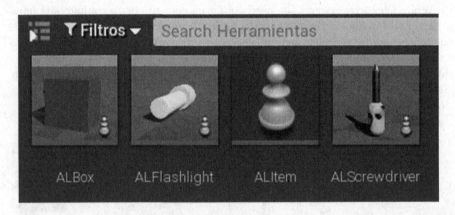

Fig. 2. The ALItem Entity used in the library to abstract the Antilatency SDK and ease the configuration of tracked entities.

The ALItem Entity, and its attached BP_AltTrackerTag Component, abstracts the technicalies of configuring the Antilatency trackers in the Unreal Engine authoring system (a task that, otherwise, should be done via the Antilantency C++ SDK). On top of this basic Entity, we built a collection of default, ready-to-use scenes, entities and Blueprints functions to build basic interactions based on physical and/or virtual positions of the objects and players in the scene (both absolute or relative to other objects) as well as events such as collisions or raycasting, and actions such as show/hide an entity, or change its color, shape, texture, or position. A *Manager* System operates over all the ALItems in the scene.

---

[4] A "pawn" typically refers to a basic, low-level game object (Entity) that can be controlled or manipulated by a player or AI.

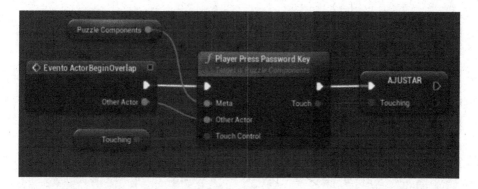

Fig. 3. Example of a Blueprints visual script to implement an interactive behavior: a user is touching a physical objects that acts as a key to open a safe in the virtual world.

Together with the TangibleVR plugin, for the purpose of the workshop, that is, to observe designers while performing a tangible mixed-reality programming task using a node-based visual language, we developed XRoom[5] an ad-hoc library of higher-level Blueprints functions and tools to support the design of a mixed-reality escape room experience at the intersection of the physical and the virtual world.

The library was organized in a set of ready-made scenes, tools, user-configurable puzzle components and associated Blueprints functions. By adding a puzzle component to a virtual entity, access is granted to the Blueprints functions of the library. For instance, Fig. 3 shows an interactive behavior pre-implemented by the library: toggle a boolean variable while a user touches an object (it could be a physical or a virtual object). Figure 4 shows an example a complex pre-defined behavior available in the library, that participants could use as-is, or remix to implement their desired behavior: a virtual element associated to a physical proxy is made visible only while a second physical object keeps contact with a third object.

3.3 Participants

We selected 6 participants (5 male, 1 other) aged 20–39 ($M = 29$, $SD = 4.5$) with various degrees of computer engineering and research expertise: two HCI researchers (PhD), and four students (three graduate and one undergraduate), all of them in Computer Science and Engineering. We recruited our participants locally, from our research group. All the participants had at least four years of programming experience and had previous experience with the creation of immersive systems ($M = 4$ years, $Mdn = 3$, $SD = 3.6$). Three participants had 5 or more years of experience with virtual reality environments, while the rest had

---

[5] The TangibleVR plugin and the XRoom library are available at https://drive.google.com/drive/folders/19md1j7xzApyo1CAOCZ8-J9-brO7VhDWS.

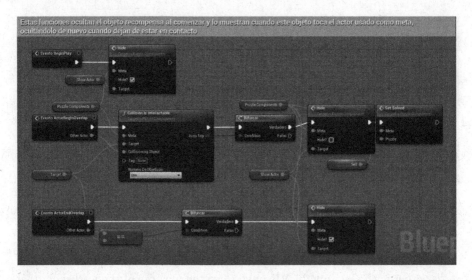

Fig. 4. Example of a Blueprints visual script to implement an interactive behavior: a virtual element associated with a physical proxy is made visible only while a second physical object keeps contact with a third object.

worked with virtual reality environments for one year. Five out of six had never used Unreal Engine before. While all the participants self-reported they were proficient in textual programming in C++, they never used visual syntaxis for programming interactive behaviors in mixed-reality applications. All the participants reported that they are currently working on the design of immersive systems in different application contexts (e.g., the use of augmented reality for dementia care or videogames) as well as the integration with tangible technologies and artificial intelligence (i.e., one-shot object recognition, hand gestures or full-body movement recognition). Four out of six participants knew and had used some kind of visual programming language: three participants had used block-based visual languages such as Scratch and one participant had used node-based visual programming for procedural modeling in Blender and Unity. Even if all the participants had virtual or augmented reality programming experience, none of them had previously programmed, let alone experienced, the use of physical objects in virtual reality. Five out of six participants had never used Unreal Engine before.

3.4   Procedure

The workshop took place in a 64m2 room equipped with a 3x3m2 Antilatency tracking surface and three workstations with HP OMEN 30L dekstop computers (32GB RAM, GeForce GTX 3080), 27in LCD displays and a Meta Quest 2. The research protocol and data collection were approved by the university research ethics board. We video recorded, through screen capturing, the design activity

Fig. 5. A participant experiencing the interaction with physical proxies in the mixed-reality escape room scenario.

and also audio recorded participants answers of the contextual interview. We took paper notes to document the observations. The schedule of the workshop was as follows:

Introduction (15 min). Participants were given a brief introduction to the purpose of this study. Participants were highly interested in the topic and they seemed thrilled to learn about visual programming languages and to provide feedback that could shape the design of future authoring tools for tangible VR. Before continuing, participants were asked to fill a consent form and provide demographic and background information: age, education, years of programming experience and experience with immersive environment programming and visual languages.

Experiencing Tangible VR (30 min). Each participants experienced the mixed-reality escape room scenario they were going to design in the guided activity (Fig. 5). This step was facilitated to raise participants' awareness, through direct interaction, about the possibilities and user experience of how it feels to walk freely in a room-scale virtual environment and to interact with their hands and physical objects, instead of standard controllers. One by one, participants were helped by one researcher to put on a Meta Quest 2 headset and they freely explored and interacted with the escape room scenario for about five minutes, using the available tracked physical objects (e.g., a torch or a box, see Fig. 5) to solve puzzles.

XRoom Training and Guided Design Activity (120 min). One researcher gave participants a primer on the Unreal Engine user interface and the Blueprints

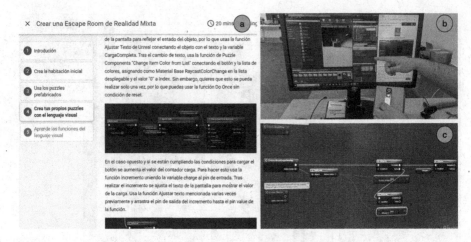

Fig. 6. The guided design activity. a) The fourth step of the tutorial in which participants created a custom puzzle: hold the hand on a physical object to charge a battery. b) A participant trying out what he was implementing with his design partner. c) An excerpt of the visual code to implement an interactive behavior: the hand is touching the physical object (i.e., the hand is colliding with the digital representation of the physical object).

visual system. Participants had previous experience with the Unity authoring environment and quickly grasped the basics of Unreal Engine. They were then grouped in three pairs. Each pair was assigned a workstation and asked to follow a tutorial that guided them through the different phases of designing the mixed-reality escape room scenario they experienced. Participants started by adding a prefabricated (prefab) room into the 3D scene. They then learned how to use prefab puzzles and, in the following step (fourth step of the tutorial, see Fig. 6a), they engaged in the guided creation of a custom puzzle using Blueprints. The dynamic of the puzzle was simple, yet crafted to guide participants' learning of Blueprints functions to program interactive behaviors with physical and virtual objects. They programmed the following behavior: a player touches a physical object (e.g., a box) in the escape room and, as long as the player holds a hand on the object, a battery (another physical object with a virtual representation) will be charged, which will be later used to solve other puzzles. Figure 7 shows the resulting Blueprints visual graph to program such behavior.

Participants were encouraged to collaborate, think-aloud and try-out what they were programming (Fig. 6b). A researcher moved around, observed participants' behavior and asked for more insights and feedback when needed. In the last (fifth) step of the tutorial, participants were left time to learn about the Blueprints functions in the XRoom library by browsing the catalog of available visual functions.

Free Design Activity (60 min). Each pair was asked to describe a meaningful scenario or an application of tangible VR (e.g., from their research experience

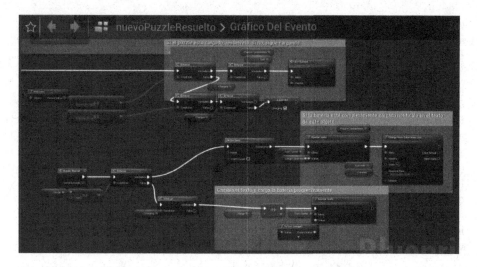

Fig. 7. The resulting visual script that implements the desired behavior of the guided design activity: charge a battery as long as the player is touching a physical object.

or to support their future work). Participants' ideas were annotated (as well as audio recorded) and, then, they attempted to implement through Blueprints some interactive behaviors to explore and materialize their ideas.

Debrief and Final Remarks (15 min). We concluded by recapitulating what was done in the workshop and its goal, asking participants for some final remark, explaining our follow-up activities and, finally, we thanked participants for their time and meaningful feedback.

4   Results and Discussion

Participants were able to complete the guided design activity and learn about the visual language and the XRoom plugin with minimal intervention. They enjoyed discovering how to program the interactive behaviors by connecting visual elements. Each group came up with a new design idea. One group (P5, P6) implemented a tangible interface to explore 3D data visualization on the globe using a physical sphere as a proxy for interaction; a second group (P1, P2) envisioned a tangible MIDI controller for music education in Virtual Reality, using physical blocks with different geometries to control music events and parameters; the third group (p3, P4) was intrigued by the opportunities of the escape room scenarios and explored the design of other mixed-reality puzzles.

Five participants (P1, P2, P4, P5, P6) constantly made parallels and tried to imagine how they would have used textual programming to implement the same feature. From this direct experience, they acknowledged that the visual programming language does lower the barrier of entry and it would be easier to use for rapid prototyping, especially for non-technical users. Participants praised the support for learning and code understanding afforded by the visual syntax, as well as for collaboration. For instance one participant reported (P2) that *"the visual appearance makes it easier to quickly grasp other programmers' intention"*.

All the participants also reported that the organization of the visual graph is not a luxury or otherwise, with more complex Blueprints, the programming space can get very cluttered. This is a common issue with visual languages as the complexity of the program grows. Participants proposed solutions that are aligned with best practices for visual programming, such as coherent and consistent use of the space (e.g., arranging dependent nodes always in a horizontal or vertical fashion), or group and collapse a set of logically related nodes into a its own subgraph, or the use of functions, repeatable and self-contained sections of logic with one execution input and output and their own graph.

Even if the time frame did not allow participants to fully implement their ideas, the two design activities allowed us to contextually observe and interact with participants, and identify four areas for future development.

Provide Layers of Abstraction. All the participants were surprised that the visual environment did not allow to switch from visual to textual programming or at least to examine the code generated through visual composition (e.g., like in the Blockly environment[6]). This is the main limitation they found to the Blueprints environment, as experienced developers. For instance, one participant (P1) reported that, coming from textual programming in Unity, he was *"amazed"* how easy was to define interactive behaviors with physical object without having to *"touch a line of code"*. However, he also felt somewhat limited by the visual syntax, and argued that he could have configured or implemented some features quickly if only he had access to the C++ code editor. That was not an option, as Unreal Engine does not combine visual and textual programming, and the developer has to choose the programming environment at the beginning. Inspired by Blueprints Function nodes and collapsible groups in a visual graph, two participants (P1, P4) proposed hybrid visual programming environments as a possible solution, with a zoomable interface that allowed programmers to enter and edit a node (or a group of nodes) at a lower level, e.g., using textual programming. This kind of *"semantic zooming"* was already proposed for the development of interactive behaviors in multimodal and multidevice systems [15] to allow source code changes without leaving the visual design environment. Develop such a hybrid environment can be, however, challenging: the visual elements of the language should correspond to a syntax that the computer can understand (i.e., how each visual element maps to code), and a compiler should be developed that can translate the visual programming code into executable code and viceversa (the compiler should be able to detect errors and provide feedback to the user such as syntax highlighting or code completion). As an intermediate level to source code editing, one participant (P4) proposed the use of templates and simplified syntaxes, such as Event-Condition-Action rules that already proved successful to program and/or configure interactive behaviors in different context, such as smart homes or robotics [22].

---

[6] https://developers.google.com/blockly?hl=es-419.

Embrace Liveness. Four participants (P1, P2, P3, P4) reported that the visual system should allow to experiment with changes in the graph without interrupting playtesting sessions or work in the visual editor itself. They anticipated opportunities for interactive and live programming [27], a paradigm that emphasizes real-time interaction between the programmer and the program being developed. Interactive programming allows developers to quickly create, test, adjust and customize new ideas in real-time, which can be particularly useful for prototyping tangible VR interactive behaviors, where the user's physical movements and interactions with the environment and physical objects are an integral part of the experience. Together with just-in-time compiling to avoid breaking the execution of the program, P2 proposed the use gizmos to highlight, in the virtual world in-editor player, the relationships of a selected element and, thus, be able to jump directly to the corresponding section of the visual graph. P2 reported that *"sometimes, without a visual aid, it is hard to keep track of which objects you are working on".* Another participant (P3) missed a functionality to test a behavior without having to move a physical object in the space, for instance by manually entering values for its position and/or orientation and see the result in the in-editor player. Lastly, a third participant (P4) missed a visual debug tool that, while testing the interactive scene in the in-editor player, would highlight the flow of execution of the code in the visual graph, such as, for instance, the nodes that are triggering events or the variables that are changing value. This would allow him to better understand the correlation between the program and the (both physical and virtual) objects in the scene.

Foster in Situ Immersive Programming. P1 suggested that, while the in-editor player is useful for quick debugging, it is also important to seamlessly try out and experiment the interactive behaviors in the immersive VR environment. It is however time consuming to put the headset on and off anytime a developer needs to make some adjustment and, thus, he envisaged the possibility for *in situ immersive visual programming*, that is, to edit parts of the visual graph (related to the interactive behavior he is testing) without exiting the virtual environment, thus avoiding to go back and forth, from the editing environment to the immersive environment for live testing. The use of immersive visual programming to create interactive scenes in situ is underinvestigated. To the best of our knowledge, FlowMatic [31], a system that provides a flow-based visual syntax for authoring reactive behaviors in VR, represents a first effort in this direction. Even if participants (8) in a user study recognized that immersive programming avoid context switching, further investigation is needed to fully understand the benefits of having a 3D space for the visualization of the visual layout of the program, compared to the classical 2D visualization provided by the Blueprints environment.

Participants felt that having to manually enter the id of tracker for the physical object was problematic, since they had to retrieve it using an external tool and, with more than one tracker active at the same time, it was not always obvious which one was the correct id. When asked, they proposed strategies to identify a tracker that involved physical manipulation like touch it, or move it a little, or shake it. This idea resonates with a similar strategy proposed in the literature to assist the programming of smart things by physical interaction [17]. While Kubitza and Schmidt envisioned the technique for a textual IDE, it could be easily incorporated in a visual environment, for instance by creating a new node in the graph, or by assigning the tracker id to an existing node, or highlight all the nodes in the program that are used to implement an interactive behavior with the selected object.

Enable Physical Demonstration Through Interactive Machine Learning. Lastly, participants felt somehow limited to program simple behaviors, mostly involving collisions (e.g., the user hand touching an objects, or a physical object colliding with a virtual object) or relative positions of objects in the space. All three groups reported that real-world interactions are difficult to express through the visual syntax and that a mechanism that supports the creation of interactive behaviors through demonstration is pivotal to support rapid prototyping, similar to the approaches that are being investigated in the Augmented Reality literature [28]. Participants expressed preferences toward a programming-by-demonstration approach especially when the interactive behaviors involved spatial relationship between objects, such as collisions or proximity-based interactions.

The discussion with participants opened up opportunities for integrating interactive machine teaching as a tactic to prototype more complex behaviors [24]. This kind of human-centered machine learning approach has been championed by systems like Teachable Machine [6] that allows the end-user development of custom classifiers from limited, user-generated examples using input sources such as a webcam or a microphone. The proposed solution, therefore would make use of the transfer learning technique to implement specialized classification nodes in the visual language from pre-trained models that would learn a behavior through physical demonstration, and give the desired output accordingly. The visual system will support the developer collecting training examples of labeled data from various sources (e.g., users' hands as detected by the VR hardware, or position/orientation of trackers connected to physical objects, or the position/orientation of the VR headset itself, or data from external hardware such as stereo cameras), train the model and, lastly, use the resulting node to perform inference on live data and produce an output event that can be connected to other nodes in the visual graph.

5   Limitations

In our contextual inquiry workshop we focused on designers and researchers with textual programming knowledge; our results may not generalize to users with no technical background. Our means of selecting the target population may have biased the results since all the participants are members of our research laboratory. However, our results are aligned with the recent literature on authoring environments for virtual reality as well as with previous results from the visual language community. Given the fact that participants develop, and have developed, interactive and immersive systems as part of their research, we are confident that our results provide new ideas to the EUD community about future designs of tools capable of easing the creation of tangible VR experiences.

Another limitation is the restricted amount of time that did not allow participants to fully implement and explore their ideas. Most of the workshop was dedicated on experiencing physical interaction in VR, getting acquainted with the visual language, learning the how to use the library and complete the guided design task. If participante were given more time to develop their ideas, which were closer to their design and research needs, we could have gathered more in-depth insights on ideas and needs that were only casually mentioned by participants. For instance, participants found shortcomings in the use of the visual syntax that, as they suggested, could be overcome by using artificial intelligence alongside visual design. Participants had troubles with the names of some functions, since they do not follow the convention of textual programming languages (e.g., the *if* conditional clause is represented by the *Branch* node in the Blueprint environment). An AI-powered assistant can provide alternatives and suggestions (visual autocompletion) and disambiguation, as well as assist in browsing libraries of existing behaviors. Due to the time constraints, however, we did not delve into this road of future development.

6   Conclusions

Emerging from a contextual inquiry workshop with six designer and researchers with programming experience, we illustrated four areas to improve the usability and usefulness of visual tools to support the prototyping of tangible VR interactive behaviors: (1) Provide layers of abstraction, (2) Embrace liveness, (3) Foster in situ immersive programming and, (4) Enable physical demonstration through interactive machine learning. While (1) and (4) can be implemented on existing authoring tools such as Unreal or Unity, (2) and (3) require more malleable and accessible technologies. Here, the Web can offer an ideal platform, considering the late advances towards the development of immersive environments (e.g., WebXR API, three.js or A-Frame) and its inherent predisposition for interactive programming. Our work carries the limitations of a time-constrained workshop with a narrow user population and we acknowledge that further research is needed in each one of the four areas for their meaningful integration into usable tools. For instance, identify benefits and challenges of immersive authoring environments when compared to 2D, desktop-based authoring tools; explore how to effectively combine visual languages together with programming-by-demonstration approaches in immersive tools and; understand the mental model of the end users while programming complex behaviors.

Acknowledgments. This project has received funding from the Spanish State Research Agency (AEI) under grants Sense2MakeSense (PID2019-109388GB-I00) and form the Madrid Government (Comunidad de Madrid-Spain) under the Multiannual

Agreement with UC3M in the line of Excellence of University Professors (EPUC3M17), and in the context of the V PRICIT (Regional Programme of Research and Technological Innovation).

References

1. Arora, J., Saini, A., Mehra, N., Jain, V., Shrey, S., Parnami, A.: Virtualbricks: exploring a scalable, modular toolkit for enabling physical manipulation in VR. In: Proceedings of the 2019 CHI Conference on Human Factors in Computing Systems, pp. 1–12 (2019)
2. Bellucci, A., Jacucci, G., Kotkavuori, V., Serim, B., Ahmed, I., Ylirisku, S.: Extreme co-design: prototyping with and by the user for appropriation of web-connected tags. In: Díaz, P., Pipek, V., Ardito, C., Jensen, C., Aedo, I., Boden, A. (eds.) IS-EUD 2015. LNCS, vol. 9083, pp. 109–124. Springer, Cham (2015). https://doi.org/10.1007/978-3-319-18425-8_8
3. Bellucci, A., Zarraonandia, T., Díaz, P., Aedo, I.: End-user prototyping of cross-reality environments. In: Proceedings of the Eleventh International Conference on Tangible, Embedded, and Embodied Interaction, pp. 173–182 (2017)
4. Beyer, H., Holtzblatt, K.: Contextual design. Interactions **6**(1), 32–42 (1999)
5. Borowski, M., Larsen-Ledet, I.: Lessons learned from using reprogrammable prototypes with end-user developers. In: Fogli, D., Tetteroo, D., Barricelli, B.R., Borsci, S., Markopoulos, P., Papadopoulos, G.A. (eds.) IS-EUD 2021. LNCS, vol. 12724, pp. 136–152. Springer, Cham (2021). https://doi.org/10.1007/978-3-030-79840-6_9
6. Carney, M., et al.: Teachable machine: approachable web-based tool for exploring machine learning classification. In: Extended Abstracts of the 2020 CHI Conference on Human Factors in Computing Systems, pp. 1–8 (2020)
7. Chang, J.S.K., et al.: TASC: combining virtual reality with tangible and embodied interactions to support spatial cognition. In: Proceedings of the 2017 Conference on Designing Interactive Systems, pp. 1239–1251 (2017)
8. Chen, M., Peljhan, M., Sra, M.: Entanglevr: a visual programming interface for virtual reality interactive scene generation. In: Proceedings of the 27th ACM Symposium on Virtual Reality Software and Technology, pp. 1–6 (2021)
9. Chu, E., Zaman, L.: Exploring alternatives with unreal engine's blueprints visual scripting system. Entertain. Comput. **36**, 100388 (2021)
10. Feick, M., Bateman, S,, Tang, A., Miede, A., Marquardt, N.: Tangi: tangible proxies for embodied object exploration and manipulation in virtual reality. In: 2020 IEEE International Symposium on Mixed and Augmented Reality (ISMAR), pp. 195–206. IEEE (2020)
11. Fiani, B., De Stefano, F., Kondilis, A., Covarrubias, C., Reier, L., Sarhadi, K.: Virtual reality in neurosurgery: "can you see it?"-a review of the current applications and future potential. World Neurosurg. **141**, 291–298 (2020)
12. Flanagan, J.C.: The critical incident technique. Psychol. Bull. **51**(4), 327 (1954)
13. Harley, D., Tarun, A.P., Germinario, D., Mazalek, A.: Tangible VR: diegetic tangible objects for virtual reality narratives. In: Proceedings of the 2017 Conference on Designing Interactive Systems, pp. 1253–1263 (2017)
14. Jordà, S., Geiger, G., Alonso, M., Kaltenbrunner, M.: The reactable: exploring the synergy between live music performance and tabletop tangible interfaces. In: Proceedings of the 1st International Conference on Tangible and Embedded Interaction, pp. 139–146 (2007)

15. König, W.A., Rädle, R., Reiterer, H.: Interactive design of multimodal user interfaces: reducing technical and visual complexity. J. Multimodal User Interfaces **3**, 197–213 (2010)

16. Krauß, V., Nebeling, M., Jasche, F., Boden, A.: Elements of XR prototyping: characterizing the role and use of prototypes in augmented and virtual reality design. In: Proceedings of the 2022 CHI Conference on Human Factors in Computing Systems, pp. 1–18 (2022)

17. Kubitza, T., Schmidt, A.: meSchup: a platform for programming interconnected smart things. Computer **50**(11), 38–49 (2017)

18. Lekić, M., Gardašević, G.: IoT sensor integration to node-red platform. In: 2018 17th International Symposium Infoteh-Jahorina (Infoteh), pp. 1–5. IEEE (2018)

19. Muender, T., Reinschluessel, A.V., Drewes, S., Wenig, D., Döring, T., Malaka, R.: Does it feel real? Using tangibles with different fidelities to build and explore scenes in virtual reality. In: Proceedings of the 2019 CHI Conference on Human Factors in Computing Systems, pp. 1–12 (2019)

20. Myers, B., Park, S.Y., Nakano, Y., Mueller, G., Ko, A.: How designers design and program interactive behaviors. In: 2008 IEEE Symposium on Visual Languages and Human-Centric Computing, pp. 177–184. IEEE (2008)

21. Myers, B.A.: Taxonomies of visual programming and program visualization. J. Vis. Lang. Comput. **1**(1), 97–123 (1990)

22. Paternò, F., Santoro, C.: End-user development for personalizing applications, things, and robots. Int. J. Hum. Comput. Stud. **131**, 120–130 (2019)

23. Raffaillac, T., Huot, S.: What do researchers need when implementing novel interaction techniques? Proc. ACM Hum.-Comput. Interact. **6**(EICS), 1–30 (2022)

24. Ramos, G., Meek, C., Simard, P., Suh, J., Ghorashi, S.: Interactive machine teaching: a human-centered approach to building machine-learned models. Hum.-Comput. Interact. **35**(5–6), 413–451 (2020)

25. Resnick, M., et al.: Scratch: programming for all. Commun. ACM **52**(11), 60–67 (2009)

26. Schiavoni, F.L., Gonçalves, L.L.: From virtual reality to digital arts with mosaicode. In: 2017 19th Symposium on Virtual and Augmented Reality (SVR), pp. 200–206. IEEE (2017)

27. Tanimoto, S.L.: A perspective on the evolution of live programming. In: 2013 1st International Workshop on Live Programming (LIVE), pp. 31–34. IEEE (2013)

28. Wang, T., et al.: Capturar: an augmented reality tool for authoring human-involved context-aware applications. In: Proceedings of the 33rd Annual ACM Symposium on User Interface Software and Technology, pp. 328–341 (2020)

29. Weintrop, D., et al.: Evaluating coblox: a comparative study of robotics programming environments for adult novices. In: Proceedings of the 2018 CHI Conference on Human Factors in Computing Systems, pp. 1–12 (2018)

30. Yigitbas, E., Klauke, J., Gottschalk, S., Engels, G.: End-user development for interactive web-based virtual reality scenes. J. Comput. Lang. **74**, 101187 (2023)

31. Zhang, L., Oney, S.: Flowmatic: an immersive authoring tool for creating interactive scenes in virtual reality. In: Proceedings of the 33rd Annual ACM Symposium on User Interface Software and Technology, pp. 342–353 (2020)

How End Users Develop Point-and-Click Games

Valentino Artizzu[1], Ivan Blečić[2], Vittoria Frau[1],
and Lucio Davide Spano[1(✉)]

[1] Department of Mathematics and Computer Science, University of Cagliari,
Via Ospedale 72, 09124 Cagliari, Italy
{valentino.artizzu,vittoria.frau,davide.spano}@unica.it
[2] Department of Civil Engineering and Architecture, University of Cagliari,
Via Marengo 2, 09123 Cagliari, Italy
ivanblecic@unica.it

Abstract. Rule-based approaches have proven effective in automating smart homes, managing IoT sensors and devices, or expressing simple web-based workflows. More recently, rules have been used to define the behaviour of point-and-click games and virtual reality experiences. In this paper, we propose an analysis of the first dataset of point-and-click games developed by end users. It includes 143 games, some created for cultural heritage promotion and others created in dedicated events. The dataset shows peculiar characteristics in the rules defining the game navigation and more general patterns in managing enumerations, integers and booleans. The dataset is publicly available for further research.

Keywords: End-User Development · Rules · Games · Trigger-Action · Event-Condition Action · Dataset

1 Introduction

Rule-based approaches in End-User Development allow the building of configurable software applications where the system's behaviour is (partially) defined by a set of rules. End users can change it by modifying these rules, making such approaches well-suited for environments where the requirements are rapidly evolving or for supporting fine-grained system customization. One of the most important application domains for rule-based approaches is the home automation [8,10,12,14,16,19], by providing user-friendly interfaces for authoring rules controlling different devices (lighting, heating, security etc.). These solutions allow creating custom rules automating tasks without writing code or technical expertise, making smart home technology accessible and flexible for many users.

Recently, rule-based approaches found application in the development of immersive experiences, such as Point-and-Click (PaC) games based on 360° videos [4,11] or customisable VR environments [2,20,21]. While datasets for studying the characteristics of rules for home and office automation are available in the literature [18,19], no data is publicly available for analysing rules

L. D. Spano et al. (Eds.): IS-EUD 2023, LNCS 13917, pp. 220–229, 2023.
https://doi.org/10.1007/978-3-031-34433-6_14

developed in this emerging domain. This paper analyses the first dataset representing PaC games defined through rules. We characterise their complexity in scenes and rules and identify patterns in rule definitions for identifying peculiarities in rule-based EUD in this particular domain. The dataset is publicly available for further research[1]. Please refer to [4,11] for information about the authoring environment and game examples.

2   Related Work

Rule-based approaches for EUD are widely explored in research. Several rule styles exist in the literature, and one of the most commonly adopted is Trigger-Action (TAP), particularly in the Internet of Things (IoT) domain at both academic [8,10,12] and commercial levels [14,18,19]. TAP is designed for users with limited programming skills, with rules taking the form of "if ⟨trigger occurs⟩, then ⟨action is executed⟩". The trigger refers to an event, such as a change in an object's state or context, that activates the rule. The action results from the trigger, such as turning off a light. TAP rules can be linked, creating complex behaviours, but this can also lead to unexpected consequences [7]. A variation includes an "else" block for alternative actions if the trigger is not satisfied [9].

Event-Condition-Action (ECA) rules have an additional intermediate part between the trigger and action, known as the condition. The condition acts as a guard, preventing the rule from executing if not verified. This usually checks the state of the environment or other context-related information. ECA rules are more expressive than TAP rules as they can associate different actions with the same trigger event and support filtering through the condition [17]. However, this increased expressiveness can also make behaviour definition more complex for end users [5]. Research has also focused on detecting and fixing bugs in rules through model checking [6,13,15,22], with current results limited to enforcing safety checks [1].

3   The Game Dataset

The games included in the dataset result from two main development activities. The first is promoting cultural heritage by professional content creators. This activity produced a large demonstration game called *Brother Rivals* [4], the biggest game in the set, including professional content creators (filmmakers, sound designers, actors etc.) but no developers. Part of the team working on such a demonstrator also created different pilots among the largest games in the repository. The dataset's second source of game definitions is five events we organised for disseminating the authoring tool involving creative volunteers in game jams. They all had a similar organisation, which we replicated in three high schools and two events dedicated to a broader audience, including 1) the presentation of the authoring platform through examples; 2) the team organisation

---

[1] https://github.com/GLab-UniCA/PaC-dataset.git.

Characteristic	Value
# of Games	143
# of Scenes	1598
# of Rules	2722
# of Actions	2961
# of Interactive Objects	2858

Fig. 1. Overview of the Point-and-Click games dataset. The left part shows a plot of the graph, including game, scene, rule and action nodes. The right part shows the node count and the colour coding used in the graph plot.

and task assignment among the participants (e.g., video-making, story definition, content composition in the EUD authoring environment); 3) the location scouting, video and photo shooting and production; 4) the game development in the EUD authoring environment, test and presentation of the results to the other teams.

PaC games in the dataset are represented as graphs. They have been authored through the PAC-PAC [4,11] platform, applying a rule-based direct manipulation approach [3]. Each game consists of a set of scenes, represented by 360° videos or images. Scenes are connected by arcs, called transitions. Each scene contains a set of interactive objects, representing elements the player can interact with and variables for maintaining the game state. For instance, a *key* is used for representing boolean values, a *counter* represents an integer, a *switch* represents an enumeration, and a *textbox* represents a string. Scenes also contain rules in the ECA format. Events are related to the player's interactions and the interactive objects' state change. A Condition is a logic predicate on an object's state or composition through boolean operators. An action specifies a change in the state of an interactive object.

The dataset contains the definition of 143 game graphs as coded by 101 end users. Figure 1 shows an overview of the resulting graphs in the left part. Most of them are small graphs, except four, which stand out as the biggest ones. Overall, the graph set contains about 1.5k scenes and 3k rules, actions and interactive objects. The exact number is available in Fig. 1, right part. Figure 2-A shows that most users coded only one game in our dataset (55). The number drops if we consider the authors of more than one game: 9 people coded 2 games, 8 coded 3 games, 5 coded 4 games, while only one or two persons coded between 5 and 9 games. No one passed the 10 games threshold.

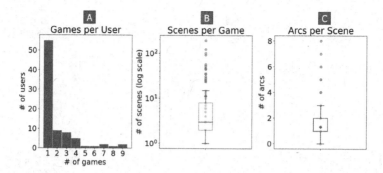

Fig. 2. A) The number of users that developed a given number of games included in the dataset. B) Distribution of the scenes per game. C) Distribution of the number of arcs (transitions) per scene.

3.1 Scenes

The games in the dataset consist mainly of small graphs, having a low number of scene nodes. As depicted in Fig. 2-B, a game has 11.17 scenes on average ($std = 48.35$), while the median value is 3. This leads to a positively skewed distribution having a Fisher-Pearson coefficient of 4.72. So, considering as small the games below the average, we have 115 small games. We have 21 medium-sized games (between 12 and 50 scenes) and 6 big games (above 50 scenes). The maximum number of scenes in a game belongs to the demonstrator *Brother Rivals* [4], which includes 191 scenes. The connections between scenes mostly depict linear paths, as 50% of the scenes have a single arc. 25% of the scenes have 2 arcs, representing simple branches in the game path. The remaining 25% represent complex branch nodes, having between 3 and 8 out-coming arcs. In summary, the average number of arcs in a scene is 1.31 ($std = 1.5$), the median is 1, and the maximum is 8.

3.2 Rules

Overall, most games in the dataset are defined using a small number of rules. The average count per game is 20.25 ($std = 48.18$), while the median is 6. Similarly to the scene distribution, rules per game are positively skewed with Fisher-Pearson coefficient of 5.68: we have only 34 games (25%) defined with more than 15 rules, 5 of them have more than 100 rules, while the maximum number of rules in a game is 435 (again the *Brother Rivals* [4] demonstrator). Figure 3-A summarises the rule distribution per game. The rule per scene distribution follows a similar trend. Each scene contains 1.81 rules on average ($std = 1.57$), while the median is 1. The distribution is positively skewed (Fisher-Pearson 4.51). The maximum count is 22, but 75% of the scenes have at most two rules (see Fig. 3-B).

We can characterize the structure of the rules in the dataset by i) counting the number of actions and ii) assessing the complexity of the conditions in the rule definition. Figure 3-C shows the number of actions per rule. Most (2711)

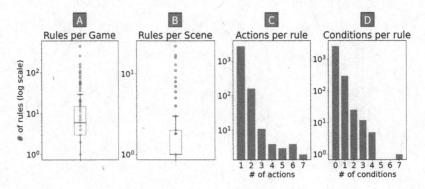

Fig. 3. Distribution of the number of rules per game (A) an scene (B). Bar charts showing how many rules have a given number of actions (C) and conditions (D).

define only one action reacting to the rule trigger. The count drops an order of magnitude if we consider rules having two actions (161) and another one for rules having three actions (11). Rules having up to 7 actions exist in the dataset, but their number is marginal.

To assess the conditions' complexity, we count the number of simple predicates on the interactive object state, connected through *and* and *or* operators. We register a trend similar to the action count: the number of rules drops a magnitude order when increasing the number of predicates (conditions) by one. The majority of rules have no condition (2556), 297 rules have a simple condition consisting of a single predicate, while we find two predicates in only 25 rules and 3 in 12 rules. The maximum number of predicates in a condition is 7. By considering together the distributions depicted in Fig. 3-C and D, we obtain that 89% of the rules in the dataset are trigger-action.

Besides characterizing the graph in terms of the different node types, it is interesting to identify behaviour patterns in the rules. To this aim, we analyzed the relationship between the interactive objects used in the rule trigger and those used in the actions. The matrix showing the co-occurrence is depicted in Fig. 4. We count a trigger-action pair for each action in rules having multiple consequences for its trigger. Two main patterns stand out in Fig. 4. The first and most prominent is that transitions are affected by changes triggered by almost all the interactive object types. The matrix in Fig. 4 has many cells with high values in the last column. Indeed, end users enable and disable transitions among scenes to control the player's progress in the game and block his/her navigation until the current enigma is not solved. However, the variety of interacting object types affecting transitions indicates also that end users created different types of enigmas controlling the game progress, exploiting almost entirely the available building blocks for this purpose. The following are examples of the enigmas we identified in different games:

- *Button:* Pressing a button unlocks a transition.
- *Keypad:* A correct code or password unlocks a transition.

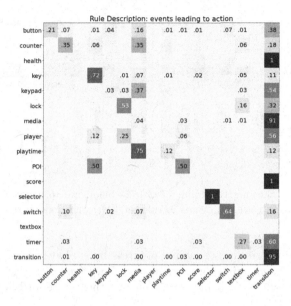

Rule Description: events leading to action

	button	counter	health	key	keypad	lock	media	player	playtime	POI	score	selector	switch	textbox	timer	transition
button	.21	.07		.01	.04		.16	.01	.01	.01			.07		.01	.38
counter		.35			.06		.35								.06	.18
health																1
key				.72		.01	.07	.01		.02					.05	.11
keypad					.03	.03	.37								.03	.54
lock						.53									.16	.32
media					.04			.03					.01		.01	.91
player					.12	.25		.06								.56
playtime							.75	.12								.12
POI				.50						.50						
score																1
selector												1				
switch	.10				.02		.07						.64			.16
textbox																
timer	.03						.03			.03			.27		.03	.60
transition	.01	.00		.00			.00	.03					.00		.00	.95

Fig. 4. Co-occurrence matrix of the interactive object types in events triggering a rule (rows) and in the associated actions (columns). The matrix shows numbers only if the co-occurrence is higher than zero, normalized and rounded to the second decimal place.

- *Lock:* Opening a lock enables a transition.
- *Media:* The end user wants that the player watches a video or listen to recorded audio before going on in the game. So the transition is enabled when the media ends.
- *Player:* The player clicks on an interactive area triggering a transition.
- *Timer:* The player goes back to the initial scene when the time is up.
- *Transition:* Triggering a transition disables another one. Mostly used to prevent the users goes back into the game graph.

The second pattern we can identify in Fig. 4 is the high values of the cells positioned along the matrix diagonal. This indicates that a trigger caused by an interactive object changes the state of objects having the same type. For instance, an interaction with a selector usually changes the currently selected option, often used in conditions (see Fig. 5). Interaction with keys often results in collecting or releasing them. Similarly, locks are locked or unlocked by triggering an interaction with them. There are interesting exceptions to this pattern. Playtime mostly affects the playback of media elements, for instance, showing further information only if the player stays in the game for a certain time. Keypads are used to let the player control the playback of audio and video media. The game plays audio (media) feedback when a counter reaches a certain value. By looking at a point of interest, a key appears.

In summary, the rule set shows that end users create mainly simple rules, exploiting 89% of the time the trigger-action paradigm. They express differ-

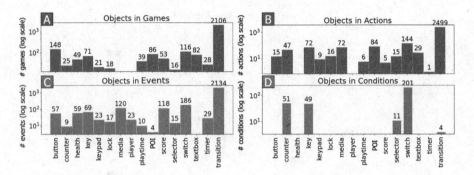

Fig. 5. Bar chart showing the count of objects belonging to a given type in A) all games, B) actions in rules, C) events in rules and D) conditions in rules.

ent enigmas for controlling the game progress by exploiting various interactive objects as triggers affecting the game navigation. Last but not least, many triggers modify objects of the same type, changing their state for implementing the gameplay.

3.3   Interactive Objects

The last question we try to answer with our analysis is about the frequencies in using interactive objects inside games and in all parts of a rule. Figure 5 shows the distribution by counting the number of interactive objects involved in games (A), events (C), conditions (B) and actions (D).

Regarding the object distribution in games (Fig. 5-A), the most used object type is the transition. We expected this, considering that it implements navigation in a PaC game. Then, end users exploit buttons, switches, textboxes, points of interest, and keys. The other objects are less frequently used. In Fig. 5, we do not report the count of media objects since they are assets referenced in other objects or in scenes, and the player is always one.

As expected, rules are triggered mostly by transitions since they implement navigation. Then, we have switches, media, keys and buttons. Figure 5-C graphically depicts such distribution. The two patterns identified in Fig. 4 explain the increased count of transitions involved in the action part of a rule (see Fig. 5-B) and the similarity in the frequencies of switches, media and keys.

Finally, the objects involved in rules conditions are a few. Most of them include a test on the state of a switch, a counter or a key. Considering that they represent an enumeration, an integer and a boolean variable respectively, we conclude that the EUD metaphor used for representing them in point-and-click games is effective. Even if available through the textbox object type, string manipulation was not considered in developing games in our dataset.

4   Discussion and Limitations

End Users Define Small and *quasi*-linear Games. The PaC games included designed throught the PAC-PAC platform and included in the dataset are small experiences, including a single puzzle to be solved by players. A large part represents either a prototype for similar enigmas included in a larger game or quick attempts created to explore the platform. The path from the beginning to the end of these games is linear, including two or three branches at maximum.

End Users Create Different Types of Enigmas. Despite the small game size, the puzzles used various interactive objects in the authoring environment. We identified some of the most recurrent patterns in Sect. 3.2. This shows that representing the game state and interaction through such objects balances the expressiveness and understandability of the EUD authoring environment.

Most Rules in the Dataset are Trigger-Action. End users seldom create rules including conditions. When they do, the condition is either a simple predicate or two predicates connected in and/or. Conditions involve only a few types of interactive objects, but the subset includes the metaphor used in these games for representing programming variables (enumeration, integers and booleans). Even if conditions are not used in most rules, dropping them (i.e., adopting a simple trigger-action paradigm) would limit the expressiveness, especially in controlling programming variables.

Interactive Objects Trigger Changes in the Game Navigation or Their Own State. We identified two main patterns in the rule developed for point-and-click games. The first indicates that almost all interactive objects trigger changes in the game navigation (i.e., on *transition* objects), which is peculiar to this specific videogame genre. The second pattern shows that end users mostly programmed reactions on the same object that generated the event. Section 3.2 reports a set of interesting exceptions in this pattern.

Limitations. There are a set of limitations on the findings reported in this paper. The first is the dataset size, which is smaller than those analysed in home routines [18,19]. The cause is the lower spread of the EUD practice in the game domain. The second limitation relates to the different types of end users who contributed to this dataset. On the one hand, we have people that exploited the platform to create promotional content for cultural and environmental heritage over a long time, contributing to different games. On the other hand, we have "casual" users that participated in the development events, which lasted about one week. This explains the large differences in the game complexity in our dataset. Finally, some patterns we identified may be peculiar to the game genre, particularly those related to the navigation mechanism.

5   Conclusion and Future Work

In this paper, we presented the first dataset of rules developed for defining PaC games by end users. We discussed the structural properties of the graphs representing games and the patterns we identified in rules and among their sub-parts, such as the relationships between the events and the consequent actions. In future work, we aim to expand the support for other game genres, extending the rule-based support for their behaviour definition. In addition, we want to open the authoring environment to the community for collecting games developed outside dedicated events.

References

1. Ariano, R., Manca, M., Paternò, F., Santoro, C.: Smartphone-based augmented reality for end-user creation of home automations. Behav. Inf. Technol. 1–17 (2022). https://doi.org/10.1080/0144929X.2021.2017482
2. Artizzu, V., et al.: Defining configurable virtual reality templates for end users. Proc. ACM Hum.-Comput. Interact. **6**(EICS) (2022). https://doi.org/10.1145/3534517
3. Barricelli, B.R., Fogli, D., Locoro, A.: Eudability: a new construct at the intersection of end-user development and computational thinking. J. Syst. Softw. **195**, 111516 (2023). https://doi.org/10.1016/j.jss.2022.111516. https://www.sciencedirect.com/science/article/pii/S0164121222001923
4. Blečić, I., et al.: First-person cinematographic videogames: game model, authoring environment, and potential for creating affection for places. J. Comput. Cult. Herit. **14**(2) (2021). https://doi.org/10.1145/3446977
5. Brackenbury, W., et al.: How users interpret bugs in trigger-action programming. In: Proceedings of the 2019 CHI Conference on Human Factors in Computing Systems, CHI 2019, pp. 1–12. Association for Computing Machinery, New York (2019). https://doi.org/10.1145/3290605.3300782
6. Celik, Z.B., McDaniel, P., Tan, G.: Soteria: automated IoT safety and security analysis. In: 2018 USENIX Annual Technical Conference (USENIX ATC 2018), Boston, MA, pp. 147–158. USENIX Association (2018). https://www.usenix.org/conference/atc18/presentation/celik
7. Corno, F., De Russis, L., Monge Roffarello, A.: Empowering end users in debugging trigger-action rules. In: Proceedings of the 2019 CHI Conference on Human Factors in Computing Systems, CHI 2019, pp. 1–13. Association for Computing Machinery, New York (2019). https://doi.org/10.1145/3290605.3300618
8. Corno, F., De Russis, L., Monge Roffarello, A.: A high-level semantic approach to end-user development in the internet of things. Int. J. Hum.-Comput. Stud. **125**, 41–54 (2019). https://doi.org/10.1016/j.ijhcs.2018.12.008. https://www.sciencedirect.com/science/article/pii/S1071581918301228
9. Coutaz, J., Crowley, J.L.: A first-person experience with end-user development for smart homes. IEEE Pervasive Comput. **15**(2), 26–39 (2016). https://doi.org/10.1109/MPRV.2016.24
10. Desolda, G., Ardito, C., Matera, M.: Empowering end users to customize their smart environments: model, composition paradigms, and domain-specific tools. ACM Trans. Comput.-Hum. Interact. **24**(2) (2017). https://doi.org/10.1145/3057859
11. Fanni, F.A., et al.: PAC-PAC: end user development of immersive point and click games. In: Malizia, A., Valtolina, S., Morch, A., Serrano, A., Stratton, A. (eds.) IS-EUD 2019. LNCS, vol. 11553, pp. 225–229. Springer, Cham (2019). https://doi.org/10.1007/978-3-030-24781-2_20

12. Ghiani, G., Manca, M., Paternò, F., Santoro, C.: Personalization of context-dependent applications through trigger-action rules. ACM Trans. Comput.-Hum. Interact. **24**(2) (2017). https://doi.org/10.1145/3057861

13. Hsu, K.H., Chiang, Y.H., Hsiao, H.C.: Safechain: securing trigger-action programming from attack chains. IEEE Trans. Inf. Forensics Secur. **14**(10), 2607–2622 (2019). https://doi.org/10.1109/TIFS.2019.2899758

14. Zapier (2022). https://zapier.com. Accessed 17 Feb 2022

15. Liang, C.J.M., et al.: Systematically debugging IoT control system correctness for building automation. In: Proceedings of the 3rd ACM International Conference on Systems for Energy-Efficient Built Environments, BuildSys 2016, pp. 133–142. Association for Computing Machinery, New York (2016). https://doi.org/10.1145/2993422.2993426

16. Manca, M., Paternò, F., Santoro, C., Spano, L.D.: Generation of multi-device adaptive MultiModal web applications. In: Daniel, F., Papadopoulos, G.A., Thiran, P. (eds.) MobiWIS 2013. LNCS, vol. 8093, pp. 218–232. Springer, Heidelberg (2013). https://doi.org/10.1007/978-3-642-40276-0_17

17. Paternò, F., Santoro, C.: End-user development for personalizing applications, things, and robots. Int. J. Hum.-Comput. Stud. **131**, 120–130 (2019). https://doi.org/10.1016/j.ijhcs.2019.06.002. https://www.sciencedirect.com/science/article/pii/S1071581919300722. 50 years of the International Journal of Human-Computer Studies. Reflections on the past, present and future of human-centred technologies

18. Ur, B., McManus, E., Pak Yong Ho, M., Littman, M.L.: Practical trigger-action programming in the smart home. In: Proceedings of the SIGCHI Conference on Human Factors in Computing Systems, CHI 2014, pp. 803–812. Association for Computing Machinery, New York (2014). https://doi.org/10.1145/2556288.2557420

19. Ur, B., et al.: Trigger-action programming in the wild: an analysis of 200,000 IFTTT recipes. In: Proceedings of the 2016 CHI Conference on Human Factors in Computing Systems, CHI 2016, pp. 3227–3231. Association for Computing Machinery, New York (2016). https://doi.org/10.1145/2858036.2858556

20. Yigitbas, E., Klauke, J., Gottschalk, S., Engels, G.: Vreud - an end-user development tool to simplify the creation of interactive VR scenes. In: 2021 IEEE Symposium on Visual Languages and Human-Centric Computing (VL/HCC), pp. 1–10 (2021). https://doi.org/10.1109/VL/HCC51201.2021.9576372

21. Zarraonandia, T., Díaz, P., Aedo, I., Montero, A.: Immersive end user development for virtual reality. In: Buono, P., Lanzilotti, R., Matera, M., Costabile, M.F. (eds.) Proceedings of the International Working Conference on Advanced Visual Interfaces, AVI 2016, Bari, Italy, 7–10 June 2016, pp. 346–347. ACM (2016). https://doi.org/10.1145/2909132.2926067

22. Zhang, L., He, W., Martinez, J., Brackenbury, N., Lu, S., Ur, B.: Autotap: synthesizing and repairing trigger-action programs using LTL properties. In: 2019 IEEE/ACM 41st International Conference on Software Engineering (ICSE), pp. 281–291 (2019). https://doi.org/10.1109/ICSE.2019.00043

Programming with Minecraft Bedrock Up: Modeling, Coding, and Computational Concepts

Anders I. Mørch[1]([email]) and Renate Andersen[2]

[1] Department of Education, University of Oslo, Oslo, Norway
`andersm@uio.no`
[2] Faculty of Education and International Studies, Oslo Metropolitan University, Oslo, Norway
`renatea@oslomet.no`

Abstract. As society gradually digitizes, the need increases for computational literacy education or the inclusion of programming and computational thinking in school curricula and teaching practices. A challenge is to reach students with little or no experience in programming but who have played digital games like Minecraft (i.e., the sandbox game). Toward that end we have developed a new teaching method, which guides students from concrete to abstract programming activities stepwise: 1) block building and modeling, 2) high-level functions, and 3) general purpose programming. The method is based on a theoretical framework Action–Breakdown–Repair and is the result of the first iteration of a design-based research (DBR) process that aims to adapt Minecraft Education and its embedded block-based programming language MakeCode to teaching introductory computer science. We demonstrate the method and report the strengths and weaknesses of the first DBR iteration, including high engagement, different levels of abstraction, challenges of understanding computational concepts in working code, and the role of a shared referent in the game world to coordinate program understanding.

Keywords: Minecraft · Programming · Modeling · Computational Thinking · Teaching Method · Action-Breakdown-Repair · Design-Based Research · End-User Development · Block-Based Programming · Levels of Abstraction

1 Introduction

The main goal of our research is to develop a method of teaching programming to students who are not primarily interested in technology but who need to understand how technology impacts society and educational processes. The rationale for the method is the gradual increase of digitalization in society, most recently seen by generative AI tools, requiring understanding of algorithms. Furthermore, the method must start with concrete activities of a practice situation, in our case a game environment, providing an engaging entry to computer science (CS) for non-CS majors. The method is part of a design-based research (DBR) process, whereby aspects of theory, design, and evaluation develop iteratively [1–3].

The other rationale for the method and the DBR process is a theoretical framework and pedagogical model, levels of abstraction and ABR model. The notion of levels

L. D. Spano et al. (Eds.): IS-EUD 2023, LNCS 13917, pp. 230–240, 2023.
https://doi.org/10.1007/978-3-031-34433-6_15

of abstraction implies two assumptions. First, to modify an application, an end-user developer must only increase their knowledge proportionally to the complexity of the modification [4]. Second, information presented at one level of abstraction must be more than the sum of the information presented at a lower level [5]. Therefore, we investigated the following abstraction levels in this study: 1) designing with building blocks, 2) building with code blocks (high-level functions), and 3) general-purpose programming and computational concepts. These levels support learners' gradual adoption of more general programming constructs.

The action–breakdown–repair (ABR) model [6–8] is a three-step process. First, the designers (here, a group of learners) create domain-specific artifacts (*action*). The design activity stops when the designers encounter a problem (*breakdown*). To continue, designers must *repair* the breakdown, and this provides opportunities for learning and teaching. Mørch [9] proposed ABR as a pedagogical model for technology use in education to bridge school learning (formal) and out-of-school learning (practical). In our work, ABR informed our teaching method, whereby actions in the game environment can lead to new understanding by shifting to another, more general, level of programming caused by a breakdown (initiated by human teacher or computer) to enable students to reflect on their activity and modify the game experience by programming at different levels of abstraction (repair).

2   Related Work

2.1   Introducing Programming and CT Using End-User Development

In the first course in programming, students are introduced to the fundamental concepts and techniques of computer programming, such as data types, control structures, and algorithms. Second, students learn how to think similarly to a programmer, referred to as computational thinking (CT) [10–13]. CT was revived in CS education after Wing's more focused redefinition of CT as a generic skill set everyone must have, naming key concepts such as abstraction, algorithmic design, decomposition, iteration, pattern recognition, and problem orientation [11]. Teachers in our country (Norway) are expected to teach CT in schools in some subjects [14], although no clear instructions or competence connect to how to do this. Accordingly, more research is needed to examine the implications of this in practice.

End-user development (EUD) is a method of software development in which end users create or modify software applications to meet their needs or preferences without the assistance of professional programmers [5, 8, 15–17]. The connection between CT and EUD has been proposed in previous work, but only a few studies have been reported [18, 19]. CT has been suggested a topic in collaborative learning [20], but there is plenty of room for more research.

2.2   Minecraft Studies

Minecraft Education (ME) is an adaptation of the popular game Minecraft for educational purposes [21], providing a digital environment where students can develop both generic and domain-specific competencies [22, 23]. ME has been found to support engagement, collaboration, the creation of authentic learning activities, and the attainment of learning outcomes [24], as well as teamwork, computer, and coding skills [25]. Studies have highlighted the game's affordances for collaboration in the open-world multiplayer game environment and for developing spatial skills by creating and interacting with 3D objects and scenarios [26]. Minecraft can be used to teach various subjects such as natural science, math, social sciences, language arts, and composition classes [27, 28]. While research on Minecraft for teaching programming is sparse, recent studies have explored its usefulness for teaching programming and coding concepts [29–31], making use of its embedded programming languages (MakeCode, JavaScript and Python) and EUD techniques. ME provides a technical framework for a gradual transition into programming and users can easily access the programming environment from the game world by direct activation [16, 32] (Fig. 1).

Fig. 1. The CodeBuilder (right) is accessed by command "C" from the game environment (left).

2.3 Teaching Methods

Three popular methods for teaching block-based programming are as follows: Use-Modify-Create (UMC), Predict-Run-Investigate-Modify-Make (PRIMM), and Parson's problems. UMC is a framework used to scaffold children's learning in three stages that define the progression of students' programming toward computational thinking [33]. PRIMM is related to UMC but extends it and emphasizes the importance of understanding existing code before changing or modifying it and organizing work around collaborative learning by reading and discussing code to create a shared understanding of how the code works [34]. Instead of starting from an existing program, Parson's problem is a way of learning to program that starts with the correct building blocks (analogous to puzzle pieces to solve a jigsaw puzzle). However, the students, themselves, must assemble the building blocks. This method aims to teach students the relationships of program constructs [35].

3 Research Method

3.1 Research Question

Based on the related work we found that further research is needed to develop a method for teaching introductory programming that is informed by EUD research and theory, and we ask: How can Minecraft be used as a EUD environment in an educational context to facilitate and motivate the learning of introductory programming, which we address in the remainder of the paper.

3.2 Research Design and Data Collection

We applied a design-based research methodology (DBR). DBR is an interventionist research method that aims to implement changes in a real-world context by combining theory building and practical action [1–3]. We used DBR to develop a teaching method for use in an educational setting. We chose McKinney and Reeves's [36] "generic model for educational research," since it is an iterative and flexible research method that guides the early stages of the DBR process, which fits our setting. The DBR model consists of three phases: 1) analysis and exploration, 2) design and construction, and 3) evaluation and reflection.

We collected data from students using a questionnaire and observation of the classroom activities. The Minecraft course lasted four weeks with one 2-h meeting per week. It was one of two seminars that comprised the practical module of a Learning, Design, and Technology course for 2nd year BA students majoring in education at a large public university in Scandinavia. We are in the early phases of our research project and have completed one full DBR cycle (16 participants; 12 questionnaire respondents). Several DBR cycles and iterations may be needed to harness the teaching method. The responses were thematically categorized using aspects of Clarke & Braun's method [37] and combining inductive (data driven) and deductive (theory driven) coding. In the next section, we provide a demonstration of the teaching method as we used it.

4 Demonstration of Teaching Method

In Minecraft, the primary aim of players is to build and interact with visual artifacts and communicate with other players by chat. In this case, the students are given the task of designing a dream house in steps that require programming and traversing levels of abstraction. We investigated the following abstraction levels: 1) designing with building blocks, 2) building with code blocks, and 3) general programming and computational concepts. These levels aim for a gradual transition into programming according to the theoretical framework we presented in Sect. 1. We show examples of each of these levels through a scenario based on observational data and reproduced snapshots.

4.1 Designing with Building Blocks

The first task took place on Day 1 and was to create a house based on a visual model (picture) provided by the teacher (Fig. 2a–b) and a set of building blocks (Fig. 2c). The students worked in groups of four and collaborated to solve the task in a shared ME world hosted on the teacher's computer. ME worlds can accommodate up to 30 simultaneous users, and an avatar represents each user (Fig. 2a). The students completed the task in about an hour. The group work included gaining a shared understanding of the overall assignment, the first task, and dividing the work into subtasks.

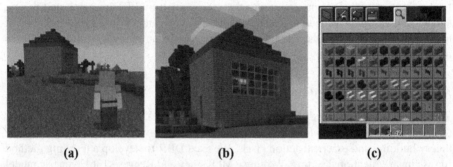

(a)   **(b)**   **(c)**

Fig. 2. a) House with an avatar who built the house by manual operations, b) same house seen from another angle; it has two windows and an entrance, and c) building blocks inventory and toolbar with four active blocks: oak planks, spruce planks, air, and glass.

Figure 2 (a–b) shows the model house that the students created in Minecraft, and the building blocks are shown in (c). None of the students found this task difficult, and all enjoyed the experience of designing and modeling, which they called "doing digital Lego." The transfer to programming was not obvious at this stage, as students did not encounter problems other than the time it took to stack blocks manually, which some considered tedious or boring. They were told at the end of the first day that block-based programming is analogous to a builder who calls out basic operations (place and destroy) to an interpreter who stacks blocks automatically to create visual structures by composition, such as a mason stacks bricks to build real houses. Furthermore, they were told that code blocks are a special type of building block that can be used to create computational structures by composition.

4.2 Building with Code Blocks

On the second day, one week later, the students were asked to recreate the house they had previously built manually—this time, using code blocks to automate construction. Each group hosted its own world so they could work outside class hours. This task was more complicated, and the teacher simplified it thus: 1) using higher-level building blocks, and 2) the blocks were given and inspired by Parson's method [35]. The code blocks are 3D graphic functions ("fill with" and "place" in Fig. 3) requiring parameters (x, y, z) and the blocks must be put in the right sequence (Fig. 3-right). To simplify the task, the students were given code blocks in a PDF document but scrambled like a jigsaw puzzle (Fig. 3-left).

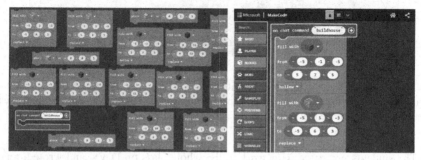

Fig. 3. Left: the students were given 16 code blocks on the second day, which when placed in the right sequence inside the "buildhouse" command block recreated the house shown in Fig. 2. The task was adapted from a YouTube video [38].

The students noticed that the blocks could be placed in many different sequences within the chat-command block to solve the task. They also noticed distinctions when they executed the "buildhouse" command, and the parameters (often inadvertently) varied from those in the given code. The teacher's on-demand scaffolding addressed these problems, suggesting *sequences* and *variables* as useful programming concepts. These topics would recur at the beginning of the next meeting in a lecture. Students gained practical experience in the game world to address unexpected situations, such as breaking out of the entrapment on their own or getting help from peers. The students could monitor their progress by comparing their results with the model house, which gave them great pleasure upon (and some frustration about) the task's accomplishment. All students completed the task and took screenshots to be part of the final report.

4.3   General Programming and Computational Concepts

In the third meeting (Day 3), the students were given the task of extending the model house toward the "dream house" that each group documented with a photo or visual image they brought to class. To complete the task, they were allowed to use higher-level code blocks, like Day 2. However, they also had to use at least one loop and one variable, and the loop preferably included a Boolean variable. Before they started, they were given a lecture on the relevant programming concepts and a few related topics with examples (e.g., how to automate the construction of a wall with two loops).

Figure 4 depicts three examples of the kind of code the groups created: a) stairs to the second floor, b) a cobblestone pathway to the front entrance that checks for the appearance of Redstone in the ground, and c) an argument for the build-house command that places the house x meters from the avatar (~x). This task was perceived as the most complex; the students preferred to use the more specific code blocks they had used before. Scaffolding at this stage included bringing to the students' attention problems they may not have discovered independently: 1) efficient code, and 2) general concepts.

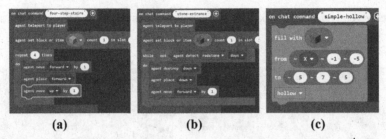

(a)   (b)   (c)

Fig. 4. From left to right: a) loop with four iterations to create stair-like path to 2nd floor, b) loop with conditional test to create cobble stoned path to house that stops when Redstone is underneath the agent, and c) variable that represents the x-value of a hollow cube.

The students presented their work to the whole class on Day 4 and wrote a report afterwards. The report asked about reflections on the experiences gained from the seminar, the extent to which the beginning activity of designing and modeling was useful, and the role of higher-level (CT) concepts in conceptualizing the programming activity.

5   Preliminary Results

We organized the empirical findings in terms of strengths and weaknesses, which were the high-level thematic codes. The first iteration of the DBR process had aims of exploration and problem finding. We summarize findings below and then elaborate them.

Strengths: Students said that the levels of abstraction (operationalized as three tasks) provided a gentle introduction to programming: everyone found the first level (modeling) easy and highly engaging. Coding felt progressively more demanding but using specialized code blocks (ME building functions) were easier than general-purpose programming blocks. Everyone collaborated when they built. Several cooperated when they programmed, but not all. Those who worked alone received more help from the teacher. Everyone said they learned something about basic programming concepts. Loops were mentioned by everyone; variables and the Minecraft agent (coding assistant) were also mentioned by several.

Shortcomings: The students could traverse all the levels, but further into the process, they lost an understanding of what they were doing. One student said, "Minecraft is a gentle way to learn programming, but I don't seem to have learned the depth of it, though." Having a shared referent (a common object of understanding) outside the computing domain (in the game world) helped as we elaborate below. The connection between visual structures in Minecraft (building and modeling) and general concepts in programming was difficult to understand despite visual similarity. Everyone found the coordinate system demanding; they struggled to place the blocks correctly when programming. No one mentioned the general (CT) concepts, such as iteration and abstraction, when asked to name what they had learned.

6 Discussion and Conclusions

In this paper, we addressed the following research question: How can Minecraft be used as a EUD environment in an educational context to facilitate and motivate the learning of introductory programming? Our main finding is a novel teaching method that enables non-programmers a gentle introduction to learning programming, which is characterized by three steps: 1) designing with building blocks, 2) building with code blocks, and 3) general programming and CT. Our method has some similarities to existing teaching methods with block-based programming. In step 2, where the students are given code blocks that they must assemble into a working code [35]. In addition, the students do not start programming from scratch; they are given an external object (model house in the game world) to reconstruct, first by building blocks and then by code blocks, inspired by modeling practice in CS education [39] applied to visual design. Finally, the students created something on their own by choosing their own object: a dream house. The method has similarities to UMC [33] and PRIMM [34], as these methods emphasize reusing and modifying program code before the learners create something new. However, in our method, adaptation (modeling) is a new activity.

Out theoretical framework informed the teaching method by a stepwise process in terms of what to do on each level and the conditions for transferring to the next. This framework emphasizes knowledge and program code as two objects that must be coordinated, and levels of abstractions for each software object that lead students into more advanced computational concepts and programming practices upon transfer.

We identified two dilemmas in our findings. First, whereas the students could traverse the three levels and complete the tasks, they could not always explain the program code they had created, which they found frustrating. One the one hand, the shared referent in the game world (model house) helped the learners to create a shared object of understanding that evolved. On the other hand, this object did not evolve to align with the technical (software) object the students created in the CodeBuilder. A cause of some disturbance was the Minecraft coordinate system. The students struggled to understand that variables (e.g., x, y, z) could be used as placeholders for constants (e.g., -5, 3, -3) and more generally arguments to use as input to the buildhouse command.

The other dilemma we identified was that the connection between visual structures in Minecraft and general programming constructs (including CT concepts) was difficult for the students to understand. On the one hand, visual artifacts (building blocks and code blocks) reveal high resemblance by following a similar composition logic based on the jigsaw puzzle metaphor and snapping. On the other hand, connecting code blocks by their names does not follow the same intuitive logic. There is no natural transition from "fill with" to repeat-loop and from integer values to variables. Intermediate levels of abstraction or increased scaffolding may be needed to make verbal transitioning more meaningful.

In summary: Our main idea is that by integrating the learning of programming in Minecraft, students can learn advanced programming concepts without being aware that they are learning them. Based on feedback from the students and evaluations of the method, we found that students could traverse all the levels, but further into the process, they lost understanding of what they were doing, or rather they did not achieve shared conceptual understanding. To address the issues and dilemmas and looking ahead, we suggest that more teaching and scaffolding are needed to harness the object of under-standing toward a shared knoweldge object of multiple levels, on the one hand, and to make the general (e.g., CT) concepts applicable to students' concrete learning activities, on the other. Future work will address the shortcomings by adding another day to the course (for teaching and practice) and designing non-player characters (NPCs) in the game world for automated scaffolding. This requires another cycle of the DBR process.

Acknowledgement. This work was supported by the Regional Research Fund of The Research Council of Norway.

References

1. Brown, A.: Design experiments: Theoretical and methodological challenges in creating complex interventions in classroom settings. J. Learn. Sci. **2**(2), 141–178 (1992)
2. Collins, A., Joseph, D., Bielaczyc, K.: Design research: theoretical and methodological issues. J. Learn. Sci. **13**(1), 15–42 (2004)
3. Hoadley, C., Campos, F.C.: Design-based research: what it is and why it matters to studying online learning. Educ. Psychol. **57**(3), 207–220 (2022)
4. MacLean, A., Carter, K., Lövstrand, L., Moran, T.: User-tailorable systems: pressing the issues with buttons. In: Proceedings of CHI 1990, pp. 175–182. ACM, New York, NY (1990)
5. Mørch, A.: Three levels of end-user tailoring: customization, integration, and extension. In: Kyng, M., Mathiassen, L. (eds.) Computers and Design in Context, pp. 51–76. The MIT Press, Cambridge (1997)
6. Schön, D.A.: The Reflective Practitioner: How Professionals Think in Action. Basic Books, New York (1983)
7. Ehn, P.: Work-oriented design of computer artifacts. Arbetslivscentrum, Stockholm (1988)
8. Fischer, G.: Domain-oriented design environments. Autom. Softw. Eng. **1**(2), 177–203 (1994)
9. Mørch, A.I.: Two 3D virtual worlds as domain-oriented design environments: Closing the educational gap with the action-breakdown-repair model. Int. J. Inf. Learn. Technol. **37**(5), 295–307 (2020)
10. Papert, S.: Mindstorms: Children, Computers, and Powerful Ideas. Basic Books, New York (1980)
11. Wing, J.M.: Computational thinking. Commun. ACM **49**(3), 33–35 (2006)
12. Weintrop, D., et al.: Defining computational thinking for mathematics and science classrooms. J. Sci. Educ. Technol. **25**(1), 127–147 (2016)
13. Shute, V.J., Sun, C., Asbell-Clarke, J.: Demystifying computational thinking. Educ. Res. Rev. **22**, 142–158 (2017)
14. Bocconi, S., et al.: Reviewing computational thinking in compulsory education. Report no. JRC128347. Publications Office of the European Union (2022)
15. Fischer, G., Girgensohn, A.: End-user modifiability in design environments. In: Proceedings CHI 1990, pp. 183–192. ACM, New York (1990)
16. Wulf, V., Golombek, B.: Direct activation. A concept to encourage tailoring activities. Behav. Inf. Technol. **20**(4), 249–263 (2001)
17. Costabile, M.F., Fogli, D., Mussio, P., Piccinno, A.: End-user development: the software shaping workshop approach. In: Lieberman, H., Paternò, F., Wulf, V. (eds.) End-user development. Human-Computer Interaction Series, vol. 9. Springer, Dordrecht (2006). https://doi.org/10.1007/1-4020-5386-x_9

18. Basawapatna, A., Koh, K.H., Repenning, A., Webb, D.C., Marshall, K.S.: Recognizing computational thinking patterns. In: Proceedings of the 42nd ACM technical symposium on computer science education (SIGCSE 2011), pp. 245–250. ACM, New York (2011)
19. Barricelli, B.R., Fogli, D., Locoro, A.: EUDability: a new construct at the intersection of end-user development and computational thinking. J. Syst. Softw. **195**, 111516 (2023). https://doi.org/10.1016/j.jss.2022.111516
20. Kafai, Y.B.: From computational thinking to computational participation in K-12 education. Commun. ACM **59**(8), 26–27 (2016)
21. Ellison, T.L., Evans, J.N.: Minecraft, teachers, parents, and learning: what they need to know and understand. Sch. Commun. J. **26**(2), 25–43 (2016)
22. Mørch, A.I., Eie, S., Mifsud, L.: Tradeoffs in combining domain-specific and generic skills' practice in Minecraft in social studies in teacher education. In: Proceedings of Fifth International Workshop on Cultures of Participation in the Digital Age, CoPDA 2018, pp. 44–52. Castiglione della Pescaia, Italy (published https://ceur-ws.org/Vol-2101/paper6.pdf) (2018)
23. Rahimi, S., Walker, J.T., Lin-Lipsmeyer, L., Shin, J.: Toward defining and assessing creativity in sandbox games. Creativ. Res. J. (2023).https://doi.org/10.1080/10400419.2022.2156477
24. Callaghan, N.: Investigating the role of minecraft in educational learning environments. Educ. Media Int. **53**(4), 244–260 (2016)
25. Karsenti, T., Bugmann, J.: Exploring the educational potential of Minecraft: the case of 118 elementary-school students. In: Proceedings ICEduTech2017, International Conference on Educational Technologies, International Association for Development of the Information Society, Sydney, Australia (2017)
26. CarbonellCarrera, C., Jaeger, A.J., Saorín, J.L., Melián, D., de la TorreCantero, J.: Minecraft as a block-building approach for developing spatial skills. Entertain. Comput. **38**, 100427 (2021)
27. Baek, Y., Min, E., Yun, S.: Mining educational implications of Minecraft. Comput. Sch. **37**(1), 1–16 (2020)
28. Andersen, R., Eie, S., Mørch, A.I., Mifsud, L., Rustad, M.: Rebuilding the industrial revolution: Using Minecraft in teacher education in social studies. In: Proceedings of the 15th International Conference of the Learning Sciences (ICLS 2021), pp. 27–34. International Society of the Learning Sciences, Bochum, Germany (2021)
29. Klimová, N., Šajben, J., Lovászová, G.: Online game-based learning through Minecraft: Education edition programming contest. In: 2021 IEEE Global Engineering Education Conference (EDUCON), pp. 1660–1668. IEEE Press, Washington, DC (2021)
30. Bile, A.: Development of intellectual and scientific abilities through game-programming in Minecraft. Educ. Inf. Technol. **27**(5), 7241–7256 (2022)
31. Kutay, E., Oner, D.: Coding with Minecraft: the development of middle school students' computational thinking. ACM Trans. Comput. Educ. **22**(2), 1–19 (2022)
32. Mørch, A.I.: Aspect-oriented software components. In: Patel, N. (ed.) Adaptive evolutionary information systems, pp. 105–123. Idea Group Publishing, Hershey (2003)
33. Lee, I., et al.: Computational thinking for youth in practice. ACM Inroads **2**(1), 32–37 (2011)
34. Sentance, S., Waite, J., Kallia, M.: Teaching computer programming with PRIMM: a sociocultural perspective. Comput. Sci. Educ. **29**(2), 136–176 (2019)
35. Parsons, D., Haden, P.: Parson's programming puzzles: a fun and effective learning tool for first programming courses. In: Proceedings of the 8th Australasian Conference on Computing Education, vol. 52, pp. 157–163. Australian Computer Society, Canberra (2006)
36. McKenney, S., Reeves, T.: Conducting Educational Design Research, 2nd edn. Routledge, Oxford (2019)
37. Michalos, A.C. (ed.): Encyclopedia of Quality of Life and Well-Being Research. Springer, Dordrecht (2014). https://doi.org/10.1007/978-94-007-0753-5

38. Minecraft Education Edition - How to Code a House. https://www.youtube.com/watch?v=APSo9qFngoM. Accessed 16 Apr 2023

39. Madsen, O.L., Møller-Pedersen, B.: A unified approach to modeling and programming. In: Petriu, D.C., Rouquette, N., Haugen, Ø. (eds.) Model driven engineering languages and systems. LNCS, vol. 6394, pp. 1–15. Springer, Heidelberg (2010). https://doi.org/10.1007/978-3-642-16145-2_1

Challenges of Enabling End-Users
to Develop Systems with AI

Daniel Tetteroo[✉]

Department of Industrial Design, Eindhoven University of Technology, Eindhoven,
The Netherlands
`d.tetteroo@tue.nl`

Abstract. With the advent of AI in research and practice, the research
community has started discussing how end-user development might be
affected. This paper aims to outline a number of challenges that might
arise when end-users aim to integrate AI in their software creations. It
examines these issues for different stages of a design process (ideation,
conceptualization, implementation and evaluation) and concludes with
an outlook towards overcoming these issues.

Keywords: artificial intelligence · end-user development · research
challenges

1 Introduction

End-user development (EUD) aims to empower end-users of technologies to create, modify and expand those technologies to fit their personal needs [16]. With
the advent of Artificial Intelligence (AI) both in research and practice, the integration of EUD and AI has been a topic of ongoing discussion [12,19]. While
AI is an umbrella term that has acquired many different meanings [21] and this
paper is not going to add an additional definition, some characteristics of AI
important for the context of this paper are: machine learning, (large sets of)
data as input, intelligent conversion of input data into (high-level) output, not
"Artificial General Intelligence (AGI)". We note that rule-based systems, sym-
bolic AI, etc. can also produce seemingly intelligent behavior, but are not in the
scope of this paper.

Fischer [10] has recently presented a vision of what the integration of EUD
and AI could look like, noting amongst others the sometimes contradicting
premises upon which both concepts are built. At the same time, he acknowledges there could be a mutually beneficial relationship between both, given serious commitment towards the EUD objective to initiate cultural transformations
that will empower all stakeholders. In order to empower end-users in working
with AI, we need to critically assess the challenges that working with AI presents
to them. Only then can we design appropriate tools and methods for end-users
to harness the power of AI for personally meaningful purposes.

© The Author(s), under exclusive license to Springer Nature Switzerland AG 2023
L. D. Spano et al. (Eds.): IS-EUD 2023, LNCS 13917, pp. 241–249, 2023.
https://doi.org/10.1007/978-3-031-34433-6_16

When considering the combination of AI and EUD, we can roughly distinguish two ends on a scale: AI for EUD and EUD of AI. The first is about using AI and/or AI-powered tools to support end-users in developing meaningful personal solutions. Examples of AI-supported software engineering have surfaced (e.g., Chat-GPT[1] and Github Co-Pilot[2]) that have the potential to greatly increase the efficiency of programming tasks, as well as to help novice programmers convert natural language expressed needs into actionable code, or help explain functionality of existing code in natural language. In contrast, EUD of AI is about how end-users can be supported to engage in customization, extension etc. of systems with AI. In a sense, this can be understood as an extension of 'traditional' EUD into a context where the technology that end-users use to create, modify or extent software incorporates (traces of) AI. AI for EUD and EUD of AI may not be mutually exclusive - in fact it is likely that AI can provide end-users with support for implementing (other) AI into their creations [1]. While AI-supported EUD is briefly discussed later, this paper focuses on the challenges that end-user developers encounter when engaging in the creation, modification or extension of AI-infused software - EUD of AI.

This paper aims to complement the work of [10] by turning from a high-level, abstract view on *what* the integration of AI and EUD could mean, towards a slightly more concrete view on *how* end-user developers might be supported in engaging with AI. Therefore, the remainder of this paper outlines a number of (research) challenges that might arise during EUD of AI. In this, the paper takes a rather pragmatic and implementation centered view, purposefully disregarding further considerations (e.g., ethical, normative) related to the use of AI that are equally important, but would cloud the scope of this paper.

2   Challenges for Integrating AI in EUD

This paper aims to explore some of the challenges that integrating AI may present to end-users, within the context of End-User Development. These challenges are explored along four typical stages of a design process: ideation, conceptualization, implementation and evaluation. While end-users might not formally organize their activities along these stages, the stages help us to separate conceptually different activities that end-users face when engaging in EUD.

2.1   Ideation

Two main challenges for end-users in ideating about the use of AI in EUD are: *having realistic expectations about what AI can do for them*, and *envisioning scenarios of use*. While these two challenges are interconnected (i.e. without a realistic understanding of AI capabilities, envisioned scenarios might be meaningless), they point towards two distinct issues.

---

[1] https://chat.openai.com/.

[2] https://github.com/features/copilot.

Realistic Expectations About AI. The impressions and expectations of the general public on the potential of AI have varied over the years [8]. These expectations might not necessarily align realistically with the capabilities of AI. AI being a suitcase term [10] and cultural popularization of AI focusing largely on loss of control to Artificial General Intelligence (AGI) [3] causes *"expectations [amongst the general public] that the technology is not (yet) able to fulfil"* [3]. In the context of EUD, a recent study where users were asked to formulate trigger-action rules for IoT applications based on their daily needs, identified a discrepancy between what users would formulate, and what was technically possible [5]. A more nuanced and realistic understanding of the technological possibilities and limitations of applying AI in EUD is thus necessary for end-users to envision realistic scenarios of use.

Envisioning Scenarios of Use. Even if users have a realistic understanding of the capabilities of AI, they might find it difficult to express scenarios of use where AI could be implemented. On the one hand, end-users might propose the use of AI in scenarios where less complex solutions suffice, or even present a better fit to their needs. On the other hand, end-users might lack an understanding of the application areas for AI in their domain. Previous studies have shown that, generally speaking, end-users are well capable of developing creative ideas for EUD in various domains (e.g., [5,20]). Yet, working with AI implies certain characteristics that may be challenging for end-users to work with, such as e.g., dynamic response behavior (changing as the system trains on new data) and limited scope (i.e. depending on the data it has been trained on). While there has been previous research on ideation of AI-supported applications with end-users (e.g., [18]), developing more structured support in the form of e.g., ideation toolkits could be helpful in overcoming the issues around envisioning scenarios of use.

2.2 Conceptualization

Breaking Down Scenarios into Conceptual Elements. End-users who have defined relevant scenarios of use for AI will need to translate these scenarios into conceptual representations. For example, a user might have envisioned *that* AI can help in controlling the sunscreens on their home to keep the inside temperature at a comfortable level. Yet, before engaging in implementation, the end-user will need to translate and break down this scenario into concrete elements that can be measured and controlled by an AI-based smart home solution (i.e., *how* AI can help in controlling the sunscreens). For example, what data can the system use to make decisions regarding lowering or raising the sunscreens? Under which conditions should the system act, and under which conditions should it refrain from acting (for example, while the windows are being cleaned)?

While this challenge of translating abstract scenarios into concrete conceptual elements is an element of any EUD project, introducing AI in this context aggravates the challenge. Recently, Corno et al. [5] have shown that end-users use different abstractions to express personalized scenarios in the context of internet of things. For example, end-users might choose to use device-centric abstractions (e.g., *"lower the sunscreens when pv power is over 2000W"*), or information-centric abstractions (e.g., *"when the sun is in the south, close the sunscreens"*) while actually aiming to elicit similar behavior from a system.

This means that end-users will need to understand the nuances of what such expressions mean for e.g., the data to which the AI needs access in order to produce the desired output. Furthermore, optimal output might not be achieved through the abstractions that users express themselves. For the above example about sunscreens, users might define system behavior in terms of incoming sunlight and room temperature. However, the system might produce more optimal behavior if additional, or different data sources (e.g., power output of the heating system, PV-power generation, weather forecast, energy price forecast, solar trajectory) are incorporated.

Managing Technological and Computational Feasibility. Related to the first challenge of the ideation phase, during conceptualization end-users might need to be supported in conceptualizing solutions that are technologically and computationally feasible and adequate. For example, and end-user in the previous example might choose to 'feed' live video data from their smart doorbell to the system, assuming it will aid in identifying the intensity and direction of incoming sunlight. A solution that is both more adequate and less computationally intensive is likely to exist, but the end-user might need to be supported in identifying it.

2.3 Implementation

Perhaps the most difficult to overcome challenges regarding AI in EUD arise in the implementation phase. Barring any 'pre-packaged' AI-fueled services that provide high-level APIs for very specific tasks (e.g., image generation, text generation), implementation of AI in EUD projects will often require in-depth technological knowledge.

Acquiring, Preparing and Selecting Data. A first challenge is the acquisition, preparation and selection of high-quality data serving as training data for an AI model. The challenges in collecting relevant training data, and the consequences of careless inclusion of unfiltered training data (e.g., introducing bias) are well known. If we would want to support end-user developers in integrating AI in their projects, supporting them in training data collection and preparation is of utmost importance. Additionally, for some contexts it might be possible or even desired to offer pre-trained models upon which end-users can expand, analogous to the Seeding, Evolutionary growth, Reseeding (SER) model [11]. The end-users would then receive a 'seeded' AI-model that has been pre-trained (*seeding*). Going further, end-users would be enabled to expand or modify the training data for the model, thereby changing its performance (*evolutionary growth*). Eventually, there might be a need for an expert to revisit, evaluate and manipulate the expanded data set that the model has now been trained upon, in order to align it with the end-user's goals (*reseeding*).

Selecting a Model. An equally important and difficult step is selecting the right model for an end-user's task. While end-users might be trained to understand the high-level differences between classes of AI models (e.g., supervised machine learning (ML) models for predictive tasks vs. unsupervised models for descriptive tasks), distinguishing between specific models within those classes and being able to select models based on their mathematical properties will likely be too daunting a task for end-users. A solution could be to offer end-users with a limited selection of models fit for specific purposes at the cost of reduced performance.

Integrating AI into Software. Finally, implementing AI in end-user programs requires technical expertise that end-users might be lacking. Even if models come pre-trained and pre-packaged, connecting them to existing software might pose a challenge to end-users. Also, various ML models will require specific ways of connecting to software, for example depending on the required input and output data. In short, the challenge here is to find and design suitable paradigms and tools for offering end-users the possibility to integrate AI in their EUD solutions.

Some of tools have already been proposed, for example [15] developed Poseblocks, a block-based programming tool that enables students to create AI-supported applications featuring body, hand and face tracking. Interestingly, the tool is based on a visual programming paradigm and framework (Scratch [17]) that have existed for a while, showing that re-purposing or integrating with existing paradigms might be a viable way of incorporating AI in EUD. Similarly, learning from approaches developed in fields related to EUD may be beneficial, such as the Authoring Artificial Intelligence (AAI) approaches common in the field of robotics [6].

2.4 Evaluation

Testing and evaluating end-user software has been a subject of research for a long time, amongst others leading to an extension of EUD called end-user software engineering (EUSE) [2]. Major efforts have been undertaken to support end-users in debugging their software creations, be it in the context of spreadsheets (e.g., [14]) or trigger-action programming (e.g., [4]).

Performance Evaluation. Where evaluating the performance of 'regular' software can already be a challenge to end-users, this challenge arguably increases when integrating AI. For simple classification tasks (e.g., determining whether a picture features a cat) evaluating AI performance is well understood and relatively straightforward: performance can be expressed as the ratio between correct and incorrect classifications. For other tasks (e.g., object detection, regression, etc.) evaluation metrics might be less straightforward. Especially when AI is applied for generative purposes, evaluation can become a lot more difficult and subjective. Finally, when using models that continuously evolve by incorporating new training data, evaluation transforms from 'a final step in the design process' to 'continuous monitoring of performance'.

Explainable AI. Beyond being able to evaluate the performance of AI, end-users will need to understand the factors that impact that performance, and how to manipulate those factors in order to improve performance. Explainable AI (XAI) is a relatively recent field of research that aims to develop methods and tools for explaining AI output in terms of its input, in ways understandable to the user. Although XAI is understood in many different ways, for EUD debugging it is essential that systems are as transparent as possible and offer explanations that do not require further human processing, i.e. what [7] call *truly explainable systems*.

Table 1. Overview of research challenges in EUD of AI.

Design process stage	Challenge
Ideation	Maintaining realistic expectations about AI
	Envisioning scenarios of use
Conceptualization	Breaking down scenarios into conceptual elements
	Managing technological & computational feasibility
Implementation	Acquiring, preparing & selecting data
	Selecting a model
	Integrating AI into software
Evaluation	Performance evaluation
	Explainable AI

3   Discussion and Conclusion

With AI permeating in more and more domains of daily life, it is important to consider how end-users might be supported to use, modify or expand AI as part of end-user development. This paper has briefly examined where challenges might arise in this process. While by no means exhaustive, the list of challenges in Table 1 can serve as an agenda for future research on the topic.

As mentioned in the introduction, this paper purposefully took an implementation centered approach in exploring challenges, disregarding some important subjects when end-users engage in the creation, adaptation or expansion of AI software. For example, end-users might run into legal or ethical trouble in collecting or curating training data for their models [13]. Especially in a corporate environment, EUD of AI might thus require close involvement of non end-user stakeholders, such as system administrators, lawyers, etc. It is thus imperative that we consider the challenge of providing end-users with the possibility to develop software with AI not merely a technological one, but approach it from a socio-technical perspective encompassing a broad range of stakeholders.

In general, addressing the challenges above will require a broad view on what constitutes EUD. Some of the challenges might be solved by technological means or by improving the user experience of existing tools. Other challenges will require educating end-users, or even designing the socio-technical context in which EUD takes place. For example, one could envision scenarios where it would be beneficial to conceptualize the above challenges in view of a "Culture of Participation" [9] consisting of a range of stakeholders (e.g., domain experts, model developers, IT-infrastructure managers, etc.) who occupy different positions in a socio-technical space. The burden of overcoming the challenges mentioned above would then no longer be placed on either the technology or the end-users, but shared amongst the different elements that make up this socio-technical space.

Not all challenges listed in this paper are of equal difficulty, and some might even be largely overcome as tools for EUD of AI mature and AI for particular tasks is offered as ready-to-use service. End-users might not even think about particular AI-fueled services in terms of AI, much like we do no longer think about search engines in terms of web pages, but in terms of content. Yet, there is a fundamental difference between *using* such services and *developing* with them in the level of understanding required from end-users. Future research should focus on uncovering these differences and on nuancing and expanding the challenges presented in this paper. By gaining a better understanding of the relation between EUD and AI, we can ensure that the development of future EUD tools and ecosystems remains committed towards the EUD objective to initiate cultural transformations that will empower all stakeholders.

References

1. Barricelli, B.R., Fogli, D.: Exploring the reciprocal influence of artificial intelligence and end-user development. In: Proceedings of the Sixth International Workshop on Cultures of Participation in the Digital Age: AI for Humans or Humans for AI?, Frascati, Italy, vol. 3136, pp. 21–29. CEUR, June 2022
2. Burnett, M.M., Myers, B.A.: Future of end-user software engineering: beyond the silos. In: Proceedings of the ICSE 2014, FOSE 2014, pp. 201–211. ACM, New York (2014). https://doi.org/10.1145/2593882.2593896
3. Cave, S., et al.: Portrayals and perceptions of AI and why they matter. Report, The Royal Society, December 2018. https://doi.org/10.17863/CAM.34502. https://www.repository.cam.ac.uk/handle/1810/287193. Accepted 19 Dec 2018
4. Corno, F., De Russis, L., Monge Roffarello, A.: Empowering end users in debugging trigger-action rules. In: Proceedings of the 2019 CHI Conference on Human Factors in Computing Systems, CHI 2019, pp. 1–13. Association for Computing Machinery, New York (2019). https://doi.org/10.1145/3290605.3300618

5. Corno, F., De Russis, L., Monge Roffarello, A.: Devices, information, and people: abstracting the Internet of Things for end-user personalization. In: Fogli, D., Tetteroo, D., Barricelli, B.R., Borsci, S., Markopoulos, P., Papadopoulos, G.A. (eds.) IS-EUD 2021. LNCS, vol. 12724, pp. 71–86. Springer, Cham (2021). https://doi.org/10.1007/978-3-030-79840-6_5

6. Coronado, E., Mastrogiovanni, F., Indurkhya, B., Venture, G.: Visual programming environments for end-user development of intelligent and social robots, a systematic review. J. Comput. Lang. **58**, 100970 (2020). https://doi.org/10.1016/j.cola.2020.100970. https://www.sciencedirect.com/science/article/pii/S2590118420300307

7. Doran, D., Schulz, S., Besold, T.R.: What does explainable AI really mean? A new conceptualization of perspectives, October 2017. https://doi.org/10.48550/arXiv.1710.00794. arXiv:1710.00794 [cs]

8. Fast, E., Horvitz, E.: Long-term trends in the public perception of artificial intelligence. In: Proceedings of the AAAI Conference on Artificial Intelligence, vol. 31, no. 1, February 2017. https://doi.org/10.1609/aaai.v31i1.10635. https://ojs.aaai.org/index.php/AAAI/article/view/10635

9. Fischer, G.: End user development and meta-design: foundations for cultures of participation. J. Organ. End User Comput. **22**(1), 52–82 (2010). https://doi.org/10.4018/joeuc.2010101901. http://www.igi-global.com/article/end-user-development-meta-design/39120

10. Fischer, G.: End-user development: empowering stakeholders with artificial intelligence, meta-design, and cultures of participation. In: Fogli, D., Tetteroo, D., Barricelli, B.R., Borsci, S., Markopoulos, P., Papadopoulos, G.A. (eds.) IS-EUD 2021. LNCS, vol. 12724, pp. 3–16. Springer, Cham (2021). https://doi.org/10.1007/978-3-030-79840-6_1

11. Fischer, G., McCall, R., Ostwald, J., Reeves, B., Shipman, F.: Seeding, evolutionary growth and reseeding: supporting the incremental development of design environments. In: Proceedings of the CHI 1994, pp. 292–298. ACM, New York (1994). https://doi.org/10.1145/191666.191770

12. Fogli, D., Tetteroo, D., Barricelli, B.R., Borsci, S., Markopoulos, P., Papadopoulos, G.A. (eds.): IS-EUD 2021. LNCS, vol. 12724. Springer, Cham (2021). https://doi.org/10.1007/978-3-030-79840-6. https://www.springer.com/gp/book/9783030798390

13. Furman, J., Marchant, G., Price, H., Rossi, F. (eds.): AIES 2018: Proceedings of the 2018 AAAI/ACM Conference on AI, Ethics, and Society. Association for Computing Machinery, New York (2018)

14. Grigoreanu, V., Burnett, M., Wiedenbeck, S., Cao, J., Rector, K., Kwan, I.: End-user debugging strategies: a sensemaking perspective. ACM Trans. Comput.-Hum. Interact. **19**(1), 5:1–5:28 (2012). https://doi.org/10.1145/2147783.2147788

15. Jordan, B., Devasia, N., Hong, J., Williams, R., Breazeal, C.: PoseBlocks: a toolkit for creating (and dancing) with AI. In: Proceedings of the AAAI Conference on Artificial Intelligence, vol. 35, no. 17, pp. 15551–15559, May 2021. https://doi.org/10.1609/aaai.v35i17.17831. https://ojs.aaai.org/index.php/AAAI/article/view/17831

16. Lieberman, H., Paternò, F., Klann, M., Wulf, V.: End-user development: an emerging paradigm. In: Lieberman, H., Paternò, F., Wulf, V. (eds.) End User Development. HCIS, vol. 9, pp. 1–8. Springer, Dordrecht (2006). https://doi.org/10.1007/1-4020-5386-X_1. http://www.springerlink.com/content/h371591g75621w53/

17. Maloney, J., Resnick, M., Rusk, N., Silverman, B., Eastmond, E.: The scratch programming language and environment. ACM Trans. Comput. Educ. **10**(4), 16:1–16:15 (2010). https://doi.org/10.1145/1868358.1868363

18. Morrison, C., Cutrell, E., Dhareshwar, A., Doherty, K., Thieme, A., Taylor, A.: Imagining artificial intelligence applications with people with visual disabilities using tactile ideation. In: Proceedings of the 19th International ACM SIGACCESS Conference on Computers and Accessibility, ASSETS 2017, pp. 81–90. Association for Computing Machinery, New York (2017). https://doi.org/10.1145/3132525.3132530

19. Paternò, F., Burnett, M., Fischer, G., Matera, M., Myers, B., Schmidt, A.: Artificial intelligence versus end-user development: a panel on what are the tradeoffs in daily automations? In: Ardito, C., et al. (eds.) INTERACT 2021. LNCS, vol. 12936, pp. 340–343. Springer, Cham (2021). https://doi.org/10.1007/978-3-030-85607-6_33

20. Tetteroo, D., et al.: Lessons learnt from deploying an end-user development platform for physical rehabilitation. In: Proceedings of the CHI 2015, pp. 4133–4142. ACM, New York, April 2015

21. Wang, P.: On defining artificial intelligence. J. Artif. Gener. Intell. **10**(2), 1–37 (2019). https://doi.org/10.2478/jagi-2019-0002. https://sciendo.com/article/10.2478/jagi-2019-0002

EUD Strategy in the Education Field for Supporting Teachers in Creating Digital Courses

Stefano Valtolina[1](✉) [iD] and Ricardo Anibal Matamoros[2]

[1] Department of Computer Science, Università Degli Studi di Milano, Milano, Italy
stefano.valtolina@unimi.it
[2] Milan Bicocca University, Milan, Italy
r.matamorosaragon@campus.unimib.it

Abstract. This paper aims to investigate End-User Development (EUD) strategies in the education field. In this area, e-learning is becoming a crucial instrument to promote the role of instructors from simply information transmitters to dynamic co-creators of knowledge among their students. Our idea is to use an e-learning platform to allow teachers to create digital courses in a more effective and time-saving way. This paper proposes a EUD strategy that uses learning objects (LOs) as primary elements. The solution aims to endow the e-learning platform with a smart chatbot to assist teachers in their activities. Defined using RASA technology, the chatbot asks for information about the course the teacher has to create based on their profile and needs. It suggests the best LOs and how to combine them according to their prerequisites and outcomes. A recommendation system provides suggestions through a machine-learning model to define the semantic similarity between the entered data and the LOs metadata. In addition to suggesting how to combine the LOs, the chatbot explains why the module is significant. Finally, the paper presents some preliminary results about tests carried out by teachers in creating their digital courses.

Keywords: End-User Development · Virtual Assistants · CUI – Conversational Interface in education · AI for HCI

1 Introduction

End-User Development (EUD) provides end users with strategies, methods, techniques and tools that allow them to act as non-professional software developers, to create, modify, or extend software artefacts [1]. The term End-User Development is not new. It stems from the field of End-User Programming [1–11]. The shift from "programming" to "development" reflects the emerging awareness that, while adapting a computer to a user's needs may include some form of programming, it certainly is not limited to it. EUD is relevant to a potentially large population segment, including most end users of traditional computer applications.

© The Author(s), under exclusive license to Springer Nature Switzerland AG 2023
L. D. Spano et al. (Eds.): IS-EUD 2023, LNCS 13917, pp. 250–267, 2023.
https://doi.org/10.1007/978-3-031-34433-6_17

In this paper, we take a specific perspective to discuss the EUD approach concerning its application in education. Using e-learning platforms aims to support teachers who can maximise the benefits of both asynchronous and synchronous learning by adopting proper EUD technology. These solutions are designed to improve professor-student communication and increase students' course satisfaction. Another encouraging aspect is that these platforms can change many teachers' and students' perceptions of lessons, homework, and their importance in education.

In this regard, we believe these platforms should evolve from easy to use in general to easy to use for developing digital courses. In this context, the teachers act as empowered users to "create" suitable and personalised lessons according to their didactic requirements and students' needs.

Although some solutions do not directly mention the use of the EUD approach, e-learning platforms are becoming an invaluable resource for educators and teachers that provides students with tools to learn at their own pace by harnessing a new model of knowledge sharing. E-Learning Management Systems (LMSs) such as Absorb, Moodle, Blackboard, Schoology, Google Classroom, Learnopoly or Elucidat (see this link for an updated list of LMS: https://research.com/software/list-of-learning-management-systems-for-schools-and-universities) are designed to help an individual to develop, manage and provide online courses and programs to learn. A key role for teachers in a virtual classroom is their effort to be innovative in their teaching methodologies without imitating what has been done previously in the traditional classroom. Being an expert in a subject is no longer enough. They have to know how to transfer their knowledge and experience differently online.

According to these considerations, this paper presents a new strategy to support teachers in creating a digital course using an e-learning platform named WhoTeach[1]. The innovative approach consists of endowing the platform with a smart chatbot to assist teachers in their activities. The idea relies on using learning objects (LOs) as fundamental elements to compose a course [12–14]. Lately, the area of research dealing with finding and recommending a list of LOs that fit specific teachers' needs and requirements is very active [13, 14]. Nevertheless, teachers highlight difficulties in effectively combining small chunks of educational material to meet the teacher's academic requirements [15, 16].

In this field, the main research question concerns how to support teachers in finding LOs that can be valuable, well-rated and suitable for the teacher's needs and how to help them to personalise and combine these materials to create the final course. Our solution aims at inserting in the development process of a digital course a EUD strategy mediated by a virtual assistant. This assistant is a chatbot defined using RASA technology, an open-source platform for creating voice or text-based virtual assistants. The chatbot asks the teachers for information about the course she/he has to create. This information and the teacher's profile suggest the best open-access LOs and how to combine them according to their prerequires and competencies that students can acquire by attending them. Suggestions are implemented using Sentence-BERT (S-BERT) [17], a machine-learning model based on Transformers for generating embedding representations helpful in capturing the semantic similarity between input data and LO metadata. Finally, the

---

[1] https://www.whoteach.it/.

chatbot not only suggests the better LOs to use but also how to combine them to create a personalised course according to the teacher's needs by levering the prerequisites each LOs specifies.

The paper is structured as follows. Section 2 describes the state of the art of learning management systems and the EUD approach they provide to teachers. To test our idea, we considered a specific course type that focuses on teaching the first foundations of programming languages or coding. This is a typical case in which teachers do not want to waste time creating lessons from scratch. Instead, they want to exploit open-accessible online resources to combine and personalise learning objects that will compose the new course. Section 3 focuses on the strategy we adopted to develop the recommendation system we integrated into our e-learning platform specifically studied to help teachers to create courses. The Section describes the model we defined for suggesting a sequence of proper LOs, a model used by the chatbot we present in Sect. 4. The Section explains how we used the chatbot to provide teachers with a EUD approach for creating a course and the interaction strategies it offers to support teachers in their activities. Specifically, we describe how the chatbot can explain its advice to avoid presenting suggestions that may be obscure to teachers. Section 5 presents some preliminary results about tests carried out in creating their digital courses. In particular, we defined and implemented a model to evaluate teachers' level of acceptance and intention to use the chatbot, extending the UTAUT model (The unified theory of acceptance and use of technology) presented in [18]. Finally, Sect. 6 sums up conclusions and future works.

2   How LMS Can Support Teachers in the Design of Courses

E-learning is a crucial strategy to support teachers in creating digital courses that can improve the effectiveness and efficiency of their educational efforts [19]. This technology promotes the role of instructors from simply information transmitters to dynamically functioning as co-creators of knowledge among their students. Some studies examine the teachers' perceptions of e-learning teaching because they are the main driver in the educational process and understand the various possibilities of implementing e-learning [20, 21].

These studies suggest that online education may be successfully implemented as a new modality of education strategy. A Learning Management System (LMS) can be the right solution to facilitate this teaching. LMS provides an indispensable set of features that support educational activities such as classroom learning and distance education. It helps make learning more interactive and fun, track student progress, create and deliver educational content, and collaborate on projects. One of the key benefits of these solutions is that they make educational processes easier for teachers. In particular, they could save teachers a great deal of time they would have spent creating new courses. The problem is particularly true in the case of basic or professional courses for the creation of which teachers would like to exploit previous knowledge or online resources without wasting too much time. For example, in this paper, we consider the design of courses for learning the foundations of coding, which could sometimes be tedious and time-consuming.

Independently by the type of lessons to create, one major problem of e-learning is that it is challenging to do well. To facilitate this issue, teachers can use authoring tools such as Absorb[2], Learnopoly[3] or Elucidat[4]. These tools provide a platform for the students and instructors to learn and highlight their skills wherever and whenever they want, at their convenience. Special features of these LMS in relation to others such as Moodle or Google Classroom are that they help teachers develop, launch and review an e-learning course. However, these systems cannot support teachers throughout the whole process of creating a new digital course.

For this reason, a research question we want to reply to in this paper concerns how to provide teachers with a EUD strategy that can assist them in searching online and open-access learning materials. Then, they need a solution for personalising and combining these materials to create the final course for the students.

Our approach uses an intelligent chatbot to assist teachers in their activities. In the literature, there are many studies regarding the use of chatbots in the educational domain [22]. [23] and [24] present investigations that focus on using conversational agents in areas such as teaching and learning, administrative assistance, assessment, consultancy and research and development. According to the review [22], chatbots are mainly applied for teaching and learning (66%). They promote rapid access to materials by students and faculty at any time and place [25, 26]. This strategy helps save time and maximise students' learning abilities and results [27], stimulating and involving them more in teaching work [28]. Furthermore, they can automate many student activities, including submitting homework, replying to emails and sending feedback on the courses followed [29, 30]. Finally, the chatbot can be used as a real personal assistant for teachers, assisting them in their daily tasks.

In our work, we promote using conversational agents not as student assistants but as mentors that can help teachers to create digital courses. The chatbot asks for information about the course the teacher has to create based on her/his profile and needs. Then it extracts and suggests the learning objects (LO) that better meet the teacher's needs. Reusing existing LOs is a valuable solution for helping teachers create courses. LOs can be viewed as building blocks a teacher can assemble to produce a course that achieves the instructional objectives. The development of LOs has brought a significant promise for creating highly personalised learning programs and has resulted in the creation of various LOs repositories worldwide. LOs promise to make the creation of courses quicker and more efficient thanks to their accessibility, reusability and interoperability in different settings.

Nevertheless, finding suitable material for the teacher's specific needs can be a headache when there are many to choose from. This plethora of materials can be seen as a disadvantage of online education and leads to paralysis of the creation process.

Moreover, the problem is how to find the right LOs and combine and sequence them to ensure that learning resources can be appropriately assembled in a course that can meet the teachers' objectives and requirements.

---

[2] https://www.absorblms.com/.

[3] https://learnopoly.com/.

[4] https://www.elucidat.com/.

2.1 A Case Study: Teaching Coding

Nowadays, knowing how to code is not just for people with computer science degrees. More and more people, companies and institutions require specific courses of this type. Specifically, we focus our attention on a particular reality taking into account organisations that act as global volunteer-led communities for teaching programming to young people. A charity called the CoderDojo Foundation operates worldwide to support various clubs[5] called CoderDojo, in which participants learn how to code, develop websites, apps, programs, and games, and explore technology in a fun and creative way. One lead volunteer typically sets up dojos, but the creation of personalised courses is, in some cases, a very time-demanding activity.

That is why the existence of online materials and resources from which to draw is a good starting point for creating a course. In the context of the CoderDojo activities, LOs refer to computer programming skills aimed at learning and using technology and the Web and developing computational thinking[6]. Our idea is to use the WhoTeach platform to allow teachers to create a course that can be offered to the students in an asynchronous way guaranteeing constant learning. In addition, they enable lessons to be carried out remotely, making it easier to carry out teaching activities, especially if there are numerous students. With this aim, our problem is how to enable teachers to create suitable and personalisable courses in a fast way while at the same time guaranteeing good quality.

3 A Strategy for Recommending LOs

Reusing learning objects (LOs) rather than their reinvention aims to save time and effort [31]. Moreover, from a quality point of view, the more a resource is reused, the more likely it is to be of high quality simply because more people will have been exposed to it and have had the opportunity to provide feedback [32]. In this paper, we focus on reusing LOs during the design phase of an online course. Expert practitioners use their experience of solving problems in the past to build on and create new solutions in new situations. These reusable solutions, which Gamma et al. in [27] named design patterns, aim to help teachers to create courses by providing them with a set of design ideas in a structured way [33].

Nevertheless, most current e-learning platforms are closed systems with owned digital materials. Different systems hardly share and reuse these materials because they are made in proprietary formats. To solve the problems of sharing and reusing teaching materials in other e-learning systems, many international organisations, including IEEE Learning Technologies Standardization Committee (LTSC), Instruction Management System Global Learning Consortium (IMS), Aviation Industry CBT Committee (AICC), Advanced Distributed Learning initiative (ADL) [34–36], and Alliance of Remote Instructional Authoring and Distribution Networks for Europe project [37], have devoted to establishing e-learning standards. Among many proposed standards, the

---

[5] https://coderdojo.com/en/.

[6] Coding: https://www.sprintlab.it/blog/coding/.

Sharable Content Object Reference Model (SCOR [38]) is recognised as the most popular one, and the IEEE-Standards Association has approved its Learning Object Metadata (LOM) [39]. Another standard, the Dublin Core[7], emerged over the years to facilitate the sharing and reuse of learning materials which establishes metadata policies and provides suggestions for using the LOs. All these standard protocols allow teaching materials for different learning management systems to be shared, reused, and integrated, but none agree on which metadata could be used for describing LOs. Some studies [40] recommend a minimal metadata set representing an LO. Still, no specific rules are indicated, whereas other surveys [40, 41] have shown that Dublin Core is suitable for describing the bibliographic side of digital resources, but LOM allows the best representation of the pedagogical aspects.

Due to its nature, we decided to use LOM for our project, but a problem remains. How to exploit this metadata to suggest proper LOs and combine them in a final course. Recommendation Systems (RS) such as the one proposed in [42–46] can leverage each resource's prerequisites or outcomes they provide to suggest a sequence of educational resources. The most promising methods for extracting these prerequisites are based on an approach that uses specific machine-learning techniques to analyse a Wikipedia page (also named wiki page) associated with each LO in which requirements and final competencies are described [47]. As explained later, we tested and extended a work presented by Angel et al. [48] among these different models. This model extracts the prerequisites from pairs of wiki pages, so it is necessary to add to the LOs metadata the URL of the related Wikipedia page that describes the content covered by the LO.

Figure 1 depicts a LO related to using Scratch, a block-based visual programming language aimed at learning coding basics for students ages 8 to 16. We linked LO to a related wiki page where we can extract some information about the characteristics of this topic. In particular, the prerequisites needed to attend this lesson or the competencies acquired by the students at the end.

3.1 Analysis of Prerequisites Between LOs

Some intelligent systems, such as [49, 50], use strategies based on machine-learning models to extract information from the LOs for indexing them according to their semantics. This paper proposes a Natural Language Processing (NLP) model that uses the "prerequisite" feature in the IEEE LOM. This model aims to learn if a LO "A" is a prerequisite for a LO "B" by analysing the field known as "description" associated with the LOs [35]. The proposed model implements the identification of prerequisite relationships between concepts in the Italian language. The system is based on the approach proposed in [48] for the PRELEARN task of EVALITA 2020 project.

According to this work, we linked each learning object - LO to a wiki page to describe the concepts it presents. Then we used this wiki page to extract metadata to evaluate if a LO is a prerequisite for another. By analysing the wiki pages and using the LOM standard, we can associate 72 features to each LO and 9 descriptive areas for categorising the information content in the teaching resource.

---

[7] https://www.dublincore.org/.

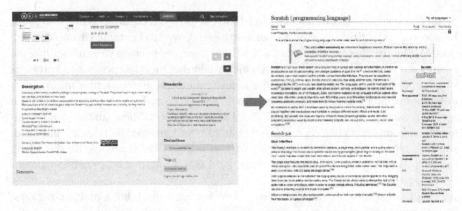

Fig. 1. On the right, the Figure presents a LO related to Scratch, a block-based visual programming language to teach the basics of coding. On the left, a linked wiki page is reported. We use this page to extract some information about the characteristics of this lesson, such as the prerequisites needed to attend it or the competencies acquired by the students at the end.

To create the LOM metadata called "prerequisite," we analysed the concepts presented in the wiki pages defining a set of metadata such as: (1) the age of acquisition of a concept, (2) the age of acquisition of correlated concepts, (3) the length of a concept description, (4) the number of mathematic expressions presented on each wiki page, and (5) the frequency of concept visualisations. With the age of acquisition (AoA) of a concept, we refer to the work presented in [51]. The study collects AoA ratings for 1,957 Italian content words (adjectives, nouns, and verbs), asking participants to estimate the age at which they thought they had learned the word in a Web survey procedure. With AoA of correlated concepts, we mean the AoA average value of the concepts that appear on the wiki page that describes a given concept. This second type of feature aims to model the relationship between pairs of concepts. In particular, it evaluates if a concept appears as a sub-string in the title or the description of the other concept.

Then, we applied our algorithm to a dataset of resources related to the CoderDojos activities. LOs refer to computer programming skills aimed at learning and using technology and the Web and developing computational thinking. The dataset contains 554 LOs, and we linked to each resource a wiki page containing the same typology of informative content. The model implements the identification of prerequisite relationships between LOs using an approach proposed in [48]. Due to the limited number of records, we achieved only an average F1 of 0.68 over the test set. Nevertheless, we are confident this result could be a good indication of the extraction model of the prerequisites. A model that we can use successfully for suggesting a sequence of proper LOS to use for creating a course.

4 EUD Strategies in Education

In the EUD approach, the problem of creating a course by combining a set of LOs can be faced through a design environment where visual entities represent the LO that need to be connected graphically to define the sequence of LOs at the base of the learning path.

Visual strategies typically used for modelling the mashup of entities can be described through the most famous systems that apply them: IFTTT, Atooma, and Yahoo's Pipes. In [52–54], the authors discuss how the first two design strategies support users without programming knowledge to define their context-dependent applications. Precisely [55] describes how these EUD strategies allow users to define desired behaviours according to their needs. Based on the results of these studies, we devised a new solution explicitly addressing enabling non-technical users to design courses by selecting proper LOs suggested by a virtual assistant personalised by a chatbot.

4.1 Graphical Interface of the Chatbot

Figure 2 describes a situation in which the chatbot asks the teacher to specify information about the course to create. The teacher indicates the duration of each lesson, the topics covered, and the specification of the prerequisites the students must have for attending the course. Regarding topics, skills and competencies, the chatbot allows adding items to the corresponding list if the user needs it. Once the teacher has entered the course information, the parsing system checks the orthographic and performs the translation into English (since the dataset is in English) via the DeepTranslator library[8].

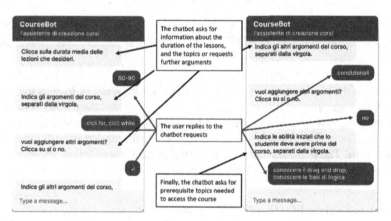

Fig. 2. Two screenshots present the chatbot interaction. In the first one, the chatbot asks the teacher for information about creating a programming course. In detail, it asks to insert: 1. The average time for each lesson, 2. The number of topics to cover, and 3. if the teacher wants to add new topics. In this example, the teacher responds "yes" and then inserts a new topic: "conditional structures". On the left in the final request, the chatbot asks to insert prerequisites the students need to know before taking the course. The teacher indicates: to know "drag and drop" and the "basics of first-order logic".

Then, the topics, the difficulty, type and duration fields are transformed into embeddings and tensors using S-BERT. Finally, the similarity between this information's tensors and each LO's metadata is measured using cosine similarity. The function used to

---

[8] Deep translator. https://pypi.org/project/deep-translator/.

compute this metric is the semantic_search from the Sentence-Transformers library[9]. The RS calculates a final SCORE by using the average of the scores of the individual metadata for each LO. The chatbot recommends the LOs based on their SCORE and presented via a graphical interface. Figure 3 shows the LOs selected by the teacher. If a LO contains exercises, the teacher can specify to repeat the activity if the student fails to finish a LO in the desired time or according to an established rating.

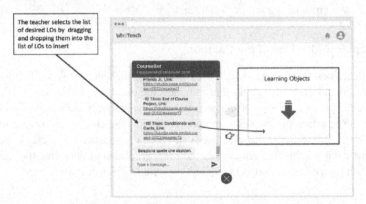

Fig. 3. In the screenshot on the right, the chatbot asks the teacher to select the LOs to insert into the final course. The teacher can drag and drop each LO into the list of LOs to insert in the final course.

To finish, the teacher has to combine the LOs in a sequence of lessons the students have to follow according to the prerequisites of each LO. Once the teacher selects a LO, the chatbot suggests a list of LOs that can be used as the following lesson according to their prerequisites. Figure 4 describes a situation where the teacher indicates the possible learning paths. The branches show the paths the student has to follow according to the evaluation obtained at the end of the previous LO.

4.2   How to Explain LO: Pull Out of the Black Box

In [56], the authors propose 18 guidelines of practical design to improve the interaction between humans and artificial intelligence. In the context of the intelligent assistant, the processes occurring in the background are based on proactive services supporting users. The results that can be achieved from the system can change over time as the underlying intelligent models are constantly being customised or updated. Thus, it is essential to maintain users' trust and acceptance, and this is why we decided to adopt a subset of these guidelines. For our purpose, we chose the guidelines G2, G13, and G14 to address best practices for prototyping intelligent assistants [56].

Exploring state-of-the-art, particularly on the G2 guidelines, techniques called interactive visualisations have been identified [57]. Intelligent assistants deal very well with information overload by minimising the effort for a given user. Their accuracy has

---

[9] Sentence-transformers. https://www.sbert.net.

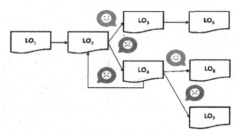

Fig. 4. The Figure presents possible learning paths the teacher has defined for the course. The sequence is suggested by the chatbot according to the prerequisites but it is the teacher who has to indicate the branching paths. The branches show the paths the student has to follow according to the evaluation obtained at the end of the previous LO. For example, if the student does not pass the test at the end of LO_2 or she/he evaluates it with a low rate, the LO_4 is proposed as a following lesson; otherwise, the student will attend the LO_3.

improved significantly in recent years, but the non-transparency to the end user has increased too. Therefore, to address this issue, interactive visualisations have been introduced to explain our assistant's "black box" suggestions. Interactive visualisations allow the chatbot to present information transparently to support the data understanding process. To identify suitable visualisations, we decided to adopt the taxonomy introduced by the authors [57], also based on the one proposed by Shneiderman [58] and Keim [59]. A proper visualisation must allow teachers to have insight into the LO content and increase transparency, acceptance and trust towards recommendations. Figure 5 presents a LO visualisation in which a set of "Best n topics" covered in the LO are shown simultaneously to the teacher.

Moreover, for each topic, the evaluation inferred by the RS according to the user's history and profile is reported. Together with the list of main topics, two alternative lists are presented. The "Correlated items" list shows issues for which the user did not provide information to the assistant. Items returned to the user have an inferred rating for which the system has determined a low affinity (Fig. 5). The "New items" list is a set of topics that other teachers considered little relevant to this LO or topics that have never been taken into account for explaining this LO. These topics can solve the cold start problem as users may find them helpful. In this case, Wilkinson et al. [60] propose selecting items with the least ratings. Finally, the explanation of LO provides teachers with a detailed description, a preview, a set of keywords and a rating provided by the teachers until now.

5   Acceptance and Intention to Use the Chatbot

To evaluate teachers' level of acceptance and intention to use the chatbot, we used the UTAUT model (The unified theory of acceptance and use of technology) [18]. This model includes eight user acceptance indicators that are well-validated in the context of a large number of studies. The UTAUT model presents four constructs that play significant roles as direct determinants of user acceptance and intent to use a new technology: 1. Performance Expectancy (PE); 2. Effort Expectancy (EE); 3. Social Influences (SI); 4. Facilitating Conditions (FC).

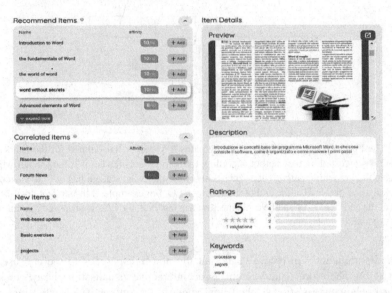

Fig. 5. Interactive visualisation strategies. The screenshot presents an explanation about a LO related to MS Word. On the left, a set of topics explains the LO content. The first list is associated with the main topics, the second is about secondary themes, and finally, the last one specifies topics other teachers considered little relevant to this LO. On the right, the explanation presents a detailed description of the LO, a preview, a set of keywords and a rating provided by the teachers until now.

Performance Expectancy measures how much an individual considers a valuable system for improving their job performance. Effort Expectancy measures how easy a system is to use. Social Influence measures the influence of colleagues, instructors, and friends on the intention to use a new technology [62, 64]. Finally, Facilitating Conditions measure how much external aid can facilitate the adoption and use of the system.

UTAUT is a generic acceptance analysis model which can be applied to different fields. To obtain a higher level of detail and a specific adaptation to our context, according to the results of these works [61, 63], we decided to use an extension model that integrates the primary constructs of the standard UTAUT model by adding these constructs: 1. Hedonic Motivation (HM); 2. Habit (H); 3. Trust (T).

The first construct measures the degree of appreciation of the system by users and how this could affect the intention to use it in the future. The second measures how much experience and the habit of using new technology can be helpful in its more concrete acceptance [63]. Finally, the Trust construct measures how much trust in the chatbot can affect its acceptance and future use.

As depicted in Fig. 6, each construct is related to other constructs specifying the hypothesis we need to study. For example, Hypothesis 1 (H1) links PE to Behavioural Intention (BI) for evaluating how much the performance expectancy positively affects teachers' intention to use the suggestions of the digital assistant. Or again, Hypothesis 6b (H6b), linking HM to PE, measures how much the degree of the chatbot appreciation can influence how much teachers consider it valuable for improving their job performance.

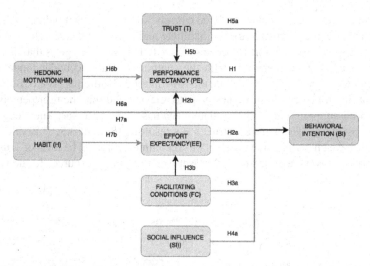

Fig. 6. Hypotheses schema. Each arrow represents a hypothesis that measures how much a construct can affect the validation of the other. For example, H6b, linking HM to PE, measures how much the degree of the chatbot appreciation can influence how much teachers consider it valuable for improving their job performance.

26 people took part in the evaluation, mainly chosen among the employees of the Social Thingum company[10] (15 employees) and students of the Department of Computer Science at the University of Milano (11 students), given the impossibility of recruiting real teachers. The participants were aged between 23 and 26 and had a master's or three-year degree in Computer Science. The participants demonstrated solid knowledge of basic programming, enabling them to simulate teachers properly for creating courses about the basics of coding. When we asked about the amount of experience they had in the past with e-learning platforms such as Moodle[11], the results were 4% for "No experience", 18% for "little experience", and 78% for having good experience with technology. Regarding testers' gender, we have a slight prevalence of males at 58% compared to the remaining 42% of females. Finally, to the question, "Have you ever used a chatbot?" Almost all answered "No," with 75%. Therefore, only 25% have ever tried to use services offered by chatbots in the past.

After administering the cognitive questionnaire and signing a document for informed consent, we asked participants to create a course about coding for a CoderDojo. At the end of the test, we provided testers with a questionnaire related to the constructs of our UTAUT model with a total of 24 questions (5 for measuring PE, 3 for EE, SI, FC, T, and HM, 2 for H, and BI). The questionnaire uses a 5-point Likert scale method to explore the study, ranging from 1 (strongly disagree) to 5 (strongly agree), respectively.

Figure 7-A reports the arithmetic mean and the standard deviation of the answers for each question of the constructs. The average of the responses relating to the Performance Expectancy construct is 3.7, therefore between indecision (3) and agreement (4) on the

---

[10] https://www.socialthingum.it/.

[11] https://moodle.org/.

Likert scale. This score can be considered entirely satisfactory, as it indicates that users consider the chatbot a valuable tool to facilitate and speed up the search for LO. The average of the construct "Effort Expectancy" is 4.1. This value suggests that the chatbot is easy to use and that interacting with the chatbot is clear and understandable. The "Social Influence" average is 3.7, while the "Facilitating Conditions" is 4.0. Both values imply that the influence of colleagues is quite relevant and that the user perceives that she/he is well-supported in using the chatbot and has all the necessary knowledge to use it without problems. The Trust construct has a resulting mean of 3.5. This value means that people have enough trust in the chatbot's recommendations. The level of Trust could grow if more LOs were added to the dataset to return more resources to the teacher's request.

	Average	SD		Average	SD
PE1	3.73	1.185	T1	3.27	1.218
PE2	3.85	1.120	T2	3.62	1.061
PE3	3.77	1.243	T3	3.62	0.983
PE4	3.73	1.041	HM1	3.58	1.137
PE5	3.76	1.165	HM2	2.88	1.143
EE1	3.96	1.038	HM3	3.77	0.992
EE2	4.15	0.925	H1	2.19	1.021
EE3	4.31	0.970	H2	1.62	1.061
SI1	3.62	0.804	BI1	2.81	1.386
SI2	3.85	0.881	BI2	2.85	1.347
SI3	3.58	1.102			
FC1	4.27	0.962			
FC2	4.36	0.757			
FC3	3.42	1.238			

(A)

Hypothesis	β	p-value	Acceptance
H1: PE → BI	0.218	0.014	Accepted
H2a: EE → BI	0.238	0.170	Not significative
H2b: EE → PE	0.847	<.001	Accepted
H3a: FC → BI	0.487	0.002	Accepted
H3b: FC → EE	0.879	<.001	Accepted
H4a: SI → BI	0.600	<.001	Accepted
H5a: T → BI	0.535	<.001	Accepted
H5b: T → PE	0.834	<.001	Accepted
H6a: HM → BI	0.623	<.001	Accepted
H6b: HM → PE	0.863	<.001	Accepted
H7a: H → BI	0.816	0.001	Accepted
H7b: H → EE	0.384	0.583	Not significative

(B)

Fig. 7. The Figure in Section A presents a table showing the mean and standard deviation of the answers to the questions of the UTAUT model. While the Figure in section B offers a table containing the results of the SEM analysis, in particular indicating which hypotheses were accepted as the final result of the test.

The average score for the "Hedonic Motivation" construct is 3.4, a pretty good result but not optimal. This result may be due to the chatbot interface's limited presence of fun and rewarding components. Unfortunately, RASA restricts the use of various graphical elements, such as animations, which could make the interface pleasant and attractive. The "Habit" construct has a low average of 2.0, indicating that the users do not frequently use chatbots. Therefore previous experience does not affect the degree of acceptance. To verify the hypotheses in Fig. 6, we used the structural equation model (SEM) [64], combining factor analysis and regression. It first constructs latent variables starting from the items that have been defined and, subsequently, estimates the regressions using the variables above. Through the results of these regressions, it is possible to verify which hypotheses are accepted and with which level of significance.

As can be seen in Fig. 7-B, the SEM model provides an estimated beta value and a p-value as an output. Beta represents the effect of the explanatory variable (the antecedent of the hypothesis) on the dependent variable (the consequent of the hypothesis) and can be either positive or negative. The p-value allows us to derive the significance level with which the hypothesis is eventually accepted. In this work, the SEM analysis was performed using Jamovi[12], an open-source tool for data analysis and the realisation of statistical tests. From the table, it is possible to observe that habit does not influence the construct of Effort Expectancy, as hypothesis H7b has not been accepted. This result means that the created assistant is easily usable even for people who use the chatbot sporadically, like the test participants. The other hypothesis that was not significant is the H2b, which implies the low average obtained for the Behavioral. This value allows us to say the final intention to use the chatbot does not depend on its level of usability. This result is an interesting indication because it suggests that the teachers considered the chatbot a helpful assistant even if its usability can be improved. All the other hypotheses were confirmed, even with a high beta value.

6 Conclusions

This paper aims to reply to some research questions. First, we investigated how to exploit a learning platform to provide teachers with a EUD approach that helps them to create a new digital course. The idea is to use an intelligent assistant to advise teachers about the e-learning modules according to their objectives. These smart suggestions are presented through a visualisation that offers LOs in an accurate, accountable, transparent and well-explained manner. The chatbot asks the teacher for the main properties of the course, including the age of the students, the difficulty and the topics covered, necessary to understand the teaching needs of the teacher. Based on the information obtained, the assistant suggests a series of LOs, which the teacher can view and select. In developing the chatbot, we tried to ensure the teacher could immediately decide on the better LOs and how to combine them. In this regard, the chatbot can describe a LO to explain its content and why it has been suggested. The implementation of the chatbot is based on the RASA framework, an open-source framework which, thanks to the use of natural language processing models, allows the creation of sophisticated chatbots. The data of the course, indicated by the teacher, were subjected to a parsing procedure to facilitate the filtering of LOs by the recommendation system. For the parsing, it was decided to use Sentence-BERT, a machine-learning model based on Transformers, to identify the LOs with the data most semantically similar to the data entered by the teacher.

In the final testing phase, a set of experiments were conducted to evaluate the chatbot's understanding ability. To evaluate the impact of the virtual assistant on the teachers' activity, we adopted an extended version of the UTAUT model to study its acceptance and intention to use it. To understand the factors driving the teachers' intention to use the digital assistant's suggestions, we recruited 26 participants. As discussed in the paper, the final results of our tests demonstrate sound effects for concerns about the acceptance of the virtual assistant. Specifically, good values concern the quality of the assistant's ability to communicate effectively, the level of perceived trust in its suggestions and finally, how the teachers' experience affects their perception of the ease of use of the assistant. Further researches aim at extending the studying involving more teachers with a broader range of competencies in other learning.

---

[12] Jamovi. https://www.jamovi.org/.

References

1. Lieberman, H. (ed.): Your Wish Is My Command: Programming by Example. Morgan Kaufmann, Burlington (2001)
2. Bell, B., Lewis, C.: ChemTrains: a language for creating behaving pictures. In:1993 IEEE Workshop on Visual Languages, Bergen, Norway, pp. 188–195 (1993)
3. Cypher, A.: Watch What I Do: Programming by Demonstration. The MIT Press, Cambridge (1993)
4. Eisenberg, M., Fischer, G.: Programmable design environments: integrating end-user programming with domain-oriented assistance. In: Proceedings of the 1994 ACM CHI Conference, Boston, MA, pp. 431–437 (1994)
5. Fischer, G., Girgenson, A.: End-User modifiability in design environments. In: CHI '90, Conference on Human Factors in Computing Systems, Seattle, WA, pp. 183–191 (1990)
6. Ioannidou, A., Repenning, A.: End-user programmable simulations. Dr. Dobb's(302 August), pp. 40–48 (1999)
7. Jones, C.: End-user programming. IEEE Comput. **28**(9), 68–70 (1995)
8. Nardi, B.: A Small Matter of Programming. MIT Press, Cambridge (1993)
9. Pane, J.F., Myers, B.A.: Usability Issues in the Design of Novice Programming Systems (Technical Report No. CMU-CS-96–132). School of Computer Science, Carnegie Mellon University, Pittsburg, Pennsylvania (1996)
10. Rader, C., Cherry, G., Brand, C., Repenning, A., Lewis, C.: Principles to scaffold mixed textual and iconic end-user programming languages. In: Proceedings of the 1998 IEEE Symposium of Visual Languages, Nova Scotia, Canada, pp. 187–194 (1998)
11. Repenning, A., Sumner, T.: Agentsheets: a medium for creating domain-oriented visual languages. IEEE Comput. **28**(3), 17–25 (1995)
12. Ruiz, J.G., Mintzer, M.J., Issenberg, S.B.: Learning objects in medical education. Med. Teach. **28**(7), 599–605 (2006)
13. Deschênes, M.: Recommender systems to support learners' agency in a learning context: a systematic review. Int. J. Educ. Technol. High. Educ. **17**(1), 50 (2020)
14. Urdaneta-Ponte, M.C., Mendez-Zorrilla, A., Oleagordia-Ruiz, I.: Recommendation systems for education: systematic review. Electronics, **10**(14), 1611 (2021)
15. Conference Name:ACM Woodstock conference Campbell, L.M.: Engaging with the learning object economy: Introducing learning objects and the object economy. In: Reusing Online Resources, pp. 53–63. Routledge (2003)
16. Cohen, E., Nycz, M.: Learning objects and e-learning: an informing science perspective. Interdisc. J. E-Learn. Learn. Objects **2**(1), 23–34 (2006)
17. Devlin, J., Chang, M.W., Lee, K., Toutanova, K.: Bert: Pre-training of deep bidirectional transformers for language understanding. arXiv preprint arXiv:1810.04805(2018)
18. Venkatesh, V., Morris, M.G., Davis, G.B., Davis, F.D.: User acceptance of information technology: toward a unified view. MIS Q. 425–478 (2003)
19. Mushtaha, E., Dabous, S.A., Alsyouf, I., Ahmed, A., Abdraboh, N.R.: The challenges and opportunities of online learning and teaching at engineering and theoretical colleges during the pandemic. Ain Shams Eng. J. **13**(6), 101770 (2022)
20. Alhumaid, K., Ali, S., Waheed, A., Zahid, E., Habes, M.: COVID-19 & elearning: perceptions & attitudes of teachers towards E-learning acceptancein the developing countries. Multicult. Educ. **6**(2), 100–115 (2020)
21. Sofi-Karim, M., Bali, A.O., Rached, K.: Online education via media platforms and applications as an innovative teaching method. Educ. Inf. Technol. **28**(1), 507–523 (2023)
22. Okonkwo, C.W., Ade-Ibijola, A.: Chatbots applications in education: a systematic review. Comput. Educ.: Artif. Intell. **2**, 100033 (2021)

23. Medeiros, R.P., Ramalho, G.L., Falcão, T.P.: A systematic literature review on teaching and learning introductory programming in higher education. IEEE Trans. Educ. **62**(2), 77–90 (2018)
24. Smutny, P., Schreiberova, P.: Chatbots for learning: a review of educational chatbots for the Facebook messenger. Comput. Educ. **151**, 103862 (2020)
25. Alias, S., Sainin, M.S., Soo Fun, T., Daut, N.: Identification of conversational intent pattern using pattern-growth technique for academic chatbot. In: Chamchong, R., Wong, K.W. (eds.) MIWAI 2019. LNCS (LNAI), vol. 11909, pp. 263–270. Springer, Cham (2019). https://doi. org/10.1007/978-3-030-33709-4_24
26. Hwang, G.J., Chang, C.Y.: A review of opportunities and challenges of chatbots in education. Interact. Learn. Environ. 1–14 (2021)
27. Gamma, E., Helm, R., Johnson, R., Vlissides, J.: Design Patterns: Elements of Reusable Objectoriented Software. Addison-Wesley, Boston (1995)
28. Lam, C.S.N., Chan, L.K., See, C.Y.H.: Converse, connect and consolidate–The development of an artificial intelligence chatbot for health sciences education. In: Frontiers in Medical and Health Sciences Education Conference. Bau Institute of Medical and Health Sciences Education, Li Ka Shing Faculty of Medicine, The University of Hong Kong (2018)
29. Molnár, G., Szüts, Z.: The role of chatbots in formal education. In: 2018 IEEE 16th International Symposium on Intelligent Systems and Informatics (SISY), pp. 000197–000202. IEEE (2018)
30. Sreelakshmi, A.S., Abhinaya, S.B., Nair, A., Nirmala, S.J.: A question answering and quiz generation chatbot for education. In: 2019 Grace Hopper Celebration India (GHCI), pp. 1–6. IEEE (2019)
31. Downes, S.: Learning objects: resources for distance education worldwide. Int. Rev. Res. Open Dist. Learn. **2**(1), 1–35 (2001)
32. Jones, R.: Designing adaptable learning resources with learning object patterns. J. Digit. Inf, **6**(1) (2004). Article no. 305
33. Goodyear, P.: Educational design and networked learning: patterns, pattern languages and design practice. Aust. J. Educ. Technol. **21**(1), 82–101 (2005)
34. ADL-1: Advanced Distributed Learning (ADL) initiative. SCORM Specifications – The SCORM Content Aggregation Model Version 1.2 (2001). http://www.adlnet.gov/scorm/his tory/Scorm12/. Accessed 7 June 2007
35. ADL-2: Advanced Distributed Learning (ADL) initiative. SCORM Specifications – The SCORM Run-Time Environment Version 1.2 (2001). http://www.adlnet.gov/downloads/dow nloadpage.aspx?ID=218. Accessed 7 June 2007
36. ADL: Advanced Distributed Learning (ADL) initiative. SCORM Specifications – SCORM Version 1.3 Application Profile Working Draft Version 1.0 (2003). http://www.adlnet.gov/ News/articles/index.aspx?ID=126. Accessed 7 June 2007
37. ARIADNE: The Alliance of Remote Instructional Authoring and Distribution networks for Europe (1998). http://ariadne.unil.ch/. Accessed 7 June 2007
38. SCORM: Sharable Courseware Object Reference Model (2003). http://www.adlnet.gov/dow nloads/downloadpage.aspx?ID=243. Accessed 7 June 2007
39. LOM: Final LOM Draft Standard (2002). http://ltsc.ieee.org/wg12/20020612-Final-LOM-Draft.html. Accessed 7 June 2007
40. Hoebelheinrich, N., et al.: Recommendations for a minimal metadata set to aid harmonised discovery of learning resources (2022).
41. Dagienė, V., Jevsikova, T., Kubilinskienė, S.: An integration of methodological resources into learning object metadata repository. Informatica **24**(1), 13–34 (2013)
42. Pang, Y., Wang, N., Zhang, Y., Jin, Y., Ji, W., Tan, W.: Prerequisite-related MOOC recommendation on learning path locating. Comput. Soc. Netw. **6**(1), 1–16 (2019). https://doi.org/ 10.1186/s40649-019-0065-2

43. Karpova, M., Shmelev, V., Dukhanov, A.: An automation of the course design with use of learning objects with evaluation based on the Bloom taxonomy. In: 2015 9th International Conference on Application of Information and Communication Technologies (AICT), pp. 138–142. IEEE (2015)

44. Siren, A., Tzerpos, V.: Automatic learning path creation using OER: a systematic literature mapping. IEEE Trans. Learn. Technol. (2022)

45. Gasparetti, F., De Medio, C., Limongelli, C., Sciarrone, F., Temperini, M.: Prerequisites between learning objects: automatic extraction based on a machine learning approach. Telematics Inform. **35**(3), 595–610 (2018)

46. Xiao, K., Bai, Y., Wang, Z.: Extracting prerequisite relations among concepts from the course descriptions. Int. J. Software Eng. Knowl. Eng. **32**(04), 503–523 (2022)

47. Liang, C., Wu, Z., Huang, W., Giles, C.L.: Measuring prerequisite relations among concepts. In: Proceedings of the 2015 Conference on Empirical Methods in Natural Language Processing, pp. 1668–1674 (2015)

48. Angel, J., Aroyehun, S.T., Gelbukh, A.: Nlp-cic@ prelearn: Mastering prerequisites relations, from handcrafted features to embeddings. arXiv preprint arXiv:2011.03760(2020)

49. Atkinson, J., et al.: Web metadata extraction and semantic indexing for learning objects extraction. In: Recent Trends in Applied Artificial Intelligence: 26th International Conference on Industrial, Engineering and Other Applications of Applied Intelligent Systems, IEA/AIE 2013, Amsterdam, The Netherlands, 17–21 June 2013. Proceedings 26. Springer, Berlin (2013)

50. Marconi, L., Aragon, R.A.M., Zoppis, I., Manzoni, S., Mauri, G., Epifania, F.: Explainable attentional neural recommendations for personalized social learning. In: Baldoni, M., Bandini, S. (eds.) AIxIA 2020. LNCS (LNAI), vol. 12414, pp. 67–79. Springer, Cham (2021). https://doi.org/10.1007/978-3-030-77091-4_5

51. Elsherif, M.M., Preece, E., Catling, J.C.: Age-of-acquisition effects: a literature review. J. Exp. Psychol.: Learn. Memory Cognit. (2023)

52. Valtolina, S., Barricelli, BR: An end-user development framework to support quantified self in sport teams. In: Paternò, F., Wulf, V. (eds.) New Perspectives in End-User Development, pp. 413–432. Springer, Cham (2017). ISBN 9783319602905

53. Ghiani, G., Manca, M., Paternò, F., Santoro, C.: Personalisation of context-dependent applications through trigger-action rules. ACM Trans. Comput. Hum. Interact. **24**(2), 33 (2017)

54. Desolda, G., Ardito, C., Matera, M.: Empowering end users to customise their smart environments: model, composition paradigms and domain-specific tools. ACM Trans. Comput. Hum. Interact. **24**(2), 52 (2017)

55. Caivano, D., Fogli, D., Lanzilotti, R., Piccinno, A., Cassano, F.: Supporting end users to control their smart home: design implications from a literature review and an empirical investigation. J. Syst. Softw. **144**(2018), 295–313 (2018)

56. Amershi, S., et al.: Guidelines for human-ai interaction. In: Proceedings of the 2019 Chi Conference on Human Factors in Computing Systems, pp. 1–13 (2019)

57. Richthammer, C., Sänger, J., Pernul, G.: Interactive visu- alization of recommender systems data. In: Proceedings of the 4th Workshop on Security in Highly Connected IT Systems, pp. 19–24 (2017)

58. Shneiderman, B.: The eyes have it: a task by data type taxonomy for information visualisations. In: The Craft of Information Visualisation, pp. 364–371. Elsevier (2003)

59. Keim, D.A.: Visual exploration of large data sets. Commun. ACM **44**(8), 38–44 (2001)

60. Wilkinson, D.: Testing a recommender system for self-actualisation. In: Proceedings of the 12th ACM Conference on Recommender Systems, pp. 543–547 (2018)

61. Venkatesh, V., Davis, F.D.: A theoretical extension of the technology acceptance model: four longitudinal field studies. Manage. Sci. **46**(2), 186–204 (2000)

62. Warshaw, P.R.: A new model for predicting behavioral intentions: an alternative to Fishbein. J. Mark. Res. **17**(2), 153–172 (1980)
63. Venkatesh, V., Thong, J.Y., Xu, X.: Consumer acceptance and use of information technology: extending the unified theory of acceptance and use of technology. MIS Q. 157–178 (2012)
64. Fan, Y., et al.: Applications of structural equation modeling (SEM) in ecological studies: an updated review. Ecol. Process. **5**(1), 1–12 (2016). https://doi.org/10.1186/s13717-016-0063-3

Author Index

L. D. Spano et al. (Eds.): IS-EUD 2023, LNCS 13917, p. 269, 2023.
https://doi.org/10.1007/978-3-031-34433-6

Printed in the United States
by Baker & Taylor Publisher Services